Shakespeare on Salvation

Shakespeare on Salvation

Crossing the Reformation Divide

DAVID ANONBY

Foreword by Gary Kuchar

◦PICKWICK *Publications* · Eugene, Oregon

SHAKESPEARE ON SALVATION
Crossing the Reformation Divide

Copyright © 2024 David Anonby. All rights reserved. Except for brief quotations in critical publications or reviews, no part of this book may be reproduced in any manner without prior written permission from the publisher. Write: Permissions, Wipf and Stock Publishers, 199 W. 8th Ave., Suite 3, Eugene, OR 97401.

Pickwick Publications
An Imprint of Wipf and Stock Publishers
199 W. 8th Ave., Suite 3
Eugene, OR 97401

www.wipfandstock.com

PAPERBACK ISBN: 979-8-3852-0299-7
HARDCOVER ISBN: 979-8-3852-0300-0
EBOOK ISBN: 979-8-3852-0301-7

Cataloguing-in-Publication data:

Names: Anonby, David, author. | Kuchar, Gary, 1974–, foreword.

Title: Shakespeare on salvation : crossing the reformation divide / David Anonby ; foreword by Gary Kuchar

Description: Eugene, OR : Pickwick Publications, 2024 | Includes bibliographical references and index.

Identifiers: ISBN 979-8-3852-0299-7 (paperback) | ISBN 979-8-3852-0300-0 (hardcover) | ISBN 979-8-3852-0301-7 (ebook)

Subjects: LCSH: Shakespeare, William, 1564–1616—Religion. | Religion and drama. | Religious thought—England. | Religion in literature. | Religion and literature.

Classification: PR3011 .A56 2024 (paperback) | PR3011 .A56 (ebook)

03/12/24

To my dear wife Kirsten, beautiful on the inside and out.
You are always my first and only love.
The greatest achievement of my life is winning your heart in marriage.
"For thy sweet love remembered such wealth brings
That then I scorn to change my state with kings."

In memoriam
My dad, Dr. John Anonby, a true Renaissance man.
You loved me so well.
For me, you are the measure of all other men.
Thank you for nurturing in me a deep love of literature and theology.

Solus Christus

Contents

	Foreword by Gary Kuchar	ix
	Acknowledgments	xiii
	Introduction	1
1	"One Drop of Christian Blood": Shakespeare's Critique of Justification by Faith in *The Merchant of Venice*	33
2	"Try What Repentance Can": Soteriological Agency and Avant-Garde Conformity in the Claudius Prayer Scene in *Hamlet*	80
3	*Hamlet*, the Discernment of Spirits, and the Sifting of St. Peter: An Elegy for Religious Violence	119
4	Vicarious Atonement and the Failure of Ethics in *Measure for Measure*	165
5	"Thy Life's a Miracle": Exorcism, Martyrdom, and Ecumenism in *King Lear*	205
	Conclusion	253
	Bibliography	267
	Subject Index	287

Foreword

IN APPARENT OUTRAGE, AN early owner of the Rosenbach copy of *Shakespeare's Sonnets* has scrawled "What a heap of Infidel Stuff" at the end of Sonnet 154, the last in the sequence (Duncan-Jones, *Shakespeare's Sonnets*, 49).[1] The response may be a reaction to any number of things, from Shakespeare's appropriation of God's self-denomination, "I am that I am" in Sonnet 121, to the parodically Trinitarian praise lavished on the young man as "fair, kind, and true," to the repeated Christological trope of putting the young man on in love as one would put on Christ in faith as in Romans 13:14, Corinthians 15:53, or Galatians 3:27 (Kuchar, "Loves Best Habit," 211–236). Such impressing of theological figures into the secular service of human praise is a reminder that Shakespeare's works are awash in religious idioms. Moreover, these practices are a further reminder that such creative misuses of religious imagery are only possible among a theologically fluent audience, one capable, for example, of appreciating the thrill of blasphemy in a manner that a non-religious audience today could not. From this standpoint, to return to the theological dimensions of Shakespeare's writing is to return not only to the highly fraught world of early modern religion, but to the whole sweep of passionately felt ethical and social problems inherent in Reformation controversy, from the questions of freedom and love to the politics of law and sexuality. Indeed, to say that Shakespeare understood religion to be the master-discourse of his culture is to say nothing more than that a twenty-first-century writer knows that psychology is a dominant discourse of self-understanding.

---

1. References to the sonnets are from Katherine Duncan-Jones, editor, *Shakespeare's Sonnets* (Arden).

Take, for example, *Sonnet 138*. Despite its ostensible cynicism and overwrought worldliness, this poem is not fully legible absent of its allusions to debates about redemption that so deeply preoccupied some of the most brilliant minds of Shakespeare's day. The result is a lyric that looks straight into the heart of the deepest possible skepticism only to glance at something beyond it, a gracefulness (if that is the right word) that is exquisitely and perhaps illegibly personal, if not wholly individual. To be sure, the paradoxes involved in this particular form of grace could only have been expressed by an actor-playwright sensitive to the ways that intense imaginative experience can change seemingly intransigent realities into, what from one perspective, looks like a mutually-redeeming shared vision, but from another, appears as a self-mocking delusion. The difference lies in whether one stands inside or outside the magic circle generated by, what is, in effect, a peculiar form of shared faith:

> When my love swears that she is made of truth,
> I do believe her, though I know she lies,
> That she might think me some untutored youth
> Unlearned in the world's false subtleties.
> Thus vainly thinking that she thinks me young,
> Although she knows my days are past the best,
> Simply I credit her false-speaking tongue;
> On both sides thus is simple truth suppressed.
> But wherefore says she not she is unjust?
> And wherefore say not that I am old?
> O love's best habit is in seeming trust,
> And age in love loves not t'have years told:
>   Therefore I lie with her, and she with me,
>   And in our faults by lies we flattered be.

The great divide between Protestant and Catholic theories of salvation, on which so many lives turned in Tudor England, finds rather subtle expression in the pun on *habit* in the exclamation, "O love's best habit is in seeming trust." On one hand, this implies that the best course of repeated action in the context of a long-term relationship is to bestow trust even when there may be cause to do otherwise. The justifying force of this witticism partly turns on its Protestant logic, on the idea that grace involves a forensic judgment of salvation on an undeservingly sinful soul. On this rather Lutheran account, what redeems the beloved and thus the relationship as a whole is that an unmerited grace, an unearned trust, is extended in the knowledge that, well, nobody's perfect. From such a standpoint, the word *habit* resonates in the context of Shakespeare's repeated echoing of Paul's figure that one puts Christ on in faith as though he were a garment in which one might be, as it were, habited. On the other hand, however, the term *habit* also recalls the Aristotelian idea that repeated actions can shape the soul over time, turning habituated forms of behavior into character. On this more Thomist account, what strengthens and thereby redeems the relationship is not just the one-sided extending of unmerited grace, but the shared action of repeatedly and playfully "lying with" rather than "to" one another. Practiced over time, such mutually shared "seeming trust" turns a potentially tense and deceitful dynamic into a kind of satisfying play, one in which both parties understand and have come to accept the underlying rules, however awkward and strange they may appear to those outside the magic circle generated by the relationship's internal dynamics. Viewed this way, the poem's wit partly turns on its playful jostling between Lutheran and Thomist perspectives in a rather unexpected context and in a self-consciously indecorous register.

If the sort of dynamics explored in *Sonnet 138* recall the mid-life antics of *Antony and Cleopatra*, the aesthetic logic of the poem repeats the paradoxes of *The Winter's Tale*, where Paulina tells Leontes (and by extension the audience) that to appreciate the "miracle" of Hermione's "resurrection" he must awake his faith. Otherwise, she warns, the statue's coming to life will look like an old tale that will be hooted at for its daft implausibility. In both cases, faith constitutes an act of shared imagination—a bestowing onto intransigent reality something that is not empirically visible but which, once bestowed, becomes recognizable and thereby real in its transforming effects on the parties involved. But to those outside the magic circle of bestowed faith, the whole process will appear absurd, like some meaninglessly perverse inside-joke. Viewed in these contexts, it becomes clear that Shakespeare's wit in *Sonnet 138* also relies on its subtle interlacing of competing theological ideas of faith and grace with theatrical ideas of acting and performance. Purposefully confusing these conceptual realms, the poem intimates how a certain kind of poetic faith proper to the theater can be (mis)applied to life in order to bring it more in line with our will. This is not to suggest for a moment that the poem is "religious," or even that its generation of the magic circle of faith is intended to be persuasive to anyone but the speaker and his beloved. What it is to suggest, however, is that the poem's articulation of the relationship's interpersonal dynamics, with its complex oscillation between irony and seriousness, are not fully legible absent of its theological background. Or more precisely, to not hear the poem's subtle allusions to major questions about how souls are saved is to remain deaf to its illegibly wry liar's paradox—to its purposeful confusing of the faith proper to theater with the forms of trust requisite to sustaining long-term (or complexly adult) relationships in life. As is so often the case in Shakespeare's plays, the line between life and art, like the one between religious and aesthetic faith, can be a thin one.

David Anonby's intervention in *Shakespeare on Salvation* is to suggest that in adopting such theological idioms the bard is not only exploiting them for literary or dramatic ends. On the contrary, he is also testing their validity as forms of human understanding, exposing them to the white-hot pressure of the dramatic machinery in plays such as *Hamlet* and *King Lear*. If a theological idea has any merit, Anonby's Shakespeare suggests, it should explain the world we live in, the dynamics of our relationships, and the effects that our morally charged actions have on ourselves and others. If a theological idea has merit, it should illuminate the here and now as well as what is yet to come. In pursuing the provocative claim that Shakespeare uses theology to think and, that in turn, his thinking casts judgment on the religious medium in which he operates, Anonby provides the first full-length study of Shakespeare's engagement with Reformation controversies over questions of salvation. In the process, he discovers a playwright concerned not only with how to tell a good story but one invested in the biggest questions of his, and perhaps any, time. This is a Shakespeare who moved in the world of Lancelot Andrewes and Richard Hooker, as well as Christopher Marlowe and Thomas Middleton, leaving us with plays where the line between pulpit and stage is often productively and consequentially elided. It is a Shakespeare entirely worth our attention as it helps explain the impossible intellectual and emotional weight borne by these plays both in their time and in ours.

GARY KUCHAR
Professor of English
University of Victoria

Acknowledgments

 Social Sciences and Humanities Research Council of Canada   Conseil de recherches en sciences humaines du Canada   Canadä

THIS MONOGRAPH DRAWS ON research supported by the Social Sciences and Humanities Research Council. Thank you to the government and people of Canada.

I wish to acknowledge Gary Kuchar for lending his erudite grasp of early modern religion to this project, and I am grateful for his personal kindness to me. I am thankful to Erin Kelly for supporting me with her capacious knowledge of non-Shakespearean drama. Thanks to my friend and colleague Holly Nelson for inspiring me to earn a PhD in early modern literature and for advising me at many turns of the development of my academic career.

I wish also to acknowledge Paul Stanwood, who taught me Renaissance literature with such profound, but understated joy when I was a young graduate student. His impact on me is abiding.

To my colleagues in the English department at Trinity Western University, thank you for making my workplace a second home for these past twenty years (with many more to come).

To Erik, thank you for championing me as my younger brother and senior academic.

To Lily, *asante sana kwa maisha na upendo yako.*

To Mom, thank you for believing in me, prioritizing my passions, and loving me so well.

To my children, Isaiah, John David, and Joy, you are the delight of my life. I love you.

Introduction

THIS BOOK EXPLORES SHAKESPEARE'S negotiation of Reformation controversy about theories of salvation. While twentieth-century literary criticism tended to regard Shakespeare as a harbinger of secularism, the so-called "turn to religion" in early modern studies has given renewed attention to the religious elements in Shakespeare and his contemporaries (Cummings, *Mortal Thoughts* 7–8). Yet in spite of the current prevalence of early modern religion studies, there remains an aura of uncertainty regarding some of the doctrinal or liturgical specificities of the period. This historical gap is especially felt with respect to theories of salvation, or soteriology. For example, Anthony Dawson concludes that Claudius's abortive attempt at repentance in *Hamlet* (3.3) is ambiguous in terms of its confessional affiliation (239). Such ambiguity invites further inquiry into historical theology. Tellingly, Claudius attempts to repent without confessing to a priest; moreover, he laments that he is unable to repent. These factors suggest reformed ideas of repentance and election or (in this case) rejection by God.

But is Claudius unable to repent or actually unwilling? Shakespeare's echoing in Claudius's prayer of Jesuit martyr Robert Southwell's poem *Mans Civill Warre* intimates a Catholic spirituality that emphasizes the freedom of the will. In other words, Claudius's failed penitence encapsulates the longstanding Reformation debate between Erasmus and Luther. While Erasmus championed the role of free will in salvation in *De Libero Arbitrio*, Luther defended the notion that human choice was of no avail in obtaining salvation in *De Servo Arbitrio*. Claudius's cross-confessional dalliance with repentance (like the many other religious scenes in Shakespeare's plays), gives very little insight into Shakespeare's own religious predilections. Rather, Shakespeare's rich layering of religious contexts and concepts often dramatizes the religious landscape of his day as pluralistic and mutually intolerant. As Brian Cummings avers, *Hamlet* holds in tension conflicting theological concepts (213). Even salvation provokes irreconcilable differences.

The exigency for my study of Shakespeare and soteriology is rooted in the historical intersection of the Renaissance and the Reformation. While the theological controversies of the patristic era were generally focused on Christology—hence the emergence of the Trinitarian creeds and the New Testament canon—Reformation disputes were typically concerned with soteriology and ecclesiology. Shakespeare's drama was written, performed, and published at the end of the same century in which Martin Luther nailed his ninety-five theses to the door of the church in Wittenberg, an action that effectively prompted the Protestant Reformation and irrevocably splintered the Western church into numerous denominational fragments. The seismic historical aftershocks of the Reformation were felt throughout Europe for centuries and arguably continue to unsettle fault lines in today's geopolitical context. It would thus be surprising if Shakespeare's art did not register the socio-political upheavals caused by the theological controversies of his age. The following study captures Shakespeare's sustained engagement with his religio-political context in four plays.

Reformation Christianity was ineluctably about salvation. Alec Ryrie, paraphrasing Susan Karant-Nunn, observes that "for Protestants, understanding of the doctrine of salvation took the place of feeling Christ's agonies" (289). The theological texts of the reformed English church attest to the primacy of soteriology as a theological discourse. In defending *The Book of Common Prayer*, Thomas Cranmer emphasized the liturgy's usefulness to soteriology because of its incorporation of vernacular scripture:

> . . .[I]n the English service appointed to be read there is nothing else but the eternal word of God: the new and the old Testament is read, that hath power to save your souls; which as Saint Paul saith, 'is the power of God to the salvation of all that believe'; the clear light to our eyes, without the which we cannot see; and a lantern unto our feet, without which we should stumble. (qtd. in Booty 359–360)

Cranmer's statement is not merely an affirmation of the Protestant principle *sola scriptura*, but also an insistence that the main preoccupation of the Bible itself is the salvation of humankind through the gospel (good news) of Jesus Christ, as Cranmer's citations of Romans suggests.

Another major architect of the English church, especially through the posthumous impact of his *Laws of Ecclesiastical Polity*, is Richard Hooker. In the first book of the *Laws*, Hooker argues that God has ceased to speak to the world since the closing of the New Testament canon because all necessary teaching about salvation is contained in scripture. Like Cranmer, Hooker suggests that the main focus of scripture is salvation through Christ:

> The main drift of the whole new Testament is that which Saint John setteth down as the purpose of his own history, *These things are written, that ye might believe that Jesus is Christ the Son of God, and that in believing ye might have life through his name.* The drift of the old [is] that which the Apostle mentioneth to Timothy, *The holy Scriputres are able to make thee wise unto salvation.* So that the general end both of old and new is one, the difference between them consisting in this, that the old did make wise by teaching salvation through Christ that should come, the new by teaching that Christ the Saviour is come. ... (115).

Hooker's comments convey the merging in soteriology of the reformed English church's Christocentric and logocentric foci.

However, Hooker's rapturous sentiments about the salutary effects of scripture fail to capture the historical realities of post-Reformation Christianity. While the sacred text of Christianity advocates salvation through a figure who meekly turned the other cheek to his torturers, the early modern religious landscape was inescapably contentious, often even violent. Shakespeare's parents lived through the bloody persecution of Protestants under Mary Tudor, and Shakespeare saw the escalating persecution of Catholics in the second half of Elizabeth's reign as tensions mounted with Spain. As I argue, Shakespeare exercised his concern over such cross-confessional hostility in *King Lear*, where he laments the inhumane martyrdom of his "cousin" (as defined loosely in the period), the Jesuit priest Robert Southwell. The very fact that martyrdom in the sixteenth century was almost universally enacted by Christians against other Christians with different beliefs speaks to the failure of early modern religion to live up to its theoretical ideals.[1] Doctrine was often a

---

1. Generally, Catholics and Protestants in the sixteenth and seventeenth centuries did not recognize each other as Christians. John Donne was a notable exception in

matter of life and death, and no mere private arena of personal opinion. Soteriology was no exception.

Much twentieth-century scholarship assumed that the religious dimensions of drama largely disappeared from the stage with the advent of the Renaissance commercial theater, but this assumption has been challenged by many scholars, including Erin Kelly. This secularizing narrative of the theater was sometimes buttressed by citing Elizabeth's "Proclamation 509, By the Queen, Against Plays, May 16, 1559," which insists that the justices of the peace "permit none [interludes] to be played wherein either matters of religion or of the governance of the estate of the commonwealth shall be handled or treated, being no meet matters to be written or treated upon but by men of authority, learning, and wisdom, nor to be handled before any audience but of grave and discreet persons" (rpt. in Pollard 302–303). Elizabeth's decree, however, does not entirely forbid religious expression in drama, but rather requires the oversight and audience of "men of authority, learning, and wisdom." And while Elizabeth's decree was certainly designed to keep the Reformation from being fought on the stage, her edict did not actually produce the effect of voiding religion from Renaissance drama.

Albeit generally less explicitly religious than medieval drama or even earlier sixteenth-century drama, the Renaissance commercial theater was a site of substantial religious thought and expression, even if such "theology" had to be muted enough or sufficiently orthodox to pass the taste tests of the royal censors. The fact that much Renaissance drama engages significantly with religion, despite Elizabeth's decree and the risky nature of public religious debate, speaks to the inextricable relationship between early modern religion and theater. Many Renaissance plays, written by a wide array of playwrights, reference religious ideas and events in a manner that assumes a general level of theological literacy of its audiences.

The scope of my project is Shakespeare and soteriology, rather than soteriology and Renaissance drama at large. In terms of his handling of religion, Shakespeare can easily be distinguished from a number of contemporary playwrights of the period, such as Thomas Dekker, who deploy religion in a fairly obvious confessional direction. Nathaniel Woodes's *Conflict of Conscience*, an interlude rather than a commercial play, is emphatically polemical, and thus even further removed from Shakespeare's

---

recognizing Catholics as Christians.

aesthetic. Playwrights such as Ben Jonson and Thomas Dekker overtly satirize their respective enemies, Puritans and Catholics. Shakespeare's satire of religion (as in *Twelfth Night*), tends to be absorbed by his more general examination of human failings such as self-righteousness, vanity, and cruelty. Still others, such as Christopher Marlowe, and to a lesser extent, Thomas Middleton, transgressively explore the violation of religious and moral norms by satirizing hypocrisy or extremism.[2] Whereas Ben Jonson converted to Roman Catholicism and then back to Protestantism, there is virtually no biographical evidence for what Shakespeare's religious preferences may have been. By comparison to most other Renaissance playwrights, Shakespeare holds his religious and skeptical cards much closer to his chest.

Recent biographical criticism has suggested that William's father John Shakespeare may have been a recusant (a Catholic who refused to conform to the Protestant Elizabethan church), and Andrew Hadfield has suggested that Shakespeare's daughter Susanna may have been a committed Roman Catholic (29–30). Be that as it may, there is really no compelling evidence that clarifies the nature of William Shakespeare's personal religious beliefs. While some have opined that Shakespeare was an agnostic or atheist, such language is largely anachronistic. In 1900, George Santayana argued that "Shakespeare. . . is remarkable among the greater poets for being without a philosophy and without a religion" (rpt. in Kermode 168). However, in the early modern period, an "atheist" was a person devoid of morals rather than someone who denied the existence of God. Atheism as we know it today is the legacy of the Enlightenment. Santayana's celebration of an irreligious Shakespeare, while misguided, contributed to the secularizing narrative about Shakespeare that was so popular throughout the twentieth century. Biographical explanations of religion in Shakespeare have been exhausted, to little avail.

Shakespeare never attended university and, thus, was not formally trained as a theologian, in the sense of being an expert on religious matters. However, Julia Lupton theorizes that Shakespeare uses religion (the master grammar of the period)[3] to think about ethical, political, and

---

2. Unlike Thomas Middleton, whose religio-politically topical *Game at Chess* landed him in prison and apparently ended his stage career, Shakespeare astutely managed to avoid getting embroiled in any controversies that would incur the wrath of the church or crown. Arguably, Shakespeare's life was more politically uneventful than the lives of some of his contemporaries in part because his deployment of religion was more subtle and politically non-committal than that of the majority of his peers.

3. Here I am adapting the titular metaphor of Brian Cummings's *The Literary*

philosophical issues, rather than to write theology (*Citizen-saints*). Her caution has helped to protect Shakespeare studies from digressing into speculative and polemical dead-ends, such as the quest for a Catholic Shakespeare. David Scott Kastan has also been reluctant to attribute personal religious convictions to Shakespeare, instead positioning him ambivalently astride the secular and the sacred (143). In some cases, however, this critical guardedness has diverted attention from the religious topography of Shakespeare's plays.

In any case, Shakespeare's personal views arguably form an incomplete basis for the theology in his plays. Although Shakespeare's voice is heard as a playwright (in some cases, collaborating with other playwrights), his plays nevertheless have a corporate aspect to them. Shakespeare was writing plays for theatrical companies in which he was a shareholder. He was not the only source of the ideas shaping the plays we now attribute to him. It is entirely possible that some of the religious perspectives in the plays derive from the corporate interests of the Lord Chamberlain's Men and the King's Men, and not from Shakespeare alone.

Therefore, my study is not concerned with Shakespeare's biography nor with his personal beliefs. These questions are beside the point of my research. My study of Shakespeare and soteriology will be confined to his drama because his biography affords so little relevant information. Exploring religion in Shakespearean drama is particularly fascinating because all we can rely on are the plays in historical context. Nevertheless, Shakespeare seems to have been interested in questions of theology. Although his drama tends to be less obviously "religious" than that of some of his contemporaries, his indifference to theological matters should not be assumed. The comparative subtlety, discretion, and dramatic integrity of Shakespeare's representations of religion do not disqualify such theology from serious scholarly inquiry and assessment.

Shakespeare embeds soteriological discourse from the Protestant and Catholic reformations in a surprisingly large number of places throughout his corpus.[4] Claudius's prayer for redemption, the gravediggers' speculation about Ophelia's salvation or damnation, and the purgatorial language of the ghost all foreground soteriology in *Hamlet*. In *The Merchant of Venice*, the willing (but possibly mercenary) conversion of

---

Culture of the Reformation: Grammar and Grace.

4. The plural term, "reformations" acknowledges the evolving, uneven, and varied nature of reform in England, as Christopher Haigh argues (12–24). Alexandra Walsham's work on Catholic reformation is also *à propos* here.

Jessica, the forced conversion of Shylock, Portia's mercy speech, and the dialectic between law and grace convey the inflammatory character of early modern soteriology. *Measure for Measure* pointedly comments on contentious aspects of penance/repentance, as well as the more confessionally unifying dogma of the vicarious atonement of Christ. Even *King Lear*, a play set in pagan Britain, is sufficiently anachronistic to concern itself with questions of evil and suffering in terms of cross-confessional theological polemics, including contemporary disputes about exorcism and martyrdom. Soteriology is clearly an important discourse in Shakespearean drama.

While Shakespeare and religion studies have all too often been derailed by largely fruitless biographical claims (Cummings, *Mortal Thoughts* 14), the better sort of Shakespeare and religion scholarship eschews biography. A number of more salient questions have given shape to some of the recent Shakespeare and religion scholarship. These include: What is the nature of Shakespeare's engagement with religion? More specifically, does Shakespeare have a dog in the theological fight, or is he better described as an impartial observer? What is the extent of religion and its controversies in Shakespearean drama? Does Shakespeare subordinate religious considerations to his dramatic art? What are the barriers to a present day understanding of the relationship between Shakespeare and religion? Lastly, what are some of the misgivings scholars have about the current "turn to religion" in Shakespeare studies? I will address these questions in turn.

So how does Shakespeare negotiate the religious sea changes of his age? Perhaps the best language for describing Shakespeare's approach to the volatile religio-political tensions of his period is the policy of Falstaff: "The better part of valour is discretion, in the which better part I have saved my life" (*1 Henry IV* 5.4.118–119). While Shakespeare engages with soteriology extensively in his plays, he refrains from committing himself to a position that would compromise his safety or alienate large sectors of his religiously pluralistic audience.[5] As Peter Kaufman avers, Shakespeare was not overtly advocating a particular theological position nor refuting one (199).

---

5. Perhaps the lack of any obvious confessional commitment in the drama was not even a deliberate strategy adopted by Shakespeare. Religious representation in the plays may represent the interests of the entire theater company, rather than just Shakespeare's individual preferences.

An avoidance of confessional affiliation, however, is not equivalent to a lack of interest in religion. As Peter Marshall insists, Shakespeare was engaged in debates about religious difference because they were a dominant feature of his culture ("Choosing" 56). David Loewenstein and Michael Witmore rightly observe that Shakespeare draws richly upon both Catholic and Protestant traditions, making it hard to discern Shakespeare's personal worldview (4). Maurice Hunt aptly refers to this cross-confessional fusion as "Shakespeare's syncretistic method," arguing convincingly that Shakespeare integrated Catholicism and Protestantism more thoroughly than any other early modern English playwright (ix). Loewenstein and Witmore suggest that Shakespeare engages with religion in an "independent-minded and flexible way," as befits a period with so much volatile religious controversy (19). Jean-Christophe Mayer likewise suggests that for Shakespeare religion was "not so much a matter of systematic allegiance as one of *constant* debating and questioning" (5).

Mayer is not alone in positing a dialectical Shakespeare. Alison Shell observes a longstanding trend in Shakespeare studies—the playwright has been championed as "profoundly religious" by some and "profoundly secular" by others (2). Shell suggests this "paradox" is owing to the inherent quality of Shakespeare's art and its effect upon audiences (2–3). However, perhaps such divergences of perspective owe more to the competing presuppositions of various audiences rather than to a historically accurate registering of Shakespeare's art. Brian Cummings's magisterial recovery of early modern religious contexts has gone a long way in debunking the secularization thesis about Shakespeare (*Mortal Thoughts*). Yet I suspect that the greater popularity Shakespeare currently enjoys over his fellow playwrights probably is owing in part to his comparatively nimble and unthreatening handling of religion.

What, then, is the nature or tone of Shakespeare's handling of religion? Jeffrey Knapp proffers a religiously informed Shakespeare, but strenuously argues that Shakespeare's handling of religion evades the pitfalls of sectarian bias (102; 171). It is easy to see why Knapp's picture of an irenic and inclusive Shakespeare has been so convincing, especially when the urbane playwright is seen against the backdrop of the bloody religious politics of his age.[6] Indeed, Shakespeare often defuses religious tensions, rather than

---

6. While my argument draws upon Jeffrey Knapp's insights into the religious pluralism of Shakespearean drama, I would caution against Knapp's idea that Shakespearean drama is inherently irenic and inclusive (14). While Knapp cites Erasmus as the model reformer for Shakespearean drama (14), this notion is highly reductive, for

inflaming them after the fashion of many of his fellow dramatists. Nevertheless, I would complicate Knapp's argument by pointing out that many of Shakespeare's portrayals of religion, especially with respect to soteriology, are inflected with coded political assessments of the often violently antithetical polemics of his period. At times, Shakespeare nuances his dramatizations of soteriology in such a way as to indicate possible positions on particular religious controversies in particular plays. These theological colorings, often veiled and oblique, however, are not uniformly Catholic or Protestant, but form a rich tapestry of religious ideas.

Such theological colorings constitute a variegated representation of confessional politics. David Bevington argues that Shakespeare evinces a "seeming wariness of Puritanism" (28). The Puritan comic butt Malvolio in *Twelfth Night* emphatically conveys Shakespeare's distaste for moralistic self-importance. However, my analysis of the first quarto of *Hamlet* illuminates that play's favorable handling of predestinarian Calvinism, suggesting that Shakespeare's perspective on Puritanism may not be quite as clear-cut as Bevington implies. However, Bevington rightly observes that Shakespeare's representations of Judaism and Islam are less nuanced than "his mediating negotiations of Catholic and Puritan" (39). In contrast, Gary Taylor suggests that Shakespeare's politics may have been oppositional, i.e., Catholic (283–314). Stephen Greenblatt also emphasizes the Catholic dimensions of Shakespeare's drama in *Hamlet in Purgatory*. However, Paul Stevens argues that the politics of *Henry VIII* (co-written with John Fletcher) are nationalistic (almost jingoistic) and highly favorable to the reformed English church (246–250). All these diverging critical opinions attest to the polyphony of confessional perspectives in Shakespeare's corpus. As Jeffrey Knapp comments (in a deft allusion to *Romeo and Juliet*), "Shakespeare would rather call down a plague on both Catholics and Protestants than take sides with either faction" (102–103).

What is the extent of Shakespeare's engagement with religion? Despite the paucity of biographical clues to Shakespeare's beliefs, Shakespeare's dramatic engagement with religious controversy is extensive. Hannibal Hamlin observes that in Shakespeare's plays "no book is alluded to more often, more thoroughly, or with more complexity and significance than the Bible" (*Bible* 3). Shakespeare alludes to every single book of the Bible, including the Apocrypha (112). Many of Shakespeare's biblical allusions

---

Shakespeare's drama bears the imprint of many reformers, both Catholic and Protestant. Nor do these various theological influences always sit comfortably with one another in Shakespeare's plays.

come from the Geneva Bible rather than from *The Great Bible* (the latter being the version used in *The Book of Common Prayer*), suggesting that Shakespeare was intimately acquainted with the biblical text not only from mandatory church worship but also from personal reading. These observations should unsettle the persistent opinion that Shakespeare was exceptionally secular in a religious world. Thomas Fulton and Kristen Poole observe a "popularization of hermeneutics" in Shakespeare's cultural context, arguing that his plays "reflect biblical fluency and engagement with contemporary exegetical debates" (2). Hamlin also indicates something of the breadth of Shakespeare's theological knowledge, suggesting that Shakespeare read from a variety of confessional positions (34). Shakespeare did in fact read cross-confessionally—my chapter on *King Lear* shows the play delicately balancing polemical Protestant and Catholic source texts.

The extent of religious representation in Shakespeare is nonetheless a matter of debate. While Hamlin, Fulton, and Poole observe the ubiquity of religion in Shakespeare, Allison Shell qualifies their findings: "For him [Shakespeare], as for few of his contemporaries, the Judeo-Christian story is something less than a master narrative" (3). It is true that Shakespeare's art is less explicitly religious than that of many of his contemporaries, in the sense of being less polemical, propagandist, or evangelistic. However, Shakespeare's softer, more nuanced approach to religion does not necessitate a conclusion that he was indifferent to the Judeo-Christian meta-narrative. Plays such as Thomas Dekker's *The Whore of Babylon* and Thomas Heywood's *A Woman Killed with Kindness* may be more polemical, even more determinedly religious, than Shakespeare's works, but they are arguably also less Christian in their overall vision and spirit (owing to their deficiencies in *caritas*).

Nonetheless, Shell is in good company when she attempts to rein in the limits of religion in Shakespeare. In 1904, A.C. Bradley virtually inaugurated the secularization thesis: "The Elizabethan drama was almost wholly secular; and while Shakespeare was writing he practically confined his view to the world of non-theological observation and thought" (40). Anthony Dawson speaks on behalf of the contributors to Jane Hwang Degenhardt and Elizabeth Williamson's collection in basically affirming the secularization thesis about Renaissance drama (236). Citing *Hamlet* as the supreme example, Dawson explores the ways in which "the theater (like Stephen Daedalus perhaps) both loses its religion and cannot escape it" (236). While the analogy of Stephen Daedalus's (and Joyce's) haunted apostacy may hold for Claudius, it is more doubtful whether the example applies across the board to Shakespeare's corpus. Commenting on the soliloquy as prayer in *Richard II*, Cummings observes that it "resembles something quite contrary to a secularization thesis: it is a religious meditation in the face of death. This is a commonplace genre of the period, not in any way restricted to ministers or the extravagantly godly" (187). If Shakespeare's religion is for the common person, and not just for the Cambridge educated theologian, it is no less worthy of scholarly inquiry.

What are some of the barriers to our understanding of Shakespeare and religion? The biggest impediment is likely to be the historical remove of the religious controversies to which Shakespeare was attending (Fulton and Poole 1). The Bible itself, like all religious texts of the period, was variously appropriated by competing theological camps (Fulton and Poole 2).[7] Soteriology, while a biblical discipline in its own right, emerges in the period as a politically charged discourse that pervades early modern culture, including the commercial theater. As Lucio says with such pluck in *Measure for Measure*, "Grace is grace, despite of all controversy" (1.2.24–25). However, for the historically minded literary critic, any attempt to discern what Shakespeare means by "grace" is likely to be slippery, especially considering how the term was invested with such diverse meanings in the period. My chapter on Claudius's prayer in *Hamlet* reveals grace to be the highly prized core of salvation—forgiveness of sin—that is attainable (or not) only through competing and contradictory pathways. As universal as the doctrine of salvation was purported to be, it lay behind barriers of religio-political controversy.

A second barrier to understanding Shakespeare and religion may be an affective resistance to the intolerance and violence characteristic of Reformation controversy (Marotti 1–2). Not only are many modern readers often limited by a widespread cultural illiteracy about religion (whether it be of the early modern past or of the pluralist, multi-cultural present), but they are also likely to have an antipathy for any kind of polemic that easily degenerates into violence—and for good reason. Such violence, after all, was the historical reality of Reformation soteriology. I would argue, however, that Shakespeare's handling of religious controversy suggests a way forward for religious difference even in today's world, where the other is often stereotyped rather than loved as a neighbor with common *humanitas*. Shakespeare's ability to engage intelligently

---

7. Hannibal Hamlin claims that biblical literacy is necessary for a critical understanding of Shakespearean drama (*Bible* 3).

with religion, while avoiding the mudslinging that is so typical of his period and ours, suggests that it is possible for religious identity to be represented in the public sphere without jeopardizing the common good.[8]

A third barrier in Shakespeare and religion studies may be the bias of a particular critic, whether such bias presents itself as religious or anti-religious. Jean-Christophe Mayer complains that studies of religion in Shakespeare have all too often been "incomplete, one-sided or partisan, whereas the cultural and religious universe around Shakespeare was fast-moving, ever-changing and largely hybrid" (5). For instance, David Beauregard's Catholic bias seems to emerge in his analysis of revenge in *Hamlet*, where he claims that "from a Catholic standpoint... the 'problem' of revenge disappears" (93). Somewhat puzzlingly, Beauregard suggests that because the ghost is from Purgatory its mandate of vengeance "can be seen as morally good" (93). The irony is that in attempting to defend a Catholic interpretation of the play, Beauregard ends up misguidedly attributing the violence in the play to Catholicism, rather than to medieval feudal culture.

Conversely, a Protestant bias is potentially discernable in Adrian Streete's claim that Protestantism is "a deeply Christocentric religion" (39). Such a claim needs to be counter-balanced by an equally emphatic recognition that early modern Catholicism is a Christocentric religion. After all, the Reformation debates were not about Christology, but about soteriology and ecclesiology. The issue of Christ's identity had been virtually settled in the Patristic debates, and subsequently celebrated by early modern Catholics and Protestants alike. Streete defends his claim for a specifically Christocentric designation of Protestantism by citing William Perkins's views on double predestination and irresistible grace (40–41). But these doctrines are more accurately soteriological rather than christological. In my analysis of the resonances of Lancelot Andrewes's proto-Arminian thought in the second quarto of *Hamlet*, I argue that Shakespeare broadens his soteriological views beyond the pale of Calvinist orthodoxies represented by popular theologians such as Perkins. In an attempt to avoid the pitfalls of sectarian bias, I have tried to absorb some of the best historiography of the early modern period—including that of Alec Ryrie on Protestantism, Alexandra Walsham on Catholicism, and Peter Marshall on both.

---

8. Julia Reinhard Lupton makes a point to this effect in discussing Shylock's status as a minority Jew in Christian Venice (*Citizen-Saints* 79).

The dichotomy between a Catholic and Protestant Shakespeare is also found in popular studies of Shakespeare and religion. For example, Graham Holderness's *The Faith of William Shakespeare*, though replete with remarkable insights into the plays, perhaps somewhat unconvincingly proffers a Calvinist Shakespeare. Meanwhile, Joseph Pearce's *The Quest for Shakespeare* concertedly argues (in the face of the current scholarly consensus) for a Catholic Shakespeare. One could almost get the impression that Shakespeare is up for theological grabs.

The literary criticism in *The Cambridge Companion to Shakespeare and Religion* edited by Hannibal Hamlin helpfully balances Catholic and Protestant perspectives, along with Jewish and Muslim discourses. The afterword in *The Cambridge Companion* is written by Rowan Williams, former archbishop of Canterbury, an editorial choice that suggests that Shakespeare is relevant to religion, putting aside the question of how much religion is relevant to Shakespeare. While this study seeks to emulate the nuanced and erudite recovery of Catholic/Protestant controversy in Hamlin's edited volume, I also engage in a limited capacity in Jewish-Christian dialogue. In my chapter on *The Merchant of Venice*, I resonate with Kenneth Gross's and Janet Adelman's grievances with early modern Christianity's persecution of Jews and Shakespeare's complicity with such prejudices, while attempting to extricate the writings of Saint Paul from these critics' allegations of anti-Judaism.

Given Shakespeare's reputation as a commercial dramatist, it is perhaps unsurprising that a dominant perspective in Shakespeare criticism suggests that he subordinates religion to his dramatic art. Allison Shell (3) and Roland Mushat Frye (239) are among those who privilege Shakespeare's drama to religion. In commenting on Claudius's prayer scene in *Hamlet*, Frye insists, "The theological material is thus not presented as an end in itself, but is digested to the needs of dramatic characterization" (239). Anthony Dawson seems to be taking his ideas and language from Frye when commenting on the same scene in *Hamlet*: "The scene dramatizes the intensity of religious emotion as it opens itself to theatrical representation, a kind of cannibalizing of the religious for theatrical purposes" (243). Dawson's argument extends the currency of Frye's thesis of 1963. Frye had further suggested, "A certain civil and temporal purification and even ennoblement may come from human affliction, rightly borne, but we should not confuse these effects so as to suppose that the plays were concerned with Christian salvation" (121–122).

Frye is correct in stating that Shakespeare's plays are not "concerned with Christian salvation" in the obvious sense that Shakespeare was not writing morality or mystery plays, nor was he writing polemical or evangelistic interludes after the fashion of Nathaniel Woodes's *Conflict of Conscience*. But as Cummings points out, the common notion that Shakespeare is a secular icon is seriously misguided (*Mortal* 8). Dawson's thesis, taken from Frye, that Shakespeare subordinates his treatment of religion to his dramatic aesthetic is ahistorical and overly simplistic. Cummings helpfully points out that in the early modern period the boundaries between the religious and secular were porous (13). Any attempt to understand Shakespeare's engagement with religion needs to acknowledge that early modern culture was pervasively religious. Dawson's suggestion that Shakespeare is "cannibalizing. . . the religious for theatrical purposes" is thus anachronistic and historically untenable. Even Frye acknowledges that "Shakespeare understood theology far better than do those who now try to convert his plays into Christian parables" (272). (My aim is emphatically *not* to co-opt Shakespeare for religious purposes, but rather to understand the religion inherent to his drama.)

Frye and Dawson's attempt to force an ontological distinction between religion and drama is not borne out by Renaissance drama itself. If anything, religion is so intrinsic to the drama of Shakespeare and his contemporaries that to try to expunge it would do a similar disservice to Shakespeare as the bowdlerizing of his texts in the nineteenth century to remove bawdy language. Shakespeare is not Shakespeare without the sex and the religion. Modern enthusiasts of Shakespeare may tend to prefer the sex to the religion, but the religion is nonetheless integral to the enduring success of Shakespeare's art.

An interesting line of thought explores Shakespeare's disillusionment, not only with religion, but also with the theater itself, thus turning the secularization thesis into something of an existential crisis. Commenting on *King Lear*, Stephen Greenblatt suggests that "the scene at Dover is a disenchanted analysis of both religious and theatrical illusions" (118). The scene in which Edgar as Poor Tom attempts to save Gloucester from suicide by having him safely dramatize (as an exorcism) the motions of self-slaughter without inflicting any actual harm is both heart-wrenching and heart-warming. One can see why Greenblatt regards this scene as conveying a disillusionment even with drama itself. However, Gillian Woods helpfully redeems this scene (and the theater) by observing the reciprocal relationship between theater and exorcism in the play: "Where the *Declaration* characterizes exorcism as mere theatre and therefore sinful, *King Lear* recasts theatre as exorcism that is salvific" (163). Here, the "secular" Shakespeare comes full circle only to find himself face to face with the "religious" Shakespeare. If *King Lear* suggests that drama can cure despair, much like a ritual of exorcism performed by a Jesuit priest or Puritan dispossessor can eject an evil presence from the human subject, then the boundaries of the religious and secular in Shakespeare are porous indeed. My research on the soteriological aspects of exorcism in early modern culture (and their relationship to Shakespearean drama) builds on Woods's insightful work.

The turn to religion in early modern literary studies has not captured the imagination of every critic, however. Alluding to Samuel Taylor Coleridge's reading of Shakespeare, Richard McCoy argues: "For all their supernatural atmospherics, Shakespeare's romances operate at a human and worldly level rather than attaining a transcendent plane. They aim to elicit 'poetic faith' rather than a faith in the divine and providential" (115). In his deft reading of *The Winter's Tale*, however, McCoy cannot entirely sever the term *faith* from its religious moorings, try as he might: "Chastened by the lethal outcome of his dark and destructive fantasies, Leontes accepts a more submissive and positive faith in things unseen, beginning his transition from bad faith to good faith. Moreover, in the long run Paulina's lie enforces Leontes' profound penitence and remorseful recognition of his wife's innocence" (137). Ironically, McCoy's neo-romantic secular reading of the play borrows its definition of good faith from Heb 11:1 and relies on soteriological concepts such as repentance to elucidate the play's meaning. The aptly named Paulina is an obvious referent for St. Paul (who was mistakenly thought by the translators of the King James Bible—published the same year as the first recorded performance of *The Winter's Tale*—to be the author of the epistle to the Hebrews). Paulina urges Leontes to prepare himself for the pseudo-resurrection of Hermione: "It is required / You do awake your faith" (5.3.94–95).

For an early Jacobean audience, the discourse of faith carries the weight of a century of passionate and sometimes bitter controversy, a context which McCoy sidelines to the detriment of his scholarship. Paulina's comment thus alludes to Luther's appropriation of Paul, which was contested by Erasmus and More. Calvin and his inheritors further codified the Lutheran doctrine of *sola fide* by requiring it to conform to the theological straightjacket of double predestination (a doctrine to which Luther had given rough outline in *De Servo Arbitrio* [*On the Bondage of the Will*], a text later repudiated by Lutherans). Further nuancing Shakespeare's citation of the Reformation contest between Protestant salvation by faith alone and Catholic salvation by a combination of faith and works is the Catholic orientation towards penance that dominates *The Winter's Tale*.

Here we see how in one play Shakespeare nuances his language with both Protestant and Catholic soteriological discourses but ultimately suggests something different than either tradition had contended, but which is nevertheless essential to his art. (In this case, as in many other moments in the plays, I am examining not only broad theological discourses, but also the particular idioms they have fostered.) While the modernist secular academy of the twentieth century often celebrated the deposition of theology from its medieval reign as the queen of the sciences, scholars today are increasingly re-awakening to the necessity of understanding religion to grasp the early modern period. Hirschfeld observes that "doctrine is itself a language, an aesthetic, and a structuring of meaning; and it remained in our period in crucial, mutual dialogue with the lived practice we associate with dramatic performance and content" (14–15). *The Winter's Tale* is a case in point.

The current "turn to religion" in Shakespeare studies has both promise and peril. While McCoy fears that "the fixation on religion" privileges cultural contexts to literary texts (xii), Ken Jackson and Arthur Marotti celebrate the opportunity to make connections between the religious tensions in the early modern world and those in our world today (*Shakespeare* 1). (My work on *The Merchant of Venice* and *Hamlet* attempts to make a little sense of such historical patterns.) Moreover, Jackson and Marotti's edited collection brings postmodern philosophy and theology to bear on Shakespeare (163–286). While these postmodern readings effectually sustain Shakespeare's cultural relevance, there is nonetheless a risk of remaking Shakespeare in our own image, rather than understanding his drama with historical accuracy.

A number of studies on Shakespeare and soteriology form an emerging subset of Shakespeare and religion scholarship. The ground-breaking work of Paul Cefalu, Debora Shuger, Sarah Beckwith, Heather Hirschfeld, Claire McEachern, and Gary Kuchar has begun to fill the lacuna in Shakespeare and soteriology. While some of these studies do not self-consciously categorize themselves under the rubric of soteriology, they all are concerned with controversy about salvation in Shakespearean drama.

Such scholarship attempts to answer a number of basic questions: What conclusions may be drawn from the scholarship on Shakespeare and soteriology? What soteriological language and concepts may we identify in Shakespeare's plays? What, if any, are the confessional affiliation(s) of the soteriological discourses in Shakespeare's plays? What is the meaning of Shakespeare's engagement with soteriology? What are some of the opportunities for and limitations of scholarship on Shakespeare and soteriology? While addressing each of these questions, I will indicate how I attempt to carry the scholarly conversation forward by newly identifying and analyzing particular soteriological discourses in Shakespeare's plays. While my volume will not be the first monograph-length study which falls under the rubric of Shakespeare and salvation, I position my work within the large gaps in the existing scholarship.

What conclusions may be drawn from the growing field of Shakespeare and soteriology? Before answering this difficult question, I will make some preliminary observations. First, Shakespeare includes a diverse array of soteriological positions in his plays. Second, Shakespeare is highly elusive when it comes to indicating his own theological positions, if any.[9] Third, the relationship between Shakespeare's soteriology and his drama can be quite complex, sometimes involving irony, parody, and other forms of generic and ethical interrogation. Fourth, Shakespeare's command of soteriology is impressive, despite Ben Jonson's quip that Shakespeare knew "small Latin and less Greek." Working within the parameters of these observations, I submit that the meaning of the soteriology in Shakespeare's plays is best determined in its specific dramatic and historical contexts. Therefore, each play or perhaps even each relevant scene could be described as having its own particular soteriological meaning. I have aimed to elicit the significance of critically important soteriological moments in several plays, but such discoveries represent only the tip of the iceberg. I have not been able to observe any broad confessional trend in the soteriological discourses throughout Shakespeare's corpus. Rather, I have detected a creative flexibility in Shakespeare's plays on the subject of salvation. Shakespeare clearly works across the Reformation divide when it comes to soteriology.

As one of the 'hot-button' issues of the Reformation, salvation was fiercely contested in Shakespeare's day, making it essential for scholarship to differentiate between conformist (Church of England), godly

9. A pun on the elusive/allusive nature of religion in Shakespeare forms the basis of Maurice Hunt's argument in *Shakespeare's Religious Allusiveness*.

(puritan), and recusant (Catholic) strains of soteriology in Shakespearean plays. Even these categories do not represent soteriologically monolithic traditions, but contain a diversity of expression within themselves, both synchronically and diachronically. In the multicultural, secular, postmodern academy, such doctrinal variations within Christianity may seem inconsequential, but it is important to remember that the narcissism of small differences is often one of the most intensely felt of human experiences. And while I do not wish to overstate the differences between Catholicism and Protestantism, early modern religion sometimes inflamed subtle theoretical divergences into full-scale war. The subtlety of Shakespeare's handling of religion contrasts refreshingly with the heated and volatile polemics so characteristic of his age.[10] Non-partisan investigation of these ideological variants within the drama is crucial to the forward momentum of Shakespeare and religion studies.

What are some of the soteriological language and concepts identified to date in the scholarship? It should not be surprising that soteriological debate figures prominently in Shakespearean drama. As Jonathan Willis observes, "Sin and salvation were the two central religious preoccupations of men and women in sixteenth-century," even as the Reformation disrupted the meaning of these concepts (1). Willis further argues, "Sin and salvation were in a theological sense great cosmic absolutes, but they were also historical constructs, born of particular social, cultural and theological contexts" (8). Scholarly attempts to recover soteriology in drama are necessarily selective due to the protean nature of the doctrine.

As such, lists of soteriological concepts quickly prove inadequate, however useful they are as a starting point. Willis gestures at the indeterminacy of soteriology in the period by concluding his provisional list of relevant concepts with ellipses: "sin, salvation, faith, works, virtue, vice, heaven, hell. . ." (13). Jesse Lander explores the vast theological terrain of *Hamlet* and emerges with a distinctly different list of soteriological constructs: "providence and predestination, free will, the Eucharist, purgatory, ghosts, prayer, burial rites, and the resurrection of the body" ("Maimed" 189). An itemization of soteriological concepts given attention in this study would include the following: justification by faith/works, sanctification, vicarious atonement, agency, predestination, election, law, grace, gospel, spiritual discernment, evil, exorcism, remorse,

---

10. While the drama of Shakespeare's contemporaries tends to be less polemical than much of the earlier sixteenth-century religious drama, there are many expressions of invective and contention in late Elizabethan and early Jacobean religious prose.

confession, repentance, penance, contrition, attrition, satisfaction, absolution, *imitatio Christi*, imputed/imparted righteousness, regeneration, ethics, conscience, conviction of sin, guilt, hypocrisy, self-righteousness, the sacraments, transubstantiation, baptism, *caritas*, forgiveness, healing, cleansing, redemption, suffering, sacrifice, death, resurrection, the body and blood of Jesus Christ, the Holy Spirit, adoption, *sola scriptura*, the priesthood of believers, and prayer. In no way does this list exhaust the soteriological concepts in Shakespeare. Wherever one turns in the drama, there is likely to be a lack of soteriological uniformity. This unruliness is to be expected, given the sheer volume and variety of the subject matter.

Nonetheless, there are a number of salient features of Shakespearean soteriology that have attracted the concerted attention of scholars. One conversation registers the tension between Catholic penance and Protestant repentance in Shakespearean drama. This tension is conveyed in my language about "the Reformation divide" in Shakespearean drama (and more emphatically in the early modern period at large). Sarah Beckwith's *Shakespeare and the Grammar of Forgiveness*, perhaps the most authoritative monograph on Shakespeare and soteriology, examines Shakespeare's romances as responses to the Reformation's replacement of the sacrament of penance with the individualistic discipline of repentance. Heather Hirschfeld's *The End of Satisfaction: Drama and Repentance in the Age of Shakespeare* argues that the Reformation's removal of satisfaction from penitence engendered a disorientation which found expression in revenge drama.

Criticism of *Measure for Measure* has proved particularly responsive to debates about penance and repentance. For example, James Knapp (256–286) and Peter Lake (*Antichrist's* 621–700) engage controversies about penitence in *Measure for Measure*. Lake's thoroughgoing analysis of popular penitential tracts about the conversion of criminals lends historical credence to his interpretation of the play's penitential politics. In her magisterial monograph on the play, Debora Shuger observes that the momentum to install a harsh Genevan form of discipline in the English church subsided during the late Elizabethan and early Jacobean periods (120). However, she suggests that "the ecclesiological repressed returned as soteriology," as became evident in severe Puritan formulations about behavioral righteousness and signs of election (120). Taking my cue from Shuger's *Political Theologies*, I explore aspects of the play's soteriology that relate to politics, thus avoiding the well-trodden terrain of penitence. My innovation is to correlate the play's discourse of substitutionary atonement with Luther's doctrine of the two realms of government, the church and the state.

Another line of inquiry seeks to discern the relative weighting of sacraments and faith, as far as salvation is concerned. David Coleman's *Drama and the Sacraments in Sixteenth-Century England* concludes that Shakespeare's plays explore the boundaries of the medieval and modern worlds, as well as the intersections of Catholic and Protestant theologies, at times demystifying the sacraments and sometimes attributing grace to soteriological signs (130). David Beauregard's *Catholic Theology in Shakespeare's Plays*, while not confined to the rubric of soteriology, nevertheless emphasizes penance and grace in terms that are distinctly Catholic and sacramental. In a highly influential study, Greenblatt considers the sacraments in *Hamlet* through the lens of anti-Catholic polemic (*Hamlet* 240). Jay Zysk masterfully argues that soteriological anxieties about the unsacramental death of Hamlet's father fuels Hamlet's revenge quest (422–443).

Rather than exploring salvation in terms of the sacraments, John Cox traces the presence of faith and biblical "salvation history" in Shakespearean drama (xiii). Cox's *Seeming Knowledge: Shakespeare and Skeptical Faith*, besides offering fascinating readings of the spirituality of most of Shakespeare's plays, compares Shakespeare's approach to faith and skepticism with the writings of seventeenth-century French epistemologists. Cox ingeniously suggests that Shakespeare's three main genres of tragedy, comedy, and history derive their distinctiveness from "Shakespeare's continuing reflection on the narrative of salvation history and its way of imagining the human situation" (xiii).

What can these studies tell us about the confessional affiliation of the soteriological discourses in Shakespeare's plays? With the obvious exception of Cox (whose theological hermeneutic seems to be more biblical and philosophical than historical) most of the authors I surveyed above from the literature on Shakespeare and soteriology evince a discernable bias in favor of pre-Reformation Catholic soteriology over the reformed soteriologies of Shakespeare's context. One of the implications of this pre-Reformation bias is that most of the current scholarship on Shakespeare and soteriology largely restricts the definition of salvation to the seven Catholic sacraments, predominantly focusing on the sacrament of penance. Such approaches also privilege ritual and liturgy to doctrine and belief in the study of soteriology. The biased nature of some of the scholarship on Shakespeare and soteriology has proved to be a defining limitation of the field, whether such presuppositions manifest as Catholic, Protestant, or secular.

The Reformation tension between Catholic and Protestant soteriologies also finds expression in John S. Coolidge's classic study, *The Pauline Renaissance in England: Puritanism and the Bible*, which has recently been qualified by Paul Cefalu in *The Johannine Renaissance in Early Modern English Literature and Theology*. Cefalu suggests that Herbert's poetry is part of a Johannine rather than a Pauline Renaissance ("Johannine Poetics" 1047). Cefalu challenges "the critical perception that soteriological and forensic Pauline-Protestant notions of justification by faith are more central to Herbert's poetry than the metaphysical Johannine themes of the divinity of Christ, God's hiddenness, and the use of scriptural-based irony and misunderstanding" (1044–45). As in Pauline inflected Herbert studies, Shakespearean religious studies of the past had a largely Protestant predilection, but it would seem there has been an over-compensation towards Catholic categories in the recent studies of Shakespeare and soteriology. Claire McEachern's *Believing in Shakespeare: Studies in Longing*, fascinated with the Protestant doctrines of faith and predestination, has helped to correct the theological balance in Shakespeare and religion criticism.

My study of Shakespeare and salvation, rather than simply retracing the well-worn controversy between Catholic penance and Protestant repentance, picks up the thread of Cefalu's distinction between the (Protestant) Pauline Renaissance and the (Catholic) Johannine Renaissance. I use Cefalu's distinction to trace in the drama evidence of Paul's emphases on faith and grace (championed by the Protestant reformers, via Augustine) and John's emphases on love and mystery (championed by medieval Catholicism and defended by early modern Catholic theologians). My research also privileges the tension between the reformed (Protestant) emphasis on divine election (double predestination), on the one hand, and the Catholic emphasis on free will (human agency) in salvation, on the other hand. I also foreground Reformation debates about justification and sanctification and their iterations in Shakespearean drama, such as the extensive debate about justification by faith/works in *The Merchant of Venice*.

While Luther and Calvin insisted that faith alone could justify, and that sanctification was instead a distinct activity proceeding salvation, Roman Catholic polemicists such as Thomas More refused to divorce justification and sanctification. In Catholic thought, *caritas* holds justifying power, and not faith alone. Shakespeare's dialectic between justification and sanctification in the romances, while drawing on both Catholic and Protestant theologies, ultimately envisions justification and sanctification as soteriological corollaries.[11] Shakespeare thus inserts these prominent Protestant concepts into a Catholic mold.

Indeed, the question of confessional affiliation is one of the subtexts of much criticism on Shakespeare and soteriology, even as it undergirds Shakespeare and religion criticism at large.[12] At times it seems as though the great Reformation divide may be discerned in the scholarship on soteriology in Shakespeare. Rather than leaning to one side or another on the question of the confessional status of Shakespeare's soteriology, this study identifies particular plays or even scenes as having a range of Protestant or Catholic inflections. Most notably, my analysis of Claudius's prayer in *Hamlet* recovers a combination of Puritan, Jesuit, and proto-Arminian discourses. This work attempts to emulate the balanced critical perspectives of Gillian Woods, who argues that *King Lear* is "an unreformed rather than a Catholic fiction" (168).

The first swing of the turn to religion tended to recover Catholic soteriologies.[13] Peter Marshall's historiography may help to explain why the question of Shakespeare's possible Catholicism has such a lingering presence in criticism, even if some of the answers proffered tend to be scant on evidence or one-sided (Mayer 5). Marshall makes the compelling observation (less obvious than it seems) that Catholics did not know they were on the losing side of English religious politics during Shakespeare's lifetime ("Choosing" 53). There was a lively hope among many English Catholics that the nation would be restored to the jurisdiction of Rome. The question of which faith was the better bet to follow was by no means settled (53). Marshall wisely observes of Shakespeare that "we cannot observe him making distinct religious choices (like a Jonson or

11. The idea and terminology of justification and sanctification being "soteriological corollaries" was suggested to me by theologian Gary Foreman.

12. Some of the soteriological studies that emphasize Catholic ideas in Shakespeare include those of Sarah Beckwith, Heather Hirschfeld, David Beauregard, Stephen Greenblatt, Gary Taylor, John Klause, Jesse Lander, Phoebe Jensen, David Coleman, Robert Bennett, and Jay Zysk. Some of the work that accentuates the Protestant dimensions of soteriology in Shakespeare includes that of Brian Cummings, Debora Shuger, Claire McEachern, Graham Holderness, John Cox, Hannibal Hamlin, Adrian Streete, and Peter Lake.

13. Gary Taylor's influential argument about Shakespeare's possible oppositional status as a Catholic (283–314) led to other influential studies emphasizing Catholic nostalgia, such as those of Stephen Greenblatt (*Hamlet* 229) and Eamon Duffey ("Bare" 47–52).

Donne) and cannot readily identify confessional statements or stances in his writings" (56). Nonetheless, the soteriological questions of his day exercised his imagination, as the burgeoning field of Shakespeare and religion suggests.

What is the meaning of Shakespeare's engagement with soteriology? Because the meaning of soteriology in Shakespeare is best discerned in particular dramatic contexts, the answers to this question are legion. Here, I will attend to one salient hermeneutical crux, the "debate concerning questions about the scope of a person's participation in his or her own salvation" (McEachern 19). A common perception is that Catholicism assumes soteriological agency, while early modern Protestantism adheres to soteriological determinism. However, Claire McEachern observes that some versions of Protestantism made allowance for human participation in the drama of salvation (37). My study of the contextual significance of Lancelot Andrewes's proto-Arminian thought to Claudius's prayer explores the significance of Protestant soteriological agency, à la McEachern.

Soteriological agency is becoming increasingly recognized as a feature of some early modern English spiritualities. Maria Devlin argues that the despair engendered by theological determinism may be a feature of reformed systematic theology, but not of "rhetorical theology," her term for persuasive preaching that enjoined its audiences to be saved (174). Devlin argues that rhetorical theology "re-opens a place for temporality, indeterminacy, and human agency" (175). Citing Martin Bucer's exemplum of Aristotle's idea of dramatic "reversal," Devlin argues that in rhetorical theology, "a reversal from sin to salvation is always possible for *me*" (189). Devlin's research is ground-breaking, in that it brings much needed qualification to common stereotypes of Protestant soteriological determinism. Shakespeare's plays seem to have registered such soteriological agency.

The current scholarship on Shakespeare and soteriology shows much promise, but also some limitations. This academic domain, like the broader field of Shakespeare and religion criticism to which it belongs, has the potential to recover a largely cautionary picture of how to handle the thorny problem of religious difference on a geo-political scale. Jackson and Marotti's *Shakespeare and Religion* and Jackson's *Shakespeare and Abraham* make some helpful theoretical connections between Shakespeare's religious context and our own. Nevertheless, there remains ample work to be done in learning from tensions between Catholicism and Protestantism in early modern Europe in order to better understand and address the often uneasy relationship in the current global context among the three Abrahamic faiths—Judaism, Christianity, and Islam. Tragically, religious difference today produces egregious violence, much like it did in the early modern period. An ignorance of the past will not serve humanity well going forward.

The integration of faith with Shakespeare scholarship is another feature of some soteriological studies of Shakespeare that can be regarded as either a limitation or an opportunity, depending on one's critical vantage point. Piero Boitani's *The Gospel according to Shakespeare* is a work of faith, as well as scholarship, and thus has a potentially narrower (or broader) audience than mainstream academic Shakespeare and religion criticism, into whose conversation I have situated my scholarship. John Cox's *Seeming Knowledge* conveys resonant insights into Shakespearean drama, along with mature spiritual perspectives that are delivered in an open-handed and hospitable manner, so as to invite a generous academic audience. Graham Holderness's *The Faith of William Shakespeare* is replete with perceptive comments on the plays, articulated in an informal style. Perhaps the Calvinist bias of Holderness's thesis does not serve Shakespeare's corpus well, but his approach offers a much needed corrective to the previous spate of determinedly Catholic approaches to Shakespeare.

A misguided hermeneutic of religious allegory has been a limitation of some past studies of Shakespeare. While Shakespeare and religion criticism has largely (and thankfully) outgrown the unwarranted religious allegorizing of some earlier generations of scholars, allegory still occasionally rears its ugly head. For example, in an otherwise erudite monograph, Robert Bennett interprets *Measure for Measure* in terms of allegory: as "scapegoat Mariana serves as a mediating Logos within the play" (138). While I am indebted to Bennett for some of his ideas about substitution, I concertedly attempt to resist unwarranted allegorizing.

Some critics are concerned with what they perceive to be the overreach of religion in Shakespeare studies. Indeed, soteriology is perhaps not an idea that excites every imagination, however prevalent I have shown it to be in Shakespeare. Richard McCoy eloquently contends for a return to a secular approach to Shakespeare: "I now see faith in Shakespeare as more theatrical and poetic than spiritual" (ix). As such, he challenges "the fixation on religion" in Shakespeare studies (xii). Religion is certainly not everyone's cup of tea, so I applaud critics such as Hannibal

Hamlin, Brian Cummings, and Jesse Lander who write about religion with appropriate scholarly rigor and historical accuracy, irrespective of their personal religious beliefs or lack thereof.

This volume builds on the substantial findings of recent Shakespeare and religion criticism but focuses concertedly on the relationship between Shakespeare and soteriology so as to yield innovations in the scholarly discourse. The methodology for my study is neo-formalist, historicist, contextualized close reading of Shakespearean plays in relation to early modern theology and drama. My hermeneutic is to read Shakespeare through the lens of contemporaneous theological controversy and to read such theology through the lens of Shakespeare.[14] I also compare some of Shakespeare's approaches to soteriology with those found in works by a number of his fellow dramatists, including major figures such as Marlowe and Middleton and minor figures such as George Whetstone and Cyril Tourneur—playwrights who afford especially helpful contextualization for the study of religion in Shakespeare. Marlowe's influence on Shakespearean drama can scarcely be overstated, even if Marlowe's protracted fascination with religion tends to be more volatile, parodic, and transgressive than Shakespeare's comparatively muted and cautious engagements. In contributing revisions to *Measure for Measure* and in collaborating on *Timon of Athens*, Middleton becomes an important referent for studies of Shakespeare and religion, especially because both of these plays evince a critique of Calvinism, despite the opinion of a number of scholars that Middleton's drama is essentially Calvinist in its orientation.

In order to understand the theories of salvation inherited by Shakespeare and his contemporaries, I bring Shakespearean drama into conversation with primary source Reformation documents by major continental theologians such as Luther, Erasmus, and Calvin, as well as those by English controversialists such as Tyndale, More, Hooker, Perkins, Southwell, Harsnett, and Andrewes. In analyzing religious references in several Shakespearean plays, as well as the theological ideas in selected works by contemporary dramatists that foreground religious controversy, I shed light on the presence and contours of Reformation

14. In my methodology, I aspire to follow the historically sensitive approaches of leading Shakespeare and religion scholars such as Hannibal Hamlin and Brian Cummings. I also have been influenced by the spiritual resonance of scholars such as John Cox, whose objective academic tone and Socratic wisdom I have tried to absorb. While I admire the theoretical prowess of Ken Jackson and Arthur Marotti, my study does not lie within the purview of postmodern literary theory.

soteriologies in the drama. To this end, I draw extensively on current criticism and theory of Shakespeare and religion, as well as recent studies of early modern religious cultures and contexts.

Certainly, I would concede that Shakespearean drama is not theology in the same formal sense as Richard Hooker's prose. Nor is Shakespearean drama engaged as directly or explicitly with theological arguments as are John Bale's plays or George Herbert's poetry. Indeed, Shakespeare writes about religion as a playwright, not a divine. But religion, after all, was the master grammar of the period, and Shakespeare demonstrates a surprising level of fluency in its discourses, as my study demonstrates. I do also recognize that a theological reading of Shakespeare necessarily involves some degree of magnification, as any specialized, theoretical reading of literature is wont to produce. But given Shakespeare's historical context, applying a Reformation theological lens to his drama is likely to be as illuminating as, say, a feminist, Marxist, deconstructionist, post-colonial, or eco-critical reading of him. While my interests and approach in this study are strongly theological, I hope that my readings are fair to the drama, even if they accentuate religion at the expense of other equally valid, and perhaps even more ubiquitous, discourses in the plays, such as gender, love, sexuality, politics, and history, though my study of soteriology intersects with each of these domains.

I also position Shakespeare's references to and images of Christ—understood by most early modern Europeans to be God incarnate, the Savior of humanity—in relation to competing Catholic and Protestant soteriologies. I further examine the presence of the Eucharistic and cruciform Catholic Christ in the drama (in part a legacy of medieval miracle and mystery plays), as well as the Protestant (largely Pauline) Christ as the object of faith, the subject of scripture, and the impetus for religious conversion (in the Reformation period often practiced as converting or reverting from Catholicism to Protestantism, or vice versa). A tension can be felt in Shakespeare's plays between the Protestant location of the gospel in scripture (and preaching) and the Catholic dispensing of salvation through the church and her seven sacraments.

This study interrogates the discourses of soteriology in four Shakespearean plays from a variety of early modern religious perspectives with a view to recovering more of the political, spiritual, philosophical, and dramatic dimensions of Shakespeare's representation of religion. More precisely, this volume seeks to discern the meaning of Shakespeare's deployment of Reformation soteriologies. My sense is that Shakespeare's rather protean depictions of soteriology enhance his dramatic purposes. Nevertheless, his representations of soteriology also seem to comment reflexively on the Reformation contexts of his age. While Shakespeare uses theological tropes largely for dramatic ends, he arguably also engages on some level with the theological controversies of Elizabethan and Jacobean England.

This study contextualizes some of Shakespeare's myriad religious references and allusions by analyzing their various relationships to competing Reformation theories of salvation. I explore how the language and concepts of faith, grace, charity, the sacraments, election, free will, justification, sanctification, and atonement find expression in Shakespeare's plays. In doing so, this volume hopes to contribute to the recovery of a greater understanding of the relationship between early modern religion and Shakespearean drama, a relationship which twentieth century criticism tended to dismiss as tenuous or to politicize as oppositional, but which the turn to religion in early modern scholarship of the past decade and a half has increasingly recognized as highly complex, sophisticated, and interdependent.

My methodology springs into action by recovering the soteriological deep structures in particular plays. In addition to analyzing the dramatic play of theological language in Shakespeare, I explore the soteriological deep structures of a number of dramas, including *King Lear*, which I argue is rooted in the violent imagery of Catholic sacramentalism. By soteriological deep structures I mean the undergirding or pervasive presence of soteriology in dramatic action, characterization, or imagery in a way that transcends mere verbal play or local allusion. For example, the relentless suffering in *King Lear* hearkens back to a bloody medieval Catholic Christology, thus rejecting a sanitized reformed soteriology. In reaction to the reverent agonies of Catholic soteriology, Calvin made salvation more confident and logical for the believer. Whereas Calvin and his codifiers were determined to emphasize the role of certainty in his keys to salvation—faith and election—Catholicism continued to signify its soteriology in terms of the violent mysteries of Christ's sufferings, whether Eucharistically or historically embodied. Gary Kuchar observes, "In the course of revising *The Institutes*, Calvin evolved a definition of faith that went from primarily meaning 'trust' to eventually meaning 'certain knowledge.' . . .Calvin made the practice of becoming assured of one's own salvation the center of his spiritual vision" (*George Herbert and the Mystery of the Word* 77–78). Whereas Calvin in his *Institutes of the Christian Religion* would locate the first cause of salvation in the inscrutable will of God which arbitrarily ("gratuitously") predestines some people to salvation and others to damnation, Shakespeare draws a soteriological parallel between King Lear's hell on earth and the sufferings of Christ. Lear's agonies thus function as a skeptical gloss on Calvin's theological voluntarism, instead intimating a recovery of the violent medieval Catholic images of the crucifixion and the sacrament of communion in which wine is transubstantiated into Jesus's blood.

The liturgical practice of exorcism underlies much of the action in *King Lear*, constituting another possible soteriological deep structure in the play. The numerous allusions to Samuel Harsnett's *Declaration of Egregious Popish Impostures* function not only as images of mental illness, but also as metaphors for the eviction of evil from the human subject, whether it be Poor Tom being transformed back into Edgar, Gloucester being freed from the "demon" of suicide, the kingdom being cleansed of its ungrateful princesses and violent oppressors, or even the eleventh-hour quasi-repentance of Edmund. I argue that the pervasive imagery of demonic possession and exorcism suggests that the Markan narrative of the Gadarene demoniac is an important source in shaping the dramatic trajectory. Stanley Wells further observes that the book of Job and the parable of the Prodigal Son from Luke 15 have been identified as "deep sources" for *King Lear* (29). Here the Lukan soteriological imagery is reversed, in that the father assumes the role of the wayward son, while the virtuous daughter Cordelia is cast in the role of redemptive father. The gender reversed Pietà, in which Lear holds the dead Cordelia in his arms, also inverts biblical imagery.

Other plays in this study show evidence of having soteriological deep structures. *The Merchant of Venice* culminates in the trial scene which conveys the forensic nature of Reformation notions of justification. Portia's (in)famous mercy speech accentuates Reformation controversy over whether salvation is a matter of *undeserved* "justice" (i.e., justification by faith, the Protestant position) or whether salvation is expressed by "deeds of mercy" (the Catholic position) (4.1.196–199). The courtroom context for this speech about salvation is no accident, for the Protestant reformers, picking up on legal biblical imagery, regard salvation as the forensic imputation of Christ's righteous to the sinner. Catholicism, following Augustine, regards regeneration as the actual impartation of Christ's righteousness to the believer. *The Merchant of Venice* thus interrogates how salvation is supposed to operate in Christian soteriology, whether through the legal transference of Christ's goodness to a believing sinner (Luther) or through the ethical renewal of the penitent (Thomas More). In depicting the court's abuse of Shylock in such strongly soteriological terms, the play would seem to challenge the ethical integrity of Luther's cherished doctrine. The play casts doubt on the formulation of salvation as a justifying forensic status precisely because the behavior of the Venetian Christians remains so cruel. A salvation that refuses to engender ethical renewal is no salvation at all.

The problematic relationship between salvation and ethics is also a major concern in *Measure for Measure*, another play with soteriological deep structures. Isabella's speech about the vicarious atonement of Christ (2.2.73–80) is parodied in the play's scenes of sexual and penal substitution. The substitution that Isabella regards as necessary for salvation, namely, the sinless Christ dying in the place of sinful humanity, is comically inverted when Angelo is deceived into sleeping with Mariana instead of Isabella and when Ragozine's head is used as a proxy for Claudio's. The ethically suspect substitutions of the bed trick and head trick seem to suggest the incongruity of grace itself. How can grace be correlated with ethics when grace forgives a multitude of egregious wrongs by a single act of penal substitution in which the innocent is afflicted on behalf of the guilty? How is it possible to envision the undeserved sufferings of Jesus Christ as the sole solution to the world's multifarious problems?

In the world of the play, however, grace is good news for devious sinners and hypocrites such as Angelo, but grace fails to reward the virtuous Isabella and Mariana according to their deserts. Both women are pressured to marry men who are vastly inferior to them morally. The play's preoccupation with penitence thus speaks to the uneasy relationship between salvation and ethics, for in the schema of grace the wicked who repent receive the rewards of the virtuous, while the virtuous themselves are subjected to the caprice of the wicked. Perhaps the play suggests that such a soteriological exchange is anything but fair.

This volume analyzes Shakespeare's engagement with both the theory and praxis of soteriology. Drawing upon the methodologies of theoretical historical theology, chapter one engages the quintessential Reformation controversy over justification by faith, chapter two probes the tenability of soteriological agency and its implications for the well-worn terrain of grace and predestination, while chapter four queries the reach and limits of the cardinal doctrine of vicarious atonement. Justification, free will, and vicarious atonement are all major foci of Reformation controversy, and these topics emerge impressively in Shakespearean drama. Chapters three and five consider Shakespeare's approach to practical theologies, namely, spiritual discernment, exorcism, and martyrdom. In essence, these are also para-soteriological theological concerns. These practical domains were just as controversial as major soteriological theory. Shakespeare's shrewd engagement with such volatile issues of practical theology is highly masterful, both in terms of literary effect and ideological nuancing.

What follows is a brief summary of the argument of each chapter in this study:

My first chapter explores the tension in *The Merchant of Venice* between Protestant notions of justification by faith and a Catholic insistence upon works of mercy. The trial scene in particular deconstructs cherished Protestant ideology by refuting the efficacy of faith when it is divorced from ethical behavior. The first chapter also examines the implications of Reformation controversy for Jewish-Christian interfaith dialogue. The second chapter situates *Hamlet* in the stream of Lancelot Andrewes's "avant-garde conformity" (to use Peter Lake's coinage), thereby explaining why Claudius's prayer in the definitive text of the second quarto has intimations of soteriological agency that are lacking in the first quarto. While the first quarto strongly evinces Calvinist predestinarianism, the second quarto may even have intimations of Molinism via intertextuality with a lyric by Jesuit Robert Southwell. The third chapter argues that *Hamlet* undermines the ghost's association of violence with religion, thus implicitly critiquing the proliferation of religious violence on both sides of the Reformation divide. Both Hamlet and the audience are invited to engage in protocols of spiritual discernment that have longstanding traditions in Catholicism. Through a sophisticated network of allusions to the apostle Peter which derive from the Bible and Southwell's *Saint Peters Complaynt*, *Hamlet* drops clues that the ghost is a demon, a spirit understood by early modern theology to be malignant.

The fourth chapter argues that Calvin's theory of the vicarious atonement of Christ, expounded so eloquently by Isabella in *Measure for Measure*, meets substantial resistance, especially when the Duke and others attempt to apply the soteriological principle of substitution to the domains of sexuality and law. The ethical failures that result from an over-realized soteriology indicate that the play corroborates Luther's idea that a distinction must be maintained between the sacred and secular realms. The fifth chapter examines controversies in the English church about the (il)legitimacy of exorcising demons, a practice favoured by Jesuits but generally frowned upon by Calvinists. Shakespeare cleverly negotiates satirical source material by metaphorizing exorcisms in *King Lear* in a way that seems to acknowledge Calvinist skepticism, yet honour Jesuit compassion. The violence in *King Lear* also speaks to the early modern reality of martyrdom through an extended allusion to Southwell's *Epistle of Comfort*.

The arrangement of the chapters is based on the chronological order of the plays discussed (based on presumed date of writing and/or first performance). While certainly not exhaustive, this volume innovatively coalesces the discourses of soteriology in particularly germane texts across Shakespeare's corpus. The plays represented include two tragedies and two comedies (*The Merchant of Venice* and *Measure for Measure* sometimes being recategorized as problem plays). My selection of plays is significant, for it includes two which are characteristically regarded as Shakespeare's most religiously inflected—*Measure for Measure* and *The Merchant of Venice*, as well as a play that twentieth century criticism considered a statement of nihilistic agnosticism—*King Lear*. In other words, salvation turns up in Shakespeare both when it is expected and when it is presumed absent. While the religious dimensions of *Hamlet* are becoming increasingly appreciated by critics, my study suggests that there may yet be new ground to break in that field.

Soteriology in Shakespeare is by no means restricted to the plays in the purview of this study. A truly exhaustive study of soteriology in Shakespeare would likely need to comment on every Shakespearean play, as well as his lyric and narrative poetry. Indeed, in the foreword to this volume, Gary Kuchar bears witness to the imprint of soteriology on Shakespeare's sonnets. Space did not allow me the comprehensiveness necessary to register all of Shakespeare's engagements with theology. The topic of soteriology could be fruitfully explored in *The Comedy of Errors* and *Twelfth Night*, both of which further engage the contemporaneous exorcism controversies. The eponymous king of *Richard II* is an ironic Christ figure who complains bitterly about the necessity of carrying his "sour cross" (4.1.234). *Othello* portrays Desdemona as innocent through her invocation of her salvation and Othello as ethically corrupt by his failure to act in accordance with the values of his Catholic baptism. *Macbeth* traces the allure of sin and the consequent elusiveness of salvation in distinctly theological terminology. *The Winter's Tale* explores the meaning of faith, while *The Tempest* probes the distinction between magic and prayer, all in the context of an expansive vision of forgiveness. Clearly, soteriology is a subject to which Shakespeare would frequently return. Arguably, the four plays I have chosen to discuss with reference to soteriology could be seen more accurately as representative rather than exceptional.

My recovery of both the ecumenical and controversial impulses in Shakespearean soteriology helps to elucidate the pervasiveness of early modern theological discourses—even in popular theatrical contexts—and aims to show how religion enhances rather than diminishes the dramatic effect of Shakespeare's art. Indeed, I suspect that the fine and discreet nuancing of religion in Shakespeare's plays is one of the reasons that many earlier critics missed so much of the religion in his drama. When in Shakespeare's Arden, it is hard to see the theological trees amongst the dramatic forests precisely because all the greenery blends so well together. Aspiring to gain a greater theological appreciation of Shakespeare's art is a worthwhile goal, in that it promises to reveal some resonant insights by one of the world's greatest playwrights into a watershed period in Western culture—the Reformation.

My research thus sheds further light on the connection between theology (the dominant early modern discipline) and Renaissance drama. In addition to illuminating Shakespeare's plays through their historical context, my study helps scholars recognize both the breadth and limitations of Shakespeare's understanding of the religious discourses of his day, possibly even giving further perspective on the theological leanings of particular plays. Because Catholics and Protestants alike can find so much familiar fodder in Shakespeare, his discerning, yet generous approach to religion affords a paradigm for interfaith (or, at least, intrafaith) dialogue that is as relevant to our age as it was to his. My research also indirectly benefits scholarship of the post-modern global context, for an understanding of the historical roots of religious disagreement can stimulate insight into the persistent problems of religious intolerance and violence. In Shakespeare's hands, even grace has a keen political edge.

This study of soteriology in the four plays I have selected has helped to furnish further evidence that Shakespeare was theologically literate, though not formally trained, and that religion is an important dimension of the *oeuvre* of the most important dramatist (arguably the greatest writer) in the Western literary canon. I also hope that I have adequately conveyed the sophistication, erudition, grandeur, and sometimes comedy of the theology in Shakespearean drama.

1

"One Drop of Christian Blood"
Shakespeare's Critique of Justification by Faith in *The Merchant of Venice*

IN THE WAKE OF 9/11, the academy began to pay more concerted attention to religion, particularly the bloody intersections of the three "Abrahamic" faiths—Judaism, Christianity, and Islam. The vexed and often violent relationship between these three monotheisms was also exhibited on the early modern stage in Marlowe's darkly comic *The Jew of Malta* and in Shakespeare's *The Merchant of Venice*. As a play preoccupied with justice, *The Merchant of Venice* probes the social and legal difficulties of navigating the competing claims of the majority religion (Christianity) and minority faiths (Judaism and, to a lesser extent, Islam). While most scholars would easily recognize *The Merchant of Venice* as one of the most religiously inflected of Shakespeare's plays, many restrict their theological purview to the play's fractious Jewish-Christian relations. However, the religious discourses in the play also engage seriously with theological controversies *within* Christianity. In his ground-breaking work on the play's early modern religious contexts, John Klause observes that "Shakespeare took special pains to introduce religion into his story where it had been for the most part absent from his literary sources" ("Catholic and Protestant" 181). Klause makes a convincing case that some of the play's Jewish-Christian tension maps onto more local Catholic-Protestant controversy (180–221). During Shakespeare's lifetime, soteriology was one of the most contested discourses in Catholic-Protestant disputation, so it should not be surprising that salvation figures prominently in such an inherently religious play. By recovering Shakespeare's engagement with soteriology in *The Merchant of Venice*, I conclude that the play critiques a central Protestant doctrine—justification *sola fide* (by faith alone). In addition to positioning the play in the religious landscape of the period, this intervention helps to explain why the Venetians act the most unethically when they are articulating their religious beliefs.

In order to see *The Merchant of Venice* as the comedy Shakespeare may have intended it to be, rather than as a bleakly offensive anti-Semitic tragedy, a critic must suspend a present day, post-Holocaust approach to the play. While I in no way wish to excuse the play's rife anti-Judaism,[1] nor to deflect attention away from either the historical or current persecution of Jews, I wish to exegete the aspects of the play's religious discourse that are constructive in recovering other early modern contexts than those which are hostile to Jews. One strategy to avoid propagating the play's anti-Jewish thinking is to recover more of the early modern theological contexts of the play. Rather than simply perpetuating the Venetians' deplorably xenophobic demonization of Jews, the religious difference in the play can be read as a subtext for Catholic-Protestant controversy. John Klause helpfully reads the play in terms of such Christian intrafaith tensions: "If then under Shylock's 'Jewish gaberdine' Shakespeare hid a militant Protestant, and if he stealthily traced a Roman collar around Antonio's neck, the conflict between the two characters, played out as it is, must reveal something of the playwright's response to the issues of persecution and intolerance as they were dramatized in the

---

1. I use the term "anti-Judaic" rather than "anti-Semitic" in order to historicize the difference between a religious and a racial antipathy. However, I respectfully acknowledge that a number of important critics use the term "anti-Semitism" in connection with the period and the play. Even though the term "anti-Semitism" originates in the nineteenth-century, some of the Jewish critics I cite below apply the term to the play and to earlier Christian thinkers such as Paul and Luther. Even though "racism" is often regarded as a twentieth-century term, Adelman convincingly argues that the play's handling of conversion appeals to "a proto-racial difference" between Jews and Christians (78). Adelman further suggests that the play's handling of religion elides religious and racial difference: "The puns through which Antonio introduces the topic of conversion into the play suggest the set of anxieties about sameness and difference, nature and nations, that the topic provokes—anxieties for which racialized thinking provided an easy remedy, whether or not racial categories were fully in place in the early modern period" (79). Referring to the Spanish Inquisition, Jens Å[set ring over capital A]klundh argues emphatically for a recognition of the racial basis of hatred towards Jews in the period: "Spanish Purity of Blood laws engendered an understanding of Jewishness as a racial category" (57).

religious politics of his day" (208). Edward Berry shifts the ideological ground of the play to suggest its anti-Catholicism: "In such a context is it possible that Elizabethan audiences might have been unsettled by the clash of two 'othernesses' in *The Merchant of Venice*: Shylock's 'Judaism' and a Venetian Catholicism, the latter as tainted in its own way by legalism as the former? Perhaps the 'mercy' that Shylock receives in forced conversions is a Catholic, not a Christian mercy" (134). Both of these critics rightly contextualize the religious conflict of the play in terms of mutual Catholic-Protestant hostility.

I would like to contribute further to Klause's discussion of the play's denominational tensions by arguing that Shylock as Jew recalls the old faith of Catholicism, and that his forced conversion to Christianity depicts the plight of English recusants during the latter part of Elizabeth's reign, when the state introduced more drastic measures to assimilate Catholics into the Protestant church of England. Shylock's forced conversion from Judaism to Christianity is a thought experiment for some persecuted English Catholics who were pressured into taking the Oath of Supremacy to Elizabeth I as the head of the church of England.[2] In creating empathy for Shylock as a persecuted Jew, Shakespeare also indicts Elizabeth's disenfranchisement of Catholics. And this is only the tip of the iceberg of the play's commentary on Christian intrafaith controversy (assuming Catholicism and Protestantism are essentially the same faith).

However, a theological reading of the play presents some serious difficulties. Indeed, it is not surprising that the reputation of Christianity fares rather poorly in most of the scholarly responses to this play. Critics have long lamented the unethical behavior of the Venetian Christians. Harold Goddard argues, "Shylock's conviction that Christianity and revenge are synonyms is confirmed" (35). René Girard makes a similar claim: "The Christians use the word *mercy* with such perversity that they can justify their own revenge with it, give full license to their greed and still come out with a clear conscience" (100). While critics have complained generally about the Venetians' anti-Semitism, scholarship has hitherto failed to adequately trace the Christians' unethical behavior to its theological underpinnings. A couple of inaccurate implications result from this paucity of theological contextualization: first, critics

---

2. Most Catholics were not required by Elizabeth to swear the Oath of Supremacy, but anyone who held public or church office was mandated to swear the Oath. The Oath thus systematically discriminated against Catholics by keeping them out of positions of influence.

sometimes leave the impression that Christianity as a whole is inherently anti-Semitic, and secondly, scholars may assume that Shakespeare believes that religion (be it Christianity or Judaism) is unethical. A more precise engagement with the play's erudite theology helps explain *why* the Venetian Christians are anti-Judaic hypocrites. Instead of regarding *The Merchant of Venice* as broadly anti-religious, I would suggest that Shakespeare specifically ascribes the Venetians' unethical behavior to their faulty soteriology.

The infamous trial scene, which forms the core of this study, is heavily invested in precise soteriological discourse, particularly pertaining to the doctrine of justification. Once recovered, this theological dimension of the play should not be surprising, for debates about justification in sixteenth-century Europe were as widespread and heated as those about racism and feminism in twentieth-century North America. The theological polarization in early modern Europe between the Catholic doctrine of justification through the sacraments of the church and the Protestant idea of justification through faith alone was also more volatile than the growing divide between the left and the right in current American politics. Shakespeare's critique of the Venetian Christians as anti-Judaic hypocrites, then, requires an awareness of his theological context in order to prevent misreading. Rather than dismissing Christianity wholesale, Shakespeare targets the untenability of a very particular aspect of Christianity, namely, the Protestant dogma of justification by faith alone.

The cardinal doctrine of the Protestant Reformation, justification *sola fide*, was conceived in reaction to what the reformers perceived as the works-based righteousness of the Catholic sacramental system. As one of the major ideological controversies of the sixteenth century, which maintained its currency well into the seventeenth century, even contributing to the conflict between Arminianism and Puritanism which helped spark the English civil wars, this divisive soteriology found frequent expression in popular drama. While Shakespeare tends to handle religious issues with greater obliqueness (but also greater sophistication) than most other contemporary drama, several of his problem plays engage quite extensively, sometimes even rather openly, with contentious soteriological discourses. *The Merchant of Venice*, in particular, concretizes popular Protestant notions of salvation in the pivotal trial scene, as seen in Portia's comment "That in the course of justice none of us / Should see salvation" (4.1). The reason Portia assumes that everyone in the courtroom buys into this soteriological truism is that it succinctly articulates the majority Protestant understanding of salvation in late Elizabethan England. While critics have often excoriated the cruelty of the Christians in their unjust legal treatment of Shylock that culminates in his forced conversion to Christianity, scholarship has neglected to trace such injustice to the soteriological underpinnings of the trial over which Portia presides. The unsavory picture of salvation that emerges in the play suggests that Shakespeare is interrogating commonplace interpretations of this central Christian doctrine. While soteriology was often one of the most cherished of early modern belief systems, Shakespeare makes Shylock's "salvation" (in terms of his coerced conversion to Christianity) the most morally objectionable moment in the play. Kenneth Gross observes, "The forced conversion [of Shylock] is Shakespeare's most conspicuous addition to the traditional pound-of-flesh legend" (6). The pejorative representation of Shylock's forced conversion (as evidenced in the revulsion of most critics to this scene) should give pause to overly simplistic attributions of anti-Semitism (or anti-Judaism) to Shakespeare.

Indeed, the forced conversion of Shylock mediates the play's soteriological discourses with a polyvalent complexity. By reading the play's coerced conversion as an analogy for the persecution of the Catholic minority, Shakespeare's intrafaith discourse comes into focus. However, Shakespeare's invocation of Catholic-Protestant controversy is not restricted to a critique of state-sanctioned inequities, but also extends to disputes over dogma. Shakespeare condemns Protestant soteriology by aligning it with the injustice of the courtroom proceedings. Portia talks *ad nauseam* about salvation during the trial and the Venetian Christians all celebrate her articulation of received Protestant dogma, even as they are all conspiring to destroy Shylock by getting him to commit apostasy, the equivalent of spiritual suicide. The play obviously points out the irony of popular religious discourses being used as a vehicle for the immoral treatment of a vulnerable minority. By situating the play in early modern theological controversy, Shakespeare locates the disparity between the Venetians' faith and their actions in their soteriology. In believing themselves saved by faith alone, the Venetians feel no obligation to corroborate their faith with the deeds of mercy (such as love of neighbor). In effect, Shakespeare critiques Luther's influential idea that faith can be notionally (practically?) divorced from ethics. Implicitly aligning himself with standard Catholic polemic (including that of Thomas More), Shakespeare rejects justification by faith as a dogma which inculcates serious violations of ethics. The miscarriage of justice in the trial scene of *The*

Merchant of Venice indicts the schism between ethics and salvation in the classic Protestant doctrine of justification by faith.

In this reading, the obvious binary in the play between law (Judaism) and mercy (Christianity) deconstructs into a more nuanced dialectic between salvation by works (Catholicism, as understood by Protestants) and salvation by faith and grace (as claimed by the magisterial Protestant reformers). While a superficial reading of the play would see the Venetian Christians as heroes and the Jewish Shylock as the villain, Shakespeare interrogates the quality of the mercy exhibited by the Christians, who in their own way, are just as vindictive and legalistic as Shylock. In Portia's extended discourse on salvation, Shakespeare similarly parrots the cultural assumption that the Protestant formulation of salvation through faith and grace is superior to the Catholic emphasis on works of charity, but he undermines this theological cliché by exposing the moral bankruptcy of the characters who espouse it and by creating empathy for those who are persecuted for their minority (Catholic) religious position.[3]

THEOLOGY AND THE STRUCTURE OF THE PLAY

In terms of its structure, the play contains three high points: the choice of the caskets, the trial scene, and the ring test.[4] The play has a chiastic structure, in that the infamous trial scene of 4.1, which is the play's center of gravity, is flanked by the casket scenes and the comic ring scene. Each of these flanking scenes speaks to the play's concern about choice, be it in the matter of love or of religion. The caskets are symbols of the choice between true and false love and the ring test is a symbol of the competing loyalties of heterosexual marriage and same-sex friendship (and possibly also between heterosexual marriage and homoeroticism).[5] The suitors who choose the wrong casket apparently love Portia for the wrong reasons, whereas Bassanio's choice of the lead casket proves that he is right for Portia. The ring test is designed to show whether Bassanio has more love for Portia or Antonio. In the course of the play, Bassanio pledges his

---

3. Of course, Catholics were not a minority in Venice, but they were in Shakespeare's England.

4. Rhetorically, the high point of the play is Shylock's speech, "Hath not a Jew eyes?" (3.1.50–69).

5. Jeremy Irons's subtle homoerotic interpretation of Antonio's relationship with Bassanio is convincingly acted in the film version of the play directed by Michael Radford.

life to Antonio but his loyalty to Portia, and it is perhaps unclear who emerges as the winner. Even though Portia gets her husband back to herself, Bassanio has never shown to her the kind of sacrificial love he articulated to Antonio in the trial scene.

While the casket and ring scenes most obviously pertain to the testing of *amor* and *eros*, these symbols also broach the more religious terrain of *caritas*. In a play so concerned with the difference between choice and coercion in matters of religion, the choice of the right casket and the safe-keeping of the wedding ring inevitably become associated with religion. As an example of the overlay between love and religion in the play, the Christians in the play speak of marriage in terms of "faith," whereas Shylock is the "infidel." Jessica's story pointedly shows the correlation between choice in love and choice in religion. Jessica feels she must choose to marry a Christian and thus renounce the faith of her fathers. Conversely, Shylock is effectively forced to become a Christian against his own will. These tragic religious conversions find a ready parallel in the comic choice of the caskets and the comic ring test.

The framing of the trial scene with the comic symbols of love (the caskets and the ring) situates Protestant soteriology in the center, even while interrogating it from a Catholic periphery. The casket scene and the ring scenes, with their obviously symbolic cast of thought, align with a Catholic sacramental theology. The Council of Trent famously interpreted Augustine's definition of a sacrament in terms of sign and signifier: "A sacrament is a visible sign of an invisible grace." Bassanio's discovery of love in the correct casket speaks to a sacramental understanding of *caritas* through its symbolic encoding. Just as mere bread and wine can constitute the body and blood of Christ, so Bassanio discovers that the leaden casket contains a love of heavenly worth. The ring test also speaks to a sacramental understanding of love through its symbolism. After all, some Puritans were averse to wedding rings because of their perceived associations with Catholic "idolatry." The conception of love (and religion) in terms of symbol is challenged by the forensic conception of soteriology in the trial scene. Broadly speaking, the play puts Catholic sacramental understandings of love in conversation with a highly Protestant iteration of salvation as justification by faith. While the received Protestant formulation of justification dominates the play's chiastic structure (in terms of theology), Shakespeare critiques the ethical deficiencies of such popular soteriology.

The choice of caskets is the quest by three ethnically distinct suitors for the key to Portia's heart (or at least her hand in marriage). But in this play, so concerned to explore the volatility of *religious* difference, each casket (and its corresponding suitor) represents a distinct religious option available to early modern Europeans. The Prince of Morocco is a Muslim, his vast wealth possibly also evoking associations with the Ottoman Empire. Although the African prince articulates his ardent love for Portia, his choice of the gold casket leaves him empty-handed, possessing nothing but a death's head. The inscription over the gold casket, "Who chooseth me shall gain what many men desire," articulates a vision of love in terms of satiety and a vision of religion as prosperity (2.7.5). From the xenophobic perspective of Portia, neither the Moroccan's wealth nor his ethnicity could woo her to his marriage bed nor to his Islamic faith.

The inscription over the silver casket, "Who chooseth me shall get as much as he deserves" (2.7.7) recalls the Catholic idea of justification by works of charity. Interestingly, the Catholic Spanish Prince of Arragon (echoes of Henry VIII's Catholic wife, Catharine, mother of Mary I?) claims he has the "stamp of merit" (2.9.38): "I will assume desert" (2.9.50). Catholics believed that, in a limited sense, people could merit grace, but Protestants greatly misconstrued the role of charity in Catholic soteriology, misrepresenting it as salvation by works. When Arragon receives the fool's head, he laments, "Are my deserts no better?," thus giving the impression that the play corroborates the Protestant view that grace is unmerited. However, the Prince of Arragon's choice of the silver casket is motivated in part by a nostalgia for an older, more just world. The Prince of Arragon laments the current disconnect between merit and reward: "And how much honour / Picked from the chaff and ruin of the times / To be new varnished!" (2.9.46–48). Much like Eamon Duffy's reading of Sonnet 73[6] (40–57), in which the speaker's longing for the "Bare ruined choirs, where late the sweet birds sang" (4) recalls the Catholic past with nostalgia, Arragon's lament for the present moral decay evokes a melancholic Catholic response to the Protestant Reformation.

There is also possibly an overlay between Judaism and Catholicism in the inscription on the silver casket. For early modern Protestants, the idea that Catholics could in some respect merit salvation by preparing their hearts for grace with acts of charity paralleled the Jewish idea of justification by works of the Mosaic Law.[7] The play also feints at an as-

---

6. Eamon Duffy's argument helped to prompt "the turn to religion" in Shakespeare studies.

7. James Shapiro observes that Protestants identified circumcision with the Law and saw faith as replacing such legalistic observance. Moreover, Shapiro explains that

sociation between old Catholic money and Jewish wealth. When Lancelot abandons his Jewish master to serve Bassanio, Lancelot suggests that Bassanio (more Protestant than Venetian Catholic) has God's grace, whereas the Jewish Shylock (associated with Catholicism) has "enough" wealth, even without God's grace: "The old proverb is very well parted between my master Shylock and you, sir: you have the grace of God, sir, and he hath enough" (2.2.143–145).

The play cavalierly dismisses Islam and Judaism as religious options for early modern Europeans through the rejection of the gold and silver caskets. The rejection of the silver casket also seems to parrot the official English anti-Catholic propaganda. The only available religious option left for England is Protestantism, and that is what the inscription on the lead casket entails: "Who chooseth me must give and hazard all he hath" (2.7.9). What Kierkegaard would later call "the leap of faith" is the secret to winning Portia. In terms of the play, the idea of giving and hazarding everything finds its clearest expression in Antonio's willingness to die for Bassanio. Antonio, in turn, describes his sacrificial love for Bassanio in terms of an allusion to Abraham sacrificing Isaac (4.1.113–114). Biblical writers variously interpreted the sacrifice of Isaac as an expression of faith or works. In the immediate context of Bassanio's choice, however, faith is the key to love, be it *amor* or *caritas*. When Bassanio correctly chooses the lead casket, he is addressed by the words on the scroll (scripture?), "You that choose not by the view" (3.2.131), which echoes the definition of faith in Hebrews 11 as "the grounde of things, which are hoped for, and the euidence of things which are not sene" (11:1, Geneva Bible). Moreover, Bassanio echoes the Calvinist doctrine of total depravity when he says to Portia, "When I told you / My state was nothing, I should then have told you / That I was worse than nothing" (3.2.256–258). Portia, too, brings together the language of depravity and faith in her statement to Arragon (which contradicts his belief in merit) that he must "hazard for my worthless self" (2.9.17). The reports of the shipwrecks of Antonio's ventures being announced in the context of Bassanio's statement of his unworthiness has the added effect of suggesting that no human effort is sufficient for salvation. Clearly, Bassanio and the other "heroic" Christians in the play more closely resemble English Protestants than Venetian Catholics.

The dialectic between "shadow" and "substance" in the respective choices of the silver and lead caskets also entrenches the rhetorical

---

English Protestants compared Paul's rejection of circumcision to Protestantism's rejection of Catholic ideas about good works (118).

polarization between Judaism/Catholicism and Protestantism. When Arragon reads the note in the silver casket, he is reminded that "The fire seven times tried this" (2.9.62). This allusion to Ps 12:6 articulates a Protestant approach to worship which emphasizes scripture rather than sacerdotal liturgy: "The words of the Lord are pure words, as ye siluer, tryed in a furnace of earth, fined seuen folde." Arragon is then further rebuked, "Some there be that shadows kiss; / Such have but a shadow's bliss" (2.9.65–66). In an antithetically parallel passage, Bassanio discovers the portrait of Portia in the lead casket. He exults:

> Yet look how far
> The substance of my praise doth wrong this shadow
> In underprizing it, so far this shadow
> Doth limp behind the substance. (3.2.126–129)

Bassanio, in religion as in love, has chosen the "substance" rather than the "shadow." Poor Arragon chose the mere "shadow." Bassanio's choice again conveys the definition of faith in Heb 11:1 as "the substance of things hoped for, the evidence of things not seen" (Authorized Version, to be slightly anachronistic). The dialectic between shadow and substance also alludes to Col 2:16–17, in which Paul disparages ceremonial religious observances in favor of a Christocentric religion: "Let no man therefore condemne you in meat and drinke, or in respect of an holie day, or of the new moone, or of the Sabbath dayes, Which are but a shaddowe of things to come: but the bodie is in Christ" (Geneva Bible). Much like Saint Paul urges the church at Colosse to abandon the observance of Jewish ceremonial law (as well as gnostic spirituality), the Protestant reformers urged Christians to abandon the cumbersome ceremonies of late medieval Catholicism. The network of biblical allusions here reinforces the Protestant understanding of salvation through faith in Christ rather than through ritualistic religious observance. Bassanio has chosen the better part than Arragon, and it shall not be taken from him. To put it another way, at first glance Shakespeare seems to be parroting the official English church theology which privileges Protestant faith over Judaic/Catholic works.

The soteriological mainspring of the play, Portia's famously controversial speech on mercy, asserts "That in the course of justice none of us / Should see salvation" (4.1.166–197). Portia's statement is the culmination of Protestant doctrine in the play, which up to this point, has been presented in a favorable light as the majority position. But the forced conversion of Shylock that follows hard on the heels of Portia's acclamation of salvation by grace has the effect of unsettling this profession of Protestant doctrine that finds such cruel expression in the actions of the play's hegemonic Christians. The persecution of Shylock in his coerced conversion to Christianity finds a ready analogy in England's Oath of Supremacy, which required English Catholics to pledge allegiance to Elizabeth as the head of the Church of England if they wanted to hold public or church office. The threats and realities of fines, imprisonment, and execution experienced by recusants are pictured in the inhumane treatment of Shylock. Shylock, however, has far less similarity to English Catholics than do the Venetian Christians to English Protestants. Nonetheless, his association with the old religion, his wealth (like that of English Catholic gentry), his adherence to salvation by works, and his obsession with flesh and blood (transubstantiation?) recall stereotypes of the recusant. The ways in which Shakespeare problematizes the (im)morality of the Christians' treatment of Shylock, thus subversively creating empathy for him, might have given early modern audiences pause over the state-sanctioned persecution of recusants, as well as Jews.

Shakespeare's religious commentary in *The Merchant of Venice*, however, is more than just veiled advocacy for recusants, as my reading suggests. Shakespeare's handling of the courtroom scene allows for a diversity of perspectives, another of which, paradoxically, is the vindication of Puritanism. Murray Levith observes a connection between Shylock and Puritanism: "In Elizabethan times, Protestant exiles who had come into contact with Calvinism, and other more local sects, developed the sober values associated with both Shylock and the Puritans" (102). Shylock's obsession with assurance over the bond and his antifestive, anti-comic spirit (like that of Malvolio in *Twelfth Night*) give the Jewish money-lender a Puritan cast. From this perspective, Shylock is a Protestant victim of persecution by Italian Catholic judges who recall the Spanish Inquisition. Whether read as pro-Catholic or pro-Protestant in its denominational orientation, the play complicates the notion of salvation by associating it with political coercion.

PAULINE AND REFORMATION FORMULATIONS OF JUSTIFICATION IN THE TRIAL SCENE

Among the most theologically literate moments in the Shakespearean corpus, the trial scene in *The Merchant of Venice* materializes and concretizes a Pauline metaphor of justification as it is refracted through Reformation controversy. Biblical scholar N. T. Wright notes that Hebrew and Greek each have one word to convey what English designates in the two words "just" and "righteous" (88). The Hebrew *tsedaqah* and the Greek *dikaios* each have strong associations with the context of a law court and are employed by biblical writers to denote "*the status that someone has when the court has found in their favor*" (Wright 90). The Latin *iustitia*, like its Hebrew and Greek forbearers, also covers the range of meanings found in the English "just" and "righteous," but the term began to incorporate many theological accretions as it passed through medieval and Reformation theological controversies, as Alister McGrath observes with such encyclopedic scope in Iustitia Dei: *A History of the Christian Doctrine of Justification*. McGrath explains that "[t]he 'doctrine of justification' has come to bear a meaning within dogmatic theology which is quite independent of its Pauline origins" (2–3). McGrath carefully nuances Reformation ideas of justification in a way that shows their greater debt to Augustine than Paul. While the Reformation is often represented as a rediscovery of Pauline soteriology, it is more accurately a recovery of Augustinian concepts of grace and a critique of Augustinian ecclesiology (188–189). In the sixteenth century, the *sine qua non* of Protestant justification was its forensic metaphor (184). The reformers' insistence on a forensic justification is thus arguably a recovery of what N. T. Wright has identified as the biblical etymology of justification as a vindication in a court of law.

McGrath observes that much early modern Protestantism was heavily influenced by Melanchthon's conception of justification:

1. Justification is understood to be the forensic declaration that the Christian is righteous, rather than the process by which he is made righteous, involving a change in his *status* before God rather than his *nature*.
2. A deliberate and systematic distinction is made between the concept of *justification* itself (understood as the extrinsic divine pronouncement of man's new status) and the concept of *sanctification* or *regeneration* (understood as the intrinsic process by which God renews the justified sinner).
3. The formal, or immediate cause, of justification is understood to be the alien righteousness of Christ, imputed to man in justification, so that justification involves a *synthetic* rather than an *analytic* judgement on the part of God. (McGrath 182)

In Melanchthon's classic conception of forensic justification, salvation is a kind of legal fiction rather than a statement of fact about a person's actual condition.

Popular English Puritan theologian William Perkins bears the strong imprint of Melanchthon's ideas about justification, as seen in Perkins's *A Golden Chain or the Description of Theology* (1592). According to Perkins, justification by faith involves a legal exchange of the believer's sin with the righteousness of Christ. As such, Perkins's definition of justification has much in common with the thinking of the magisterial Protestant reformers:

> Justification hath two parts: remission of sins and imputation of Christ's righteousness. Remission of sins is that part of justification whereby he that believeth is freed from the guilt and punishment of sin by the passion of Christ. . . .Imputation of righteousness is the other part of justification, whereby such as believe, having the guilt of their sins covered, are accounted just in the sight of God through Christ's righteousness. The form of justification is, as it were, a kind of translation of the believer's sins unto Christ and again Christ's righteousness unto the believer by a reciprocal or mutual imputation.... (*Work of William Perkins* 233)

The forensic nature of Perkins's justification is encapsulated in the quintessential Protestant word *imputation*. In Perkins's thinking, following Luther, Melanchthon, and Calvin, Christ's righteousness is "imputed" rather than imparted to the believer. A sinner who trusts in Christ's sufferings, death, and resurrection on her behalf is accounted righteous on Christ's merit, not on her own. Hence Luther's famous idea that a believer is simultaneously a saint and a sinner. Perhaps we might say that Luther's believer is a living paradox, an ethical contradiction.

The strongly forensic nature of justification in Lutheran thought, which considers a person righteous even if she acts like nothing of the sort, surfaces among the Venetian Christians. The Venetians consider themselves soteriologically solvent merely by virtue of the fact that they are Christians. Their religious label entitles them to ridicule and persecute Jews and Moors, giving them a privileged status over others, regardless of how they might compare ethically as fellow human beings. Indeed, the courtroom scene celebrates a Protestant doctrine of justification by faith, irrespective of "justice" itself: "in the course of justice none of us / Should see salvation" (4.1.196–197). The Venetians are imputed righteous by their faith even though they fail to perform good works. The Venetians meet all three criteria of justification that McGrath identifies as central to early modern Protestant dogma:

1. The Venetians understand justification "to be the forensic declaration that the Christian is righteous, rather than the process by which he is made righteous, involving a change in his *status* before God rather than his *nature*" (182).

2. The Venetians make a "deliberate and systematic distinction. . . between the concept of *justification* itself (understood as the extrinsic divine pronouncement of man's new status) and the concept of *sanctification* or *regeneration* (understood as the intrinsic process by which God renews the justified sinner)" (182).

3. The Venetians see the "formal, or immediate cause, of [their] justification [as]. . . the alien righteousness of Christ, imputed to man in justification, so that justification involves a *synthetic* rather than an *analytic* judgement on the part of God" (182)

Shakespeare, however, deconstructs each of these three salient features of Protestant justification into critiques of the Venetians' self-justified separation of religion and ethics.

1. Portia may, in effect, enunciate "the forensic declaration" that the Venetians are "righteous," and they may gloat in their "*status* before God," but Shakespeare points out the glaring irony that their "*nature*" remains unchanged. Their actions do not match their words.

2. The Venetians' confidence in their "justification," extrinsically conceived, makes them neglect "the concept of *sanctification* or *regeneration*." None of the Christians in the play question their own salvation, even though their behavior is devoid of any concomitant ethical renewal. They fail to forgive Shylock as they believe themselves to have been forgiven (or as Jesus forgave his Roman executioners and Jewish accusers).

3. The Venetians' "justification involves a *synthetic* rather than an *analytic* judgement on the part of God." Shakespeare seems to be pointing out the inconsistency of the Venetians' believing themselves to be approved by God, even though they fail to love their neighbor.

Put another way, the Venetian Christians are distinctly unlike Christ. Rather than showing the same mercy to Shylock that the Venetians believe they have themselves received from God, the Venetians use the doctrine of justification as a pretext for exerting their spiritual smugness over a Jew who threatens to unsettle their religious hegemony. In short, Shakespeare subjects the Protestant doctrine of justification to a scathing critique in *The Merchant of Venice*. The doctrine is weighed in the scales and found wanting.

The fact that the play becomes most morally objectionable at the point where it becomes most soteriologically invested is all too telling. This contradiction becomes Shakespeare's means of interrogating the ethical implications of the Protestant doctrine of justification by faith in the play's infamous courtroom scene. Much like Catholics who were alarmed that Luther's dogma was opening a theological Pandora's box, Shakespeare seems to be questioning the very justice of the Protestant notion of justification. As their flagrant anti-Judaism would suggest, the Venetian Christians seem content to dull their consciences with Luther's notion that one's salvation need not be evidenced by any ethical improvement. What Luther intended as God's gift to a conscience tormented by self-condemnation came to be promoted as a moral shortcut to self-justification. The irony is that Luther's intention was to locate the Christian's confidence completely away from self and entirely in the person of Christ.[8] The Venetian Christians, with their repugnant superiority complex and self-satisfaction, instead convey the worst aspects of religious self-justification.

Now I will demonstrate how the Pauline courtroom metaphor for justification, which finds expression in Reformation conceptions of forensic righteousness, is the theological subtext informing the trial scene in *The Merchant of Venice*. Antonio is the accused who has been unable to repay his debt to Shylock. Shylock insists on his right to cash in on the bond which Antonio pledged to him as a condition for borrowing

---

8. *The Book of Homilies* captures the Christo-centric intentions of Lutheran justification, particularly in the sermon, "Of the Salvation of All Mankind": "[O]ur faith in Christ (as it were) saith unto us thus, It is not I that take away your sins, but it is Christ only, and to him only I send [you] for that purpose, forsaking therein all your good virtues, words, thoughts, and works, and only putting your trust in Christ." According to this classic Church of England homily, faith itself is not actually the basis of salvation, but rather Christ alone is the one who saves. Faith brings the sinner to Christ, but it is always Christ who saves the individual. The soteriological emphasis is *solus Christus* rather than *sola fide*.

Shylock's money. The absurd nature of the bond, "a pound of flesh," does not seem to matter to Shylock, who is intent on revenge, nor to Antonio, who in his melancholy all too easily sees himself as "a tainted wether of the flock, / Meetest for death" (4.1.113–114). Antonio's friends, conflicted in their strategies for liberating Antonio, simultaneously hurl anti-Judaic slurs at Shylock and beg him to be merciful. Even the Duke seems perplexed about the legal conundrum before him, appealing to Shylock's better nature rather than simply throwing the case out of court because of its ridiculously barbaric premise. The city state of Venice was financially dependent on legal aliens such as Shylock, so his case must be handled according to the normal protocols of law, as repellent as Shylock's case is to the Venetians.

As the judge, the plaintiff, the accused, and the courtroom audience all are fumbling the case, failing to make any meaningful justice from the tangle of legal technicality, financial exploitation, religious persecution, proto-racism, and revenge—Portia enters—a *deus ex machina*, as it were. Although she is not actually a judge, but an imposter, she takes the case in hand with a confidence that no one else in the courtroom can manage to convey. Perhaps surprisingly to a modern audience, one of the first things Portia does is to shift the case from financial or contractual or even constitutional grounds to theology. Instead of beginning with Venetian law as it pertains to business dealings between citizens and legal aliens, Portia appeals to religion, even though the person she is trying to persuade to her position belongs to a different faith than hers and that of the entire courtroom audience. Portia assumes that there is enough commonality between Christianity and its parent faith, Judaism, to draw Shylock into her interfaith dialogue.

> The quality of mercy is not strained.
> It droppeth as the gentle rain from heaven
> Upon the place beneath. It is twice blest:
> It blesseth him that gives and him that takes. . . .
> But mercy is above this sceptred sway.
> It is enthronèd in the hearts of kings;
> It is an attribute to God himself,
> And earthly power doth then show likest God's
> When mercy seasons justice. Therefore, Jew,
> Though justice be thy plea, consider this:
> That in the course of justice none of us
> Should see salvation. We do pray for mercy,
> And that same prayer doth teach us all to render

> The deeds of mercy. I have spoke thus much
> To mitigate the justice of thy plea,
> Which if thou follow, this strict court of Venice
> Must needs give sentence 'gainst the merchant there. (4.1.181–184; 190–202)

As it turns out, the speech falls on deaf ears, remaining a monologue rather than producing the kind of rational exchange Portia had hoped. Critics often note that texts from both the Hebrew Bible and the New Testament support the idea that God is merciful, that he seasons justice with mercy, and that God's people are to be characterized by mercy. Even though the play (at least superficially) dichotomizes Judaism as law and Christianity as mercy, the continuities between the Hebrew Bible and the New Testament challenge such a simple binary. The penitential psalms, which came to occupy such a privileged position in Christianity, convey God as eminently merciful, if transcendently majestic. The flavor of this theology may be found in Portia's speech, hearkening back to such texts as Psalm 130 (Luther's favorite): "Lord, heare my voyce: let thine eares attend to the voice of my praiers. If thou ô Lord, straitly markest iniquities, ô Lord, who shal stand? But mercie is with thee, that thou maiest be feared" (130:2–4). The prayer to which Portia refers is, of course, the Lord's prayer, particularly the line, "And forgiue vs our dettes, as we also forgiue our detters" (Matt 6:12). But the biblical text which really underscores Portia's rhetoric, and which she manipulates into a dagger to stab in Shylock's back, is the pronouncement in James (Luther's "epistle of straw"), "For there shalbe iugement merciless to him that sheweth no mercie, & mercie reioyceth against iudgement" (2:13). Portia will later allude to this text when she exerts the full force of her power over Shylock: "For as thou urgest justice, be assured / Thou shalt have justice, more than thou desir'st" (4.1.312–313).

The domain of theology that Portia is particularly determined to draw to Shylock's attention is soteriology:

> Though justice be thy plea, consider this:
> That in the course of justice none of us
> Should see salvation.

While there are many biblical proof texts that could be provided in defense of Portia's contention that no human being justly deserves salvation, her comment taps into a broader soteriological discourse on the doctrine of justification which undergirds this trial scene in the play. Portia's careful positioning of the words *justice* and *salvation* in opposition to each other pointedly recalls Reformation debates about justification. The reformers, like Saint Paul, were determined to tease out the method by which God could be just, while at the same time acquitting humanity of its sins. Perhaps of greater concern to the reformers was the related puzzle of how humanity could be justified in the sight of God (*coram Dei*), even though it was still patently sinful. The fact that this discourse on justification occurs in the courtroom scene is no accident, for both St. Paul and the reformers were inclined to imagine justification in forensic terms.

Does Portia's theology deliver the salvation it promises? Shylock's hardened response to Portia's appeal to mercy forestalls any immediate hope of a reasonable compromise between Antonio and Shylock's competing claims. In fact, the trial escalates into increasingly tense appeals to Shylock for mercy, which he rejects ever more emphatically. Portia seems to be bungling the trial just as badly as the Duke, despite her confidence that she would see it to an effective resolution. The Venetians do not know how they got into this wretched predicament, but it seems that Antonio must die, submitting his breast to the excision of a pound of flesh. Portia has failed the Venetians, and her soteriology apparently amounts to nothing more than specious nonsense.

And then Portia suddenly redeems the trial from its miscarriage of justice, rescuing Antonio's life and putting the "villain" on the defensive. And just how does Portia achieve this legal sleight of hand in which she reverses the roles of the defendant and the plaintiff? How does she so successfully get Shylock on the defensive and Antonio on the attack? Soteriology. The rhetorical mainspring of the play, Portia's doctrine that "in the course of justice none of us / Should see salvation" is finally playing itself out. By what means does this almost magical, eleventh-hour reversal come about? The long-anticipated deliverance comes about through the mere mention of "One drop of Christian blood":

> Tarry a little; there is something else.
> This bond doth give thee here no jot of blood;
> The words expressly are 'a pound of flesh'.
> Take then thy bond. Take thou thy pound of flesh.
> But in the cutting it, if thou dost shed
> One drop of Christian blood, thy lands and goods
> Are by the laws of Venice confiscate
> Unto the state of Venice. (4.1.302–309)

How can "one drop of Christian blood" effect such an overwhelming victory in a court of law, turning the tables of justice back to rights? Again, soteriology. In light of Portia's earlier determination to set the trial on a soteriological footing, "one drop of Christian blood" arguably transposes into "one drop of Christ's blood." (Shakespeare's borrowing from Marlowe will help me substantiate this interpretation below.)

For Saint Paul, Augustine, and the Protestant reformers, Christ's blood was regarded as uniquely salvific. In Romans, Paul develops his idea of the justifying power of Christ's blood: "But God setteth out his loue towarde vs, seing yt while we were yet sinners, Christ dyed for vs. Muche more then, being now iustified by his blood, we shal be saued from wrath through him" (Rom 5:8–9). Augustine affirms this Pauline understanding of justification through Christ's blood in *De Trinitate*: "we are justified by the blood of Christ, and we are reconciled to God by the death of His Son" (391). In the 1559 *Institutes of the Christian Religion*, Calvin incorporates Christ's blood into his definition of justification: "Justification, moreover, we thus define: The sinner being admitted into communion with Christ is, for his sake, reconciled to God; when purged by his blood he obtains the remission of sins, and clothed with righteousness, just as if it were his own, stands secure before the judgment seat of heaven" (533). Calvin envisions Christ's blood as the salvific agent which ensures the believer's vindication at the divine assize.

However, soteriological disagreement was a major impetus behind the division of the Western church during the Reformation. In his commentary on Galatians, Luther celebrates the justifying power of Christ's blood in rapturous terms: "For he might have satisfied for all the sins of the world by only one drop of his blood; but now he hath shed it plentifully, and hath satisfied abundantly" (*Selections* 110). Luther's statement, while arguably Pauline in its sentiment, sent out shockwaves of controversy. For William Tyndale, who transplanted much of Luther's theology onto English soil, while adding his own distinctive emphases, soteriology is a hill to die on, a watershed issue that separates the true from the false church. In 1530, Tyndale wrote in *An Answer to Sir Thomas More's 'Dialogue'* that he considered Roman Catholic soteriology to be a detraction from the justifying power of Christ's blood.

> That the pope and his spirits be not the church, may this wise be proved. He that hath no faith to be saved through Christ, is not of Christ's church. The pope believeth not to be saved through Christ: for he teacheth to trust in holy works for the remission of

> sins and salvation; as in the works of penance, enjoined in vows; in pilgrimage; in chastity; in other men's prayers and holy living; in friars and friars' coats; in saints' merits; and, the significations put out, he teacheth to believe in the deeds of the ceremonies and of the sacrament, ordained at the beginning to preach unto us, and to do us service, and not that we should believe in them and serve them. And a thousand such superstitiousnesses setteth he before us, instead of Christ to believe in; neither Christ nor God's word, neither honourable to God nor serviceable unto our neighbour, nor profitable unto ourselves for the taming of the flesh; *which all are the denying of Christ's blood.* (39–40, italics added)

For Tyndale, the Roman Catholic doctrines of and aides to salvation are antithetical to Christ's atoning blood. Ralph Werrell explains the cast of Tyndale's soteriology in terms of "a continuity between the Old and New Testaments" (24): "As with the sacrifices of the Old Testament, it was the sprinkling of the blood that made the sacrifice effective; so, for the Christian it is the Holy Spirit's sprinkling of Christ's blood on us that makes Christ's sacrifice effective to remove our sin" (Werrell 25). Werrell also observes, "Theologically, but not sacramentally, the Blood of Christ occurs 441 times in Tyndale's writings" (25).

Thomas More responded to Tyndale with exasperation and with his characteristic vitriol[9] against Protestantism in *The Confutation of Tyndale's Answer* (1532–1533). Commissioned by Bishop Tunstal, More wrote in English to protect the Catholic laity from Tyndale's Lutheran innovations (Schuster 1264). In an attempt to undermine Tyndale's Lutheran soteriology, More challenges Tyndale to admit that God punished David's sin of adultery with Bathsheba and his murder of Uriah, even though God had forgiven David (210). From there, More proceeds to argue that Christ's blood is actually not sufficient to justify unless it is also accompanied by penance:

> Now yf he [Tydnale] graunte that god punyssheth the synne not wythstandynge the repentaunce of the penitent, and the remyssyon of his dyspleasure: then graunteth he and so must he graunte, y^t all be it one droppe of Crystes precyouse blode had ben suffycyent to satysfye for all the synnys of this whole worlde / and for all the payne also that were in any wyse dew to the same: yet hath it not pleased hym so to order it. (210)

---

9. Louis A. Schuster notes with respect to the heated debate between Tyndale's *Answer* and More's *Confutation* that "More used over two hundred words to answer every ten of Tyndale's" (1259).

For More, "one droppe of Crystes precyouse blode" in fact does *not* have the unaided power to justify the sinner. More goes on to argue that penitential satisfaction for sin is necessary because without such earthly or purgatorial pain, people would not have any aversion to sin (210–211).

Eventually this controversy about the justifying potency of just "one drop" of Christ's blood found its way into Renaissance drama. The final scene of *Doctor Faustus* is Marlowe's most poignant, with its sense of the inexorable passage of time, Faustus's desperate longing for relief, the obduracy of a *deus absconditus* to his prayers for mercy, and the chilling entrance of the devils who have finally come to make good on his blood pact with the devil. Faustus's plea for salvation falls on deaf ears: "See, see where Christ's blood streams in the firmament! One drop would save my soul, half a drop" (14.75–76). In Marlowe's imagination, faith placed in Christ's blood (quintessential Protestant soteriology) is impotent to save the beleaguered Faustus from his bond to the devil. Marlowe seems to take fiendish pleasure in satirizing the most cherished Protestant ideologies of the period—*sola fide, sola gratia,* and possibly even *solus Christus*—fusing farce and tragedy to great effect.

When Portia introduces the concept of "one drop of Christian blood" as the loophole through which she will rescue Antonio and condemn (or at least threaten) Shylock, Shakespeare is potentially alluding to the theological controversies found in Doctor Faustus's failed salvation, and perhaps also to the longstanding theological disagreement about the role of Christ's blood in salvation waged by Luther and Tyndale against More. Faustus imagines his pact with the devil to be binding, to the point where even Christ's blood cannot free him from his demonic tormentors. In *The Merchant of Venice*, all the characters regard Antonio's "bond" to Shylock as having the same kind of effectuality, even though there is perhaps a degree of comic absurdity to it being taken so seriously. The fact that Shakespeare is able to save Antonio with the mere mention of "one drop of Christian blood" counterpoises strikingly with Faustus's inability to find deliverance from "one drop" of the blood of Jesus himself. That a Christian's blood—with its overtones of martyrdom—has more power in *The Merchant of Venice* than Christ's blood had in *Doctor Faustus* perhaps suggests Shakespeare's greater orthodoxy in religion compared to his dramatic predecessor and inspiration.[10]

---

10. Perhaps there is an irony in the fact that the resolution of *The Merchant of Venice* comes from *not* shedding any Christian blood rather than in creating martyrs. From a Catholic perspective, which ascribes a salvific force to martyrs' blood, there may be

BLOOD LIBEL AND THE PERSECUTION OF JEWS

The play's fixation on "one drop" of blood not only has christological associations, but also invokes the blood libel against Jews, as part of the ongoing persecution of Jews throughout medieval and early modern Europe (which sadly continues in the modern world). In the sixteenth century, Europe had its highest number of ritual murder accusations directed by Christians against Jews (Hsia, *Myth of Ritual Murder* 3). In this proto-racist and anti-Judaic mythology, some Christians falsely believed that Jews murdered Christian children to use their blood in magic rituals (2). This so called "blood libel" was a form of paranoia distinct from, but not unrelated to host desecration charges against Jews. In late medieval Europe, there are records of crowds attacking Jews after a Jew allegedly defiled the bread used in the Mass (Rubin 88). Some Christians falsely believed that Jews, wishing to cause Christ further suffering, would desecrate the host, understood to be his transubstantiated body.

The association of Jews and blood informed numerous aspects of the persecutory rhetoric against Jews. Sometimes this rhetoric would result in Jews being tortured and killed (Bynum 68). Even though Jews had been expelled from England, Jews were stereotypically played with a red beard in early modern English drama, and this practice is reminiscent of Herod and Judas being attired in red wigs in medieval German passion plays to indicate the color of blood (Felsenstein 31). Shylock was played with a red beard by Richard Burbage, his first actor, the precedent lasting all the way to the eighteenth century (Felsenstein 31). Other myths about Jews included the degrading rumor that Jewish men menstruated and that Jewish people commonly experienced hemorrhoidal bleeding (35). All of these persecutory stereotypes are signalled in the play's notion that Shylock wants to shed Christian blood.

However, the most significant theological idea behind the association of Shylock with blood and "a pound of flesh," is the Jewish identity marker of circumcision (Shapiro 114). Shylock's devilish desire to cut out Antonio's heart reimagines the Jewish ritual of circumcision in pejorative terms. The play thus unfortunately caters to common anti-Judaic stereotypes. It is little wonder that the play continues to find itself struggling to extricate itself from charges of unconscionable anti-Semitism. As much

---

a kind of anti-atonement logic here. From the perspective of Protestantism, however, which claims to locate salvation exclusively in the blood of Christ, the lack of Christian martyrdom in the play may highlight the vicarious locus of atonement in Christ.

as I love Shakespeare, I am deeply saddened by those aspects of the play that commiserate with contemporary anti-Judaism. Even the emergence of philo-Semitism on the English landscape during the reign of James, later culminating in Oliver Cromwell's readmission of the Jews, was motivated by a disingenuous desire to profit from Jews and to convert them to Christianity (Katz 164, 167).[11] Perhaps my soteriological reading of the play is my attempt to redeem it from some of its inherent anti-Judaism.

COERCED CONVERSION: INDICTMENTS OF ANTI-JUDAISM AND ANTI-CATHOLICISM

For many modern audiences, Shylock's forced conversion to Christianity undermines the theology of mercy and justification that Portia expounds so eloquently. The play sends out strongly mixed messages about Christianity by suggesting that God is merciful, on the one hand, and that Christians are justified in exacting revenge, on the other hand. Seen in the light of its early modern context, the play seems to celebrate the Christians' vindictiveness, rather than calling them to conform to the principle of mercy to which Portia gives mere lip service. For Luther, the doctrine of justification was of such central importance, that anyone who did not adhere to his understanding of it was effectively an enemy of the faith—the demonized other. In his commentary on Galatians, Luther inveighs, "For if the article of justification be once lost, then is all true Christian doctrine lost. And as many as are in the world that hold not this doctrine, are either Jews, Turks, Papists or heretics" (*Selections* 106). In Luther's mind, the Jew and the Catholic become conflated into one common enemy because they do not believe in justification by faith alone. Here Luther seems to turn justification on its head by interpreting Christ's universal offer of salvation as a dogma which alienates not only Jews and Muslims, but also the majority of other Christians. The hegemony which the Venetian Christians enforce through Portia's rhetoric of mercy recalls the theological hegemony Luther constituted by privileging his own doctrine of justification over all other theology.

---

11. David Katz notes that the earliest proposal for the readmission of the Jews was made by Sir Thomas Sherley, the younger, to James. Sherley was one of the personalities made famous by John Day, William Rowley, and George Wilkins's play, *The Travels of the Three English Brothers*, first performed in 1607 (163). In the play, there is a negatively stereotypical Jew named Zariph who is patterned after Shylock.

The Venetians think they are being merciful by sparing Shylock's life and remitting the confiscation of half of his wealth by the state. Perhaps even Antonio thinks himself merciful when he donates the other half of Shylock's wealth which the state awarded him into a trust fund for Lorenzo and Jessica, with the stipulations that Shylock bequeath his entire estate to his daughter who has converted to Christianity and that he, too, becomes a Christian, whether or not he wants to. Barbara Lewalski's (early career) countenancing of Shylock's conversion fails to address the immorality of the coercion involved in his adoption of Christianity. *Pace* Lewalski and other critics who attempt to render Shylock's conversion in positive terms, I would insist that the idea of a forced religious conversion and its concomitant violation of the human conscience is something revolting and untenable, a kind of spiritual rape. Barbara Lewalski effectively notes the tension between Jewish law and Christian grace in the play (338), but her allegorical reading has the unpalatable effect of rewarding the Venetians' anti-Judaism, even theologically justifying their demonization of Shylock. While Lewalski astutely reads some of the theological subtext of the play, her conclusion that Shylock's forced conversion to Christianity "is not antisemitic revenge" is untenable from an ethical perspective (341). Lewalski's typological reading of the play, however, accurately perceives early modern theology and sentiment: "Now that Shylock's claim to legal righteousness has been totally destroyed, he is made to accept the only alternative to it, faith in Christ" (341). The individual's inability to fulfill the law and her inherent need for grace form the backbone of Luther and Calvin's ideas about justification by faith. The play grounds the trial scene in such Reformation dogma.

Hugh Short, in an essay entitled "Shylock is Content: A Study in Salvation," argues that Shylock willingly converts to Christianity. In arguing this idea, Short is aware that he is pushing against the weight of an entrenched academic consensus: "That last condition has aroused the wrath of contemporary audiences, but it defies logic to contend that this stipulation is one last outrageous bit of hypocrisy meant to further torment Shylock" (210). Short insists that "Shylock speaks the truth when he says he is content," and suggests that Laurence Olivier's departure from the stage "with a final despairing cry of pain" is a misinterpretation (211). I strongly disagree with Short's rehabilitation of Shylock's conversion, chiefly because it goes entirely against the grain of Shylock's characterization and worldview throughout the play. Why would Shylock be truly "content" to become a Christian when the Venetians are doing little else than exacting revenge on him? Indeed, Jessica's conversion to Christianity strikes Shylock as nothing less than treachery. The play conveys Jessica's theft of her father's most precious possessions as part of her conversion to Christianity, thus giving a strong impression of her moral duplicity in abandoning the faith of her fathers. Why would Shylock then willingly convert to such a hostile community of faith? As Kenneth Gross suggests, "There is a strange refinement of cruelty in Antonio's proposal" (109). Although Shylock says, "I am content" (4.1.390), he clearly is not in a celebratory frame of mind as pretends to become a Christian. Instead of indicating delight in his incorporation into the majority faith, he says,

> I pray you, give me leave to go from hence.
> I am not well. Send the deed after me,
> And I will sign it. (4.1.391–393)

A willing conversion would be celebratory; his forced conversion is like the onset of the plague.

Some might argue that a forced conversion is to be preferred to a death sentence and the confiscation of one's entire wealth (the alternative fate which Portia lays before Shylock). However, for a deeply spiritual or religious person, the coerced renunciation of one's most cherished beliefs is an act of violence against the self from which it may be impossible to recover. Short's counter-argument is thus unconvincing: "As he [Shylock] says, he is not well, but he is on the road to health" (211).

Shylock's statement of religious conversion, "I am content," is highly ironic, even tragic. Marianne Novy observes that the phrase is a precise echo of Thomas Cranmer's recantation under duress (26). Novy further argues that the allusion to Cranmer's forced recantation and subsequent burning for heresy under the Marian regime "juxtapose[s] the Christian/Jewish issues of the play more immediately with heresy trials within Christendom" (28). Novy's research dovetails with my thesis that the play at times engages Catholic-Protestant controversy under the guise of Christian-Jewish relations.

However, the primary meaning of the trial scene is the forced conversion of a Jew by Christians, a dramatization of a tragic historical reality. John Gross's interpretation of Shylock's response to his conversion is à propos: "they are the words of a man who is sick at heart, not the words of a man who believes that he has been set on the path to salvation" (76). John Gross notes that "the enforced conversion seems to have been a Shakespearean addition to the story: no hint of it can be found in *Il*

Pecorone or any of the other probable sources" (76). Even the Venetians regard his conversion as sweet revenge rather than an adoption into a community of faith. Graziano's cruel comment underscores the gross immorality of the hegemonic Venetian Christians in requiring Shylock to convert:

> In christ'ning shalt thou have two godfathers.
> Had I been judge, thou shouldst have had ten more—
> To bring thee to the gallows, not the font. (4.1.394–396)

Emphatically, Shylock's forced conversion is a collusion by the majority faith against the conscience and self-identity of the minority.

In his ground-breaking work on Jewish conversion to Christianity in early modern England, Jens Åklundh observes that "from the Elizabethans to the close of the seventeenth century a gradual weakening of the barriers towards Jewish conversion is noticeable" (63). In reading the literature written in England by Jewish converts to Christianity, Åklundh concludes that there was no systematic forced conversion of Jews during Shakespeare's time: "The writings of the Jewish converts in this period [the late sixteenth and the seventeenth centuries] do not convey any sense of being pressured to convert. There existed no organized efforts to convert the covert *conversos* living in England since the 1590s, which according to Lucien Wolf was 'in every sense an open secret' to the English government" (46). Åklundh suggests that both Marlowe and Shakespeare were "influenced by Iberian attitudes towards *Conversos*, a category of Jewish converts which, as Miriam Bodian asserts, 'were not destined to be absorbed into Christian society'" (56). The forced conversion of Shylock, then, is more of a Spanish than an English phenomenon. The dramatic appeal of forced conversion seems to have waned by the end of the early modern period. In George Granville's *The Jew in Venice*, an adaptation of *The Merchant of the Venice* in London in 1700, the forced conversion of Shylock is conspicuously absent (Åklundh 61).

If the forced conversion of Shylock is more indicative of the fate of Jews in Spain than in England (Jews having been mostly eliminated from England by this time), Shylock's forced conversion emphatically speaks to the predicament of the persecuted English Catholic minority. The forced conversion of Jews, while a common feature of the Spanish Inquisition, finds an analogy in the forced conversion of Catholics to the church of England. Such flagrant violation of the individual conscience of the minority brings the play's anti-Judaism closer to home through the ready analogy of Catholic and Jew. English recusants often preferred to pay heavy fines rather than to participate in a form of religion which violated their conscience. Jesuit priests steeled themselves against inevitable death by hanging, drawing, and quartering rather than capitulate to an imposed religious consensus to which they could not subscribe in good conscience. John Donne took great pains to argue in *Pseudo-martyr* that a Catholic who refused to swear the Oath of Allegiance to James was not actually a true martyr. But some Catholics disagreed, seeing the Oath of Allegiance as a violation of conscience.

Shakespeare's portrayal of Shylock being subjected to a forced conversion certainly recalls the persecution of Jews before and during the Spanish Inquisition, at which time many Jews became *conversos*, or converts to Christianity, to escape expulsion from Spain. The Spanish Inquisition regarded *conversos* with suspicion, persecuting them in the belief that their coerced conversion to Catholicism was not sincere. However, in Shakespeare's England there were very few Jews left after their expulsion by Edward I in 1290. James Shapiro estimates that in early modern England, there were "never more than a couple hundred [Jews] at any given time" (Shapiro in Levith 101). For Shakespeare's audiences, the Jewish other being forced to convert against his will would have stretched their minds to foreign settings like Spain. Of course, there was the notorious case of Elizabeth's doctor, Lopez—a *converso*—being executed on disreputable charges of conspiring to poison the queen.

But the most obviously persecuted minority in late Elizabethan England were Catholics. Through his portrayal of the persecution of Jews, Shakespeare invites his London audiences to consider the heinous nature of religious coercion that is commonly occurring in England against Catholics, within the safety of a xenophobic illustration of the Jewish Shylock. Kenneth Gross speculates that Shakespeare may have heard first-hand stories of persecuted Jews and associated them with familiar cases of persecuted Catholics: "Such stories might have combined in Shakespeare's imagination with thoughts about the lives of recusant Catholics in England, their fear and nostalgia, their daily experience of secrecy and equivocation in public, and their troubled fascination with martyrdom—*things that the poet more certainly knew about*, even if the question of his own religious affiliation remains vexed" (152, italics added). Shakespeare's portrayal of Shylock being forced to convert to Christianity transplants the egregious injustices of the Spanish Inquisition onto English soil, where Catholics, somewhat like Shylock, were required to attend the state church and take communion and have their children baptized into a faith against their will, with the threat of financial penalties, imprisonment, or even torture and death, for those who would not comply. Shylock's forced conversion thus becomes a thought experiment for the persecuted English recusant.

For early modern English audiences, the play's greatest religious relevance pertained to its interrogation of the persecution of Catholics. But in the play's enduring stage history and critical reception, the religious issue that usually comes to the forefront is the widespread persecution of Jews by Christians during medieval, early modern, and especially modern Europe. The polarization of critical responses to the play's portrayal of the persecution of Jews suggests something of the drama's subtlety. While critics such as Lewalski and Short read the play as the triumph of Christianity, Janet Adelman and Kenneth Gross read the play (perhaps more convincingly) through Jewish eyes as the failure of Christianity. Janet Adelman concludes that the play speaks to historical Christianity's immoral treatment of Jews:

> . . .Antonio is the play's epitome, and the epitome of the relationship that the play unwittingly discloses between Christian and Jew. For the play cannot know its own fear and guilt about Christianity's relation to the Jews—its ancestry in a Judaism it has disavowed, its bloody persecution of the Jewish remnant, its continual need to find a justifying difference from the Jew— and so it creates the figure of the monstrous Jew to seal off that knowledge. And once that knowledge has been foreclosed, the debt to the Jew—the debt the play encodes as three thousand ducats for three months—need never be repaid. (133)

And herein lies the ugly side of the play's religion which conflates salvation with racism. The xenophobia which characterizes the Venetians, whether they are relating to a Moroccan prince or a Jew, inevitably emerges in their soteriology. Portia's command that Shylock must not shed "one drop of Christian blood" has the repugnant implication that Christian blood is somehow more valuable than Jewish blood. The Spanish Inquisition was obsessed with "pure-blood laws" (Adelman 80), meaning that Spaniards were not to become ethnically contaminated with the blood of Jews or Moors. The play thus misappropriates Pauline and Reformation ideas about the forensic justification of the sinner through Christ's blood to suggest that salvation is achieved by the Christian's militant triumph over the religious and ethnic other. Indeed, this derailment of Christian theology is not far off the mark, historically speaking. The same Luther who came to experience such profound relief from his tortured conscience through the doctrine of justification by faith uttered some disturbingly anti-Semitic statements that had very unfortunate afterlives.[12]

Nonetheless, in his early *Lectures on Romans*, Luther speaks with a surprising degree of respect for Jews:

> . . .many display an amazing stupidity when they are so presumptuous as to call the Jews 'dogs' or accursed or whatever they choose to name them, though they themselves do not know who or of what sort they themselves are before God. They should feel compassion for them fearing that they themselves may have to take similar punishment, but instead they rashly heap blasphemous insults upon them. (314)

Luther is emphatic that Jews should never be subjected to forced conversion: "They [the theologians of Cologne] want to convert the Jews with force and invective. May God be against them!" (314). Antonio, like the anti-Judaists whom Luther opposes, calls Shylock a dog and subjects him to a forced conversion. Even Luther would disapprove.

Both pro-Shylock and anti-Shylock critics have suggested that the knife he wields is emblematic of circumcision. But as Janet Adelman contends, the knife also evokes the longstanding slur against Jews as "Christ-killers," further contributing to the play's anti-Judaism (111). The fact that Shylock is at times "humanized" does not atone for the play's anti-Judaism, much like audience sympathy for Othello fails to redeem his tragedy from anti-black racism (111). Referring to Portia's prohibition of Shylock shedding "Christian blood," Adelman further contends that "the blood distinction in 4.1 is founded securely on the theological moment—the killing of Christ—that decisively and permanently separates Jews from Christians" (128). As I argued earlier, the "one drop" of Christ's blood is what amounted to Antonio's immediate salvation. Here, Adelman implies that "the killing of Christ," that is, the shedding of his blood, is what bars Shylock from salvation in the early modern imagination.

---

12. The Nazis disseminated Luther's anti-Semitic 1543 tract, *On the Jews and Their Lies* (Ryrie, *Protestants: The Faith that Made the Modern World* 266). While Ryrie clarifies that Naziism was in no way Christian (266), Ryrie observes that more German Protestants cooperated with Hitler than opposed him (265). Dietrich Bonhoeffer, a Lutheran theologian, opposed Hitler's genocide of the Jews and even participated in an assassination attempt against him. Bonhoeffer was sent to a concentration camp, being hanged shortly before Hitler committed suicide.

A more accurate soteriology would recognize the scriptural claim that Christ died for the sins of the entire world, rather than attributing his death to particular religious or ethnic groups.

PAUL, LUTHER, AND THE PROBLEM OF ANTI-JUDAISM

If *The Merchant of Venice* itself is an ambivalent and vexed foray into Jewish-Christian relations, along with the polarized interpretations it elicits from "Christian" and "Jewish" critics, then my attempt to cross such a theological divide must necessarily be another feeble gesture. Yet I would suggest that Adelman's argument that Christ's death divides Christian and Jew, while true to the soteriology of the play, does not accurately reflect Pauline soteriology. Although Adelman seems to have history on her side, i.e., that Christianity has tended to vilify Jews as culpable for their Savior's death, her theology is arguably drawn from medieval and early modern anti-Judaism (including that of the Venetian Christians) rather than from the New Testament. In terms of the xenophobic soteriology of the play, which (as Adelman recognizes) conflates Christ's blood with a Christian's blood, Christian salvation expresses itself as Christian hegemony. In this mindset, the Jew is thus an "infidel," as Graziano declaims (4.1.330), excluded from salvation and the scapegoat of Christian greed, intolerance, and hypocrisy. But in Pauline theology, Christ's death is imagined as having the power of creating a community of faith that will transcend gender, class, and ethnic barriers: "For all ye yt are baptized into Christ, haue put on Christ. There is nether Iewe nor Grecian: there is nether bonde nor fre: there is nether male nor female: for ye are all one in Christ Iesus. And if ye be Christs, then are ye Abrahams sede, and heires by promes" (Gal 3:27–29). The early moderns occasionally recognized these ideas in theory, if not in practice. As the footnote to the 1560 Geneva Bible glosses this passage, "So that Baptisme succedeth Circumcision, and so through Christ bothe Iewe and Gentile is saued." For the editors of the Geneva Bible, momentarily taking their cue from Paul, rather than from historical Christian anti-Judaism, Christ's death unites Christian and Jew in a common salvation.

While early modern audiences may have imagined Shylock's forced conversion to Christianity as a *de facto* salvation, their scriptures would have explicated soteriology in a rather different tone. St. Paul imagines Christ as suffering because of Paul's own sin, rather than as a kind of ethnic or national inheritance of Jewish guilt. (After all, Jesus and Paul are both Jews.) Rather than incurring guilt on his own Jewish race, Paul sees his early behavior in persecuting Christians (out of a desire to maintain the purity of Jewish orthodoxy) as an occasion for Jesus to exhibit mercy towards him: "This is a true saying, and by all meanes worthie to be receiued, that Christ Iesus came into the worlde to saue sinners, of whome I am chief. Notwithstanding, for this cause was I receiued to mercie, that Iesus Christ shulde first shewe on me all lo[n]g suffring vnto the ensample of them, which shal in time to come beleue in him vnto eternal life" (1 Tim 1:15–16). In Paul's case, the persecutor became the persecuted, but in Shylock's case, the persecuted became the persecutor. The hegemonic Venetian Christians, who likely had not been threatened with injustice before this moment in court, are guilty of egregious wrongdoing (the doctrine of justification, notwithstanding!), in that their systemic persecution of Jews created the monster that is Shylock. Shakespeare's play, along with church and world history, seem to bear out Adelman's contention that "the killing of Christ" is the event "that decisively and permanently separates Jews from Christians." However, Saint Paul, the greatest theological interpreter of Jesus found within the Christian tradition, would suggest otherwise. For Paul, Christ's death is the event which provides salvation for all people, including those of his own ethnicity and the gentiles he so passionately proselytized.

Not all critics share such a generous view of Paul's influence on the play. Kenneth Gross suggests that the anti-Judaism in the play actually derives from Paul:

> Does *The Merchant of Venice* point to an antisemitic or anti-Judaic impulse, a distorting prejudice against Jewish tradition, that stands inescapably at the heart of Christianity, especially the tradition of Christian thought that is shaped by the writings of Saint Paul? I am thinking of the divisive logic of Paul's vision of Jewish tradition, his reappropriations of Jewish symbolism and his hyperbolic, reductive pictures of Jewish Law, especially his evocation of both the Law's impotence and its powers of condemnation; he points to its 'evil-mindedness,' as Hans Jonas says, and its links to the realm of the demonic. (143)

Gross answers his question in the affirmative: Paul is indeed a specter lurking behind the play's anti-Judaism:

> Reading the trial scene in *Merchant*, one can feel Shakespeare reminding us of the dramatic occasions for the Pauline dialectic, its anxious projections and contingent simplifications. Portia's all-too-apparent manipulations of the oppositions of law and mercy or sin and promise, for example, suggest the more political aspects of Pauline thinking. One feels there the violence that can inhabit Pauline spiritualization, though Portia's speeches can also remind one of Paul's reimagining of the grounds of spiritual affiliation and hermeneutical freedom. The play suggests how the oppositional logic of Pauline typology helps to contain even as it gives form to both fear and guilt; this includes fear of Christian tradition's intimate links to the very Jewish scriptures it condemns and guilt over the violence it directs against living Jews. (144)

Gross accurately draws attention to the historical mistreatment of Jews by the Christian church (I would also inculpate secular regimes such as Nazism or other faiths such as Islam), as well as to the play's anti-Judaism and its identification of Shylock with Jewish Law. Does all of this amount to a Pauline derivation of the play's anti-Judaism? I suggest not. If Paul is at all behind the play's anti-Judaism, I would argue it is in his misappropriation by early modern Christianity.

When Shylock repeats his claim during the trial, "I stand here for law" (4.1.142 cf. 4.1.203), he allegorizes the Pauline idea that "the letter killeth, but the Spirit giueth life" (2 Cor 3:6). Indeed, Shylock legally attempts to kill Antonio for his failure to make good on his debt. Certainly, Paul's ideas about the Law emerge at this point in the play, but do such ideas amount to a demonization of the Law or, worse yet, anti-Semitism? Saint Paul may suggest that the letter of the Law kills, and that the Law itself has been nailed to the cross of Christ (Col 1:14), but nowhere does Paul convey the Law as demonic. Rather, Paul describes his personal struggle with sin in Romans 7, admitting that the Law is good and spiritual, but that he himself is sinful: "Wherefore the Law is holie, and the commandement is holie, and iuft, & good" (Rom 7:12). Paul does not demonize the Law, but his own sinful nature: "O wretched ma[n] that I am, who shal deliuer me from the bodie of this death!" (Rom 7:24). In Paul's personal experience, obedience to the Law could not save him because of his own proclivity towards sin. For Paul, only the life of the indwelling Holy Spirit could effect the ethical transformation he so zealously sought previously by adhering to Jewish Law.

Kenneth Gross's accusation that Paul "links" the Law "to the realm of the demonic" misreads Paul's complex understanding of the Jewish law. The ethical sections of Paul's epistles reaffirm all of the ten commandments (the core of *Torah* [the Jewish Law]), with the exception of Sabbath observance. Gross's claim comes close to suggesting that Paul advocates antinomianism, a charge from which both Paul and the Protestant reformers were anxious to defend themselves, even if the apostolic and Reformation teachings about grace were sometimes distorted in the direction of antinomianism. Some of Luther's more extreme statements excluding works from salvation arguably made him vulnerable to the charge of antinomianism, but Paul's internalization of the ethical dimensions of the Law through the Holy Spirit operating in the believer effectively discredits Gross's caricature of Paul's soteriology.

Unfortunately, *The Merchant of Venice* maps the Jewish Law onto a Jew who is himself demonized, thus effectively demonizing the Jewish Law. The Law of the play is a caricature of Jewish Law, with its outrageous enforcement of the bond of "a pound of flesh." The pound of flesh is a crude caricature of the Jewish rite of circumcision, itself a kind of "synecdoche" for Jewish Law, to use a term which I cannot attribute to its proper source. Graham Holderness suggests that "Shylock's cruelty is also a kind of forced conversion of Antonio to Judaism, a circumcision, taking literally what St. Paul says about circumcising the heart rather than the body" (150). While Holderness's comment astutely points out the self-contradiction in Shylock's appeal to Law to inflict violence, his designation of Shylock's mistreatment of Antonio as "forced conversion" fails to recognize that the parameters of this interfaith conflict are very unfairly assigned in the play. Typically, a forced conversion occurs when the majority view forces itself upon the minority, or perhaps when one minority forces itself upon another. Shylock, far from securing a conversion of Antonio to Judaism, is himself functioning from a minority position amidst a Christian hegemony. To suggest that Shylock is guilty of the same kind of spiritual abuse as the Venetians is to minimize the persecution that he has experienced as a minority Jew. Nonetheless, just as Jews have been a persecuted minority in Christendom, so too, have Christians often been persecuted minorities throughout their history.

But if the play demonizes the Jewish Law and the Jew, such anti-Judaism owes more to Luther than to Saint Paul. In his commentary on Galatians, Luther addresses the Law as though it were his enemy: "Indeed thou art my tormentor, but I have another tormentor, even Christ, which shall torment thee to death; and when thou art thus bound, tormented and suppressed, then am I at liberty. Likewise if the devil scourge me, I have a stronger devil, which shall in turn scourge him and overcome him. So then grace is a law, not to me, for it bindeth me not, but to my law; which this law so bindeth, that it cannot hurt me any more" (*Selections* 126) With great overstatement and parodic fancifulness that verges on blasphemy, Luther metaphorically calls Christ and/or grace a "devil" who will torment the accusing Satan and nullify the legal charges against Luther. Luther's association of the Law with the demonic emerges in the caricatures of Jew and Jewish Law in the play.

Luther's reputation has suffered because of his anti-Semitism, but is it fair to interpret Paul, himself Jewish, as anti-Semitic? Julia Lupton helpfully clarifies that the consensus in New Testament scholarship is that Paul is *not* speaking against Jews when he condemns those who practice circumcision. Rather, Paul's hostile rhetoric is directed towards those who claim to be Christians yet are demanding Gentile converts to Christianity to follow the Jewish Law (*Thinking* 233–234). In writing to the Galatians, Paul reserves the most violent rhetoric for those in the church who would require Gentile Christians to follow the Jewish Law. Paul imagines emasculation to be an apposite punishment for those who would insist on a Christian's circumcision: "And brethren, if I yet preache circumcision, why do I yet suffer persecution? Then is the sclander of the crosse abolished. Wolde to God they were euen cut of, which do disquiet you" (Gal 5:11–12). Paul even suggests excommunication for those Christians who would seek their righteousness from adherence to Torah: "Ye are abolished from Christ: whosoeuer are iustified by the Law, ye are fallen from grace" (Gal 5:4).

However, when Paul writes in Romans about the Jews as those of his own ethnicity who have concluded that Jesus is not the Messiah (the Christ), he speaks with a combination of respect and sorrow. Paul conveys a deep sense of personal turmoil over the fact that most of his fellow Jews do not subscribe to his high view of Jesus:

> I say the trueth in Christ, I lye not, my conscience bearing me witness in the holie Gost, That I haue great heauines and continual sorowe in mine heart. For I wolde wish my self to be separate from Christ, for my brethre[n] that are my kinsmen according to the flesh, Which are the Israelites, to whome perteineth the adoption, and the glorie, and the Couenantes, and the giuing of the Law, and the seruice of God, and the promises. Of whome

are the fathers, and of whome concerning the flesh, Christ came,
who is God ouer all blessed for euer, Amen. (Rom 9:1–4)

Luther, who took his theology so extensively from Romans and Galatians, seems to have conflated the respectively distinct groups of "Jews" referred to in these epistles. The circumcisers of the Galatian epistles, at whom Paul directs his unmitigated antagonism, are in fact a Christian faction undermining Paul's Christology, not orthodox Jews. The actual Jews Paul speaks of in Romans are a group he disagrees with substantively, but whom he nonetheless respects and cares for, even if his agenda to convert them would strike many modern readers as patronizing. Luther, whose anti-Judaism is a commonplace, apparently misappropriated Paul by misreading the antipathy Paul had for Judaizing Christians in Galatians as antagonism for Jews themselves. If Luther had paid closer attention to Paul's considerably more positive (albeit uneven) assessment of Jews in Romans 9–11, he might have avoided the pitfall of anti-Judaism or at least he might have realized that anti-Judaism was not an apostolic initiative, but a later development within Christianity. Luther's attempt to map Judaizing tendencies onto Catholics also allowed him to justify his extreme rhetoric against them, after the model of Paul's castigation of the circumcision party of Galatian Christians. In regarding the doctrine of justification by faith as the *sine qua non* of Christianity, Luther assumed he had the divine mandate to write invective against those who understood justification differently, be they Jews who adhered to *Torah* or Catholics who championed sacraments and good works.

My attempt to vindicate Paul from Kenneth Gross's charge that Paul is responsible for the play's anti-Judaism can take interfaith dialogue only so far, however. For as Lupton points out, "Paul's break from the Law reminds us that Paul's teachings were heterodox with respect to the larger Jewish communities of the ancient world" (*Thinking* 243). Indeed, from an orthodox Jewish perspective of the first centuries of the common era, Christianity is nothing more than a virulent Jewish heresy. The Jewish identification of Christianity as "heresy" (to use a familiar Christian category) should not be eclipsed by the fact that Christianity came to be and still is the world's largest religion (even as the high birth rates of many Muslim societies are causing sociologists to project that Islam may soon surpass Christianity numerically). In an earlier essay, Lupton suggests that Shylock's alien status in Venice is an outworking of Pauline theology in the Christian *polis*: "In creating a *normative Jew* living as a *tolerated exception* in a Christian state, Shakespeare draws on the historical resources of Pauline typology, with its emphasis on the legal integrity and historical function of Israel in the unfolding drama of redemption" (*Citizen-Saints* 79). However, the Venetians' toleration of Shylock's Jewishness is tenuous at best, ultimately succumbing to the brute force of anti-Semitism. I would suggest that this Venetian (and English) intolerance of Jews has more to do with medieval and early modern anti-Judaism and proto-racism than with Pauline soteriology. Lupton's reading of the Pauline influence on Shakespeare's portrayal of Shylock is more favorable than Gross's or Adelman's assessments, but even Lupton's comments convey the magnitude of the complexity of any attempts to reconcile Jewish and Christian notions of soteriology: "Invited to eat with the Gentiles, Shylock also 'draws back and separates himself,' actively choosing in this case to remain within the world defined by Jewish law. Shakespeare borrows from Paul the negative judgment on the ethical, soteriological, and civil limits of such a retreat, but he equally borrows from Paul a sense of the social, emotional, and legal coherence—the lived normativity—of that world" (*Citizen-Saints* 84). While I appreciate Lupton's attempt to nuance Paul's understanding of Jewish Law, her assumption that the representation of Law in *The Merchant of Venice* is quintessentially Pauline needs qualification. For the demonic associations of the Law come to the play through medieval and early modern prejudices rather than from the New Testament.

ABRAHAM AND ISAAC AND THE FAITH/WORKS CONTROVERSY

The metaphor of blood sacrifice which recurs in the trial scene of the play alludes to both the Hebrew Bible as well as to Pauline and Reformation notions of justification. Antonio's reference to himself as "a tainted wether of the flock, / Meetest for death" (4.1.113–114) is an allusion to Abraham's (near) sacrifice of Isaac (Halio 49 n1). Antonio's insistence on self-sacrifice answers Bassanio's own offer of his life to meet the terms of Antonio's bond to Shylock: "The Jew shall have my flesh, blood, bones, and all / Ere thou shalt lose for me one drop of blood" (4.1.111–112). The play employs the biblical allusion to suggest that Antonio "as the intended sacrificial victim may parallel Isaac, notwithstanding the reference to himself as a 'wether' (=ram), i.e., the substitute," or "scapegoat" of Leviticus 16 (Halio 49 n1).[13]

In Christian typology, Abraham's sacrifice of Isaac came to prefigure God's willing sacrifice of his beloved only Son, and Jesus's obedience to death on a cross fulfilled the death that Isaac only paid symbolically.[14] New Testament writers interpreted Abraham's sacrifice of Isaac in rather divergent ways, which later fueled controversy between Reformation-era Protestants and Catholics over the relative importance of faith and works in salvation. In his extended discourse on faith in Romans 4 which exegetes the life of Abraham, Paul avoids mentioning the sacrifice of Isaac. Instead, Paul refers to Abraham's faith in trusting God to fulfill his promise of making Abraham the father of many nations, despite Abraham and Sara's advanced age. In Paul's hermeneutic, Abraham is the iconic figure of justification by faith, which Paul sees as the antithesis of justification by works:

> For if Abraham were iustified by works, he hathe wherein to reioyce, but not with God. For what saith the Scripture? Abraham beleued God, and it was counted to him for righteousnes. Now to him that worketh, the wages is not counted by fauour, but by dette, But to him that worketh not, but beleueth in him that iuftifieth the vngodlie, his faith is counted for righteousnes. (Rom 4:2–5)

---

13. While early modern paintings of the sacrifice of Isaac, such as those by Caravaggio, convey the abject terror of the ordeal, the incident had a rather different meaning in the context of the ancient world. Yahweh, the God of Abraham, asked Abraham to sacrifice Isaac as a test of Abraham's loyalty to him, but dramatically intervened, commanding Abraham in an audible voice to desist from killing his beloved son. And while modern readers of this story often conclude that Yahweh is yet another capricious tribal deity, the differences between Abrahamic religion and the other ancient near east faiths come to light through this text. Whereas the tribal deities of the fertility religions routinely required actual infanticide to guarantee generous crops and protection from enemies, Yahweh's intervention in the sacrifice of Isaac clearly distinguishes him from the bloodthirsty Canaanite tribal deities. The advent of monotheism and the birth of Judaism followed in the wake of Abraham's concept of a God who does not need to be appeased by human sacrifice.

14. Ken Jackson argues that the binding of Isaac in Genesis 22 is a deep source for *The Merchant of Venice* (96). Jackson reads the story of Abraham being first asked by God to sacrifice Isaac and then later being suddenly commanded by God to desist from killing Isaac as an expression of the two aspects of the Law, which both kills and exhibits mercy (105–107). In Jackson's reading, Shylock does not receive the second call of the Law to mercy (107). Jackson also argues that Shakespeare uses the Abrahamic story as "a means to preserve a certain religious subject formation in a world that seeks to do it harm" (111). Jackson is correct to point out that in the play, this threat comes from "Christian (Hegelian?) universalizing impulses" (111).

For Paul, Abraham's faith justifies him, rather than obedience to the Law of Moses, which came hundreds of years later, and which became the enduring core of Judaism.

In Reformation controversy, the New Testament dialectic between Law and faith/grace was applied to Catholic-Protestant disagreement about the respective roles of faith and works in salvation. Paul's discourses on justification by faith in Romans and Galatians formed much of the theological impetus of the Protestant Reformation. In his Preface to Romans, Luther gives biblical pride of place to this Pauline text: "This epistle is in truth the most important document in the New Testament, the gospel in its purest expression" (*Selections* 19). Although Luther regarded the Mosaic Law in rather pejorative terms as tormenter of the conscience, Calvin saw the Law more positively in terms of its fulfillment in Christ's perfect life (Wright 244). Yet both Luther and Calvin gravitated to a Pauline understanding of the Law as being superseded, or at least transcended, by faith in Christ. Luther and Calvin mapped Paul's discourse about the Jewish Law onto late medieval Catholic sacramental theology, including penitential works of supererogation, suggesting that such Catholic works were unnecessary for salvation, on the model of Paul's abrogation of much of the Jewish ceremonial Law by simple faith in Christ.

The epistle to the Hebrews, attributed by the editors of the Authorized Version to Paul, but more accurately recognized by the Geneva Bible as being of uncertain authorship, interprets Abraham's sacrifice of Isaac as an expression of faith. Indeed, the story of Abraham forms the backbone of the "hall of faith" chapter, Hebrews 11, which was of such importance to the Protestant Reformation: "By faith Abraham offred vp Isaac, when he was tryed, & he that had receiued the promises, offred his onely begotten sonne. (To whome it was said, In Isaac shal thy sede be called) For he considered that God was able to raise him vp euen from the dead: from whe[n]ce he receiued him also after a sorte" (Heb 11:17–19).

The epistle of James, however, interpreted Abraham's sacrifice of Isaac in terms that Luther found threatening to his beloved doctrine of justification by faith. James emphatically suggests that works are necessary for salvation:

> But wilt thou vnderstand, ô thou vaine man, that the faith which is without works, is dead? Was not Abraham our father iustified through works, when he offred Isaac his sonne vpon the Altar: Seest thou not that ye faith wroght with his workes & through the workes was the faith made perfite. And the Scripture was

> fulfilled which saith, Abraham beleued God, and it was imputed vnto him for righteousnes: & he was called the friend of God. Ye se then how that of workes a man is iuftified, and not of faith onely. (Jas 2:20–24)

James's inclusion of works in salvation was anathema to Luther. As Luther opined, "the epistle of St. James is an epistle full of straw, because it contains nothing evangelical" (*Selections* 19). Luther's reforming impulse led him to advocate for a canon within a canon, although less radically than Marcion, a Pauline enthusiast of the second century. So great was Luther's investment in the doctrine of justification by faith that he was willing to redefine the 1500 year old scriptural heritage of Christianity to make it square with his dogma of justification.

Calvin, however, attempted to reconcile James with Romans, and his influence can be discerned in the lengthy marginalia of the Geneva Bible with reference to Jas 2:14:

> S. Paul to ye Romains and Galatians disputeth against the[m], which attributed iustification to the workes: & here S. Iames reasoneth against them w[hich] vtterly conde[m]ne workes: therefore Paul sheweth the causes of our iuftificatio[n], and Iames the effects: there it is declared how we are iustified: here how we are knowen to be iustified: there workes are excluded as not the cause of our iuftificatio[n]: here they are approued as effects proceding thereof: there they are denied to go before them that shalbe iustified: and here they are said to followe them that are iustified.

In Calvin's *ordo salutis*, justification and sanctification are distinguishable, yet inextricable. Here the Geneva commentators uphold such dogma by citing faith as the cause of salvation and good works as the effects of salvation.

THE DIVORCE BETWEEN SALVATION AND ETHICS IN PROTESTANT SOTERIOLOGY

Protestantism's differentiation of justification and sanctification, however, opened up theology to some unfortunate distortions, such as antinomianism. McGrath argues that the development of Pietism[15] was a reaction to

---

15. Alister McGrath defines Pietism as an "approach to Christianity, especially associated with German writers in the seventeenth century, which places an emphasis

the moral laxity that followed in the wake of the Protestant Reformation (*Justification* 238–240). The idea that ethics could be notionally divorced from salvation was not welcomed by the Catholic church. The council of Trent upheld Augustine's understanding of justification as regeneration, effectively subsuming the Protestant doctrine of sanctification under the aegis of justification. For Catholicism, as for James, faith could not be defined apart from ethics.

Doctrinally, the split between grace and ethics may ultimately be pinned on Luther. As McGrath argues, Luther's distinctive theological innovation was to suggest that in being justified by faith, "man is *intrinsically* sinful yet *extrinsically* righteous" (182). In Luther's formulation in *Lectures on Romans*, God gives his own righteousness to the believer, even though the human does not deserve it: "For the righteousness of God is the cause of salvation. Here, too, '*the righteousness of God*' must not be understood as that righteousness by which he is righteous in himself, but as that righteousness by which we are made righteous (justified) by Him, and this happens through faith in the gospel" (18). Through faith, God's righteousness is imputed to the believer, even though she is still sinful. Luther actually celebrates the paradox of a sinner being deemed righteous by God: "The saints in being righteous are at the same time sinners; they are righteous because they believe in Christ whose righteousness covers them and is imputed to them, but they are sinners because they do not fulfill the law and are not without sinful desires" (*Lectures on Romans* 208). For Luther, the split between ethics and salvation, rather than a compromise of religious integrity, is the essence of grace itself. In his *Preface to the Complete Edition of Luther's Latin Writings* of 1545, Luther recounts his awakening to the idea of justification by faith arising from his study of Rom 1:17: "There I began to understand that the righteousness of God [*iustitia Dei*] is that by which the righteous lives by a gift of God, namely by faith. And this is the meaning: the righteousness of God is revealed by the gospel, namely, the passive righteousness with which merciful God justifies us by faith" (*Selections* 10–11). The word "passive" seems to have created problems for Protestantism, in that it sometimes created a *laissez-faire* approach to religion, as its Catholic critics (such as Thomas More) feared. Perhaps Luther's overstatement of his dogma exacerbated Protestantism's struggle to inspire spiritual and moral maturity.

---

upon the personal appropriation of faith and the need for holiness in Christian living. The movement is perhaps best known within the English-language world in the form of Methodism" (*Christian Theology* 453).

In his *Preface to the New Testament,* Luther brazenly insists that salvation must be divorced from ethics: "Understand this, that a man is given righteousness, life, and salvation by faith; and nought is required of him to give proof of this faith" (*Selections* 17–18). Catholicism, following St. James, would object. Shakespeare, too, seems to object. At least, the ethical paucity of the Venetian Christians seems to undermine the credibility of their beloved dogma of justification by faith alone.

Luther's definition of salvation as distinct from ethics, however, is not tantamount to antinomianism. In his *Treatise on Good Works* (1520), Luther insists that the cardinal work a required of a Christian is simply to believe in Christ. In Luther's mind, faith is the ground of all good works. Without faith, there can be no good works. The fact that this treatise includes significant commentary on the decalogue indicates that Luther's intent is emphatically *not* reducible to antinomianism. Rather, Luther's target is the Catholic Church's works of supererogation, which he dismisses as pointless unless inspired by faith.

RICHARD HOOKER'S ATTEMPT TO MEDIATE CATHOLIC AND PROTESTANT VIEWS ON JUSTIFICATION

Richard Hooker's views on justification are important to consider in reference to *The Merchant of Venice* because Hooker's attempt to bridge the chasm between Puritanism and Catholicism may be reflected in the play's theological discourse. Although Hooker's sermons on Habakkuk were not published until 1612, Hooker preached them in 1586 (McGrath 291), well before the play was written and first performed in 1596-97 and before the play was published in 1600. Although Hooker was a dissident voice against the Calvinist majority of his day, his episcopal, proto-Arminian theology went a long way to establishing what later came to be understood as Anglican orthodoxy. It is fitting that among his sermons on Habakkuk is *A Learned Discourse of Justification, Works, and how the Foundation of Faith is Overthrown,* for the book of Habakkuk is the source of the phrase, "the iuste shal liue by his faith" (2:4). This phrase from Habakkuk reverberated in Rom 1:17, Gal 3:11, and Heb 10:37-38, eventually becoming a slogan of the Protestant Reformation. Hooker's argument that Catholics, including the pope himself, could be saved despite the inaccuracy of their soteriology, was a rather ecumenical gesture in the sixteenth century—an overture that was not well received by his

Puritan detractors. McGrath suggests that "Hooker attempts to construct a mediating doctrine of justification between Catholicism and Protestantism, which avoids the discredited eirenicon of double justification" (291).

Unlike Luther, who felt that all who failed to uphold "the article of justification... are either Jews, Turks, Papists or heretics" (*Selections* 106), Hooker suggested that those who lived in "popish superstitions" (v) were not to be disbarred from salvation merely because they do not subscribe to justification by faith alone. Hooker rhetorically discredits the common Protestant notion that Catholics are beyond the pale of salvation:

> ...there is no difference in the world between our [Catholic] fathers and Saracens, Turks, or Painims, if they did directly deny Christ crucified for the salvation of the world.
> But how many millions of them are known so to have ended their mortal lives that the drawing of their breath hath ceased with the uttering of this faith: "Christ my Saviour, my Redeemer Jesus!" And shall we say that such did not hold the foundation of Christian faith? (vi)

Hooker, with his keen sense for irenicism, imagines how he might reconcile the apparent discrepancy between St. Paul and St. James's teachings on justification, which are reflected in the soteriological impasse between Protestantism and Catholicism:

> Did they [Catholics] hold that without works we are not justified? Take justification so that it may also imply sanctification, and St. James doth say as much; for except there be an ambiguity in some term, St. Paul and St. James do contradict each other, which cannot be. Now, there is no ambiguity in the name either of faith or of works, both being meant by them both in one and the same sense. Finding therefore that justification is spoken of by St. Paul without implying sanctification when he proveth that a man is justified by faith without works; finding likewise that justification doth sometimes imply sanctification also with it; I suppose nothing more sound than so to interpret St. James as speaking not in that sense, but in this. (vii)

Hooker seems to be suggesting that part of the problem in Protestant and Catholic soteriological controversy is a misunderstanding of each other's terminology. Whereas Protestants (including Hooker himself) were intent on distinguishing between justification and sanctification, Catholics had one term—justification—that accounted for both of these phenomena. Hooker suggests that if Paul and James can be squared by rightly understanding each of their definitions of justification, then Catholics and Protestants can make better headway in understanding each other's soteriology.

Hooker's formulation of justification is a little cumbersome, notwithstanding his critique of the doctrine of double justification articulated by the council of Trent. Hooker distinguishes between two types of righteousness gained in justification, on the one hand, and two types of sanctification experienced by the Christian, on the other hand. The two forms of justification by faith include imputed and actual righteousness, and the two forms of sanctification include "habitual" and "actual" holiness. In this formulation, Abraham was justified by faith for believing God (imputed righteousness) and justified by faith for his willingness to offer Isaac as a sacrifice (actual righteousness or "virtue"). In a twofold conception of sanctification, Hooker envisions the indwelling of the Holy Spirit as the "habitual" sanctification located in every believer, whereas the "actual" sanctification is the kind of exemplary love and character exhibited by mature saints.

It is doubtful that Hooker's idea of twofold justification and twofold sanctification is any more streamlined than Trent's idea of double justification. Yet it is clear that Hooker is carefully wrestling with the relationship between justification and sanctification in a way that tries to reconnect salvation with ethics. Ethical transformation was of paramount concern to the council of Trent, whose encoding of double justification was likely a reaction to Protestantism's doctrine of justification *sola fide*. Hooker, perhaps a close to Trent as to Luther, is determined to reincorporate ethics into salvation. Hooker believes that his formulation of justification and sanctification "showeth plainly how the faith of true believers cannot be divorced from hope and love; how faith is a part of sanctification, and yet unto sanctification necessary; how faith is perfected by good works, and yet no works of ours good without faith; finally, how our fathers might hold, we are justified by faith alone, and yet hold truly that without good works we are not justified" (vii). Hooker's attempt to close the gap between Protestant and Catholic views on justification was certainly ambitious, if a little convoluted.[16]

---

16. Recent attempts to harmonize Catholic and Protestant understandings of justification have met with unprecedented success. The 1999 *Joint Declaration on the Doctrine of Justification* by the Lutheran World Federation and the Catholic Church claims to have resolved the supreme doctrinal impasse of the Reformation. The Declaration

Something of Hooker's concern to see salvation conceived in harmony with ethics seems to lie behind Shakespeare's critique of standard Protestant notions of justification in *The Merchant of Venice*. The terms of the theological debate in the play seem to be more Protestant than Catholic, despite the ostensible Catholicism of the Venetians. Yet the play's critique of Protestant dogma, like its critique of the persecution of some Catholics pressured to swear the Oath of Supremacy against their consciences, suggests that the play has a certain degree of Catholic sympathy. Portia's deft manipulation of the law to her own religio-political agenda perhaps intimates Elizabeth's strong grip on the English church. Elizabeth, determined to keep Puritans and Catholics alike from derailing her political agenda, used coercion to keep the loyalty of her subjects. The hostile responses that most critics today have to Portia speak to the effectiveness of Shakespeare's religious critiques in the play. Just as most modern audiences recoil in anger at Portia's failure to demonstrate to the alien the mercy she so articulately requires of him, the play rather scourgingly points out the irony that in the sixteenth century the doctrine of salvation became a means of branding the religious minority as the enemy. In early modern Europe, one drop of Christ's salvific blood was violently substituted with the rapacious shedding of Catholic, Protestant, Jewish, and Muslim blood.

FROM *CARITAS* TO *EROS*: SHAKESPEARE ANTICIPATES SECULARISM

The last act of the play attempts to come to terms with the intractable religious disagreements that plague early modern Europe. The eerie tenuousness of the success of Jessica and Lorenzo's marriage speaks to the vexed complexity of any attempt at religious reconciliation between

articulates a rapprochement between the Catholic and Lutheran faiths, at least in terms of this thorny issue: "The understanding of the doctrine of justification set forth in this Declaration shows that a consensus in basic truths of the doctrine of justification exists between Lutherans and Catholics" (5.40). The document further exempts current Lutheran and Catholic views on justification from the mutual anathemas of the Protestant and Catholic Reformations: "Thus the doctrinal condemnations of the 16th century, in so far as they relate to the doctrine of justification, appear in a new light: The teaching of the Lutheran churches presented in this Declaration does not fall under the condemnations from the Council of Trent. The condemnations in the Lutheran Confessions do not apply to the teaching of the Roman Catholic Church presented in this Declaration" (5.41). More recently, Methodist and Reformed denominations have also subscribed to the ecumenical document.

early modern Jews and Christians, or even between English Catholics and Protestants. The lyrical scene of Jessica and Lorenzo evaluating their relationship under the light of the moon and stars, serenaded by the harmony of the spheres, is undermined by a series of classical allusions. Perhaps the conversion of a Jewess to Christianity for the sake of marriage will yield a union no less tragic than that of Troilus to his faithless Cressida, Thisbe to her ill-fated and despairing Pyramus, Dido to her wandering and glory-bound Aeneas, or Medea to her neglectful Jason. Jessica cannot really believe her Christian husband would actually love a proselyte to his faith:

> In such a night
> Did young Lorenzo swear he loved her well,
> Stealing her soul with many vows of faith
> And ne'er a true one. (5.1.17–20)

The subtext of this humor is a cynical awareness that religious difference is an enduring reality that can divide even the closest of lovers, families, and friends.

The ring test is a more comic analogy for competing loyalties in religion, but its tragic overtones nonetheless persist. Portia playfully chastises Bassanio for parting with his wedding ring. Portia describes the significance of the wedding ring in soteriological terms as "A thing stuck on with oaths upon your finger / And so riveted with faith unto your flesh" (5.1.168–169). The simultaneous reference to an "oath" and "faith" suggests the Oath of Supremacy that was so problematic for English Catholics. In Portia's witty banter, the competing loyalties of wife and best friend become an analogy for the competing loyalties of conscience and state experienced by recusants. The melancholy situation of a Jewess committing apostasy for the sake of marrying a Christian and the comic situation of Bassanio being discovered *sans* wedding ring both illustrate the precarious religious situation in England in which Catholics and Protestants could be members of the same family, while holding religious views which made them mutual enemies.

The sad case of Henry and John Donne comes to mind. Henry died in prison for harboring a Jesuit priest, whereas his brother John took the opposite path of becoming ordained in the Protestant state church (at the behest of James I), even composing a piece of propaganda (*Pseudo-Martyr*) that denied the martyrological status of those executed for refusing to swear the Oath of Allegiance to James.[17] From a Catholic perspective, John Donne spat on the grave of his dead brother. From a Protestant perspective, Henry Donne died a pointless death.

In this play which so concertedly tackles religious controversy, Shakespeare nonetheless conveys an impatience with religious violence. Earlier, I interpreted Bassanio's choice of the lead casket in terms of a Protestant understanding of faith, despite the sacramental overtones of the symbolism of the casket. However, the dialogue in the lead casket scene reverts to a Catholic perspective in places. Bassanio says to Portia, "Let me choose, / For as I am, I live upon the rack" (3.2.24–25). Portia's response to Bassanio steers the rhetoric into Catholic waters: "Upon the rack, Bassanio? Then confess / What treason there is mingled with your love" (3.2.26–27). Here the audience (and especially Shakespeare)[18] would likely be thinking of Catholic martyrs such as Southwell, a Jesuit priest who was executed for treason the year before Shakespeare started writing *The Merchant of Venice*. As the romantic banter continues, Portia playfully assumes the role of an interrogator, urging Bassanio to "confess and live" (3.2.35). Bassanio then redirects the conversation from politics and religion back to love:

> 'Confess' and 'love'
> Had been the very sum of my confession.
> O happy torment, when my torturer
> Doth teach me answers for deliverance! (3.2.35–38)

Shakespeare thus turns the tragic scenario of a religious criminal being tortured and martyred (i.e., a "treasonous" English Catholic) into a comic confession of love. Through this generic transposition, Shakespeare highlights the absurdity of Protestant/Catholic violence and, by implication, all religious violence. If a Catholic should not be tortured for his beliefs, neither should a Jew or a Muslim be persecuted by the Protestant majority.

Earlier, I also suggested that Shakespeare's handling of the soteriology in the play conveys a more orthodox position than that of Marlowe in *Doctor Faustus*. But orthodoxy is never really quite the right word for Shakespeare. Even as Shakespeare highlights the injustice of the

---

17. James insisted that the Oath of Allegiance was not persecutory towards Catholics, but rather a means of ensuring their loyalty to him as monarch. The Pope, however, considered the Oath to be a coercive abjuration of a Catholic's faith.

18. Shakespeare and Southwell were "cousins," as the term was loosely used in the period.

persecution of Catholic and Jewish minorities, and even as he interrogates the disconnect between ethics and doctrine in received Protestant soteriology, the play may not really be looking to religion to resolve these conflicts. Despite its erudite theology, the play is a romantic comedy of sorts, not a religious treatise. Like *The Tempest*, it is a revenge tragedy transposed into romance (or, in this case, romantic comedy). The love of Antonio for Bassanio and the love between Portia and Bassanio compose the salutary affective core of the play (if we are able to extricate ourselves from the pathological mutual *ressentiment* of Shylock and Antonio). For all his theological acumen, Shakespeare may be anticipating the modern secular world by privileging romantic love over religion. Though Portia is certainly a mouthpiece for religious dogma in the play, she (like John Donne in his early poetry) uses religious terminology to convey the force of her romantic love. Portia articulates her love for Bassanio in terms of a religious conversion: "Myself and what is mine to you and yours / Is now converted" (3.2.166–167). In a play where Jessica and Shylock's religious conversions are depicted so disturbingly, the one type of "conversion" that really shines is the turn to romantic love. If religion is the problem, then perhaps love is the answer.

The Merchant of Venice not only contains significant soteriological content but can even be read fruitfully against the soteriological backdrop of the period. A soteriological assessment of this play also helps to mitigate some of the more unsavory aspects of the play's stereotypes of Jews, Muslims, Puritans, and Catholics, even if it does deflect such negative dogma onto the magisterial reformers and the Protestant (largely Calvinist) religious establishment of late Elizabethan England. And while ethics may be more germane to Shakespearean drama than nice theological distinctions, *The Merchant of Venice* appropriates soteriological controversy in order to negotiate the morally fraught fissures in the religious landscape of early modern England. In its empathic treatment of religious minorities, Shakespeare's play challenges the more oppressive elements of the ideological consensus.

2

"Try What Repentance Can"
Soteriological Agency and Avant-Garde Conformity in the Claudius Prayer Scene in *Hamlet*

PETER LAKE'S COINAGE "AVANT-GARDE conformity" (131) describes a strain of English church thought associated with Lancelot Andrewes that may have significant implications for Shakespeare's soteriology. While Shakespeare and religion criticism of the first decade of the millennium was often pre-occupied with identifying Recusant Catholic or crypto-Catholic dimensions in Shakespearean drama, more recent scholarship has recognized that the religious contexts and discourses at work in Shakespeare's *oeuvre* resist such simplistic overgeneralizations.[1] Claudius's prayer offers yet another proof of Brian Cummings's assessment of

---

1. Anthony Dawson concludes that Claudius's abortive attempt at repentance in *Hamlet* (3.3) defies confessional affiliation: "whether the scene etches a Catholic, Calvinist, or 'Anglican' perspective on repentance is never clear" (239). Such ambiguity, however, calls for further inquiry into historical theology. What Dawson refers to as "Anglican" thought is in fact defined by such ambiguity, for Cranmer was a genius of ambiguous formulation. Rather than using Dawson's rather amorphous term "Anglican," I prefer Peter Lake's more nuanced label, "avant-garde conformist," defined below. Other figures besides Cranmer, such as Richard Hooker and Lancelot Andrewes, perpetuated ambiguity in the English church's approach to soteriology, while figures such as William Perkins tried to entrench soteriology in staunchly (Puritan) Calvinist terms. Jonathan Willis observes that soteriology was a contested and evolving discourse in the Reformed English church: "Sin and salvation were in a theological sense great cosmic absolutes, but they were also historical constructs, born of particular social, cultural and theological contexts, their meanings subtly shifting as those contexts themselves underwent incessant transformation" (8).

Hamlet: "the play confronts us with competing and often contradictory theological languages" (213). The polyphony of theological influences on Shakespeare demands careful attention to sources that have been hitherto neglected, such as popular sermons. Lancelot Andrewes's sermons delivered in the year leading up to the first performances of *Hamlet* are one such theological source that enrich our understanding of Shakespeare's religious context. Lancelot Andrewes becomes an especially important figure to place in conversation with *Hamlet* because Andrewes's celebration of free agency in salvation represents a line of thinking *within* the contemporary English church that is more often associated with Thomism or Jesuit Molinism. Instead of placing *Hamlet* in a tug-of-war between Puritanism and Catholicism, as previous generations of Shakespeare scholars were inclined to do, I am eager to recover minority views within the English church (such as Lancelot Andrewes's) as possible ingredients in the theological potpourri that is *Hamlet*.

Some of the features of Andrewes's "avant-garde conformist" theology include a celebration of unlimited atonement (meaning that Christ died for everyone, not just for the elect), an inclusive soteriology, a high view of the sacraments, an emphasis on repentance and amendment, and an eschewing of predestination (Lake 131). All of these "Arminian" views figure prominently in Andrewes's sermons on Cain, delivered about a year before the traditional dating of the first performance of *Hamlet*, and over a decade before the followers of Dutch theologian Jacobus Arminius published the definitive statement of Arminius's views posthumously in the *Remonstrance* of 1610. Peter Lake's term for proto-Arminian *English* theological thought and praxis is "avant-garde conformity," which is characterized by all of the theological perspectives attributed above to Andrewes, long before such views became the official orthodoxy of the English church during the tenure of the Arminian-minded archbishop William Laud.[2] Hence the oxymoronic descriptors "avant-garde" and

---

2. While Peter Lake regards Andrewes as an important bridge between the similarly minded Richard Hooker and William Laud (131), Peter McCullough astutely posits that Andrewes might be more accurately regarded as the godfather of avant-garde conformity than Hooker himself (393). McCullough points out that Hooker and Andrewes were almost the same age and that it was Hooker's early death that relegated him to the Elizabethan period, whereas Andrewes enjoyed the apex of his career under the favor of James, with Andrewes continuing to exert significant influence posthumously on Laud (381–382; 393). However, McCullough has discovered that many of the views that Hooker conveys in his *magnum opus* find expression in Andrewes at an earlier date: "Not only do we find here—in March 1590—Laudianism *avant la lettre*, but we also have avant-garde conformity *avant The Lawes of Ecclesiasticall Polity*" (384). Although

"conformist." For Andrewes was articulating a minority position during the predestinarian high-point of the church in the late Elizabethan era, but three decades later Andrewes's theology would become official (albeit highly controversial) Caroline church polity, thanks in large measure to Andrewes's posthumous influence on Laud's churchmanship.[3]

By situating *Hamlet* in the stream of Andrewesian "avant-garde conformity," I hope to explain why Claudius's prayer in the definitive text of the second quarto (Q2) has intimations of soteriological agency that are lacking in the first quarto (Q1). Indeed, the possibility of agency in the prayer scene in Q2 is vital to the conception of freedom in the entire play. In remaining unrepentant, Claudius disavows himself of responsibility for his fratricide. In identifying himself as the fallen sparrow of providentialist Calvinism, Hamlet also relinquishes responsibility for his actions. As such, the play exposes the ethical incoherencies of predestinarian thinking and argues for the importance of freedom not only to soteriology but to all salient human choices.

Catholic ideas in Claudius's prayer work in tandem with avant-garde conformity to promote an understanding of soteriological agency that resists predestinarian determinism.[4] Shakespeare alludes to a poem by English Jesuit Robert Southwell, "Mans Civill Warre," to nuance Claudius's decision along the lines of Catholic thought. From the one side of Claudius's conversation with God that the audience is privy to, Shakespeare reveals the operation of amazing grace, if not Calvinist irresistible grace. To use the Jesuit language of Molinism, Claudius experiences *sufficient* grace, but such grace never becomes *efficient* because Claudius does not embrace it. Possible intimations of Molinism in Claudius's

---

a minority voice in the English church of the 1590s, Andrewes becomes an important figure whose views later came to dominate the church.

3. Given its theological context, it is not surprising that *Hamlet* explores the tension between divine providence and human free will in salvation. Philip Benedict observes that "the years around 1600... were the high-water mark for predestination in English theology" (qtd. in Curran 7).

4. *Hamlet*, in its Thomistic regard for human agency in repentance, works towards healing the rupture between soteriology and ethics caused by reformed thought. Paul Cefalu's identification of a "systemic problem of integrating English Reformed soteriology... and ethical practice" informs my discussions of *The Merchant of Venice* and *Measure for Measure* (*Moral Identity* 2). Cefalu argues that "the difficulty of finding a place for ethics in the *ordo salutis* [was]... a challenge facing all theologians and literary authors who set out to theorize the relationship between justification and sanctification" (7). *Hamlet* responds to the reformed impasse between soteriology and ethics by recovering human agency, thus attributing greater ethical responsibility to human action.

prayer thus corroborate the high view of soteriological agency found in the strains of Andrewesian avant-garde conformity in the soliloquy. In *Hamlet*, free will strikes a louder chord than predestination.

Finally, by comparing *Hamlet* to its afterlives in Middleton's *The Revenger's Tragedy*, I intend to show more clearly through a non-Shakespearean *dramatic* control text how Claudius's impenitence emerges as his deliberate choice. Whereas the Duke in Middleton's play finds himself in the same soteriological quandaries as Claudius, the Duke's glib approach to repentance reveals him to be a Calvinist reprobate who is devoid of soteriological agency. In contrast, Claudius agonizes over his decision whether or not to repent, revealing himself to be a subject with vital soteriological agency. The grace Claudius envisions is greater than all his sin, but the choice to receive or reject that grace ultimately remains his own.

In short, this theological question has far reaching implications for the entire play: Is Claudius unable to repent or merely unwilling to repent? If Claudius is actually unable to repent, i.e., if he is being denied the prevenient grace necessary for conversion, the prayer scene would designate Claudius as one of Calvin's reprobates, one of the unelect doomed by God to damnation. However, if Claudius actually has agency in this process, if he genuinely has the capacity to repent by coming clean before divine and human authorities, then his failed salvation is ultimately his own premeditated decision, rather than an arbitrary rejection by God. Avant-garde conformist and Catholic theologies would construe Claudius as deciding to refuse God's generous offer of grace. Nevertheless, whether Claudius's spiritual desolation is a bed of his own making or the fate of a predestined reprobate, the symptom of his impenitence remains the same: a hard heart like Cain's which is impervious to the gentle stirrings of grace.

LANCELOT ANDREWES'S CAIN AND *HAMLET*'S CLAUDIUS

Possible intimations of Lancelot Andrewes's twenty sermons on the sin of Cain delivered at St. Giles's, Cripplegate, between February 1598 to February 1599, close to the inception of *Hamlet* (traditionally dated to 1599–1600), suggest that important proto-Arminian ideas operate among the play's polyvalent theological discourses. These sermons were published posthumously in 1657 in *Apospasmatia sacra, or, A collection of posthumous and orphan lectures.* While Shakespeare obviously did not have access to the printed version of these sermons, their oral delivery coincides with the genesis of *Hamlet*, whether or not they were a direct influence on the play. These sermons represent an important proto-Arminian discourse that positions Cain's fratricide as a willing rejection of God's grace rather an indication of his reprobation according to Calvinist double predestination. There are allusions to Cain's murder in the King's prayer in the first quarto of *Hamlet* of 1603 (Q1) and in Claudius's prayer in the second quarto of 1604–05 (Q2). The first quarto likens the King to a reprobate Cain in terms that are strongly Calvinistic. However, while the second quarto again alludes to Cain, the predestinarian contours of Claudius's prayer are softened by hints of soteriological agency.

The affinities between Andrewes's Cain and Claudius in Q2 are striking. Both are fratricides, both remain impenitent despite stirrings of conscience, and most significantly, both are confronted with a compelling picture of a merciful God but nonetheless fail to obtain salvation. The main point of Andrewes's year long exposition of Cain's sin is to create a vision of a gracious God who freely forgives any penitent sinner. Yet this expansive vision has a decidedly polemical agenda to overturn the Calvinist conception of double predestination and the alternatives of laxity and despair that Andrewes felt such theology inculcated. Claudius's picture of God resonates with aspects of Andrewes's gracious God who is keenly responsive to human agency. Nonetheless, the ultimate futility of Claudius's attempt to experience redemption suggests that latent strains of Calvinist thought remain intrenched in Claudius's belief system. Shakespeare's Claudius, who likens himself to Cain at the outset of the prayer scene, negotiates the controversial space between Andrewes's willingly impenitent, yet divinely courted Cain and the rejected, reprobate Cain of Calvinism. In other words, the prayer scene conveys a tension between an Andrewesian proto-Arminianism and Calvinist double predestination.

Claudius begins his prayer with a self-referential allusion to Cain:

> O, my offence is rank: it smells to heaven;
> It hath the primal eldest curse upon't—
> A brother's murder. (Q2 3.3.36–38)[5]

---

5. For my base text I am using the Arden 3 edition of *Hamlet*, based on the second quarto of 1604–1605. In doing so, I follow the scholarly consensus that Q2 is an earlier, and therefore more authoritative iteration of *Hamlet* than F. I recognize that this consensus is currently being challenged, by no less a critic than Terri Bourus, who posits

This allusion has obvious referents in morality plays and in Shakespeare's own reading of the Geneva Bible. The Geneva Bible footnotes represent Cain in classical Calvinist terms as a "reprobate": "This is the nature of the reprobate when[n] thei are reproued of their hupocrisie, eue[n] to neglect God and despite him" (Gen 4:9, fn h). From the Calvinist perspective of the editors of the Geneva Bible, Cain is a doubly predestined "reprobate" who has no hope of salvation. This Calvinist picture of Cain certainly underscores aspects of Claudius's thought:

> Pray can I not:
> Though inclination be as sharp as will,
> My stronger guilt defeats my strong intent
> And like a man to double business bound
> I stand in pause where I shall first begin
> And both neglect. (3.3.38–42)

Claudius is here the Geneva Bible's self-tormented Cain who is under the severe judgment of God. The most salient Calvinist moment in Claudius's prayer is captured in his logic of repentance:

> Try what repentance can—what can it not?—
> Yet what can it, when one cannot repent? (3.3.65–66)

The biblical *locus classicus* for a failed repentance is Esau's inability to regain his birthright in Genesis 27, glossed as follows in Hebrews 12:17: "For ye knowe how that afterward also when he wolde haue inherited the blessing, he was reiected: for he founde no place to repentance, thogh he soght *the blessing* with teares." Esau, like Cain, was an archetypal reprobate in the Calvinist imagination. Claudius, as a fratricide like Cain and a failed penitent like Esau, absorbs both of these biblical figures into his self-concept.

Competing with these Calvinist images of Cain as "reprobate" in Claudius's prayer are perhaps intimations of Andrewes's proto-Arminian Cain, a sinner who chooses his course of action while being constantly warned and wooed by a loving God who desires to redeem him. Andrewes pays lip service to the Geneva Bible's identification of Cain as a "reprobate," but Andrewes carefully redefines reprobation in Arminian terms as willing capitulation to and persistence in sin, rather than the Calvinist idea of double predestination, of being selected by God for

---

that F is based on an older version of the play than is Q2 (210). When I quote Q1, I also use the Arden 3 edition of that text.

destruction. Andrewes dilates on "a difference between the Children of God and of the Devill, between the reprobate and the regenerate; that in the godly there is *peccatum volans*, but not *dominans*, sin ruleth but reigneth not" (403).

Perhaps the most revolutionary feature of Andrewes's biblical exposition is not his picture of Cain, but his avant-garde conformist picture of God in constant, passionate pursuit of the salvation of the sinner. Andrewes's picture of God represents a determined alternative to the dominant Calvinist soteriology of the late Elizabethan church. Andrewes's God is in loving pursuit of the wayward Cain, the first child ever born to human parents:

> ...we are to observe these three qualities whereby God draweth men to repentance, *his goodness, and his long suffering, and patience, Romans* the second chapter and the first verse, which goodness of God towards *Cain* appears herein, that having already used perswasions and preservative physick to keep *Cain* from sinning, he contents not himself, but ministreth medicine curative now he hath sinned. (418)

Andrewes further grounds his attempt to save Cain in New Testament theology right out of the epistle to the Hebrews:

> ...if the blood of *Abel* had a voice to speak unto God; then the blood of Christ Jesus must needs have a more powerfull voice, because it *speaketh beter things than the blood of Abel, Hebrews* the twelfth chapter and the twenty fourth verse; for the blood of *Abel* cryed for Justice, but Christ's blood cryeth for Mercy... . (428)

Such discourse on justification by faith in Christ's blood would find a ready welcome in both Calvinist and proto-Arminian circles, but what follows so shockingly deviates from reformed thought that one can only imagine the scandal Andrewes's words may have stirred among his first auditors. After classically restating the doctrine of salvation *sola fide* (in terms reminiscent of the Elizabethan homily "On the Salvation of All Mankind"), Andrewes proceeds to articulate something that sounds so much like justification by works that it might as well have been sourced from The Council of Trent:

> ...If when we doe evill it will plead to God for vengeance; then if wee doe any good work, much more shall it speak to God for us. And God as he is inclined to mercy, rather than to vengeance,

will rather hear the voice of our good works, than of evill, because our good works speak better things than our wicked actions. (428)

In attributing salvific merit to good works rather than to mere faith, Andrewes here undermines justification by faith, and along with it, much of the groundwork of the magisterial Protestant Reformation. Andrewes's rhetoric in this passage is almost indistinguishable from (if less nuanced than) the Catholic soteriology that the Protestant reformers were so intent on uprooting. It is no wonder that when Laud later implemented much of Andrewes's theological vision that it had such a polarizing effect on the English church and nation, even contributing to the eruption of civil war. The controversial tenor of Andrewes's discourse speaks to just how volatile a biblical allusion to Cain in *Hamlet* might be in its original cultural moment.

If Andrewes attempts to swing the theological pendulum too close to Rome for the liking of most of his compatriots, he is nevertheless determined to advocate for a picture of God that he deems more loving than that of Calvinism:

> But the error of *Cain* stands herein, not that he is perswaded that his sin is great, for murther no doubt is a great sinne, but that he thinketh it so great *as it could not be pardoned*; as if Gods mercy were not great enough for his sinne were it never so great; Cain's error then as we see, is *Major iniquitas quàm propitiatio*. Which error God doth most of all detest.... (438)

For Andrewes, Cain's fratricide was not unforgivable, but rather Cain's desperate belief that God could not pardon his murder is what barred him from salvation. For Andrewes, the idea that God is unwilling to forgive *any* penitent sinner is so repellant that he considers it a cardinal sin to imagine God in such ungracious terms. Calvinist double predestination is clearly the target of Andrewes's controversial rhetoric.

Another of Andrewes's sermons, "Of the Power of Absolution," preached at Whitehall on March 13, 1600, taking John 20:23 as its text, attempts to unite an expansive vision of a forgiving God with a mandate for the church to dispense forgiveness. Arguing on the basis of patristic authority that clergy (but not laity) have the authority to absolve sinners, Andrewes attempts to restore "the keys" of absolution to the English church (95) in a way that suggests a movement back to Roman Catholic ecclesiology and away from Luther's priesthood of all believers. A contemporary letter by Rowland Whyte records that Andrewes's sermon created quite a stir at court, "for such doctrine was not usually taught here," and this sermon seems to have been the occasion for Andrewes having to defend himself to the secretary of state, Robert Cecil (qtd. in Stevenson 121). Nonetheless, Andrewes is careful to attribute the forgiveness of sins ultimately to God: "For of remitting sin He taketh the ground from Himself and not from any other, and therefore that more naturally; but of retaining it, the cause is ministered from us, even from our hardness, and heart that cannot repent" (89).

Andrewes once again uses the case of Cain to argue that because of the bounty of God's grace, no sinner need fear that her sin is too great to be forgiven: "So that no man shall need to say his 'sin is greater than can be remitted,' as Cain did, since that assertion is convinced to be erroneous; for his sin may be forgiven that slew Abel though his brother, seeing St. Peter saith that theirs was not greater than might be forgiven that slew the Son of God" (96–97). This sermon on absolution, dating from the same year as the first staging of Shakespeare's *Hamlet*, simultaneously upholds a high view of God's grace and a high view of human agency, even to the point where human beings collaborate with God in administering divine forgiveness.

SAMUEL HARSNETT AND AVANT-GARDE CONFORMITY

Samuel Harnsett is another figure of avant-garde conformity who has potential relevance to Claudius's prayer in *Hamlet*. Harsnett's closest connection to Shakespeare is his *Declaration of Egregious Popish Impostures* (published in 1603), a major textual source for the demonology in *King Lear*. Based on F. W. Brownlow's redating to 1594 of Harsnett's sermon against predestination delivered at Paul's Cross, Peter McCullough makes a convincing case that Lancelot Andrewes may have arranged for Harsnett to speak on such a controversial topic (391). Again, I am not making a claim that Harsnett's sermon directly influenced *Hamlet*, for the homily was not published until 1656. Nonetheless, Harsnett's sermon is an important public statement of avant-garde conformity that resonates with aspects of Claudius's prayer, further highlighting the controversial dimensions of *Hamlet*'s theology.

The polemical nature of Harsnett's sermon is patently clear throughout, and the tone is inflammatory, arrogant, and at times repellent, even when discussing something as beautiful as unlimited atonement. The text of Harsnett's sermon is Ezekiel 33:11: "As I live (saith the Lord) I delight not in the death of the wicked" (121). What begins as a lovely statement of God's salvific posture towards humanity quickly deconstructs into a parody of Harsnett's theological opponents:

> To conclude: let us take heed and beware, that we nei[t]her, (with the *Papists*) rely upon our *free will*: nor (with the *Pelagian*) upon our *Nature*: nor (with the *Puritan*) *Curse God, and die*, laying the *burthen* of our *sins* on [h]is shoulders, and the *guilt* of [t]hem at his everlasting doore. . . . (165)

For Harsnett, and apparently also for Andrewes (who may have commissioned Harsnett's sermon), the only valid theological orientation is avant-garde conformity, which represents the happy medium between the extremes of Puritan predestinarianism and the Catholic will to works of supererogation. However, the most focused target of Harsnett's polemic is the Calvinist doctrine of double predestination:

> There is a conceit in the world (beloved) speakes little better of our gracious God, then this: and that is, That *God should designe many thousands of soules to H[e]ll b[e]fore they were, not in eye to* t[h]eir faults, but to his own absolute will and power, and to get him glory in their damnation. This opinion is growne huge and monstrous (like a *Goliah*) and men doe shake and tremble at it; yet never a man reacheth to *Davids* sling to cast it downe. In the name of the *Lord of Hosts*: we will encounter it; for it hath reviled, not [t]he Host of the living God, but the *Lord of Hosts*. (133–134)

According to Harsnett, the doctrine of double predestination is incompatible with scripture's picture of a loving God who desires to save people from their sins. So abhorrent is supralapsarian reprobation to Harsnett that he considers it a menacing heresy to the church, much like Goliath was a formidable challenge to the Jewish armies until David opposed him with a slingshot. In Harsnett's metaphor, avant-garde conformity is the minority theological position (David) which is divinely ordained to supplant the majority Calvinist hegemony in the English church (Goliath).

Although Harsnett's sermon has remained in relative historical obscurity, it represents an important statement of proto-Arminian soteriology in that it anticipates the landmark Arminian *Remonstrance* of 1610, itself one of the most significant continental reactions to Calvinism.

Harsnett's list of Arminian tenets *avant la lettre* includes robust statements of unlimited atonement, resistible grace, conditional election, soteriological agency, and universal love (the love of God for all people). Harsnett is advancing a soteriology that claims to be everything that Calvinism is not:

> This last branch of Gods protestation, (*I delight not in the death of any sinner*) I resolve into six Consequences, as *Links* depending on this *Chain*.
> 1. God's absolute will is not the cause of *Reprobation*; but sin.
> 2. No man is of an absolute necessity the childe of *Hell,* so as by God's Grace, he may not avoid it.
> 3. God simply willeth and wisheth every living *Soul* to be saved, and to come to the Kingdom of *Heaven*.
> 4. God sent his Sonne to save every *Soule,* and to bring it to the Kingdom of *Heaven*.
> 5. God's Son offereth Grace effectually to save every one, and to direct him to the Kingdom of *Heaven*.
> 6. The neglect and contempt of his Grace, is the cause why every one doth not come to *Heaven*; and not any privative Decree, Counsel, or determination of God. (148–149)

Besides anticipating the most important statement of Arminian thought in theological history (the *Remonstrance* of 1610), Harsnett is here offering a proto-Arminian response to Perkins's *A Golden Chain* (1591).[6] Perkins's work had been a landmark expression of English Calvinist soteriology, with its famous parallel diagrams of supralapsarian double predestination in the form of links on a chain.[7] When Harsnett presents his soteriological tenets "as *Links* depending on this *Chain*," he is self-consciously parodying and attempting to refute Perkins's

---

6. Harsnett's proto-Arminian doctrines were conceived in reaction to the Calvinist conceptions of double predestination, irresistible grace, and limited atonement (i.e., Christ died only for the elect, not for all humanity). Such Calvinist doctrines were notorious only to Calvin's detractors, but not to those who considered themselves elect. Calvin's ideas drew fire from those who wanted to understand Christ's sacrifice more broadly as an expression of God's love for all humanity rather than for the chosen few. Claire McEachern helpfully captures how the Calvinist doctrine of predestination variously elicits responses of offense and consolation: "The notion that salvation is predestined has many harrowing aspects, but considered as a myth of recognition, its appeal is unparalleled" (39).

7. Debora Shuger calls Perkins "the leading Puritan theologian of Shakespeare's day" (125).

predestinarian theology that held strong sway over major sectors of the late Elizabethan clergy and laity.

Claudius's attempt at repentance in the prayer scene has all this polarized soteriological controversy between Calvinists and avant-garde reformers in the background, at least for theologically literate members of the audience (in other words, anyone who was educated or who paid attention in mandatory church attendance). *Hamlet* seems to be steering a course between these antagonistic positions, making concessions to either party when it suits the dramatic exigencies at hand.

THE SOTERIOLOGIES OF CLAUDIUS'S PRAYER

In *Hamlet*, the proto-Arminian contours of grace emerge from the crucible of the theater. In watching *The Mousetrap*, Claudius is forced to see a crime analogous to his own staged before him and before his court. His conscience is pricked by the performance, and he turns to prayer as a way to resolve the inner torment (and the fear of public humiliation) that he cannot escape. Claudius's prayer is the moment where the drama achieves the potential to turn from a bloody tragedy to a redemptive tragi-comedy. But, alas, the grace for which Claudius yearns seems to elude his grasp. More accurately, Claudius's near brush with salvation reveals that grace is available to him, but that he has the agency to receive or reject such cooperative grace.

The Claudius prayer scene resonates with a number of aspects of Andrewes's pictures of Cain and of God, regardless of any assumptions about influence or the lack thereof.

> What if this cursed hand
> Were thicker than itself with brother's blood?
> Is there not rain enough in the sweet heavens
> To wash it white as snow? Whereto serves mercy
> But to confront the visage of offence?
> And what's in prayer but this twofold force
> —To be forestalled ere we come to fall
> Or pardoned, being down? Then I'll look up:
> My fault is past. (Q2 3.3.43–51)

Claudius here imagines himself much like an Andrewesian Cain. Though his guilt is great, Claudius suggests in this section of his prayer that salvation is within his grasp, so great is God's mercy towards the penitent sinner, albeit the murderer of his own brother. Also, Claudius's concept of God as staggeringly merciful evokes the essence of Andrewes's proto-Arminian God whose unlimited atonement is freely available to all who repent. The first conclusion of the prayer rests on such a proto-Arminian assumption of God's mercy.

> Help, angels, make assay.
> Bow, stubborn knees, and heart with strings of steel
> Be soft as sinews of the new-born babe.
> All may be well. (3.3.69–72)

Claudius's attempt at prayer initially concludes with an understanding of himself as redeemable and a belief in God as inexhaustibly merciful. In short, the initial peroration of the prayer suggests a number of the hallmarks of avant-garde conformity: unlimited atonement, universal salvation contingent merely upon repentance, the vindication of penitence by amendment, and an urgent sense of personal responsibility for co-operating with God to maintain one's own salvation.

Though heavy laden with guilt, Claudius is clearly arrested by this opportunity to be forgiven by God: "Is there not rain enough in the sweet heavens / To wash it white as snow?" Claudius believes that God is good; so good, in fact that he will forgive any sin, including murder. This is not a mindset of unbelief, but rather an imagination which regards God as having a capacious love for his erring creatures. Instead, Claudius's unbelief is directed towards himself. Claudius doubts *his own* willingness to exchange the spoils and pleasures of sin for the freedom from guilt available to him through repentance. Not only does Claudius believe in the efficacy of God's mercy, but he also believes in the power of prayer to procure grace from the Almighty:

> And what's in prayer but this twofold force
> —To be forestalled ere we come to fall
> Or pardoned, being down? Then I'll look up. . . .

Claudius recognizes that he is "down," that he has fallen into grave iniquity. He reasons that through prayer he can "look up" to God to find the mercy he so desperately needs. Claudius's reference to gazing upwards in prayer connotes the idea of the penitent imaginatively beholding (through the Ignatian meditation technique of composition of place) Christ crucified for him or her. Claudius's reference to upward directed prayer may also be an allusion to John 3:14–15: "And as Moses lift vp the serpent in the wildernes, so must the Sonne of man be lift vp, That whosoeuer beleueth in him, shulde not perish, but haue eternal life." Indeed, avant-garde conformist soteriology construes the cross of Christ as the antidote for the sin of the entire world, and Claudius would not be remiss to avail himself of such grace, murderer though he may be.

The major turn in the soliloquy (like the *volta* in a Petrarchan sonnet) is enjambed in middle of line 51: "My fault is past." For a brief moment, Claudius luxuriates in the feeling of being forgiven by God. Having confessed his sin, Claudius reasons that he is in the clear. But not for long. He realizes that he cannot pray without meaning it, without putting actions behind his words. The glorious prospect of forgiveness entails a condition that Claudius finds too frightening to concede. He realizes that he cannot consider himself absolved of bloodguilt without repenting, which for Catholicism would require satisfaction and for Protestantism would require restitution (as much as may be possible in the case of an irrevocable act like murder). Claudius realizes that confession of sin cannot be used as a self-serving bribe to attain divine forgiveness, while bypassing the necessary amendment of life.[8] A confession cannot be mere words or mere intention, but must result in penitential action, *viz.*, a personal ethical transformation. A confession of mere words leaves the "bosom black as death," which for Calvinists would mean unregenerate total depravity, for Catholics would suggest mortal sin, and for avant-garde conformists would entail a refusal of proffered grace.

The second turn of the soliloquy occurs in the silence between the last line and the postscript. When Claudius convinces himself that "All may be well," he realizes that grace is available to him, if only he will take it. In terms that are strikingly proto-Arminian, Claudius seems to believe that God's persistent offer of pardon still stands, though he is ambivalent about availing himself of it. It is interesting that Claudius's assessment is not to blame God for predestining him to damnation, but rather to blame *himself* for not putting the weight of his personhood behind the foregoing confession of sin. He does acknowledge that he "cannot repent," though he seems to want to. Claudius is internally conflicted, self-divided. Experientially, this double-mindedness feels like an inability to repent, but Claudius's final assessment of his prayer (in the addendum after his

---

8. In the Elizabethan Homily "Of Repentance and True Reconciliation unto God," penitence is described in a four-step process know as the "short ladder" of repentance: contrition, confession, faith, and amendment (*The Second Book of Homilies*, xx). See also Eleanor Prosser (185).

soliloquy) lays the blame more accurately on his faulty "thoughts" (innermost motives). Honesty demands Claudius's conclusion that such self-exoneration is rooted in self-deception.

Is Claudius's self-deception all the greater for having turned down a pivotal opportunity to receive grace? It would appear so. Why does Claudius's attempt to be rid of his sin entangle him in it further? By his own admission, his heart is not in his confession, for he is unwilling to make the necessary changes in his life that would corroborate such a confession. In this case, such integrity would require him to turn himself in for murder (and likely capital punishment), starting with telling Gertrude the truth. Instead, he proceeds to scheme the murder of the son to cover up the murder of the father. Are Claudius's awareness of his wrong and the sensitivity of his conscience really to be regarded as ennobling features when he so quickly proceeds to hide his crime and to conspire another felony? Perhaps not. Claudius tragically rejects his moment of grace because it would come with the cost of painful self-exposure. His willful persistence in wrongful behavior suggests a lethal degree of self-deception. Having rejected grace, Claudius's only option is another murder, "The present death of Hamlet. Do it, England! / For like the hectic in my blood he rages / And thou must cure me" (4.3.63–65). Having rejected the divine anodyne of forgiveness, Claudius sees his only "cure" in escalating violence. Shakespeare creates a sense of urgency for Claudius's moment of grace by having Hamlet waiting in the wings, ready to murder him. In an interesting reversal, Shakespeare makes the villain more righteous than the tragic hero, who, in a demonic parody of the mass, has steeled himself towards murderous revenge with the darkly parodic Eucharistic words, "Now could I drink hot blood" (3.2.360). Claudius is given the opportunity to deal with his sins in a responsible, redemptive way. If he does not, Hamlet is poised in this scene to fulfill the stock function of the Renaissance drama avenger.[9]

9. Samuel Johnson was appalled by the diabolical malice in Hamlet's desire to damn Claudius to hell (Wimsatt 140). Samuel Taylor Coleridge, however, disagreed with Johnson's assessment of Hamlet's cruelty. Instead, Coleridge attributed Hamlet's decision to delay his vengeance on Claudius to simple procrastination. For Coleridge, Hamlet's stated desire to preclude Claudius from salvation "was merely the excuse Hamlet made to himself for not taking advantage of this particular and favorable moment for doing justice upon his guilty uncle, at the urgent instance of the spirit of his father" (Coleridge in Kermode 435). Johnson's ethical abhorrence of Hamlet's anti-soteriological reasoning is reflected in the arguments of critics such as Eleanor Prosser (*Hamlet and Revenge*) and René Girard (*A Theatre of Envy*), whereas Coleridge's favorable reading of Hamlet's revenge is perhaps intimated in David Beauregard (*Catholic Theology in Shakespeare's Plays*).

The Book of Common Prayer requires that all who would partake of communion must first repent of their sins and be in charity with their neighbors.[10] Judith Maltby makes a compelling case that many of the laity in the Elizabethan English church were willing conformists to the liturgy of the prayer book (2). Maltby also argues that the prayer's book's use of the vernacular and its scripts for communion "surely had far more widely felt repercussions than the soteriological debates" between "predestinarians and 'Arminians'" (4). Indeed, the prayer book signals that salvation is embodied, experienced praxis more than it is doctrinal theory.

Claudius knows that his impenitence precludes him from the spiritual nourishment of the Eucharist and the forgiveness that it embodies. (Avant-garde conformity regarded the sacraments as having at least the potential for the universal dispensation of salvation.) Claudius concludes that he is unable to repent and that he is doomed to remain in a state of spiritual desolation. However, the question remains as to whether Claudius is unable to repent or merely unwilling to repent. Towards the

---

10. Even though Cranmer inflected the liturgy in *The Book of Common Prayer* with some Calvinist leanings, as in its prescription for Communion in terms of Calvin's virtualism, the text clearly does not obviate human agency in matters of faith. The "Commination" in particular frames repentance as a free choice that has contingent outcomes. In terms of praxis, reformed spirituality was not as fatalistic as many scholars (such as David Marno) have made it out to be. Maria Devlin helpfully distinguishes between the determinism of systematic (reformed) theology and the contingency of "rhetorical theology," the latter being a posture commonly adopted by clergy in counseling their parishioners (174–175). Devlin's rediscovery of human agency in the Elizabethan and Jacobean church is corroborated by my assessment of the conditional forgiveness offered in *The Book of Common Prayer*. Much like the prayer book helps to realign a largely Calvinist English church with Catholic ideas of agency, *Hamlet* also works to reconcile popular Calvinist soteriology with longstanding Catholic ideas of free will.

From the perspective of "rhetorical theology," Claudius's failure to repent is more likely to be evidence of his unwillingness to cooperate with grace than an inability to access salvation. Devlin suggests that "divines disallowed their patients from performing the kind of interpretation of their own lives that critics are eager to perform on the lives of Faustus and Macbeth" (185). Claudius, however, performs precisely this kind of autopsy on his abortive will to repent, assuming that he cannot repent because he has not met the necessary preconditions for salvation. "Rhetorical theology" would tell Claudius otherwise. Claudius need not see himself as a doomed reprobate or the victim of disastrous life choices. The courage it takes to repent may in fact be within his grasp. As Devlin explains: "In rhetorical theology, a reversal from sin to salvation is always possible for *me*" (189). Even from the perspective of *applied* reformed soteriology, Claudius's deferral of repentance can possibly be seen as his own choice, the consequences of which he will face in the bloody final act of the play. Devlin's observation that the morality play assumes human agency in salvation is also true of the tragedy *Hamlet*. In my soteriological reading, Hamlet and Claudius are not tragic victims because they are fated to be, but because at crucial junctures they tragically choose to resist grace.

end of his prayer, he circles back once more to that nebulous crisis point of repentance where he hopes to access grace:

> . . .Help, angels, make assay.
> Bow, stubborn knees, and heart with strings of steel
> Be soft as sinews of the new-born babe.

The closest Claudius ever gets in his soliloquy to addressing God directly is in his supplication to angels as intermediaries. Earlier, he had imagined himself as confessing to God, "Forgive me my foul murder," but he had refrained from actually making the confession to God out of fear that he was not sincere, i.e., that he could not follow through with the obvious implications of such an admission of wrongdoing. At this elusive moment of grace, Claudius now asks angels to assist his heart in mustering the sufficient integrity required in dealing with an omniscient Deity. His prayer to angels (itself a Catholic gesture, as Klause observes [186]) metamorphoses into an apostrophe to his own body to kneel and his heart to soften. He is able to kneel, thus performing the external sign of repentance enjoined in the Eucharistic prayer of repentance in *The Book of Common Prayer*. The following apostrophe to his heart conveys his aspiration to achieve the internal transformation necessary to a restored relationship with God: "heart with strings of steel/ Be soft as sinews of the new-born babe." Claudius reasons that if he can allow his hard heart to be softened by grace, then his innocence will be restored, and he will be forgiven: "All may be well." Claudius's image of a new-born babe also suggests that he is attempting to recover the salvific innocence of his own baptism.

If the soliloquy had ended here, the audience, like the observing Hamlet, might have been persuaded that Claudius had been restored to a state of grace. His postscript to the soliloquy, however, reveals that his exercise has been a failed prayer rather than a moment of conversion. Unlike the biblical and Southwellian Peter, Claudius does not emerge from his prayer "conuerted" (Luke 22:32). Claudius ultimately laments the inefficacy of his prayer and repentance:

> My words fly up, my thoughts remain below.
> Words without thoughts never to heaven go. (3.3.97–98)

Sadly, Claudius has searched his own soul and found it undeserving of God's grace.[11] Claudius seems to assess himself as a reprobate, one devoid

---

11. Even if Claudius refuses to address his crime in a morally responsible manner, John Cox observes that Claudius's soliloquy/prayer is the only reliable indication to

of the Holy Spirit, and thus unable to pray to God as adoptive, forgiving Father, à la Paul. Perhaps Claudius finds himself guilty of the sin that Andrewes attributed to Cain: a belief that his sin is too great for God's mercy. In the end, Claudius seems to prove himself to be a reprobate, even if in the Arminian sense of relentlessly resisting God's kindly promptings to repentance.

THE PREDESTINARIAN CALVINISM OF THE KING'S PRAYER IN THE FIRST QUARTO OF *HAMLET* (1603)

Any theologically informed reader of the prayer scene in the first quarto (Q1) will quickly realize that its soteriology varies significantly from that of the second quarto (Q2) and folio (F), producing a strikingly different picture of both Claudius and God. The avant-garde conformity that is so essential to the prayer in Q2 is conspicuously lacking in Q1, where Calvinist soteriology instead predominates. Textual theories to date prove inadequate in identifying the precise authorial connection between the earliest and later texts of *Hamlet*, so the source of the Calvinist soteriology in Q1 remains enshrouded in mystery. However, the very contrasts between the Q1 and Q2 texts reveal just how avant-garde conformist Q2 actually is. The theological contrasts between the King's prayer in the first quarto of *Hamlet* and Claudius's prayer in the second quarto prove invaluable in determining whether Claudius's impenitence is the result of predestined reprobation or free agency.

Hamlet that Claudius is, in fact, guilty of the elder Hamlet's murder (159). The ghost's messages are inadmissible as evidence in determining Claudius's guilt; therefore, Hamlet cannot be certain that Claudius is actually guilty until Hamlet sees him struggling to confess his sins in prayer. The irony is that although Claudius's soliloquy is inefficacious as prayer or repentance, his speech act reveals the truth to Hamlet.

Moreover, even the audience who heard the words of Claudius before Hamlet enters, like Hamlet, cannot be sure what this posture might signify: it's possible, if not probable, that it is not just an outward, but also an inward, sign of Claudius' spiritual state. On top of all this, the possible efficacy of the act of kneeling in prayer is unclear to Claudius *himself*: it may be play acting—a performance of prayer (and so, as Ramie Targoff says, very un-Augustinian ["Performance" 55])—but his attempt to "make assay," while it will fail, seems in some way genuine: Claudius is giving it a real shot, though there may be just a hint here that Claudius knows he is only performing. The uncertain meaning of Claudius' action, for Hamlet, for Claudius, and for the audience, is quite marvelous. Perhaps the play of agency finds its greatest dramatic expression in this *general* confusion of outward and inward signs and in our uncertain grasp of their meaning in the moment of this performance of prayer.

Throughout the twentieth century, most scholars believed that the first quarto was a memorial reconstruction of the play—an authorially unauthorized "bad quarto." As such, Q1 has typically been regarded as bearing less textual authority than Q2 (1604–05), despite Q1's status as the first printed edition of *Hamlet*. However, recent scholarship has challenged the assumption that Q1 is a "bad quarto" based on a memorial reconstruction. Terri Bourus suggests that the Q1 *Hamlet* may be Shakespeare's first play, originally dating from the late 1580s (181).[12] Following Bourus's ideas to their logical conclusion, Dennis McCarthy argues that the Shakespearean authorship of Q1 refutes the hypothesis of the *Ur-Hamlet* (98). The textual history of *Hamlet* is a long and complicated affair, subject to diverse interpretations and rampant speculation (and beyond my area of specialization), so I will refrain from attempting to solve the problem of whether Q1 is by Shakespeare, a theatrical script, a memorial reconstruction, or a creation by another playwright such as Thomas Kyd.[13]

Nonetheless, a parallel study of the prayer scene in Q1 and Q2 yields some remarkable theological findings, and I will continue to privilege the Q2 to the Q1 text, even if both are by Shakespeare because Q2 (seemingly accurately) claims on its title page to be an authorial revision and expansion of an earlier version of the play (Lesser 70).[14] I also adhere to the traditional perspective that Q2 is aesthetically superior to Q1. Also, Q2 is arguably more theologically nuanced than Q1. The strongly Calvinist flavor of the King's prayer in Q1 contrasts strikingly with the agency in Claudius's prayer in Q2. Jesse Lander astutely argues that Q1 is inflected with hints of popularism, polemicism, and Calvinism (120–124) and that the text imagines that "Hamlet is indeed God's minister" of divine retribution (142). By engaging in a close textual comparison of the respective prayer scenes in Q1 and Q2, I suggest that Shakespeare seems to have deliberately distanced himself from the Calvinism of the Q1 prayer,

---

12. Bourus's arguments about Q1 *Hamlet* being an early play by Shakespeare himself have even convinced Gary Taylor that he was mistaken in believing that Q1 was a memorial reconstruction (Bourus xii–xiii).

13. In addition to these textual possibilities, Paul Menzer speculates that Q1 may be a text intended for touring (47). In assessing numerous explanations for the textual origins of Q1, Menzer feels unable confidently to champion one particular theory (47).

14. Zachary Lesser challenges the Arden 3 editors of *Hamlet*, Ann Thompson and Neil Taylor, for their "unediting" philosophy which caused them to avoid positing a textual theory for the relationship between Q1 and Q2 (213). Lesser insists that the need to discover a textual theory for Q1 outweighs the perils of such an undertaking (218–219).

instead reimagining the prayer in Q2 as Claudius's crisis moment of soteriological agency.

The comparatively Calvinist flavor of the King's prayer in Q1 is readily apparent to a theologically informed reader:

> O that this wet that falls upon my face
> Would wash the crime clear from my conscience!
> When I look up to heaven I see my trespass,
> The earth doth still cry out upon my fact.
> Pay me the murder of a brother and a king
> And the adulterous fault I have committed.
> O, these are sins that are unpardonable!
> Why, say thy sins were blacker than is jet—
> Yet may contrition make them as white as snow.
> Ay, but still to persever in a sin
> It is an act 'gainst the universal power!
> Most wretched man, stoop, bend thee to thy prayer;
> Ask grace of heaven to keep thee from despair. (Q1 10.1–13)

The Calvinist overtones and buzzwords in this passage abound. The King's reference to "this wet that falls upon my face" indicates that he is crying in remorse for his sin, a behavior that is not mentioned in Q2. The reference to penitential tears connects the King to the ubiquitous "tears poetry" that was predominantly Protestant by the time of Shakespeare, but which had Catholic origins.[15] Allusions to the Geneva Bible also abound in the Q1 prayer, further indicating its Calvinist orientation. The term "trespass" is an allusion to the Lord's Prayer. Similarly, the phrase, "The earth doth still cry out upon my fact" is an allusion to the Cain story in Genesis 4:10, "the voyce of thy brothers blood cryeth vnto me from the grounde." The language of "murder" and "the adulterous fault" strongly echo the ten commandments, the moral law which Protestants favored to the medieval Catholic seven deadly sins. The reference to "sins that are unpardonable" smacks of Calvinist reprobation, whereas the idea that "Yet may contrition make them as white as snow" is more broadly Protestant. "Contrition" is the key to Protestant repentance and this term is not used in Q2. The gloss for the word "contrite" in the Geneva Bible Psalm 51:170 "is a wounding of ye heart, proceding of faith, which seketh vnto God for mercie."

Catholic ideas of satisfaction or even Protestant concepts of amendment are conspicuously absent in Q1. In contrast, Claudius in Q2

---

15. See Gary Kuchar's *The Poetry of Religious Sorrow in Early Modern England*.

expends much emotional energy on anticipating the behavioral changes that he knows must accompany his feelings of penitence. The reference (in Q1 and Q2) to being made "white as snow" is an allusion to Psalm 51, the penitential psalm *par excellence*. The language in Q1, "but still to persever in a sin" recalls the Calvinist doctrine of perseverance, but here negatively suggests reprobation. "Most wretched man" alludes to Saint Paul's self-assessment as the chief of sinners: "O wretched man[n] that I am, who shal deliuer me from the bodie of this death!" (Romans 7:24 cf. 1 Timothy 1:15). The first round of the prayer concludes, "Ask grace of heaven to keep thee from despair." The opposition of "grace" with "despair" strongly suggests the Calvinist doctrine of predestination, for "despair" was the lot apportioned to those who were *not* elected unto salvation.

The postscript to the King's prayer in Q1 also has a more Calvinist flavor than the corresponding lines in Q2:

> My words fly up, my sins remain below.
> No king on earth is safe if God's his foe. (Q1 10.32–33)

Claudius's postscript to his prayer in Q2, in contrast, suggest the important role of his own agency in accessing or resisting salvation:

> My words fly up, my thoughts remain below.
> Words without thoughts never to heaven go. (Q2 3.3.97–98)

In Q1 the King's "sins remain below," whereas in Q2 Claudius's "thoughts remain below." In Q1 the emphasis is on the King not being forgiven by God, whereas in Q2 the focus is on Claudius's lack of sincerity. The King of Q1 finds that "God's his foe," denoting a strong sense of reprobation, or rejection by God. The twofold reference to Claudius's faulty "thoughts" in Q2 is missing in Q1, and suggests that in Q2 Claudius, rather than God, is to blame for the murderer's own failure in accessing forgiveness. In contrast, the "despair" the King feels in Q1 connects not only to his feeling of drowning in moral failure, but also to his idea that "God's his foe," i.e., that the King is a reprobate.

A comparison of the concluding rhyming couplets from Q1 and Q2 makes clear that Shakespeare did not use the predestinarian Calvinist template in Q1 for Claudius's prayer in Q2. Whether the predestinarianism of Q1 is to be regarded with suspicion as an interpolation from an authorially unauthorized memorial reconstruction or as a feature of an early play by Shakespeare himself, the fact remains that Q2 lacks the predestinarian emphasis of Q1. I argue that the changes from Q1 to Q2 created a greater role for human agency and perhaps a movement to a more Catholic or avant-garde conformist understanding of grace in Q2.[16] The greater sense of openness and contingency in Q2 stems from the fact that Claudius's despair is not a result of God's inhospitality to him (as in Q1), but rather is a result of Claudius's unwillingness to relinquish his sins. Such renunciation of sin would be the requisite course of action for him reconciling with "heaven." The language in Q1 of "sins that are unpardonable" and "despair" suggests that God is barring the King access to forgiveness. Even the hopeful possibilities raised by "contrition" and the prayer for grace are foiled by the antagonism of God. The Q1 prayer, markedly unnuanced compared to that of Q2, lacks any clear indication of the King's *unwillingness* (choice) to relinquish his sins. In turn, Shakespeare grants greater soteriological agency to Claudius in Q2, even if Claudius fails to use it responsibly.

Q1'S PREDESTINARIANISM VERSUS Q2'S AGENCY

The predestinarianism of Q1 is by no means confined to the King's prayer, but rather pervades the entire play. Conversely, Q2 celebrates the soteriological freedom of its protagonists. Even though Q2 puts predestinarian language in the mouth of Hamlet, the dramatic arc of the play suggests that both Claudius and Hamlet are acting as free agents with respect to their salvation (or lack thereof, as the case may be).[17]

Q1 presents a favorable, predestinarian Hamlet through the Queen's perspective on her son. In Q1, Horatio tells the Queen the news of Hamlet's marvelous return from banishment and his escape from death *before* the King and Leartes (*sic*) discover Hamlet's return. This ordering of events privileges the Queen's perspective on Hamlet. Indeed, the Queen's pious proclamation sets the tone for Hamlet's status as an elected recipient of divine favor. The Queen exclaims, "Thanks be to heaven for blessing of the Prince!" (14.31).

16. The rhyming couplet's allusion to a poem by the Jesuit Robert Southwell (discussed below) is found only in the Q2 and F versions, further suggesting that Shakespeare presented a more Catholic, or at least more ecumenical, version of grace in Q2 than that of Q1. The allusion to Southwell focusses on Claudius's internal conflict, again foregrounding the issue of agency rather than predestination.

17. I am building on Jesse Lander's idea that in Q1 Hamlet is God's messenger to depose Claudius (142), but my focus here is rather on the soteriological determinism of Q1 versus the soteriological agency of Q2.

In contrast, in Q2, Claudius and Laertes hear of Hamlet's return before the Queen does. Q2 thus puts a more complex spin on Hamlet's ethical status by having Claudius and especially Laertes give their responses to Hamlet's return before Gertrude gives her perspective. Laertes's enraged response to Hamlet reflects the grief Laertes feels in seeing his sister's mental health collapse because of Hamlet's murder of their father, Polonius. In Q2 we next see Gertrude having to inform Laertes of Ophelia's tragic death—possibly a suicide. In Q2, we have to wait until Ophelia's funeral to see Gertrude's motherly response to the return of Hamlet. In other words, Q2 casts the returning (and avenging) Hamlet in a much more questionable light than does Q1. Whereas the Hamlet of Q1 is divinely favored, the Hamlet of Q2 is ethically suspect.

The apex of Q1's predestinarian dramatization of Hamlet and the King is found in Hamlet's response to Horatio's suggestion that Hamlet should listen to his own misgivings and not enter into the duel. Hamlet overrules Horatio's wise counsel with a reference to predestination:

> If danger be now, why then it is not to come. There's a predestinate providence in the fall of a sparrow. Here comes the King. (17.44–46).

The reference to the King hard upon the heels of the "predestinate" falling sparrow suggests that *both* Hamlet and the King are predestined, the one to salvation, the other to damnation. The King, as "God's foe" is destined for perdition (10.33).

Moreover, Hamlet, already declared by the Queen to be a beneficiary of God's favor, predictably dies a godly death in Q1, a sure sign of election in Calvinism:

> Farewell, Horatio. Heaven receive my soul. *Dies.* (17.111)

In contrast, the King dies without an opportunity to pray, but with the knowledge that his murderous schemes have backfired with the death of his beloved Queen. In Q1, Leartes's pronouncement on the King has a theological force because of its juxtaposition with Hamlet's distinctly pious death: "O, he is justly served" (17.98). Hamlet is elected positively, unto salvation, while the King is predestined negatively, unto damnation.

The parallel passage in Q2 about the providence of a falling sparrow from Matthew 10:29, albeit lyrically resigned to fatalism, omits the thorny Calvinist term "predestinate":

> We defy augury. There is special providence in the fall of a sparrow. If it be, 'tis not to come. If it be not to come, it will be now. If it be not now, yet it will come. The readiness is all, since no man of aught he leaves knows what is't to leave betimes. Let be.
> (5.2.197–202)

Hamlet claims that he is not given to superstition, perhaps not even to fatalism—"We defy augury." However, Hamlet proceeds to articulate a theological determinism which is virtually indistinguishable from fatalism. For Hamlet, the meaning of Matthew 10:29 is not that God loves him in all of his frailty and vulnerability (as its biblical context would suggest), but rather that Hamlet believes he should not interfere with the status quo because to do so would resist God's foreordained plan for the world. Hamlet believes that things will play out exactly as they are supposed to, so all he can do is try to be ready for the inevitable. "Let be" becomes a quasi "Amen" for this meditation on foreordination. As Doctor Faustus muses, "*Che serà, serà*" (*Doctor Faustus* A text 1.49).[18] Although Q2's term "special providence" would seem to suggest a gentler side of God's sovereignty than Q1's more obviously deterministic "predestinate providence," for Hamlet himself the difference in the terms is perhaps negligible, so committed is he to a fatalistic theology.

There is obviously a Calvinist flavor to Hamlet's meditations, even in Q2. The term "special providence" is a favorite of John Calvin's and he uses it copiously in the *Institutes* (see especially Book 1, chapters 16 and 17). In a passage that is markedly similar to Hamlet's meditations above in Q2, Calvin argues as follows:

> And it has to be observed, first, that the providence of God is to be considered with reference both to the past the future; and, secondly, that in overruling all things, it works at one time with means, at another without means, and at another against means.
> (1.17, page 123).

Hamlet articulates his providential theology earlier in Q2, as well. In fact, there is a growing sense of fatalism in his ideology that climaxes in his reference to the fallen sparrow. When Hamlet narrates his fortunate escape from being executed in England, he attributes his survival to providence:

---

18. Faustus translates this Italian proverb, "What will be, shall be," and then proceeds to replace his studies of divinity with deviltry, "Divinity, adieu!" (A 1.50). Whereas Faustus responds to theological determinism with a desire to practice unlawful arts, Hamlet abandons his own agency by waiting passively for God's will to be done.

> There's a divinity that shapes our ends,
> Rough-hew them how we will. (5.2.10–11)

Horatio here agrees with Hamlet's providentialist theology. Hamlet further attributes to providence his luck in having his father's signet ring with him on the boat, giving him the ability to seal Rosencrantz and Guildenstern's fate: "Why even in that was heaven ordinant" (5.2.48). At this point, however, Horatio does not affirm Hamlet's providential explanation, but instead remarks, "So Guildenstern and Rosencrantz go to't" (5.2.56). Hamlet's rejoinder is anything but reassuring: "They are not near my conscience. Their defeat / Does by their own insinuation grow" (5.2.57–58).

THE REFUTATION OF PREDESTINARIAN THOUGHT IN Q2

What this exchange shows us is that in Q2 the theological determinism is more obviously Hamlet's than the play's. It emerges especially in Hamlet's ruminations with Horatio, and Horatio does not always affirm the veracity of Hamlet's growing fatalism. In Q2, Hamlet claims to be acting in accordance with deterministic providence, but the play ironizes Hamlet's growing self-understanding as God's pawn. Far from acting as the blessed messenger of divine retribution (Jesse Lander's interpretation of the Hamlet of Q1), the Hamlet of Q2 is revealed as ethically suspect for excusing his violence with theological rationalization. While Hamlet blames Rosencrantz and Guildenstern for their own demise, he attributes to God's foreordination his own decision to have them executed. In this way, Hamlet thinks he can exculpate himself for the ruthless turn he plays upon his childhood friends. Even Hamlet's best friend cannot entirely excuse such cruelty. In exposing the ethical incoherencies of Hamlet's predestinarian thinking, the play may convey intimations of avant-garde conformity.

The dramatic trajectory of Q2 ironizes the very fatalism that Hamlet increasingly believes in. Hamlet claims to be acting under divine control, but he is actually attempting (unsuccessfully) to abandon his own agency by laying his actions at the door of providence. Hamlet justifies his callous cruelty to Rosencrantz and Guildenstern with providentialist rhetoric, and there are many other indications in the play that his theological thinking is faulty. Hamlet is similarly callous to Ophelia, who herself is posturing with religion to assist in Claudius's and Polonius's sifting of

Hamlet. Hamlet apparently justifies his cruelty to Ophelia as part of his attempt to ascertain the veracity of the Ghost's message (which is also religiously inflected). Hamlet's cruelty to Ophelia discredits both his moral character and his theology. Moreover, Hamlet shows an appalling lack of remorse when he kills Polonius, but then immediately proceeds to rebuke his mother for her sexual intimacy with Claudius. Q2 more effectively nuances the dysfunction and complexity of Hamlet's relationship with Gertrude (material exploited to the uttermost by Sigmund Freud and Ernest Jones), whereas the Queen in Q1 piously blesses Hamlet and believes that the King is a murderer. In Q2 it is unclear whether Gertrude even believes Hamlet's message that Claudius is a murderer or if she thinks Hamlet is insane. In Q2 Gertrude is obviously traumatized by Hamlet's spiritual bullying of her, again showing that Hamlet's theological rhetoric is invalidated by his unethical behavior. Hamlet attempts to relinquish responsibility for his actions on the basis of his predestinarian thought, but he ends up hurting most of the people nearest him.

Finally, Hamlet's death in Q2 lacks the formulaic sense of spiritual closure that seals his predestined election in Q1. Hamlet's spiritually ambiguous death in Q2 is further evidence that the play interprets Hamlet's providentialist theology with a hermeneutic of suspicion. In Q2, Hamlet does not clearly position himself spiritually in his death, for he is more concerned about casting his vote for Fortinbras than about making a final overture to God. Hamlet's dying words in Q2, "The rest is silence" (5.2.342), are a conspicuous departure from the spiritual certitude of Q1's "Heaven receive my soul." In Q2, Horatio spiritualizes Hamlet's death with the prayer, "flights of angels sing thee to thy rest" (5.2.344), but this benediction is not representative of the way Hamlet actually died. In Q2, Hamlet is by no means a shining example of *ars moriendi*, or what the godly called a good death. Hamlet has given up, apparently resigning himself to fate, as seen in his spiritually ambiguous death, where he seems more preoccupied with state succession to an opportunistic foreign ruler (Fortinbras) than with his own salvation.

In Q1, Hamlet's predestinarianism is vindicated by the play, both in terms of Hamlet's election and the King's reprobation. In Q2, however, Claudius is not a one-dimensional reprobate, but rather a complicated person who has made some regrettably unethical decisions, and who ultimately chooses to persist in his self-deception. Try as he may, Claudius cannot escape the burden of his own decisions. The Hamlet of Q2 may himself subscribe to a predestinarian theology, but the play itself refutes

Hamlet's own worldview. However, the Hamlet of Q1 is a predestinarian, and the play basically affirms his providentialist theology along Calvinist lines. Nevertheless, Q2 persistently ironizes Hamlet's references to providence by showing how Hamlet uses such theology to justify his cruelty to others. In attempting to jettison his own agency and to lay the blame for his actions upon God, the Hamlet of Q2 ends up discrediting his own revenge quest and even his own theology. Whereas Q1 conceives "predestinate providence" in terms of the King falling into a trap of divine retribution and of exculpating Hamlet's violence, the Hamlet of Q2 is misled by his own predestinarian theology into walking into the trap of the duel with Laertes. More significantly, the Hamlet of Q2 erroneously relinquishes his agency to theological determinism, yet seems unable to recognize that by refusing to take responsibility for his cruel actions he leaves behind a trail of broken hearts and lives.

Hamlet's theological determinism also makes him increasingly vulnerable to the highly deliberate machinations of evil devised by Claudius. As Hamlet tries to relinquish himself of agency, Claudius deviously seizes the opportunity to get the upper hand against him. Whereas Claudius exercises his agency in rejecting grace, Hamlet misguidedly tries to divest himself of the burden of freedom, which is perhaps what Dostoevsky's Grand Inquisitor (but not Dostoevsky himself) would have him do. In denying freedom, Hamlet forecloses the possibilities of grace. In misusing his freedom, Claudius likewise cuts himself off from grace. For only by accepting responsibility for their wrong actions can Claudius and Hamlet hope to mitigate the unwelcome consequences of their violent behavior. Here we see that the theology in the prayer scene is the fuel for the play's persistent concerns about the ethical implications of decision making. The soteriological agency of Claudius's prayer scene becomes a microcosm for the existential dilemmas of all the characters in the play, for every decision is an avowal of personal responsibility. Any of the characters' attempts to disavow responsibility for their own actions result in escalating conflict.

CLAUDIUS'S PRAYER AS AN ETHICAL FAILURE

Despite the obvious contrasts between the predestinarian theology of Q1 and the intimations of soteriological agency in Q2, some critics persist in regarding Claudius's impenitence in Q2 as the result of Protestant theological determinism. Not all critics would agree with me in assessing the failure of Claudius's prayer as an ethical failure. David Marno uses an obscure devotional author John Norden as the basis of a reading that locates Claudius's failure to pray in the sin of distraction: "if following Norden we describe it [Claudius's failure to pray] as a failure of attention, it becomes clear that the problem with the king's attachment to Gertrude or the crown isn't a sin because it goes against human or divine law but because it distracts Claudius from his prayerful turn to God" (84). Marno's idea that Claudius is precluded from salvation because he cannot stop thinking about Gertrude shifts the focus away from his very real guilt in violating "human or divine law" by committing both fratricide and adultery. While Marno is no doubt accurate in assessing Claudius as distracted while trying to pray, Marno's privileging of "attention" over "intention" in prayer seems to muddy the waters for any critic trying to get a helpful ethical understanding of this dramatic moment (83–84). Marno's argument has the equivocal effect of making it seem like Claudius's spiritual failure is due to poor technique in prayer rather than to his ominous volitional turn against the good. If Claudius is "distracted" in prayer, it is because he is not willing to face himself as he really is (or to sustain the self-knowledge he is acquiring in prayer) by allowing the necessary spiritual and ethical redirection of his life.

The most helpful part of Marno's sequence on Claudius is Marno's isolation of the issue of agency in repentance. He argues that Claudius's inability to repent is a microcosm of the larger Protestant theology of salvation *sola gratia*: "Claudius needs to repent in order to be able to pray, and yet he needs to pray in order to be able to repent. At this point the problem he is facing is not merely his personal predicament. Rather, Claudius recognizes the problem that is at the core of early modern Christianity: the limit of personal agency in devotion" (79). Marno concludes that the reason for Claudius not receiving grace is hermeneutically inaccessible (81). Nevertheless, he is eager to interpret Claudius's inability to repent as theologically deriving from the reformed doctrine *sola gratia* (81–82).

However, the limitations that Marno places on theological speculation are inconsistent with his own argument that assumes Claudius is operating under Calvinist notions of grace. Marno is in fact speculating when he argues that Claudius's inability to repent is an effect of the deterministic, closed system of Calvinist doctrines of grace.[19] However, it is not a foregone conclusion that Shakespeare is depicting grace in exclusively Calvinist (or Catholic) terms. I would suggest that avant-garde conformist conceptions of grace as requiring the cooperation of human agency are valid alternative theological backdrops to this scene of Claudius failing at prayer. Such proto-Arminian thought has much in common with Augustine's "cooperative grace" and Aquinas's free will. If Claudius freely rejects salvation, then his prayer may suggest avant-garde conformist (or even Catholic) perspectives on grace which assume human agency. *Contra* Marno, the scene of Claudius at prayer resists stereotypes of deterministic Protestant soteriology as often as it welcomes them. If there are lingering Calvinist hints of reprobation in Claudius's prayer, they are vigorously countered by proto-Arminian and Catholic views of grace.

SOUTHWELL'S *MANS CIVILL WARRE* AND CLAUDIUS'S IMPENITENCE

Marno accounts for the hints of Calvinism in the Q2 prayer scene, and I have identified the opposing perspectives of avant-garde conformity. Is there any room left for the presence of Catholicism in the usurping king's meditations? Claudius's allusion to Robert Southwell would seem to suggest so.

Catholic theologies in *Hamlet* have been studied much more exhaustively than the resonances of avant-garde conformity in the play. Perhaps in some cases it may be difficult to extricate the Catholic from the avant-garde conformist influences on the play. Nonetheless, the very similarity between avant-garde conformist and Catholic views of soteriological agency (though Harsnett does distinguish between them in passing) is no barrier to my arguments about proto-Arminian resonances in *Hamlet*. If anything, the Roman and avant-garde English traditions seem to be working in tandem in the play.[20] In conveying the importance of

---

19. Claudius is not exactly powerless to renounce his privileges as a usurper. By way of analogy, Duke Frederick in *As You Like It* gives up his usurped position to live a religious life. Moreover, domestic tragedies show murderers accepting the justice of the death penalty as a punishment. Therefore, when Claudius says he "cannot" repent, he has dramatic examples to suggest otherwise.

20. Shakespeare seems to show a tacit respect for the Catholic sacrament of penance and the Protestant ritual of repentance, even as he conflates them theologically and

the freedom of the human will to receiving or rejecting grace, both of these traditions make a similar mark on *Hamlet*. The allusion to Jesuit Robert Southwell's "Mans Civill Warre" in Claudius's prayer (found in Q2 and F, but not in Q1), as well as the likely influence of Southwell's *Saint Peters Complaynt*, intimate a Catholic dimension of grace in the Claudius prayer scene. The Southwellian allusion, like the avant-garde resonances in the play, highlights Claudius's soteriological agency.

Southwell begins his lyric, "Mans Civill Warre," with a depiction of the tumultuous spiritual struggle of choosing between virtue and the sins of the flesh with lines that become the basis of Claudius's recapitulation of his own soliloquy:

> My hoveringe thoughtes would fly to heaven
> And quiet nestle in the skye
> Fayne would my shipp in vertues shore
> Without remove at Anker lye
> But mounting thoughts are haled downe
> With heavie poyse of mortall loade
> And blustringe stormes denye my ship
> In vertues haven secure aboade. (1–8)

Claudius's despairing postscript to his soliloquy is a compressed echo of Southwell's lyric.[21]

> My words fly up, my thoughts remain below.
> Words without thoughts never to heaven go. (3.3.97–98)

Shakespeare's pronounced allusion to Southwell's lyric at the end of Claudius's soliloquy connects this dramatic moment to Catholic ideas about grace.[22] Like Southwell's poem, Claudius's soliloquy is an extended

---

liturgically, for both Claudius and Hamlet are exposed as immoral by their respective violations of penitence. While I acknowledge that the oppositional positioning of penance and repentance may produce distortion by diminishing the awareness that penance involves repentance for Catholics, Sarah Beckwith's *Shakespeare and the Grammar of Forgiveness* productively distinguishes between these practices and their representation in Shakespearean drama. Nonetheless, on the crucial issue of agency, representations of both penance and repentance have much in common in the Claudius prayer scene.

21. I am indebted to John Klause for alerting me to Shakespeare's allusion to Southwell's "Mans Civill Warre," but the theological and literary analysis of Shakespeare's intertextuality is my own (173).

22. Scott Pilarz observes that although many of Southwell's lyrics "never specifically refer to sacramental confession," that Southwell was nonetheless concerned to inculcate a desire for penance in his poetry (248). The Council of Trent distinguishes between mere sorrow for sin—"attrition"—and sorrow for sin that results in reconciliation

deliberation between a right and wrong choice, giving Claudius's internal debate a faintly Catholic cast. Just as Southwell's persona cannot raise his thoughts heavenwards to the throne of grace because he is weighed down by sin, so Claudius cannot raise his cogitations to God in prayer because he feels the heavy gravity of his sin.

There are certainly some Calvinist overtones in Claudius's language (as Marno rightly observes), most notably Claudius's questions about repentance, "Try what repentance can—what can it not?— / Yet what can it, when one cannot repent?" (3.3.65–66). But even a classic reformed understanding of such inability to repent (presumably because of double predestination) is modified by Shakespeare's allusion to Southwell's lyric, "Mans Civill Warre." Southwell describes the inner conflict between "reason" and "phancy," between "sences" and "vertues" as resulting in "the captive will" (15–19). Southwell describes the inner struggle between choosing "sence" and "god" as a state of conflict (like Romans 7), a "Civill fraye... where halves must disagree" (27; 22–23). The speaker's frustration that "halves must disagree" is poignantly echoed in Claudius's self-description as "a man to double business bound" (3.3.41). The speaker in "Mans Civill Warre," though not confessing to a priest, is painfully deliberating over whether to follow the path of virtue or sin. Claudius is similarly engaged in a private struggle between telling the truth and living a lie. The concluding line of Southwell's lyric—"Sell not thy soule for brittle joye" (32)—anticipates the kind of apostrophe Claudius directs towards himself in an effort to extricate himself from sin—"Try what repentance can—what can it not?" Yet whereas Southwell's persona remains virtuously poised in battle against the onslaught of temptation, Claudius is afraid to save his soul by renouncing the world he has unlawfully gained. Claudius's decision to reject grace thus counterpoints Southwell's lyric.

Claudius's "inability" to repent, then, may not be a definitive theological self-assessment of his reprobation, but rather a symptom of a "captive will" (Southwell) that is enchanted by the strong pull of his sensual desires for his brother's wife and crown, making him unwilling to receive grace. Southwell's speaker moralizes that "Dame pleasures drugges are steept in synne" (29). In antithetical parallelism to Southwell's devout persona,

---

through the sacrament of penance—"contrition" (Pilarz 247–248). According to Pilarz, the sorrow for sin in Southwell's penitential poetry always has a sacramental *telos*, even if not articulated explicitly (248). For example, *Saint Peters Complaynt*, Southwell's *magnum opus,* does not include any references to auricular confession but the poem nonetheless envisions Peter's contrition as "penance" (line 461). The detailed attrition in Claudius's prayer strikingly resembles the contrition in *Saint Peters Complaynt*.

Claudius sinfully chooses Queen Gertrude ("Dame pleasure"?) over grace. Whereas Marno assumes (à la Calvinism) that Claudius lacks agency in accessing grace, I would argue that the allusion to Southwell suggests that Claudius ultimately exercises his agency by rejecting the prevenient grace that has brought him to this crucial moment of reconsidering his past sins/crimes. Southwell's self-conflicted speaker and Claudius may be at the same fork in the road, but each of them chooses a different path.

The fact that Shakespeare alludes to Southwell's poem as a way of framing Claudius's choice to reject forgiveness suggests that the scene resonates with Catholic ideas about the nature of grace. If Claudius's statement that he "cannot repent" smacks of Calvinism, the allusion to Southwell corrects Claudius's self-assessment of predestined reprobation by reframing Claudius's inability to repent as an *unwillingness* to repent. Claudius realizes that he cannot expect to have God's sympathetic ear while Claudius's "thoughts remain below." This allusion to Southwell— "But mounting thoughts are haled downe / With heavie poyse of mortall loade"—grounds Claudius's prayer in his own agency with respect to grace, as is the case with Southwell's speaker. Although in a continued state of spiritual conflict, Southwell's persona resolves to remain faithful to God as the poem draws to a close, signalling that divine grace is sufficient for resisting temptation, if only one will cooperate with grace: "Sell not thy soule for brittle joye" (32). Tragically, Claudius makes a different choice than the Southwellian penitent he echoes, serving as a cautionary picture of the Catholic idea that grace is available to all, but that it only takes effect in those who receive it.

CLAUDIUS AND MOLINISM

Shakespeare's allusion in Claudius's prayer to a poem by the Jesuit Robert Southwell on a crisis spiritual decision also potentially nods at the contemporary controversy raging between the Jesuits and Dominicans on the relationship between providence and grace. The Jesuit-Dominican controversies engaged a number of similar concerns about the relationship between grace and human agency that propelled the avant-garde conformist and Calvinist controversies in England. (Hence my contention that Catholic and proto-Arminian sources are working in tandem in *Hamlet*.) Spanish Jesuit Luis de Molina, who died in 1600 (the traditional year of *Hamlet*'s first performance), was concerned to uphold the freedom of the human will in matters of salvation, especially in the face of perceived Protestant soteriological determinism. His idea that human beings must choose to receive grace in order for grace to be efficacious was offensive to the Dominicans, who emphasized that grace in itself is efficacious for salvation. Molina, in turn, feared that the Dominicans were complicit in theological determinism by formulating grace as entirely efficacious, even without the cooperation of the human will (Pohle). Molina's most celebrated and controversial idea was that of "middle knowledge," his attempt to reconcile divine foreknowledge and human free will. Molina speculated that through his "middle knowledge," God could know not only what choices a human being would make, but also what choices a human being would make in different circumstances (Laing). According to Molina, God's providence in this actual world also accounts for contingencies that might have occurred in any number of possible worlds. Molina believed that human beings are still free to receive or reject God's sufficient (not efficient) grace, but God interacts with each individual on the basis of God's knowledge of what decisions that person would have made in different circumstances.

Hamlet's attribution of contingency to grace resonates with Molina's belief that salvation is contingent upon the co-operation of the human will. Without conscripting Shakespeare to all of the finer points of theological disputation, it is possible that some of the broad strokes of the Jesuit-Dominican controversy might have reached Shakespeare, if only indirectly through the work of English Jesuits like Southwell. In any case, my argument that the grace Claudius experiences is sufficient, but not efficient, suggests that competing Jesuit-Dominican perspectives on grace can each find themselves in the text. Also of potential relevance to Claudius's self-divided state of mind is Molina's notion of middle knowledge. From the perspective of Molinist theology, God knows that Claudius will not repent, but he also knows what decision Claudius would have made if the circumstances were different. Claudius is so compelled by the prospect of forgiveness that he plans to repent—that is, until he realizes that repentance would cost him his wife and crown.

Linked to the contingency of Claudius's decision, then, are yet other contingencies. Would Claudius have repented if he did not love pleasure and power as much as he does? Would he have repented if he had been publicly exposed? Would he have repented eventually, maybe even on his deathbed, if there had been time to prepare for it. Claudius himself imagines both getting away with his sins and being forced to testify against himself. He first toys with a superficial repentance in which he will keep his wife and crown and then with a more thorough version of penance which will require him to relinquish everything he holds dear. Claudius's processing of his choice to repent through various contingent scenarios further enhances the audience's sense of the (im)possibilities of grace, possibly resonating with Molina's idea of "middle knowledge" that was so controversial around the time of *Hamlet*.

Even if it might be difficult to prove the influence of Molinism on *Hamlet*, the play at times seems to conceive of grace as contingent on human agency, a central concern of Molina and other Jesuits. To use the language of Molinism, the sufficient grace that Claudius finds so tantalizing never becomes efficient grace because Claudius will not consent to its operation within him. In *Hamlet*, as in Molinism, the efficacy of divine grace appears to be contingent upon the co-operation of the human will. *Hamlet*'s exploration of the theology of contingency thus reflects current Catholic controversy—as well as avant-garde conformist thought—alongside the predestinarian theologies of leading Puritans such as William Perkins.

AN AFTERLIFE OF CLAUDIUS'S PRAYER SCENE IN MIDDLETON'S *THE REVENGER'S TRAGEDY* (1606)

By interrogating *Hamlet* from the divergent theological vantage points of avant-garde conformity, Calvinism, and Molinism, we find that some important ethical features of the play come to the fore, notably the extent of Claudius's and Hamlet's culpability and the degree to which these characters are willing to change for the better. But how does the soteriology of the Q2 prayer measure up to that of other *dramatic* sources? Perhaps the best dramatic control text for our purposes would be *The Revenger's Tragedy* because of its persistent parody of *Hamlet*'s soteriology.

A comparative study of *The Revenger's Tragedy* and *Hamlet* further reveals Claudius's impenitence to be an expression of his soteriological free will. While *The Revenger's Tragedy* echoes a number of scenes from *Hamlet*, the most relevant to the discourse of soteriology is its parody of Claudius's prayer and Hamlet's diabolical revenge. As if *Hamlet* were not violent enough, *The Revenger's Tragedy* amplifies Hamlet's tragic violence to the point of comic absurdity. *The Revenger's Tragedy* works to flatten out the moral landscape of the play, to the point where human agency is nothing more than a compulsion to evil. For where there is no conscience, there can be no freedom of the will. Departing from the nuanced view of human agency required for repentance in *Hamlet*, *The Revenger's Tragedy* instead satirizes repentance as either a comic impossibility (the Duke) or a contrived social more in a world of religious hypocrisy (Gratiana).

Middleton's play abounds with soteriological discourse, much of it satirical. Indeed, there is arguably more soteriology in *The Revenger's Tragedy* than in *Hamlet*, serving as yet another sign that soteriology is by no means confined to Shakespearean drama, but may in fact be more prolific (on the whole) in non-Shakespearean drama. While *The Revenger's Tragedy*'s preoccupation with chastising sexual immorality takes a page out of *Hamlet*, especially the closet scene with Hamlet and Gertrude, the brightest afterglow of *Hamlet* in Middleton's play is the recasting of Claudius's prayer scene.

In this scene that parodies Claudius's prayer, Vindice has told Lussurioso that the Duchess is in bed with his bastard brother Spurio. Lussurioso, thinking to avenge the dishonoring of his father's bed, proceeds to strike Spurio dead, only to find instead their father the Duke in bed with the Duchess. (Hamlet, too, wants to kill Claudius for killing his father and dishonoring his father's bed.) The Duke speaks in self-defense in terms that are an obvious echo of Claudius's prayer scene in *Hamlet*:

> O, take me not in sleep. I have great sins.
> I must have days,
> Nay months, dear son, with penitential heaves,
> To lift 'em out and not to die unclear.
> O, thou wilt kill me both in heaven and here. (2.3.9–13)

This speech recasts the scene of the avenging Hamlet refraining from murdering the praying Claudius, as well as the Ghost's complaint to Hamlet that he had been killed without an opportunity to repent.

The Duke's speech invites audiences to compare him to Claudius, also a murderer and an adulterer. (The Duke is a serial killer, whereas Claudius tries to cover up one murder with a second.) The Duke does not want to be killed in a state of unconfessed sin (as the elder Hamlet was), nor in a state of impenitence (Claudius after prayer). As it were, the Duke tries to beat Hamlet at his own revenge game. The Duke is now in the (sexual) position that Hamlet had hoped to find Claudius when wanting to murder him—"in th'incestuous pleasure of his bed" (*Hamlet* 3.3.90). (Ironically, the philandering Duke is in this moment atypically found sleeping with his lawful wife.) When Lussurioso is about to kill him, the Duke aspires to prolong his life with the plea, "O, thou wilt kill me both in heaven and here." Here the Duke uses the (anti-) soteriological reasoning of Hamlet's delay tactic to make a pitch for his self-preservation.

Hamlet delays in killing Claudius because Hamlet desires to kill Claudius "both in heaven and here"—not just to murder his body, but also to damn him eternally. Claudius's life is ironically prolonged because of his attempt at prayer, precisely because Hamlet does *not* want Claudius to be saved. The Duke borrows this soteriological discourse from *Hamlet* to beg Lussurioso to spare his life and his soul. In the event, the Duke's life is temporarily saved, not because of his plea for salvific mercy, but because of his correcting of his mistaken identity. However, neither Claudius nor the Duke benefit from their narrow escape from death. (Claudius is unaware of being in mortal danger, whereas the Duke faces his own mortality.) Claudius emerges from his prayer thinking that he will forfeit heaven to prolong his illicit power and pleasure in his temporal kingdom. The Duke likewise receives his wish at another chance to live, but instead of repenting he soon proceeds to plan yet another adulterous assignation, which turns out to be a fatal trap devised by Vindice. Similarly, Claudius dies in his second attempt (this time successful) to murder Hamlet.

The Duke's dalliance with repentance after nearly being killed by his son is distinctly noncommittal compared to Claudius's tortured self-examination. The superficiality of the Duke's spiritual reasoning contrasts with the agonized decision making process of Claudius, further indicating that Claudius is acting as a free soteriological agent in the prayer scene. Indeed, the Duke's soteriology is highly suspect. In a parody of the Lord's prayer, the Duke believes that in forgiving Lussurioso, the Duke will himself be forgiven. The Duke presumes to expect forgiveness from God without even repenting:

> It well becomes that judge to nod at crimes
> That does commit greater himself and lives.
> I may forgive a disobedient error
> That expect pardon for adultery
> And in my old days am a youth in lust.
> Many a beauty have I turned to poison
> In the denial, covetous of all.
> Age hot is like a monster to be seen;
> My hairs are white and yet my sins are green. (2.3.122–130)

The Duke believes he will be forgiven simply by forgiving others who have committed lesser sins, without any amendment on his own part. However, Claudius knows that he cannot be pardoned if he clings to his sins. Despite adopting religious language, the Duke is merely a narcissistic psychopath. The Duke is not seriously considering repentance—his religious language is merely a ruse to continue in his lifestyle of exploiting and murdering women. Claudius, however, is a man with enough of a conscience that he needs to dull it in order to go on living a lie. Yet even in the cruel world of these tragedies, notorious sinners are given a soteriological lifeline—repentance. In fact, both *Hamlet* and *The Revenger's Tragedy* assume that the necessary precondition for forgiveness is repentance, whether the sins be Gratiana pimping her daughter or Claudius's murder and adultery.

The Duke's speech, far from being a genuine attempt to repent, is a specious smokescreen for self-justification. MacDonald P. Jackson argues that the Duke's speech is a reworking of Claudius's prayer into a more narcissistic vein:

> But whereas Claudius's desperate monologue serves to show the conscience-stricken human being inside the suave usurper, and so prepares the audience emotionally for the postponement of revenge, the glibness of the Duke's confession reveals an automaton, whose imminent gruesome destruction by Vindice and Hippolito we can approve, and even relish. (544–545)

Jackson's use of "automaton" for the Duke is *à propos*, suggesting that either the Duke is so one-dimensional that he lacks agency or that he is so thoroughly given over to evil that all of his will has hardened into perverted compulsions.

Claudius, in contrast, seriously considers repenting, but either cannot (Calvinism) or does not want to (avant-garde conformity and Molinism). Claudius, however, is no automaton, and his willing choice to persist in his chosen course of destructive action is the result of a further refinement of self-deception in the face of the increased self-knowledge that he experienced in prayer. It is this deliberate rejection of insight and self-knowledge that renders Claudius unable to come to terms with his culpability by repenting. The Duke, whether a glib villain or automaton, lacks the requisite agency to repent, and thus serves as a foil to Claudius, whose impenitence is the result of his own agency. By comparing *Hamlet* to its afterlife in *The Revenger's Tragedy*, Claudius's tortured impenitence emerges more clearly as his own freely elected course of action. If the Duke in Middleton's *Revenger's Tragedy* shows strong signs of Calvinist reprobation, Claudius embodies an agonized tension between predestinarian soteriology, on the one hand, and avant-garde conformity and Molinism, on the other hand.

CODA: AGENCY AND GRACE

The scene of Claudius at prayer is arguably the most significant soteriological moment in Shakespeare's entire corpus. The scene, chiastically situated in the middle of the play, radiates out to its beginning and end. As the dramatic crux, the scene encapsulates so much of what the entire play has to say about ethics, grace, agency, repentance, and forgiveness. In effect, the choice before both the praying Claudius and the avenging Hamlet is the same: either to forgive oneself and the other or to face the bitter consequences of unforgiveness. The failure of grace, or more accurately, the failure of Claudius to receive grace, is the pivotal moment of the play, inexorably leading to its bloody denouement. Once Claudius decides not to repent, the deaths of Polonius, Rosencrantz and Guildenstern quickly follow. Eventually, Ophelia, Gertrude, Claudius, Laertes, and Hamlet will be added to that number.

But the forgiveness imagined in Claudius's spiritual crisis nonetheless works to soften the play's impulse to revenge, contributing to the tragedy's transcendent afterglow. Even if Claudius remains unable to forgive himself, and even if Claudius and Hamlet remain at enmity with each other to the bitter end, the possibility of forgiveness invoked in Claudius's prayer reverberates in Hamlet and Laertes's choice to forgive each other. Laertes may be a lesser figure, but he offers, at a crucial moment, and in telling words, a striking counterpoint—another spiritual possibility: "Exchange forgiveness with me, noble Hamlet" (5.2.313). Like *The Tempest*, *Hamlet* is an exquisite exception to the revenge drama because it privileges forgiveness to retaliation, even if such forgiveness is not always realized in the play itself. The play, then, refutes the ghost's rhetoric of revenge, but broadly affirms its soteriology. Nevertheless, in *Hamlet* we do not have a play of consummate forgiveness and reconciliation, but a tragedy of the violent outworking of impenitence.

Grace strikes an important note in *Hamlet*. When Polonius indicates that he will treat the players "according to their desert," Hamlet is appalled by Polonius's lack of grace:

> God's bodkin, man, much better! Use every man after his desert and who shall scape whipping? Use them after your own honour and dignity—the less they deserve the more merit is in your bounty. (2.2.465–470)

Hamlet's comment captures the prodigality of God's grace (unmerited favor on sinful humanity) as it was conceived across a broad spectrum of early modern theologies. Late sixteenth-century Calvinists, avant-garde conformists, and Molinists alike celebrated God's grace. The crucial difference between their soteriologies lay in their respective beliefs about whether such grace could be freely accessed universally or whether it were reserved for the elect, irrespective of merit or will.

The resonances of avant-garde conformist thought in Claudius's prayer suggest that the possibility of agency is important not only to the play's soteriology but also to the entire drama. Like the avant-garde reformers of the English church in the 1590s such as Andrewes, Hooker, and Harsnett, the play proposes to expose the ethical incoherencies of predestinarian thinking. In referring to the "special providence in the fall of a sparrow" (5.2.197–198), Hamlet relinquishes responsibility for his actions. Claudius too attempts to disavow responsibility for his actions, but ultimately finds that he cannot escape the burden of his past decisions. Both Hamlet and Claudius find themselves trying not to act, to make excuses for their passivity. In Claudius's soteriological crisis, acting is terrifying, but his evasion of choice is itself a choice which forecloses any creative possibilities. As such, the play's soteriology becomes a vehicle for the characters' existential dilemmas. The co-existence of Calvinist, Catholic, and avant-garde conformist vocabularies in Claudius's prayer draws attention to the agony of his decision making and to the tragic ethical consequences of his choices.

3

Hamlet, the Discernment of Spirits, and the Sifting of St. Peter
An Elegy for Religious Violence

IT WOULD BE DIFFICULT to overstate the importance of the Bible in shaping early modern literature, including Shakespearean drama. In England, the Bible had been widely available in the vernacular for several generations before Shakespeare wrote *Hamlet*. As such, recent criticism has tried to recover the biblical heritage in Shakespeare.[1] Thomas Fulton and Kristen Poole successfully defend the premise of their study of Shakespearean biblical allusion, namely that "Shakespeare himself, deeply attentive to words and language, lived in the midst of this popularization of hermeneutics, and his plays reflect biblical fluency and engagement with contemporary exegetical debates" (2). In other words, Shakespeare was not merely conversant with biblical narratives and cadences, but also

---

1. Even after the publication of Naseeb Shaheen's compendious *Biblical References in Shakespeare's Plays* (1999), a number of important studies of Shakespeare's use of scripture have demonstrated that the presence of the Bible in Shakespeare has not been exhaustively studied. Hannibal Hamlin's *The Bible in Shakespeare* (2013) interfaces biblical discourse with Calvin's sermons, highlighting the intertextual complexity of Shakespeare's biblical allusiveness. More recently yet, Thomas Fulton and Kristen Poole's edited collection, *The Bible on the Shakespearean Stage: Cultures of Interpretation in Reformation England* (2018), has advanced the study of biblical allusion in Shakespeare by exploring various hermeneutical frameworks available in England and registering how some of these methods are at work in Shakespearean drama.

with many of the politically volatile appropriations of those texts and aesthetics by competing theological factions.

While the mid-twentieth century showed some engagement with Shakespeare and religion, the fin-de-siècle saw some important work come to light by Jonathan Dollimore, Gary Taylor, and Debora Shuger and Claire McEachern.[2] In the first decade of the millennium, "the turn to religion" came into full swing (and has not showed signs of abating). Stephen Greenblatt's *Hamlet in Purgatory* (2001) became an important text, even if to refute. While the twentieth century saw a plethora of Freudian readings of *Hamlet*, based on Ernest Jones's influential study, there has been in the first two decades of the twenty-first century a renewed interest in the religious dimensions of the play, possibly reflecting something of the cultural shift that philosopher Richard Kearney describes as "anatheism," or the return to religion after atheism. As David Scott Kastan avers, "Theology has replaced psychology as the favored tool to penetrate the heart of the mystery that is *Hamlet*" (118). In particular, soteriology looms over the play as one of its most weighty and conflicted discourses. As Kastan asserts, "It is now a commonplace that the problem of *Hamlet*, the problem *for* Hamlet, is his uncertainty about the nature of the ghost, an issue that can be decided (or perhaps can't) by turning to religious debate in the sixteenth century on the question of salvation" (118). This study intervenes in the critical debate over the nature of the ghost by interrogating *Hamlet's* handling of spirituality vis-à-vis biblical allusion.

A robust body of literature on spiritual discernment would have helped Hamlet navigate his epistemic uncertainty over the identity of the ghost. Accordingly, Hamlet uses *The Mousetrap* to perform a lay (not secular) version of *discretio spirituum*, or discernment of spirits, in an attempt to determine the origin of the ghost—angelic, demonic, or human.[3] *Discretio spirituum*, believed to be a divine charism enabling

---

2. See Jonathan Dollimore's *Radical Tragedy: Religion, Ideology and Power in the Drama of Shakespeare and His Contemporaries* (1993), Gary Taylor's "Forms of Opposition: Shakespeare and Middleton" (1994), and Clair McEachern and Debora Shuger's edited collection *Religion and Culture in Renaissance England* (1997). Gary Taylor's article makes a strong case that Shakespeare may have been a Catholic, an argument which maintained its momentum for over a decade.

3. John Dover Wilson suggests that the ghost has three possible identities: according to Catholics it may be a spirit from Purgatory, according to Calvinists it may be a demon, and according to skeptics like Reginald Scot, it may be a figment of Hamlet's troubled imagination (61–63). I lean into what Dover identifies as the "Protestant" position, but I actually substantiate my interpretation via a largely Catholic body of spiritual discourse. Greenblatt's *Hamlet in Purgatory* has done much to revive what

a priest to discern a demonic presence, had a well-developed protocol in early modern Catholic spirituality. Hamlet arguably gestures at the ecclesiastical practice of *discretio spirituum* when he tries to discern the identity of the ghost. While Hamlet himself at times considers the possibility that the ghost may be a demon from hell tempting him to commit a violent act, he (ambivalently) comes to believe the identity the spirit claims for itself—his father's ghost visiting him from Purgatory.

I acknowledge that a reading of the play which regards the ghost on its own terms as the spirit of Hamlet's father from Purgatory has strong textual support, but I am not interested in following this line of evidence in the present study because Anthony Low and Stephen Greenblatt have masterfully made that case. I also acknowledge that the medieval and early modern code of family honor and filial piety required the avenging of the murder of a loved one. The advantage of the filial piety reading of the ghost and its call for revenge is that it accentuates some of the profound discourse in the play about an archetypal father-son relationship, which has always been part of the enduring appeal of *Hamlet*. Conversely, the advantage of my demonological and theological reading of the ghost is that it accentuates aspects of the play that have received less attention recently and that it elucidates the ethical status of the ghost in a play that critiques its own investment in violence. One could argue that the play contains self-contradictory readings of the ghost in terms of both filial piety/codes of honor and demonology/theology. In other words, the play gives conflicting indications that the ghost is somehow both a demon and Hamlet's father's ghost from Purgatory. Perhaps this contradiction in the play speaks to the hypocrisy of European men exacting revenge in the name of family honor while still claiming to be Christians. According to this line of thought, the syncretism in the play reflects the syncretism in medieval and early modern European culture.

However, I will argue that the play resists Hamlet's faith in the ghost by alluding to the biblical narratives about Saint Peter, particularly the cock crow and Peter's diabolical "sifting," to indicate that Hamlet is a victim of spiritual deception who is under the influence of a demon.[4]

Wilson refers to as the "Catholic" interpretation of the ghost.

4. Eleanor Prosser convincingly argues that the ghost is a demon (142). In passing, she notes that the cock crow "is the voice of grace" (100). I build on Prosser's brief observation by noting that the Petrine imagery of the cock crow and spiritual sifting work in concert with the play's persistent concern with *discretio spirituum*. My focus is on the methodology by which Hamlet and the audience discern the identity of the ghost, namely the play's Petrine imagery.

This Petrine imagery (relating to Peter), deriving from both the Bible and Jesuit Robert Southwell's *Saint Peters Complaynt*, operates as a deep source through which the play critiques both the ghost's injunction to avenge and Hamlet's compliance with it. Much like Peter is "sifted" by Satan in disavowing Christ, only to come to his senses upon hearing the cock crow, Hamlet is ensnared in a disastrous course of revenge by the rhetoric of the ghost, despite the cock crow that sheds light on the spirit's suspect origins.[5] By probing Shakespeare's exegetical spin on biblical and Southwellian Petrine allusions, I am combining biblical hermeneutics with cross-confessional polemics. Using Peter as a sword that cuts in both Catholic and Protestant directions, the play highlights the spiritual danger that the ghost poses to Hamlet.

By considering *Hamlet* in the light of this early modern biblical spirituality (rather than modern psychology), I suggest the ghost emerges as a demon who deceptively encourages violence by means of religious rhetoric. To substantiate this theory, I examine a spectrum of views about the relationship between demons, ghosts, and revenge in three other early modern plays. While *Hamlet* partakes of the Senecan revenge tradition set forth in other contemporary plays (most notably Thomas Kyd's *The Spanish Tragedy*), the theological orientation of *Hamlet* identifies the ghost as a demon in Christian, rather than classical terms, and thus more particularly engages both Hamlet and the audience with the protocols of *discretio spirituum*.[6] In contrast to the one-dimensional avenging spirit "Revenge" in *The Spanish Tragedy*, the ghost in *Hamlet* calls for more robust powers of discernment. Shakespeare's own *Titus Andronicus*, as a revenge drama in the Senecan tradition of *The Spanish Tragedy*, is another play which associates revenge with demons, mostly by relying on anachronistic theological imagery. In *Titus Andronicus*, however, the demonic is restricted to the level of imagery, rather than extending to the *dramatis personae*.

---

5. Below I extensively discuss the relationship between the term "sifting" in the Bible, *Doctor Faustus*, and *Hamlet*.

6. For my base text, I am using the Arden 3 edition of *Hamlet,* which is based on the Second Quarto of 1604–1605, and which is edited by Ann Thompson and Neil Taylor. For my control text, I am using the Arden 3 *Hamlet: The Texts of 1603 and 1623*, based on the First Quarto and the Folio, also edited by Ann Thompson and Neil Taylor. My text for Thomas Kyd's *The Spanish Tragedy* is the Arden edition edited by Clara Calvo and Jesús Tronch. For *Titus Andronicus*, I use The Oxford Shakespeare edition edited by Eugene Waith. For Cyril Tourneur's *The Atheist's Tragedy*, I cite The Revels Plays edition edited by Irving Ribner.

To give further evidence to those who are skeptical of my demonological reading of the ghost, I discuss a counter-example of a ghost from Cyril Tourneur's *The Atheist's Tragedy* who tells its son *not* to avenge its murder by its brother. Tourneur's play, as a possible afterlife of *Hamlet*, emphatically condemns revenge on religious grounds, thus implying that the ghost in *Hamlet* is malignant. Yet the critique of revenge in *Hamlet* itself is there all the same, expressed in more muted and sophisticated terms. By undermining the ghost's association of violence and religion, *Hamlet* implicitly critiques the proliferation of religious violence on both sides of the Reformation divide. In particular, the ghost of Robert Southwell, who was martyred five years before the traditional dating of *Hamlet*, haunts the play with an uncanny awareness of the spiritual deception that allowed early modern Christians to kill each other in the name of the state.[7]

HAMLET: A SPIRITUAL PLAY

It is striking just how spiritual a play *Hamlet* is. Granted, the play is not as supernatural as its forerunner, Marlowe's *Doctor Faustus*, but for a play which is so often touted as a harbinger of modernity, *Hamlet* is replete with a host of arcane spiritual beings. In addition to the ghost's three appearances, the play makes numerous references to angels and demons. As such, *Hamlet* registers its spirituality by taking seriously the interface between non-physical intelligent beings and humans. In comparison to these supernatural intermediaries, Christ figures quite diminutively in the play, with the only major reference to him (other than dominical scriptural allusions) being Marcellus's fanciful notion that the cock crows all night during the season in which "our Saviour's birth is celebrated," making it impossible for spirits to haunt (1.1.158). A cock crow does in fact silence the ghost in the first scene of *Hamlet* (1.1.146), subtly hinting that the ghost in question may not be as friendly as its paternal appearance may cause Hamlet to believe it to be.

---

7. Mary Tudor burned Protestants at the stake as "heretics," whereas Elizabeth hanged, drew, and quartered Jesuit priests as "traitors." The Elizabethan regime regarded Jesuits as a dangerous political threat to the crown.

HAMLET AND *DISCRETIO SPIRITUUM*

When the ghost appears in the guise of Hamlet's greatly beloved father, Hamlet is confronted with a spiritual vision that requires extraordinary powers of discernment. On the one hand, the ghost is urging revenge, which is clearly an immoral, arguably even a diabolical message (except for audiences of revenge dramas who have suspended their disbelief). On the other hand, the ghost speaks as Hamlet's father, appealing to Hamlet's love for him, his mother, and even the Catholic faith. Hamlet's strong love for his father clouds his judgment to the point where Hamlet is willing to converse with the ghost, even if it may turn out to be a demon. Both the audience and Hamlet find themselves in a hermeneutical crux that involves the discernment of spirits. Hamlet engages in a process of *discretio spirituum* that has affinities with well-established biblical and ecclesiastical traditions. *The Mousetrap* is Hamlet's attempt to apply the principles of spiritual discernment to his epistemic crisis:

> The spirit that I have seen
> May be a de'il, and the de'il hath power
> T'assume a pleasing shape. Yea, and perhaps
> Out of my weakness and my melancholy,
> As he is very potent with such spirits,
> Abuses me to damn me! I'll have grounds
> More relative than this. The play's the thing
> Wherein I'll catch the conscience of the King. (2.2.533–540)

Hamlet, humanist prince that he is, uses the theater as a medium for *discretio spirituum*.[8]

HAMLET'S DELAY AND *DISCRETIO SPIRITUUM*

The play as a whole (not just the play within-the-play) queries the notion of spiritual discernment. Indeed, the ghost's message to Hamlet puts him

---

8. Kurt Schreyer argues that *Hamlet*'s references to Purgatory are influenced by representations of hell and Purgatory in the mystery plays, particularly the Doomsday plays. Schreyer observes that the Doomsday plays separate the sheep from the goats in final judgment, a practice of ultimate *discretio spirituum* in Schreyer's analysis. Schreyer argues that Shakespeare uses a medieval formulation of *discretio spirituum* for his dramatic purposes in delaying Hamlet's revenge (134). The emphasis in my analysis of the relationship between Hamlet's delay and *discretio spirituum* is not on Shakespeare's dramatic intent in pacing the play, but on how the protocols of spiritual discernment (both medieval and early modern) reveal the ethics of Hamlet and the ghost.

in a Catch-22, for if the ghost comes from Purgatory, speaking on behalf of God, then Hamlet would do well to obey it expeditiously. Conversely, if there is the slightest chance that the ghost is a demon, then Hamlet best exercise the utmost caution by testing the spirit.

Popular devotional manuals advised immediate and unflinching obedience to God. Robert Parsons, in his manual of Catholic devotion, *Book of Christian Exercise* (1582), which was so successful that it was plagiarized with minor Protestant adaptations by Edmund Bunny, inveighs passionately against "delaye of resolution" in matters of faith (371). Parsons warns that people may lose their opportunity for salvation if they delay in heeding the voice of God. According to Parsons, "one of the greatest and most dangerous deceites, and yet the moste ordinarie and vniuersall, that the enemie of mankinde dothe vse towards the children of Adam" is to urge "the importance of delaye, in a matter so weightie, as is our co[n]uersion, and saluation" (371–372). Parsons argues that to delay in matters of salvation is to play into the hands of Satan. This kind of rhetoric would put extreme pressure on someone like Hamlet, who is struggling to discern if the ghost is speaking with divine authority or if it is attempting to undermine his salvation. Clearly, *discretio spirituum* was a high-stakes undertaking in early modern spirituality.

However, if the ghost is a demon, then the best thing Hamlet could do is to reject the ghost immediately and entirely. If he cannot discern whether the ghost is speaking on behalf of God or the devil, he must delay in acting upon its advice until he is able to achieve spiritual insight. Indeed, the whole question of Hamlet's "delay" made famous by Samuel Taylor Coleridge, as well as Johann Wolfgang von Goethe's notion of Hamlet having "a great action laid upon a soul unfit for the performance of it," may be quite beside the point, if we are to scrutinize the ethics of the ghost's injunctions (Goethe qtd. in Kermode 426). In other words, Hamlet may be the most ethical when he pauses to test the ghost's admonition to revenge, and he may be the most unethical when he precipitously seeks to obey it. Margreta de Grazia, questioning whether it is accurate to interpret Hamlet as delaying, brilliantly argues that the reason for the critical tradition's preoccupation with Hamlet's delay derives from the eighteenth-century critics' (especially Samuel Johnson's) discomfort with Hamlet's desire to send Claudius to hell (159): "Once emptied of its execrable intent, Hamlet's excuse for sparing Claudius at prayer becomes one among many stalling tactics. Procrastination becomes his salient, indeed his defining trait" (165). I would argue that Hamlet does in fact delay, but that his delay is due not merely to procrastination, but also to his *ad hoc* engagement with the procedures of *discretio spirituum*. The outcome of the play suggests that Hamlet might have been justified to ignore the ghost's advice to memorialize it through revenge. Tragically, Hamlet fails in his attempt to spiritually discern the ghost.

HAMLET AND HISTORICAL APPROACHES TO *DISCRETIO SPIRITUUM*

Spiritual discernment was often a complex business, sometimes only achieved in hindsight. The delay in Hamlet's ability to discern the identity of the ghost is understandable, considering the sheer variety and sophistication of many of the traditional perspectives on *discretio spirituum*. The tradition of spiritual discernment on which Hamlet might have drawn is so vast that I will select only some of the most salient voices from the Bible to post-Tridentine Catholicism. Many of these landmark texts are relevant to Hamlet's epistemic crisis in determining the identity of the ghost.

In the Greek New Testament, discernment is signified by *diakresis*, which is a revelatory gift of the Holy Spirit (Sluhovsky 169). The ecclesiastical Latin term *discretio* refers both to natural "moderation" and the divine charism of spiritual insight (172). In the Pauline corpus, discernment of spirits is a gift given by the Holy Spirit to certain members of the church for its edification and protection (1 Corinthians 12:9–10). Apparently, some of the Pauline churches believed that the Holy Spirit endowed certain individuals with the ability to identify and exorcise demons.

Athanasius's *Life of Antony* (356 CE), as one of the most supernatural expressions of historical Christian thought, represents an important patristic perspective on *discretio spirituum*. An early desert father, Antony purportedly battled solo against many assaulting demons, armed merely with prayer, fasting, and the scriptures. Antony became legendary in his ability to discern and repel demons. Despite his athletic spirituality, Anthony formulates a rather simple rule for discernment:

> It is not difficult, with God's help, to distinguish between good and bad spirits. The holy angels are friendly and calm in appearance because they do not fight nor will they cry out nor will anyone hear their voice.... Then our mind is no longer disturbed

but becomes gentle and calm, illuminated by the angels' light. (31)

According to Antony, the presence of a demon can be detected by the disturbance it causes to the human temperament:

> The ferocious expressions of these most wicked creatures [demons], their terrifying sounds and vile thoughts, . . .immediately strike fear into the soul and numb the senses, producing hatred in Christians, depression and lethargy in monks, nostalgia for family, fear of death, desire for sin, lack of enthusiasm for virtue, dullness of the heart. (31)

The disturbance that the ghost causes in Hamlet's psyche suggests that according to Antony's test of discernment, the ghost may be a malignant spirit.

Jean Gerson is an important late medieval theologian writing on the topic of *discretio spirituum*, particularly in *De Distinctione Verarum Visionum a Falsis* (*On Distinguishing True from False Revelations*) (1402). Unlike Antony, Gerson felt that spiritual discernment could not be reduced to an easy formula: "there is for human beings no general rule or method that can be given always and infallibly to distinguish between revelations that are true and those that are false or deceptive" (335). Because of the epistemic uncertainty of spiritual discernment, Gerson advises that practitioners be theologians who are well conversant in scripture. Gerson further advises his readers not to act impulsively on a revelation, but to subject it to the tests of time and patience before acting on it:

> It is my opinion that we are obliged in all matters, but especially in this investigation, not to make hasty conclusions. *We are to delay our verdict until after the fullest investigation*, unless it is easily apparent that deception or foolishness is involved. . . . For a demon can sometimes start out with many truths, and in the course of time when he has persuaded people, then he adds what is deceptive. This he can do either to deceive an individual person, or to attack miraculous events of our religion on which the faith is based. (363, itallics added)

This classic text on spiritual discernment affords insight into Hamlet's epistemic crisis, for the ghost wants Hamlet to act with precipitous violence, whereas Hamlet's proclivity to delay in order to discern the identity of the ghost resonates with longstanding protocols of *discretio spirituum*. Neither the fact that the ghost truthfully identifies the murderer of Hamlet's father nor its religious rhetoric are infallible evidence of its reliability. According to Gerson, a demon can communicate a lethal combination of half-truths, which are all the more deceptive for their partial veracity. Gerson's criteria for spiritual discernment vindicate Hamlet's delay but cast suspicion on the identity of the spirit.

The Life of Saint Teresa of Ávila (1565) is another important source of *discretio spirituum* by one of the most mystical figures of the Catholic Reformation. Like Gerson, St. Teresa advocates conformity to scripture as an important spiritual test. To these, she adds the ethical test, the accountability test (sharing with her confessors), and the ecclesiastical test (conformity with church dogma). One test which is conspicuously lacking in Teresa's case is the community test, for Teresa's peers often failed to endorse her revelations, except retroactively when the Catholic church exonerated her by making her a doctor of the faith. Teresa recounts how the devil even counterfeited visions of Jesus, which left her feeling "troubled, nauseated, and restless" (200). In contrast, the transformative impact of her true revelations authenticated their reliability, however bizarre or misunderstood they may have been, even by some of her confessors:

> I could not believe, therefore, that if the devil were doing this in order to deceive me and drag me down to hell, he would adopt means so contrary to his purpose as to take away my vices and give me virtues and strength instead. For I clearly saw that these visions had made me a different person. (202)

Again, Teresa's criteria for the discernment of spirits speak to Hamlet's situation, for the ghost fails the ethical, scriptural, and ecclesiastical tests by demanding murder. In trying to keep the ghost's visitation a secret, Hamlet also fails to use Teresa's accountability test. The long-term effects of the ghost's message on Hamlet are escalating violence and psychological disorder, rather than such healing properties as Teresa attributed to her good revelations. The fact that the ghost appeared in the likeness of Hamlet's father provides no certainty of its goodness, if (as Teresa claims) a demon can impersonate even Jesus Christ.

One of the most influential writers on spiritual discernment in the early modern period was the founder of the Jesuit order, St. Ignatius of Loyola. His *Spiritual Exercises*, written in Spanish between 1522–1524 but first published in Latin in 1548, extensively guide the spiritual practitioner in discerning between good and evil spirits. The basic premise of his methodology, similar to that of St. Antony, is the idea that a good spirit produces consolation in the human subject, whereas an evil spirit, desolation:

> I call consolation every increase of faith, hope, and love, and all interior joy that invites and attracts to what is heavenly and to the salvation of one's soul by filling it with peace and quiet in its Creator and Lord. (316.3)

An evil spirit works in opposition to the good spirit, producing desolation:

> I call desolation what is entirely the opposite of what is described in the third rule, as darkness of soul, turmoil of spirit, inclination to what is low and earthly, restlessness rising from many disturbances and temptations which lead to want of faith, want of hope, want of love. The soul is wholly slothful, tepid, sad, and separated, as it were, from its Creator and Lord. (317.4)

Ignatius complicates his methodology of discernment by analyzing the deceptive qualities of an evil spirit: "It is a mark of the evil spirit to assume the appearance of an angel of light. He begins by suggesting thoughts that are suited to a devout soul, and ends by suggesting his own" (332.4).

The syncretism in the ghost's message to Hamlet, which appeals both to Hamlet's love for his father and for God, but then urges Hamlet to commit murder, speaks to this Ignatian awareness of demonic deception that can begin with the good but conclude in evil. Ignatius further suggests that an evil spirit can counterfeit the motions of consolation produced by the good spirit: "The evil spirit consoles for purposes that are the contrary [to the good spirit], and that afterwards he might draw the soul to his own perverse intentions and wickedness" (331.3) When the ghost appears the last time to Hamlet, it once again encourages Hamlet to execute its vengeful intentions, but also to comfort Gertrude. Indeed, the ghost seems to be communicating the kind of pseudo-consolation that Ignatius attributes to evil spirits when deceiving and tempting people to sin.[9]

While Luther's biography includes vivid assaults from Satan, generally Protestant clergy dealt more at arm's length with the demonic than did the spiritual directors in the Catholic tradition. Calvin's skepticism about the miraculous elements of Christianity also extended to his views on spiritual discernment. Given Calvin's cautiousness and inexperience with those gifts of the Holy Spirit that are miraculously

---

9. On the one hand, the ghost is asking Hamlet to watch over his soul like a good Pauline subject. On the other hand, the ghost is calling for Hamlet to engage in Senecan revenge. No wonder Hamlet is becoming psychologically unhinged.

executed, it is perhaps not surprising that his definition of the discernment of spirits lacks any reference to unveiling the demonic, but is instead restricted to recognizing human imposters, as he suggests in his *Commentary on 1 Corinthians*:

> The discerning of spirits, was a clearness of perception in forming a judgment as to those who professed to be *something*. (Acts 5:36.) I speak not of that natural wisdom, by which we are regulated in judging. It was a special illumination, with which some were endowed by the gift of God. The use of it was this: that they might not be imposed upon by masks, of mere pretences, but might by that spiritual judgment distinguish, as by a particular mark, the true ministers of Christ from the false. (12:8)

Calvin's definition of the discernment of spirits would afford little help for those attempting to practice exorcism or for someone like Hamlet, who is confronted with a supernatural being of uncertain origin. The reformed church in general was inexperienced in dealing with the demonic, although John Darrell, a fanatical Puritan dispossessor, and John Foxe, author of the *Actes and Monuments*, were two notable exceptions as Reformed clergy who performed exorcisms and experienced opposition from their superiors in doing so.

Nonetheless, the reformed traditions did in fact have methodologies of spiritual discernment, even if these practices were not as robust as those of their Catholic counterparts. Claire Copeland and Johannes Machielsen "testify to the importance of *discretio spirituum* to Catholics and Protestants alike" (5). However, the Reformed church was less likely to suspect the insinuation of a demon than to engage in a grueling regimen of self-examination to determine whether or not one is among the elect. The title of John Forbes's treatise bears witness to such experimental theology: *how a Christian man may discerne the testimonie of Gods spirit, from the testimonie of his own spirit, in witnessing his adoption* (1616). Forbes's version of spiritual discernment becomes so convoluted that he imagines it is possible for someone to be illuminated by the Holy Spirit and yet not to be an elect child of God:

> Whereby it is plaine that there is no possibilitie in man of receiving or acknowledging any part of that mysterie of godlynes, without the spirits working. And yet, albeit this be the work of the spirit, yet doth it not prove him in whom it is, to be the childe of God. (23)

Theologies such as Forbes's shifted the emphasis in *discretio spirituum* away from traditional practices of discerning between good and evil spirits to deciphering one's own soteriological status in relation to double predestination. This reformed version of spiritual discernment tended to produce intense soteriological introspection.

In contrast to the reformed English church, the medieval and early modern Catholic church had a robust apparatus for detecting and eliminating demons from the afflicted human subject. A prerequisite for ministering to demoniacs was the divine grace (*gratia gratis data*) of *discretio spirituum* (Sluhovsky 169). A priest must be able to diagnose an affliction as demonic before proceeding with the rite of exorcism. However, the grace of *discretio spirituum* was proven to be useful in navigating a host of spiritual phenomena, not merely demonic possession. Even mystical visions could be evaluated through a process of spiritual discernment. Bernard of Clairvaux warned that religious zeal and even the love of God needed to be regulated by discernment in order to safeguard falling into error: "The more eager the zeal, the more vigorous the spirit, the more generous the love, so also the greater the need for more vigilant knowledge to restrain the zeal, to temper the spirit, to moderate the love" (qtd. in Sluhovsky 172). According to Bernard of Clairvaux, unregulated spirituality is vulnerable to the insinuation of the demonic (Sluhovsky 172).

St. Bernard's warning that the zeal and love of a spiritual person need to be tempered by wisdom is à propos for Hamlet. Hamlet's judgment is so clouded by love for his late father that he is willing to converse with a spirit that he thinks may be a demon simply because of its likeness to his father. Hamlet's reckless zeal in counting his life and soul as nothing, simply so he may speak with the ghost, suggest that his spirituality is not properly tempered by discernment. Hamlet's love for his father makes him particularly vulnerable to the ghost's diabolical message of revenge. The double meaning of *discretio* in Latin as both "moderation" (natural wisdom) and as supernatural charisma of discernment (172) conveys exactly what Hamlet requires in responding to his vision of the ghost. *Discretio* is also what Hamlet is lacking, as seen in his impetuous response to the ghost.

Girolamo Menghi, the most prolific Italian writer on exorcism in the late sixteenth-century, consolidated the symptoms of demonic possession into a list of seven signs, including a supernatural ability to speak another language, knowledge of the future, inexplicable bodily strength, hatred of the sacred, despair, blasphemous anger, and vomiting sharp materials (Sluhovsky 193). Confusingly, Menghi admitted that some of these signs could occasionally be the result of divine grace rather than demonic inspiration (193). Indeed, the first three signs are performed by biblical characters through the power of the Holy Spirit. Menghi even cautioned that a demon could appear in the guise of Christ, Mary, or a saint (193), as was the case with St. Teresa. Thus, a supernatural gift of discernment may be necessary to determine the origin of a spiritual vision that seems to be benign or even sacred.

In the case of Hamlet, the vision of a spirit who looks and talks like his father would need to be authenticated by *dicretio spirituum*. The ghost's likeness to his father cannot be taken at face value, but (according to ecclesiastical protocol) the vision must be tested to safeguard Hamlet from spiritual danger. The effects of the ghost on Hamlet in producing confusion and melancholy, as well as inciting escalating violence suggest that the spirit may indeed be demonic in origin, at least according to some of Menghi's criteria, including hatred, despair, violence, and blasphemous anger.

PETRINE NARRATIVES AS A DEEP SOURCE FOR *HAMLET*

In conveying the possible demonic identity of the ghost, *Hamlet* does not confine itself to early modern spirituality but also maps out a sophisticated network of biblical allusions. This double-barreled approach to *discretio spirituum* is not surprising, considering that early modern religious culture was saturated in scripture. What *is* perhaps surprising is that the play's use of biblical allusions is even more politically volatile than its appropriation of early modern spirituality. Shakespeare appropriates the Bible (and biblically inspired poetry by Robert Southwell) to make trenchant commentary on Elizabethan politics, particularly the use of religious violence.[10]

---

10. Richard Wilson comments on the symmetry between the three cock crows announcing Peter's denial of Jesus and the three invocations of the cock crow in *Hamlet* ("Imminence" 14). (More accurately, Peter denies Jesus three times before the cock crows twice [Mark 14:30].) Wilson astutely argues that the Petrine imagery of the cock crow frames "the Ghost's call for revenge as another betrayal of Christ" (14). I build on Wilson's insightful passing comment to make my case for extensive interplay between the biblical Petrine narratives and *Hamlet*. Wilson also suggests that the imagery of the cock may be a "rebuke... to the ghost of Robert Southwell" for his figuration of the cock crow in *Saint Peters Complaynt* as a call for Catholic "revenge" on Elizabeth (14).

Two unmistakable Petrine allusions in *Hamlet*—the cock crowing during the first scene and Claudius's statement regarding Polonius (but ultimately targeted at Hamlet), "we shall sift him" (2.2.58)—form the scaffolding of a larger network of faint Petrine echoes throughout the play. Both of these biblical allusions pertain to the apostle Peter's diabolical testing and spiritual failure in denying Jesus three times. Likewise, these Petrine allusions signal to the audience of *Hamlet* that the ghost may be demonic. In the 1535 Coverdale Bible, Jesus warns Peter, "Satan hath desyred after you, that he might siffte you euen as wheate." The Satanic nature of the testing of Peter (though it was human taunts that actually provoked Peter's denials of Christ) becomes a template for the "sifting" of Hamlet by Claudius and Polonius, but ultimately by a spirit that may be a demon. In the biblical Petrine narratives, Jesus prophesies that a cock crow would signal Peter's three denials of his Lord. The biblical cock crow is thus a divine indicator that Peter has capitulated to Satanic temptation. The Petrine resonances of the cock crow in *Hamlet*, along with Marcellus's association of the cock crow with the celebration of Jesus's birth, warns the audience that the ghost in question is a thing of darkness.

Jesus's warning to Peter that Satan wants to "sift" him is found only in Luke, as Calvin observes in his commentary on his harmony of the synoptic gospels. While Calvin regards Peter's overweening self-confidence and his uninformed zeal as contributing to Peter's failure, Calvin also sees Luke as unique among the evangelists in connecting Peter's failure to Satanic testing (Luke 22:31). Moreover, Calvin interprets Jesus's statement as safeguarding the fallen Peter from despair. Third, Calvin sees all of the disciples as being diabolically tested by witnessing the mistreatment of Jesus in his passion.

Robert Southwell interprets the spiritual failure of Peter mostly in terms of the apostle's cowardice, but also to his capitulation to diabolical oppression. This Satanic element in Peter's spiritual failure emerges in several stanzas of *Saint Peter's Complaynt*, most notably the following:

> The dispossessed devels that out I threw,
> In *Jesus* name, now impiously forsworne,
> Triumph to see me caged in their mew,
> Trampling my ruines with contempt and scorne,
> My perjuries were musick to their daunce:

However, I think Wilson's brief comment about Southwell misrepresents the spirit of *Saint Peters Complaynt*. Southwell never advocates for Catholic revenge against Elizabeth, but rather patient endurance in the face of persecution.

And now they heap disdaines on my mischaunce. (607–612)

In Southwell's imagination, Peter denying Jesus is a collaborative performance with the demons the apostle had previously exorcised. Calvin's and Southwell's interpretation of the diabolical nature of Peter's "sifting" resonates with the spiritual darkness of the ghost who likewise tempts Hamlet.

The Petrine imagery also reinforces the play's overarching opposition to using violence to achieve religious or personal gains. Peter, who uses a sword to cut off the high priest's servant's ear in the Garden of Gethsemane, is rebuked by Jesus for using violence to defend him. Peter, like Hamlet, must learn that violence is not a legitimate means to secure preferred religious outcomes (such as the rescue of Jesus or the vindication of Hamlet's father). Peter, too, through his own bitter experience of spiritual failure, learns the value of refining suffering, as his epistles attest.[11] Likewise, Hamlet suffers affectively from his capitulation to the demonic allure of violence.

In *Hamlet*, the ghost is about to speak when the cock crows, causing the ghost to retreat in silence. As everyone knows, the ghost appears in the image of Hamlet's recently deceased father, the former king. Also of importance is the religious symbolism of the cock crowing. Marcellus comments on this supernatural visitation:

> It faded on the crowing of the cock.
> Some say that ever 'gainst that season comes
> Wherein our Saviour's birth is celebrated
> This bird of dawning singeth all night long,
> And then, they say, no spirit dare stir abroad,
> The nights are wholesome, then no planets strike,
> No fairy takes, nor witch hath power to charm,
> So hallowed and so gracious is that time. (1.1.156–163)

The irony is that if the cock crowing at Christmas reveals the sacredness and safety of that holiday, the cock crowing presently is unable to stop a "spirit" from stirring "abroad" at night. The cock crowing in *Hamlet* nevertheless exposes the spiritual darkness of its preternatural visitor and its message of revenge.

---

11. Gary Kuchar argues that Southwell uses alchemical imagery to convey the refinement of Peter from sinner to rock of the church, thus building on Nancy Pollard Brown's idea that *Saint Peters Complaynt* follows the pattern of post-Tridentine penance (Kuchar, "Alchemy," 158–179).

D.C. Allen observes that the cock was an important medieval symbol of divine illumination, and the cock crow in *Hamlet* both parallels and counterpoints this well-established tradition:

> For centuries the cock had been famed for his instinctive knowledge of light, not only of the lesser light but of the divine light. In this relationship he was associated with the priest as an expeller of darkness and of evil, as a victor over the lions of Hell. But while he reminded men of their duties to God and awakened them from their secular slumber, he also warned them of the coming of Christ and urged them to prepare for the Day of Judgment. (Allen 102)

Marcellus's comment on the cock crow in *Hamlet* conveys the pacific christological dimensions of this medieval tradition. The cock crow in *Hamlet* has an exorcizing function in that it causes the ghost to shrink away in fear, thus offering a salutary warning that the ghost is a malignant spirit, a harbinger of violence.

The most famous cock crow in all literature, and certainly in biblical literature, is the one that announces Peter's three denials of Jesus, just as Christ had prophesied. The cock crow in *Hamlet* is explicitly linked to Jesus and his disciples through Marcellus's commentary. At the sight of the ghost, Marcellus's fear-stricken imagination turns to the comforts of his "Saviour's birth," celebrated at Christmas. However, nothing could be farther from Christmas than the eerie darkness of the moment in which the ghost appears. The biblical narratives of the cock crowing also occurred during "the very hour, and the power of darkenes," Jesus's metaphorical description of being deserted by his disciples, betrayed by one of them (Judas), denied by another (Peter), and apprehended by the religious authorities (Luke 22:53).

The cock crow in the first scene of the play allusively associates Hamlet with Peter's inability to be loyal to Jesus, despite just having been warned by Jesus of the danger of Peter's own perfidy. Peter's impetuously claims his loyalty to Jesus: "Lord, I am ready to go with thee into prison, and to death" (Luke 22:33). Jesus responds by prophesying that this very night Peter will deny him three times, Peter having completely forgotten the individual warning Jesus spoke to him, as well as the Eucharistic liturgy inaugurated earlier that evening, "do this in reme[m]brance of me" (Luke 22:19). The parallels with *Hamlet* are striking, for when the ghost commands, "remember me" (1.5.91), Hamlet responds with the confident impetuousness typical of Peter:

> Yea, from the table of my memory
> I'll wipe away all trivial fond records,
> All saws of books, all forms, all pressures past
> That youth and observation copied there
> And thy commandment all alone shall live
> Within the book and volume of my brain
> Unmixed with baser matter. (1.5.98–104)

Hamlet's reference to "the table of my memory" has distinct Eucharistic overtones. Hamlet's statement alludes to Luke 22:19 (often inscribed on communion tables) and communion is commonly referred to as "the table."[12] This Eucharistic reference further connects this scene to the play's Petrine imagery. In the event, Peter cannot retain his fidelity to Jesus under pressure (despite having just shared the last supper with him), and the question that the play brings to the fore through his Petrine imagery is whether or not Hamlet can or even should remain steadfast to the ghost's memory. However, Shakespeare's Petrine imagery of perfidy becomes distinctly ironized with reference to Hamlet, for if Peter had been better off attending to Jesus's warning to remember him, Hamlet might have been justified to ignore the ghost's advice to memorialize it through revenge.

Numerous other parallels and counterpoints between the Petrine cock crow and the cock crow in *Hamlet* link the drama with scripture, giving the audience clues to the play's religious politics. The cock crows at the appearance of the ghost of Hamlet's father, who has been recently murdered, much like the cock crow in scripture closely precedes the murder of Jesus. The cock crows in the first of three ghost scenes in Hamlet (there are yet other appearances of the ghost ante-dating the action of the play), whereas the biblical rooster crows after Peter has denied Christ three times. The biblical rooster crows when Peter fails to remember his loyalty to Jesus (and also to the Eucharistic sacrament of remembrance), whereas the Shakespearean cock crows before the ghost asks Hamlet to remember him. Barnardo mentions that the ghost was about to speak when the cock crowed, whereas the biblical cock crows after Peter had articulated his denial of Christ three times. Horatio says that when the cock crowed, the ghost "started like a guilty thing / Upon a fearful summons" (1.1.147–148). Similarly, Peter, after denying Christ several times, went away guilty, weeping bitterly. Horatio later explains to Hamlet that

---

12. Protestants objected to the Catholic idea of "an altar," preferring instead the communion table.

the ghost had "A countenance more in sorrow than in anger" (1.2.230). This sorrow parallels both Peter's grief over his own perfidy, as well as the desolations experienced by Jesus, "a man ful of sorrows" (Isaiah 53:3). The ghost beckons Hamlet to follow it alone, and in the biblical narratives only John and Peter follow Jesus into the high priest's courtyard, and only Peter ends up denying Jesus in that place.

Although perhaps more tenuous, other parallels between the Petrine and Hamletian stories may be observed. The ghost asks Hamlet's companions to "Swear!" three times that they will not divulge his appearance; likewise, Peter denies Christ three times, even with oaths and curses. When asked if he were Jesus's disciple, Peter swears that he does not know Jesus. All these connections between the cock crow in *Hamlet* and the Petrine cock crow suggest that Shakespeare is bringing the play into conversation with the biblical Petrine narratives.

PETRINE IMAGERY AND DRAMATIC IRONY

The main point of all these deft allusions to the Petrine cock crow is that Hamlet is in grave spiritual danger from the ghost. Moreover, the Petrine resonances of the cock crow function as dramatic irony. Although Hamlet is a scholar, he does not discern the implicit biblical warning in the cock crow. Horatio seriously considers the possibility that the ghost is dangerous and that it could induce madness in Hamlet, possibly even to the extent of suicide. But Hamlet is blind to the danger the ghost may pose because of its appearance in the likeness of his father. However, the Petrine imagery of the cock crow signals to the biblically literate audience members that Hamlet, like Peter, is acting with reckless over-confidence in the face of grave spiritual danger. The Petrine imagery gives the audience insight into the spiritual danger posed by the ghost, insight which Hamlet fails to realize, despite the fact that he has been educated at Wittenberg, the university made famous by Martin Luther's ninety-five theses. Dramatic irony allows the audience to see the biblical warning implicit in the cock crow, a warning to which Hamlet the scholar remains obtuse. The play thus involves the audience in some of the practices of *discretio spirituum* in which it engages Hamlet.

Deceived by all of the ghost's religious rhetoric, Hamlet is in danger of committing murder, to which temptation he eventually succumbs a number of times. Similarly, Peter over-estimates his faith, and yet under the influence of spiritual testing unadvisedly uses violence to defend Jesus and then himself denies his Lord. (Peter cuts off the high priest's servant's ear in an attempt to defend Jesus, but Jesus rebukes Peter for his violence and heals Malchus's ear.) Both Hamlet and Peter emerge as characters deceived by religious zeal to commit acts of violence. The application of this biblical imagery for the play's original audience is obvious enough during a period in which violence was dispensed by the state against those who held minority religious beliefs. In an early modern context, religion was the justification for the powerful to inflict violence on the vulnerable. Religious belief was also the category according to which the beleaguered minorities were targeted and persecuted, as in the case of recusants during Elizabeth's later reign. *Hamlet*'s use of biblical allusion contests such unjust expressions of violence in the name of the state.

ROBERT SOUTHWELL'S *SAINT PETERS COMPLAYNT* AND *HAMLET*

The parallels and counterpoints between biblical Petrine narratives and *Hamlet* are extensive, and this allusive network expands significantly when triangulated with Robert Southwell's *Saint Peters Complaynt*. In his ground-breaking study of "tears poetry," Gary Kuchar (building on and counterpointing the seminal work of Alison Shell) argues that Southwell virtually inaugurated the genre of penitential poetry as it came to be expressed in the English Renaissance religious lyric, exerting a powerful influence on subsequent poets such as John Donne, George Herbert, Aemilia Lanyer, and Richard Crashaw (*The Poetry of Religious Sorrow in Early Modern England*). Critics are increasingly coming to recognize Southwell's influence on Shakespeare as well, but the extent to which *Saint Peters Complaynt* informs *Hamlet* has not been adequately appreciated. In addition to encouraging recusants, Southwell was writing for a wide audience that included both Catholics and Protestants. His work was widely read and imitated across confessional lines, so John Klause's scholarship that demonstrates Shakespeare's significant borrowing from Southwell is highly convincing. John Klause observes that the cock crow in *Saint Peters Complaynt* is echoed in the first scene in *Hamlet* (*Shakespeare, the Earl, and the Jesuit* 155). Peter Iver Kaufman compares the religious anxieties of Hamlet with those of Southwell's poetic personae, particularly the eponymous figure of *Saint Peters Complaynt*:

"Southwell's subjects had as much difficulty struggling with irresolution as did Hamlet" (140). Building on these preliminary identifications of allusions to *Saint Peters Complaynt* in *Hamlet*, I propose that Shakespeare's *magnum opus* sustains an extensive conversation with the biblical and Southwellian narratives of the apostle Peter's testing and fall. I further suggest that these allusions convey the play's ideas about *discretio spirituum*, particularly with reference to the identity of the ghost.

In Southwell's poem, there are three stanzas about the significance of the cock crowing, one for each of Peter's denials of Jesus (Pilarz 260). The echoes of *Saint Peters Complaynt* in *Hamlet*, like the biblical Petrine allusions, reinforce the play's critique of the ghost's message of revenge and of Hamlet's spiritual failure in subscribing to it. However, in encouraging recusants to remain loyal to their faith in a hostile context, Southwell's poem enriches the play's Petrine imagery with Catholic political resonances. Peter Davidson and Anne Sweeney connect Southwell's poem to the political situation in England in the last two decades of the sixteenth century (xvii): "Southwell's Peter is a biblical character 'ventriloquised' to speak as a contemporary man" (xvii). Davidson and Sweeney further observe the pastoral intention of Southwell's poetry, "distributed in secret, written in hiding to sustain the adherents of an illegal religion" (xx). The spiritual failure of Hamlet may thus reflect the predicament of recusants, who, like Peter may be tempted to deny their faith under duress. The ghost asks Hamlet to "remember" his father by wielding the sword, but Hamlet does not pause to consider that there may be more constructive ways to honor his father's memory. *Hamlet*'s allusions to *Saint Peters Complaynt* speak to Elizabethan Catholics who find themselves in a context where they may be tempted either to resist violently the regime that has persecuted their faith or to abandon themselves to an apostate despair.

Saint Peters Complaynt, published posthumously in 1595, the year of Southwell's own martyrdom, depicts Peter as a figure of extreme remorse and self-recrimination. Adapting Luigi Tansillo's *Lagrime di San Pietro* (1560) to an English recusant audience, Southwell combines the aesthetics of Petrarchan love poetry with his own polemical and pastoral aims as a Jesuit missionary to England. In spite of its general appeal, Southwell's poem also speaks particularly to the extreme pressures experienced by English Catholics to abandon their faith by capitulating to the enforced Protestant worship of the Elizabethan church. Citing Peter as an exemplum of a saint who faltered from his faith under duress, Southwell offers a coded warning/encouragement to English Catholics to be true to their pope and liturgy. In Southwell's hands, Peter—the first pope—becomes an important figure of contrition, as well as a subtle reaffirmation of papal authority, should any English Catholics be tempted to let Elizabeth's exigencies trump the supremacy of their own church.

Southwell transforms the impetuous, but sincere disciple of the gospels into a figure of pensive self-hatred and self-recrimination. Following Kaufman, I suspect that Southwell's relentlessly self-loathing Peter was an inspiration for Shakespeare's Hamlet (140), whose introspective and self-divided habits of thought are also excruciatingly painful and exquisitely refined. Therefore, Hamlet draws his make-up not only from the well-meaning, yet impetuous Peter of the gospels (as in his impulsive killing of Polonius) but also from the agonizingly remorseful, self-critical persona of Southwell's extended lyric (as in Hamlet's soliloquies). The Southwellian Peter is revealed through dramatic irony, for in the poem itself, Peter is locked in a moment of intense spiritual failure, but the Catholic readership knows that his penitence will successfully result in his restoration to apostleship and the papacy.

As with its biblical echoes of Peter, the play's Southwellian Petrine imagery is rather extensive, further contributing to the play's religious politics. If the ghost, upon hearing the cock's crow, "started like a guilty thing / Upon a fearful summons" (1.1.147–148), Southwell's Peter conveys extreme self-hatred: "Blush craven sott, lurke in eternall night: / Crouch in the darkest caves from loathed light" (119–120). Hamlet laments that his father was killed "grossly full of bread / With all his crimes broad blown, as flush as May" (3.3.80–81). Southwell's Peter regards himself as a chief of sinners, even doubting the name Cephas (Rock) that Jesus punningly gave Simon Peter when he called him: "A rock of ruine, not a rest to stay, / A Pastor, not to feed, but to betray" (173–174). Peter despises his own double-mindedness: "Prowesse nor love lodg'd in divided brest" (178). Similarly, both Claudius and Hamlet lament their mixed motives and apparent inability to achieve their nobler desires. Claudius, in particular, sees himself "like a man to double business bound" (3.3.41). Hamlet's misogyny also finds a parallel in Southwell's Peter, who laments, "A puff of womans winde bred all my feare" (150). Peter's self-disparagement over denying Christ because of the taunts of a maiden becomes part of Southwell's political agenda to urge Catholics to subordinate the demands of Elizabeth (the Virgin Queen) to those of Pope Pius V who had excommunicated her in 1570 with the papal bull *Regnans in Excelsis*. Even though Southwell insisted at his execution that he was a loyal subject of Elizabeth, his poem suggests a veiled resistance to the religious hegemony of the Elizabethan settlement.

THE COCK CROW IN *SAINT PETERS COMPLAYNT*

Each of the three sixain stanzas about the cock crowing in *Saint Peters Complaynt* represents one of the three denials of Jesus made by Peter. This section of Southwell's extended lyric makes a particularly strong imprint on *Hamlet*. In each of these stanzas, Peter speaks in apostrophe to the rooster, as though to atone for the three denials of Jesus that Peter had earlier articulated. In the first of the stanzas, Peter laments that "Thy crowing did my selfe to me bewray" (261). In an inversion or parody of the Petrine cock crow, the cock crow in *Hamlet* scares the ghost away, and metaphorically sheds light on its nefarious message of revenge. The ghost's message, a kind of anti-*Evangelium*, plants in Hamlet an obsession with retribution that ends up testing Hamlet to the extreme, bringing to the surface both his basest faults and noblest virtues. If Southwell's Peter sees himself unfavorably in a mirror by hearing the cock crow, then Hamlet is laid bare by committing himself to the ghostly injunction to remember and avenge.

In the second of Southwell's stanzas addressed to the cock, Peter apostrophizes, "O bird, the just rebuker of my crime, / The faithfull waker of my sleeping feares" (265–266). Southwell's Peter is rebuked for his "crime" of faithlessness to Jesus by the cock crow, whereas Hamlet is alerted to the legal "crime" of Claudius's fratricide and regicide, as well as his mortal sin of adultery. The awakening of Peter's "sleeping feares" by the prophesied cock crow also finds a parallel in *Hamlet*, for when the ghost tells Hamlet that Claudius murdered his father, Hamlet responds, "O my prophetic soul! / My uncle!" (1.5.40–41). Much like Jesus's prophecy of the cock crowing anticipates Peter's confrontation with his worst fears of failure, Hamlet intuitively prophesies (discerns) his father's murder, as it were. Hamlet's reference to his own "prophetic soul" corresponds to his earlier response to Horatio's description of the ghost:

> My father's spirit—in arms! All is not well;
> I doubt some foul play. Would the night were come.
> Till then sit still my soul—foul deeds will rise
> Though all the earth o'erwhelm them to men's eyes. (1.2.253–256)

The description of the ghost fills Hamlet with the conviction that any injustice in his father's death will be brought to light, paralleling the prophetic statement of Jesus that reveals the infidelity and cowardice lurking in Peter's soul.

In Southwell's third stanza about the cock crowing in *Saint Peters Complaynt*, Peter prayerfully laments:

> O milde revenger of aspiring pride,
> Thou canst dismount high thoughts to low effects:
> Thou mad'st a cocke me for my fault to chide,
> My lofty boastes this lowly bird correctes" (271–274).

In Luke's gospel, immediately after the first Eucharist and just before Jesus's betrayal, mock-trials, torture, and crucifixion, the disciples argue about which of them is the greatest. Knowing that Peter is in particular danger of satanic temptation and testing, Jesus warns Peter accordingly that he is about to be "sifted." Peter responds that he is willing to be imprisoned and executed for Jesus, but Peter's precipitous denials of Jesus indicate that Peter is highly vulnerable because of an aggrandized self-estimation. After his spiritual failure, Southwell's contrite Peter refers to Jesus as the "milde revenger of aspiring pride" (271).

If Peter believed himself ready for public defense of Jesus in the face of grave danger, he was proven wrong by the cock's crow. Hamlet, too, overestimates his resolve to fulfill the ghost's command of revenge. The return of the ghost mid-way through the play indicates Hamlet's dilatory response to the ghost's urgent message. The ghost appears to Hamlet a second time to warn him to fulfill his task of revenge and to leave Gertrude to heaven and her conscience:

> Do not forget! This visitation
> Is but to whet thy almost blunted purpose. (3.4.106–107)

The ghost reappears shortly after Hamlet refrains from killing Claudius at prayer, and it is tempting to consider that perhaps this supernatural agent disapproves of Hamlet having passed up the perfect opportunity to slay Claudius. The network of Petrine echoes in the play, however, sheds light on the ghost's command as a kind of anti-gospel (or ante-gospel?) of the *lex talionis*. Whereas Jesus rebukes Peter for using his sword to defend Jesus, the ghost urges the principle of retribution enshrined in Mosaic law—an eye for an eye, a life for a life. The play's Petrine imagery thus provides an ironic commentary on both the ghost's message of revenge and the notion of religious violence in general. While Hamlet thinks the right thing for him to do is to speedily follow the ghost's command to act violently, the Petrine resonances of the cock crow function ironically to warn of the spiritual dangers of such a violent course of action.

THE LEGACY OF SOUTHWELL IN *HAMLET*

The significant Petrine imagery *Hamlet* borrows from *Saint Peters Complaynt* powerfully evokes not just the biblical Peter but also the recent memory of Southwell's heroic martyrdom, thus speaking to the plight of recusants. By taking Petrine imagery from Southwell, Shakespeare is tacitly honoring Southwell's memory. Southwell, as a figure who courageously maintained his religious convictions in the face of grave danger, apparently without succumbing to the temptation to repay violence in kind, is an appropriate counter-example to both Peter and Hamlet.[13] It is not simply a long lost Catholic past that *Hamlet* is grieving (as in Eamon Duffy's reading of Sonnet 73), but the very present injustice against courageous champions of a religious minority. Perhaps the Petrine imagery that *Hamlet* borrows from *Saint Peters Complaynt* suggests that neither violence nor cowardice are viable options for beleaguered Elizabethan Catholics. They are certainly not viable options for Hamlet. If anything, Southwell's Peter presents contrition as the appropriate response to spiritual failure, including violence. Hamlet is noticeably deficient in this spiritual virtue, shirking off responsibility for Polonius's, Rosencrantz and Guildenstern's, and Ophelia's deaths.

History tells us that Southwell heeded his own warning not to succumb to external or internal pressures to compromise his faith. Unlike the biblical Peter who denies his Lord after a three year period of intimate discipleship, and unlike the Peter of *Saint Peters Complaynt*, who represents a recusant who cannot live with himself after abandoning the Roman Catholic Church, Southwell endured many extensive periods of brutal torture without ever compromising his convictions or betraying other Catholic priests or worshippers to his torturer Richard Topcliffe. Southwell's strengths of faith and personhood are further confirmed

---

13. If we are to believe his rhetoric in *An Humble Supplication to Her Majesty*, Southwell arguably was not in favor of the Babington Plot or a Spanish invasion. Nonetheless, his Jesuit superiors were planning violence against the Elizabethan regime and he likely would have been aware of these plans. Victor Houlistan gives a sense of how slippery the historical witness is to the nature of the Jesuit mission in England (77–104).

by his psychological resilience after being subjected to long periods of solitary confinement. After all this brutal injustice, he spoke graciously at the scaffold of the Queen whose regime had broken his body but not his spirit. In return, he was hanged, drawn, and quartered. Southwell may have been one of the most courageous martyrs of the sixteenth century. Even if Southwell's dying tribute to Elizabeth was *de rigueur*, in that he was fulfilling a cultural script expected of victims of execution (Mary Queen of Scots did something broadly similar), his death displays both heroism and grace. Southwell's Peter laments, "I liv'd; but so, that saving life, I lost it" (224). Southwell would never have to live with the same regret. In alluding to *Saint Peters Complaynt*, the cock crow in *Hamlet* reminds the audience of the courage of martyr Robert Southwell.

But perhaps this panegyric reading of Southwell is one-sided. Southwell is also associated with the terrible burden of memory at the cost of life. When the ghost admonishes, "remember me," Hamlet responds, "Remember thee? / . . .thy commandment all alone shall live / Within the book and volume of my brain" (1.5.91; 95; 102–103). This passage may be linked to the burden the old faith placed on those born into it. The charge to remember the father at the risk of one's own death parallels the demands Southwell is placing on his fellow Catholics. Here, Hamlet remembering his father is analogous to the burden of memory in mourning the recently lost faith. The ghost's distinctly Catholic language suggests a yearning for a return to a Catholic past—and the very high cost of such nostalgia.

The ghost's rhetoric not only speaks to religious violence but also to the weighty burden of remembering the Catholic past and the danger associated with bringing such dreams to reality. In other words, the charge to remember could be read as analogous to the charge that Southwell was placing on fellow Catholics, especially in *An Epistle of Comfort*, whose deceptive title obscures its polemical exhortation of Catholics to martyrdom (Kuchar, "Compassion" 140). Even as it celebrates Southwell's courage, the play also interrogates the association of mourning and violence by stressing the burden of fidelity to a cause that *might* lead to one's own death. Even John Foxe articulated concerns about the culture of martyrdom, and John Donne argued in *Pseudo-Martyr* that the age of martyrs had passed (much like Calvin argued that the miraculous gifts of the Holy Spirit had ceased). The predominantly Protestant culture of Shakespeare's England often evinced an anti-martyr mindset, sometimes as a response to perceived excesses in Catholicism.[14] Richard Wilson argues that *Venus and Adonis* functions as an allegorical "critique of martyrdom" (301). Perhaps a strain of the same anti-martyrological sensibility can be discerned in *Hamlet* in the crushing demands the ghost puts on the tragic hero.

While Shakespeare's borrowing from Southwell subtly honors the martyr's memory, *Hamlet* nonetheless seems to acknowledge that the cost of memory for Catholics is high indeed, perhaps too high. That burden to remember would resonate powerfully for those sympathetic with the old faith. It would also cost some of them more than perhaps Shakespeare felt was reasonable. In any case, Shakespeare (unlike several other playwrights) was adept at keeping himself out of the crosshairs of the Protestant Elizabethan state. A cynical (realistic?) reading of the play could imagine Shakespeare not only as honoring Southwell but also critiquing him. Accordingly, the ghost is a liability either way, demon or not. Even if he is Hamlet's father, the burden the ghost places on his son is cruel. Likewise, Southwell's expectation that Catholics should be willing to die in an effort to restore England to Rome might be construed as an excessively costly agenda.

THE "SIFTING" OF PETER/HAMLET

If the reverberation of Southwell's martyrdom elicits mixed responses from the play, *Hamlet*'s Petrine imagery likewise deconstructs into both Catholic and Protestant hermeneutics. In the play, Peter is not only remembered as the rock of the church and the first Catholic pope, but also as a coward who lapses under satanic testing. Much like Peter denies Christ at the moment of his Lord's deepest need, Hamlet falters under the heavy burden of the ghost's command to remember it.

Shakespeare seizes on two Petrine moments, the cock crowing and the "sifting" of Peter, as ways of metaphorizing the spiritual and psychological distress which the ghost's injunction to revenge foists upon Hamlet. Like the Petrine allusion to the cock crow, the Petrine allusion to "sifting" suggests that the ghost is a demonic figure. Claudius articulates the concept of diabolical testing when he says, "we shall sift him" (2.2.58). The *OED* entry for "sift" (2. *fig.* a.), "To make trial of (a person)," notes

---

14. As exceptions to this general pattern of Protestant suspicion of martyrdom, some plays depicted Elizabeth as a martyr or saint figure, such as Thomas Heywood's *If You Know Not Me, You Know Nobody* and Thomas Dekker's *The Whore of Babylon*.

that in early quotations, this word takes its usage from Luke 22:31, especially in the 1535 Coverdale Bible, "Satan hath desyred after you, that he might siffte you euen as wheate." The context for this statement follows the very first celebration of the Eucharist, when Jesus warns Peter of imminent spiritual danger.

The 1560 Geneva Bible, an important source for *Hamlet*, uses the verb "wynowe" instead of sift: "Simon, Simon, beholde, Satan hathe desired you, to wynowe you, as wheat" (Luke 22:31). The basic idea of the Coverdale translation is maintained in the Geneva version, but the subtle difference is instructive. The *OED* defines "winnow" (v. 1. b. *fig.*) as follows: "To subject to a process likened to the winnowing of grain, in order to separate the various parts or elements, esp. the good from the bad; hence, to clear of worthless or inferior elements."

In his commentary on Luke 22:31, Calvin observes the violence involved in "sifting," both in pre-modern agrarian practice and in Jesus's metaphor for spiritual affliction:

> The metaphor of *sifting* is not in every respect applicable; for we have elsewhere seen that the Gospel is compared to a *winnowing-fan* or *sieve,* by which the *wheat* is purified from the *chaff* (Matthew 3:12;) but here it simply means to toss up and down, or to shake with violence, because the apostles were driven about with unusual severity by the death of Christ. This ought to be understood, because there is nothing in which Satan takes less delight than the *purification* of believers. Yet though it be for a different purpose that he shakes them, it is nevertheless true, that they are driven and tossed about in every direction, just as the *wheat* is shaken by the *winnowing-fan.*

As Calvin suggests, sanctification or purification is achieved by the gospel in separating the wheat from the chaff. Calvin also observes that Jesus employs the same violent metaphor of sifting to describe Satan's affliction of Jesus's disciples, especially Peter. Whereas testing either reveals a person's flaws or gives her an opportunity to transcend them, sanctification involves a transformative response to affliction. In puzzling over the connection between demonic affliction and divine sanctification, Calvin conveys a similar line of thinking to Jesuit spirituality, in which desolation, although the work of the devil, can help to produce in the human subject humility and dependence upon God. Calvin knows that the devil has no interest in sanctification, but Calvin seems to suggest that diabolical testing, with all of its violent "sifting," paradoxically can be used by God for the ultimate benefit of the saint. Peter would be a case in point—his recovery from spiritual failure helped equip him to lead the church after the ascension of Christ. The sifting or winnowing that occurs in Hamlet also seems to metaphorize a double-edged process of diabolical testing and spiritual refinement, itself perhaps a metaphor for the religious situation of the recusants, who were pitted between the conflicting agendas of Elizabeth and the pope.

The rhetoric of "sifting" can be found in a number of early modern religious texts. One such piece is the anonymous ballad entitled *Daniels siftyng in these our dayes: aptly applyed to the true Preachers of the Gospell* (1572). This ballad likens Puritan preachers of the gospel to the biblical character Daniel in his ability to use divine wisdom to "sift" (i.e. discern) the corrupt Babylonian culture in which he lived. The ballad champions Puritan preachers overcoming "popery" as analogous to the heroes of the Hebrew Bible in their concerted opposition to idolatry. In other early modern texts, "sifting" represents the practice of correct biblical hermeneutics, as in John Mayer's work, *A commentarie vpon the New Testament representing the diuers expositions therof, out of the workes of the most learned, both ancient fathers and moderne writers, and hereby sifting out the true sense of euery passage, for the benefit of all that desire to read with vnderstanding...*(1631). One of the most bizarre treatises on the theme of sifting is the anonymous *Satan Sifting: OR, THE OYL of JOY, For the SPIRIT of HEAVINESS* (1692). Although this strange piece comes almost a century after *Hamlet*, its preoccupation with being "sifted" by Satan arguably bears the imprint of the biblical treatment of Peter as well as the diabolism of Faustus. This work functions as a manual of *discretio spirituum*, warning that the devil may send wicked thoughts like "fiery Darts" into the mind, thoughts which are best repelled as unwelcome intrusions (156).

"SIFTING" IN MARLOWE'S *DOCTOR FAUSTUS*

The *OED* cites that Marlowe's *Doctor Faustus* uses "sift" in this sense of testing by Satan. In the A-text of *Doctor Faustus*, an old man rebukes Faustus for his necromancy, but Faustus decides to persist in his service to the demon Mephistopheles, even tormenting the virtuous old man with black magic. The old man pleads with Faustus to repent of his grave sins and avail himself of salvation:

> Break heart, drop blood, and mingle it with tears,
> Tears falling from repentant heaviness
> Of thy most vile and loathsome filthiness,
> The stench whereof corrupts the inward soul
> With such flagitious crimes of heinous sins,
> As no commiseration may expel
> But mercy, Faustus, of thy Saviour sweet,
> Whose blood alone must wash away thy guilt. (A Text, 13.39–46)

Faustus rejects the old man's rebuke, vengefully repaying him with a demonic affliction.

The old man is indeed afflicted by his demonic adversaries, but emerges victorious through his faith in Christ:

> Sathan begins to sift me with his pride.
> As in this furnace God shall try my faith,
> My faith, vile hell, shall triumph over thee.
> Ambitious fiends, see how the heavens smiles
> At your repulse and laughs your state to scorn!
> Hence, hell! For hence I fly unto my God. (13.113–118)

Marlowe's language of sifting is heavily invested in the idea of diabolical testing from Luke 22:31, and Marlowe's precedent seems to have influenced Shakespeare's usage in *Hamlet*.

The idea of "sifting" that reaches *Hamlet* through the Coverdale Bible and Marlowe suggests the dangerous possibility of being drawn into sin and perdition through the wiles of Satan. The fact that Claudius articulates his intention to "sift" Polonius in order discover the cause of Hamlet's madness[15]—"we shall sift him" (2.2.58)—gives the king a metaphorically diabolical resonance as the main villain of the play. In *Doctor Faustus*, the old man complains of beings sifted by Satan, but the overarching action of the play presents Faustus himself as the main object of demonic testing and temptation. A similar pattern occurs in *Hamlet*, for

---

15. *Contra* the Arden 3 editors in 2.2.58n, I think Claudius's intended object of sifting could refer to Hamlet as well as to Polonius, for Hamlet is the concerted focus of the king's fears. But even if the Arden 3 editors are correct in suggesting that the intended object of Claudius's sifting is Polonius, my point still stands, for Claudius is using Polonius as the first of a number of agents to test and, ultimately, destroy Hamlet. Even when Claudius's sifting is mediated through other characters, it is always ultimately directed towards Hamlet. Corambis (Polonius) states in Q1 that Hamlet is the object of his testing: "I'll try him every way" (7.203). This passage in Q1 confirms that both Claudius and Polonius are sifting Hamlet.

Claudius articulates his intention to "sift" Polonius (an old man), even though Hamlet is the ultimate target of Claudius's machinations.

However, while *Hamlet* retains some of the supernaturalism of Marlowe's *Doctor Faustus*, Shakespeare's play refrains from overtly staging demons. (The ghost is not overtly a demon, but possibly one disguised as "an angel of light.") Instead, the villain is one who has allowed himself to be enticed by the passion of adultery and the violence of murder. Claudius, while immoral, is a human criminal, not a literal demonic villain, as is the case with Mephistopheles. Of course, one of the salient questions for Hamlet is whether the ghost commanding him to kill Claudius is a demon tempting him to commit murder or a spirit from Purgatory justifying vigilante capital punishment. But the play does not offer an easy solution to the identity of the ghost, thus softening any spiritual inheritance in *Hamlet* from the starkly polarized supernatural world of *Doctor Faustus*, where angels and demons literally vie for the allegiance of the human subject, after the pattern of the medieval morality, mystery, and miracle plays. In *Hamlet*, a drama of Renaissance humanism, the enemy for both Claudius and Hamlet lies *within*, rather than in an obvious external demonic presence.

"SIFTING" AND SANCTIFICATION

In early modern theology, the idea of sifting presents something of a logical conundrum, for while Satan is the one who tempts and afflicts the righteous, God seems to foil the devil's efforts to destroy the saints by instead refining their character through such afflictions (as is the case with the old man in *Doctor Faustus*). So while Claudius's sifting of Hamlet (at times mediated through Polonius or Rosencrantz and Guildenstern) maps onto the biblical allusion of Satan sifting Peter's faith, suggesting that Claudius is the enemy and Hamlet is the nascent saint, the testing of Hamlet by Claudius produces very mixed results, as far as Hamlet's ethical character is concerned.[16] And while Hamlet is certainly the most famous of Shakespeare's tragic heroes, somewhat like Saint Peter was elevated among the apostles as the first pope (in the Catholic imagination),

---

16. The language in the play also suggests that Hamlet is testing Ophelia, at least in the mind of Polonius. Polonius warns Ophelia of Hamlet's sexual temptations by using the vocabulary of sifting: "Pooh, you speak like a green girl/ Unsifted in such perilous circumstance" (1.3.100–101). The irony is that while Hamlet is being tested, he is also testing Ophelia.

neither character's track record suggests anything nearly as auspicious as the critical or religious traditions would respectively claim for them. Peter's road to the papacy involves a three-fold denial of Christ *in extremis*, and Hamlet's path to revenge (filial piety?) litters the stage with the lives of eight people, including his own.

"SIFTING" AND *DISCRETIO SPIRITUUM*

Hamlet's delay in obeying the ghost's injunction to kill Claudius, rather than serving as an index of Hamlet's cowardice, is an indication that Hamlet is appropriately testing the spirits though a traditional practice of *discretio spirituum*, a protocol to which Stephen Greenblatt refers (210). In the Petrine narrative, Satan tries to sift Peter, but Peter gains discernment after his personal failure. So Hamlet, at first subjected to testing (sifting) by the ghost, later interrogates the ghost by subjecting its message to the sifting revelations of the theater.

The fact that the ghost reappears after *The Mousetrap* exposes Claudius's guilt (at least in the perception of Hamlet and Horatio) suggests that the ghost disapproves of Hamlet's efforts to test its spiritual source. The ghost wants Hamlet to act impetuously and rashly, not with careful deliberation and examination of motive. The agonizingly introspective Hamlet that we have come to know and love (and sometimes hate) is not the Hamlet mandated by the ghost. The ghost wants swift, precipitous action; Hamlet wants to consider his options carefully. The ghost wants a Hamlet like the impetuous Peter of the gospels; the play often gives us a Hamlet more like Southwell's self-absorbed and self-recriminating Peter.

As a trope, *The Mousetrap* has important soteriological implications. Alison Shell explains the Augustinian overtones of Hamlet's dramatic ruse to expose the king's guilt:

> The notion of mousetraps catching sinners would have been a natural metaphor for everyday life to yield, but it also carried reminiscences of St Augustine's aphorism *Muscipula diaboli, crux Domini* (The devil's mousetrap, the cross of the Lord); this poses the paradox that the cross, epitomizing human sin, is a mousetrap set for Christ by the devil, but that Christ's sacrifice has the effect of trapping the devil. (151)

Shell further argues that Hamlet "himself has been caught in the mousetrap of the trope" (152). The trope thus works ironically, for Hamlet, in trying to expose Claudius's guilt, incites the king's wrath, ultimately resulting in Hamlet's own death. On a literal level, then, Shell is correct in suggesting that Hamlet is caught in his own mousetrap.

However, the soteriological resonances of the Augustinian metaphor also work to extricate the ghost's soteriology from its message of revenge. After staging *The Mousetrap*, Hamlet's litmus test for the ghost, Hamlet feels he is justified in believing the ghost. The irony is that Hamlet's failure to spiritually discern the outcome of *The Mousetrap* ends up destroying him. While the play-within-the play exposes Claudius's guilt, it also has the effect of entrenching Hamlet in his determination to exact revenge, which is exactly what the ghost wanted. Unfortunately, Hamlet's choice to avenge his father's death is the very demonically motivated action that ends up destroying Hamlet and a host of others. The fact that Hamlet is misled into murder by *The Mousetrap* (starting with Polonius) tellingly suggests a failure of spiritual discernment. Hamlet is unable to extricate the salutary effect of the play in exposing Claudius's guilt from Hamlet's own violent response to the revelation of Claudius as murderer. Hamlet's confused reaction to the revelations of the theater recalls the traditional warning among the masters of *discretio spirituum* that the most dangerous lies are half-truths. Hamlet now not only believes the true message spoken by the ghost that Claudius is the murderer, but also the lie implied by the ghost that it is God's will for Hamlet to avenge his father's murder.

THE DIABOLICAL CAST OF REVENGE

Whereas Hamlet thinks he is sifting the ghost, the ghost is also sifting Hamlet. The result of Hamlet's faith in the ghost—now certified by *The Mousetrap*—is sheer moral ugliness in Hamlet. The humanist prince is now in danger of becoming a conventional Renaissance avenger like Hieronimo. Worse yet, Hamlet's determination to fulfill the ghost's command of revenge gives Hamlet an almost diabolical cast:

> 'Tis now the very witching time of night
> When churchyards yawn and hell itself breaks out
> Contagion to this world. Now could I drink hot blood
> And do such business as the bitter day
> Would quake to look on. (3.2.378–382)

Hamlet's delight that "'Tis now the very witching time of night" when "hell itself breaks out / Contagion to this world" directly opposes Marcellus's idea that the season "Wherein our Saviour's birth is celebrated" is so blessed that "no spirit dare stir abroad, /. . .So hallowed and so gracious is that time" (1.1.158–163). Margreta de Grazia is no doubt correct in suggesting that Hamlet at his most cruel recalls the stage devils that populated medieval drama (193). The irony is that although Hamlet thinks he has successfully discerned the spirit of the ghost as truthful, Hamlet's resulting malice suggests that the spirit has actually deceived (oppressed?) Hamlet. Hamlet's reference to drinking blood suggests a demonic parody of the Mass, and Hamlet's monstrous violence here reflects poorly on the spirit which occasioned it, to say the least.

Hamlet's response to Claudius at prayer further suggests that the ghost is bringing out the worst in Hamlet, "sifting" him in the most destructive sense of the term. When Hamlet has the opportunity to kill the praying Claudius, Hamlet surprisingly refrains from exacting revenge. However, his reason for delaying Claudius's death is to punish him not only temporally, but also eternally:

> Up sword, and know thou a more horrid hent
> When he is drunk, asleep or in his rage,
> Or in th'incestuous pleasure of his bed,
> At game a-swearing, or about some act
> That has no relish of salvation in't.
> Then trip him that his heels may kick at heaven
> And that his soul may be as damned and black
> As hell whereto it goes. (3.3.88–95)

Hamlet hopes to avenge his father's murder by exceeding the harm done to his father, and Hamlet imagines he can do so by killing Claudius in a state of mortal sin, thus sending him to eternal torment in hell. Here a fitting response to Hamlet might be Jesus's rebuke of Peter, "Get thee behind me, Satan" (Matthew 16:23). (We are not accustomed to diabolical inspiration coming from either Peter or Hamlet, but here we have it in both.) Samuel Johnson was justifiably appalled by the malice of the soliloquy Hamlet delivers while watching Claudius at prayer: "This speech, in which Hamlet, represented as a virtuous character, is not content with taking blood for blood, but contrives damnation for the man that he would punish, is too horrible to be read or uttered" (qtd. in Gottschalk 155).

Hamlet thinks he can test the ghost, but instead the ghost seems to be "sifting" Hamlet, transforming him into an agent of destruction. A further dramatic irony is that while the villain Claudius has been dallying with a prayer of penitence to God, the tragic hero responds with an impulse to damn Claudius. Hamlet as hero and the ghost as alleged victim now appear in a more sinister light than the perpetrator of the actual murder. In following the ghost's anti-soteriology of revenge to its logical conclusion, Hamlet becomes uncomfortably like a stage devil. The patently negative impact of Hamlet's faith in the ghost clinches the play's indictment of revenge.

OBJECTIONS TO THE GHOST-AS-DEMON THEORY

Any reader well versed in the English revenge drama tradition will realize that it is conventional to include a ghost that calls for revenge. Thomas Kyd's *The Spanish Tragedy*, an important source play for *Hamlet*, is a case in point. One could argue that Hamlet is no more ethically unhinged than Hieronimo. Moreover, one could argue that the ghost in *Hamlet* is merely continuing the tradition of the vengeful ghost from *The Spanish Tragedy*, which Kyd, in turn, borrowed from Senecan tragedy. In other words, a skeptic of my argument might ask if there is anything especially demonic about the ghost in *Hamlet*. Why is the discernment of spirits so particularly important in interpreting the ghost in *Hamlet*?

The demonology in *Hamlet* is distinct from that of its Senecan-inspired forebearers, *The Spanish Tragedy* and Shakespeare's *Titus Andronicus*. In *Hamlet*, demonology is understood more in terms of early modern theology than classical drama, registering the ghost as a formidably deceptive evil spirit. I will also discuss Cyril Tourneur's *The Atheist's Tragedy* as a case study of what a Christian ghost might actually be like, as opposed to the duplicitous and vengeful spirit in *Hamlet*. These four plays, taken together, reveal a spectrum of perspectives on the demonic. *Hamlet*'s ghost emerges as the most hermeneutically resistant of all these revenge figures, one which contemporary audiences might unmask only by careful deliberation, i.e., by the discernment of spirits. If, after considering these dramatically based counter-arguments, a reader still does not find my demonological interpretation of the ghost convincing, I hope she will at least concede that *Hamlet* asks the audience to take seriously the *possibility* that the ghost may be a demon.

THE SPANISH TRAGEDY AND THE DEMON OF REVENGE

Two important source plays for *Hamlet*, Thomas Kyd's *The Spanish Tragedy* and Shakespeare's own *Titus Andronicus*, convey the demonic nature of revenge, and *Hamlet* bears this imprint, although with some important alterations. Kyd's *The Spanish Tragedy* associates revenge with a ghost and with hell, further suggesting that ghost in *Hamlet* may also be cast as a demon. In Kyd's play, Revenge is personified as a supernatural being who accompanies the Ghost of Don Andrea on his mission to achieve vengeance on his murderers. Together, Revenge and the Ghost form the chorus of the play. Kyd's underworld is classical, not Christian, and the Ghost of Andrea travels from the Elysian fields to earth through the gate of horn. The Revenge figure in Kyd's play is some kind of demon or fury, as his violent rhetoric suggests:

> I'll turn their friendship into fell despite,
> Their love to mortal hate, their day to night,
> Their hope into despair, their peace to war,
> Their joys to pain, their bliss to misery. (1.5.6–9)

Revenge's very candor indicates the destruction he is about to unleash in the play. Like the ghost in *Hamlet*, Revenge portrays itself as using violence to serve justice.

By association, Kyd's Revenge figure is likened to a demon through his influence on Hieronimo, whose attempt to avenge the murder of his son Horatio is driving Hieronimo mad:

> The ugly fiends do sally forth of hell,
> And frame my steps to unfrequented paths,
> And fear my heart with fierce-inflamed thoughts. (3.2.16–18)

Hieronimo, like Hamlet, is considered mad by those who observe him, but like Hamlet, he does not consider himself mad. Hieronimo holds a dagger and noose, the stock signs of the suicide, suggesting that like Hamlet, he is suicidal, but ultimately prefers the option of revenge.

In addition to associating revenge with hell, Kyd's play links revenge to a supernatural agent and love, a pattern which is reflected in *Hamlet*. The Ghost of Don Andrea gives legitimacy to his revenge quest by claiming the motivation of love:

> Awake, Revenge, if love, as love hath had,

Have yet the power or prevalence in hell! (3.15.12–13)

Similarly, the ghost in *Hamlet* appeals to Hamlet's love for his father as the basis of revenge:

> If thou didst ever thy dear father love—
> ...—Revenge his foul and most unnatural murder! (1.5.23,25)

Whereas the Ghost of Don Andrea is accompanied by a supernatural being of Revenge from the classical hell, Shakespeare combines the demonic avenger and the human victim in the person of the one ghost.

In keeping with the medieval and early modern Christian worldviews of Shakespeare's play, the ghost is cast in a new light as either a wronged victim from Purgatory or a deceiving spirit from hell. The audience is thus forced to determine the origin of the ghost through its own process of *discretio spirituum*. In Kyd's play, Revenge is more obviously a demon or fury bent on destruction. The metatheatricality of Kyd's *The Spanish Tragedy* also influences Hamlet, but whereas Kyd's play-within-the play becomes the machinery for executing revenge, *The Mousetrap* is Hamlet's best attempt at discerning both the ghost and Claudius. In Kyd, the play is the site of the retaliatory murders, whereas in *Hamlet*, the play exposes Claudius' guilt.

At the end of *The Spanish Tragedy*, Revenge is again identified as a demon from classical hell.

> GHOST: ...Against the rest how shall my hate be shown?
> REVENGE: This hand shall hale them down to deepest hell
>   Where none but Furies, bugs and tortures dwell. (4.5.26–28)

Kyd's play makes clear that revenge is hellish in origin and execution, even if *The Spanish Tragedy* imagines hell in largely classical terms. *The Spanish Tragedy* also creates an entertaining spectacle of revenge—replete with Hieronimo biting out his tongue! The many bodies that litter the stage at the end of *Hamlet* similarly undermine the validity of the ghost's message of revenge, implying that Hamlet was unwise to heedlessly follow the ghost's dictates. However, the mood at the end of *Hamlet* is more soberingly cathartic than the bloodbath which consummates *The Spanish Tragedy*.

THOMAS KYD'S BIBLICAL IRONY AND REVENGE

The ironizing of revenge in Kyd's play does not come from its Senecan spirituality, but rather from a subtle injection of biblical irony. Here is where Kyd seems to have had an important impact on *Hamlet*, which also uses biblical imagery (the Petrine narratives) to undermine revenge. Like *Hamlet*, *The Spanish Tragedy* associates revenge with religious rhetoric, and like *Hamlet*, Kyd's play undermines such an attempt to justify violence with religion. Meditating on vengeance, Hieronimo appears with a book in hand, which Clara Calvo and Jesús Tronch believe to be a copy of Seneca's plays (3.13.0 SDn). Hieronimo reads, "*Vindicta mihi*," which is Latin for "Vengeance is mine" (3.13.1n). The source for Hieronimo's statement is Romans 12:19 in the Vulgate:

> non vosmet ipsos defendentes carissimi
> sed date locum irae
> scriptum est enim
> mihi vindictam ego retribuam dicit Dominus

While the Pauline and Mosaic texts (Paul is citing Deuteronomy 32:35) proscribe revenge for humans, claiming that only God is justified in avenging, Hieronimo self-deceptively reasons that he is doing God's work in exacting revenge:

> Ay, heaven will be revenged of every ill,
> Nor will they suffer murder unrepaid.
> Then stay, Hieronimo, attend their will,
> For mortal men may not appoint their time. (3.13.2–5)

Kyd thus injects an element of biblical irony into his discourse of revenge by showing that Hieronimo thinks he is acting in accord with God's will, but that his chosen path of revenge is actually scripturally proscribed by both the Hebrew Bible and the New Testament.

Kyd sets a precedent for *Hamlet* in ironizing Hieronimo's biblical hermeneutic which legitimizes revenge with religious rhetoric. The ghost urges Hamlet to avenge his father's death as an act of love and filial duty, enjoining Hamlet to murder with sacramental rhetoric.[17] However, the

---

17. One of the strategies the ghost uses to convince Hamlet to attempt Claudius's murder is to aggravate Hamlet's sense of justice by emphasizing that the old Hamlet died without having the last rites administered to him. The ghost complains that he was "Cut off even in the blossoms of my sin, / Unhouseled, disappointed, unaneled, / No reckoning made but sent to my account / With all my imperfections on my head" (1.5.76–79). The ghost's rhetoric is distinctly sacramental in that it complains of having

ghost's devout mention of Purgatory and the sacraments are part of its attempt to deceive Hamlet into exacting revenge, an action clearly proscribed by Jewish and Christian scriptures. All of the recent attempts to recover the Catholic past of England in the ghost's sacramental rhetoric have seemingly missed the more obvious irony that the play conveys: revenge, while appealing, is clearly forbidden by the very faith that the ghost marshals in its defense. Using similar irony as Kyd, Shakespeare thus undermines the ghost's religious credentials by showing both its deceptiveness and Hamlet's religious hypocrisy in believing it.

What makes the discernment of spirits so particularly relevant to the ghost in *Hamlet* is that it claims to be a spirit from Purgatory and that it invokes the sacraments. There is nothing nearly so complicated about Kyd's Revenge figure. A ghost claiming to be from Purgatory would elicit potentially divisive responses from a contemporary audience which contained both Protestants who disbelieved in Purgatory and Catholics who adhered to it. Moreover, the ghost's association of Christian rhetoric with violence calls for more careful scrutiny than the baldly vengeful ghosts and remorseless avengers that Kyd inherited from Seneca. Part of what makes *Hamlet*'s critique of violence so powerful is its appropriation of biblical imagery to undermine the ghost's claims to religious authority. While *The Spanish Tragedy* seems (on the whole) to revel in the violence inspired by the classical demon Revenge, *Hamlet* takes pains to unmask the demonic identity of the ghost which advocates revenge. Indeed, a classical *daimon* is a less formidable being than a deceptive evil spirit, as understood by early modern biblical spirituality. By identifying the ghost as demon in Christian, rather than classical terms, *Hamlet* is able to make a more convincing and sustained indictment of violence than *The Spanish Tragedy*. Kyd's minor experimentation with biblical irony becomes an important strategy in *Hamlet*, where the Petrine narratives function as a deep source to critique the very revenge genre itself. As a result, the tragic *denouement* of *Hamlet* produces a more sobering response than the finale of *The Spanish Tragedy*.

---

been denied the opportunity to confess his sin to a priest or to God, to partake of the Mass, and to receive extreme unction (anointing with oil). The ghost implies that because he was not given the opportunity for salvation due to being murdered that Claudius deserves to be murdered and damned. The ghost claims to be imprisoned in Purgatory, but the implication is that it wants Claudius to go to hell.

THE CHRISTIAN HELL OF *TITUS ANDRONICUS*

In *Titus Andronicus*, Shakespeare tried his hand at a Senecan revenge play in the genre of *The Spanish Tragedy*. *Titus Andronicus*, like *The Spanish Tragedy*, portrays revenge as the discourse of hell, further suggesting that the vengeful ghost in *Hamlet* belongs to an infernal tradition. While *Titus* is set in imperial Rome, its vision of hell and the demonic is ultimately more Christian than classical, thus anticipating the "christening" of the revenge play that Shakespeare would undertake in *Hamlet*. And while there is a reference to the classical underworld early on in *Titus* (1.1.88), and while classical allusions abound in the play, the anachronistic topical references to early modern religion are more plentiful in *Titus* than in *The Spanish Tragedy*. For example, the villainous Aaron the Moor employs anti-Catholic rhetoric:

> Yet, for I know thou art religious,
> And hast a thing within thee called conscience,
> With twenty popish tricks and ceremonies.... (5.1.74–76)

Catharine Belsey aptly comments that "in one unexpected lapse Roman suddenly means Roman Catholic" (129).

Whereas it is the play-within-the-play that exposes the perpetrator of Old Hamlet's murder, in *Titus Andronicus* it is Ovid's *Metamorphoses* that gives Lavinia the opportunity to attest to the rape she suffered. The play-within-the play in *Titus* instead serves as an opportunity for Titus to trick Tamora and her sons into believing that their costumes have deceived Titus, when, in fact, he is plotting his revenge against them. In an obvious echo of Kyd, Tamora disguises herself as Revenge, while Chiron plays the part of Rape, and Demetrius, of Murder. In Tamora's rhetoric, Revenge is figured as a supernatural being from hell:

> I am Revenge, sent from th'infernal kingdom
> To ease the gnawing vulture of thy mind
> By working wreakful vengeance on thy foes. (5.2.30–32)

This rhetoric unites Tamora the villain and Titus the putative hero by showing that their common motivation is revenge. This mutual desire for revenge contributes to Titus' ethical ambivalence. The moral ambiguity of the heroic avenger, in turn, becomes a major feature of *Hamlet*.

I suspect that the villainous Tamora, who employs her sugary sexuality to work violence owes something to the notorious biblical character, Jezebel. But the supreme villain of the play is the comic psychopath, Aaron the Moor, who associates himself with devils, albeit in a skeptical vein:

> If there be devils, would I were a devil,
> To live and burn in everlasting fire.
> So I might have your company in hell,
> But to torment you with my bitter tongue. (5.1.147–150)

Here we have Aaron imagining hell at its worst, not a classical hell, but a Christian hell, in which Satan (deriving from the Hebrew word for *accuser*) tempts human beings into error and then mocks them for their weakness, all in an experience of eternal agony.

The discourse of hell and demons in *Titus Andronicus* remains on the level of imagery, rather than materializing in character and setting. In *Hamlet*, however, a vengeful spirit—arguably a demon—appears right on stage, demanding the audience's fullest attention and powers of discernment. The metaphorical demons of *Titus Andronicus* become a more puzzling reality in *Hamlet*. The demonic imagery in *Titus* contributes to its gruesomeness, but the play's ironizing of revenge is perhaps more dramatic than theological. In contrast, the demonology of *Hamlet* is filtered through Petrine biblical imagery, allowing the play to transcend the violence to which it has been inured.

The classical hell of *The Spanish Tragedy* and the imagined Christian hell of *Titus Andronicus* set a precedent for *Hamlet*. The presupposition that viewers of *Hamlet* would have from previous encounters with revenge drama would be that revenge is demonic, even if irrepressibly entertaining. *Hamlet* engages the demonic with greater gravity as a formidable entity which must be subjected to a rigorous regime of spiritual discernment. By deconstructing the demonic with biblical imagery, *Hamlet* emphatically registers violence as immoral.

THE ATHEIST'S TRAGEDY: AN AFTERLIFE OF THE GHOST OF *HAMLET*

If some readers may be inclined to persist in regarding the ghost as an emissary from Greenblatt's Purgatory rather than from hell, perhaps a counter-example of a distinctly Christian ghost from another contemporary playwright might help to convince skeptics of my demonological reading. Cyril Tourneur's *The Atheist's Tragedy* (published in 1611) is arguably an afterlife of *Hamlet* that recasts the ghost in Christian terms as an outspoken counselor against revenge. But even if Tourneur is speaking to the English revenge drama tradition as a whole and not to *Hamlet* in particular, its critique of revenge is nonetheless highly relevant for *Hamlet*. From this perspective, it is as if Tourneur is telling Hamlet what a "Christian" ghost would actually advise—patience—unlike the avenging spirit in the likeness of old Hamlet who demands precipitous revenge. The subtitle of Tourneur's play, *The Honest Man's Revenge*, vindicates Charlemont's decision not to avenge the murder of his father by his uncle, "Now I see / That *patience is the honest man's revenge*" (5.2.277–278). By recasting *Hamlet*'s ghost in such predictable Christian terms, Tourneur's play becomes an important critical commentary on *Hamlet* as a revenge play. In effect, Tourneur's play retroactively implies that the ghost in *Hamlet*, with its preoccupation with revenge, is not a spirit sent by God from Purgatory, but rather a demon hellbent on murder.

The ghosts in both *Hamlet* and *The Atheist's Tragedy* reveal that the departed father's death was a murder, but the former commands violence and the latter, forbearance. The ghost of the murdered Montferrers appears to his son Charlemont in a dream to reveal that he has been killed, but strongly cautions against revenge:

> Attend with patience the success of things,
> But leave revenge unto the King of kings. (2.6.22–23)

The ghost of Montferrers later appears again to Charlemont at the very moment Charlemont decides to kill the murderer D'Amville and his son Sebastian in vengeance. At this crisis point in the plot, the ghost of Montferrers urges Charlemont to desist from his violence against the fallen Sebastian, much like the angel of the Lord stops Abraham from slaying Isaac at the last possible moment. The ghost's message is again a paraphrase of Romans 12:19:

> Let him revenge my murder and thy wrongs
> To whom the justice of revenge belongs. (3.2.33–34)

Charlemont's response reveals his internal conflict between the pacific demands of his faith and his visceral desire for revenge:

> You torture me between the passion of
> My blood and the religion of my soul. (3.2.35–36)

Whereas the ghost in *Hamlet* appeals simultaneously to both Hamlet's religion and his passion for revenge, the ghost in *The Atheist's Tragedy* extricates the rhetoric of faith from violence. Tourneur's play thus suggests that the ghost in *Hamlet* unethically syncretizes violence and religion. In recasting the ghost of the murder victim as an advocate for peace, Tourneur effectively reveals the ghost of *Hamlet* to be inconsistent with basic Christian principles, despite its religious rhetoric. Whereas the ghost of Montferrers appears a second time to prevent Charlemont's intended vengeance, the final visitation of the ghost to Hamlet is intended to spur his dull revenge. The ghost in *Hamlet* inflames Hamlet's passion for revenge in the name of religion. Tourneur's play decidedly objects to such a conflation of religious zeal and violence.

The multiplicity of skeptical and believing perspectives on the phenomenon of Montferrers's ghost also picks up the theme of the discernment of spirits from *Hamlet*. The various perspectives on the ghost in Tourneur's play—skeptical, benign, and demonic—reflect the spectrum of beliefs about spirits in early modern popular religious culture. But whereas Montferrers's ghost is revealed to be a good spirit, Tourneur's play suggests by diametric contrast the possibility that the ghost of *Hamlet* is a demon. Charlemont initially doubts the veracity of his dream in which the ghost of Montferrers first appears to him, thinking that his imagination may have been disrupted by the effects of what today would be called Post Traumatic Stress Disorder, but then the ghost appears to both him and a fellow soldier, who shoots it with his musket, the ghost remaining unharmed. Charlemont takes the Musketeer's experience in failing to kill the ghost with a gun as corroboration of the ghost's reality and of the veracity of its message. Here the play is parodying Hamlet's epistemic uncertainty over the nature of the ghost who appears to him in the likeness of his father.

When Charlemont returns from war to find that his fiancée has been coercively married to D'Amville's impotent son Rousard, Charlemont's presence is unwelcome to D'Amville, who had staged Charlemont's death to facilitate said marriage. The stage direction here reveals the idea of skepticism regarding ghosts and demons: "*Enter* CHARLEMONT; D'AMVILLE *counterfeits to take him for a ghost*" (3.2.17 s.d.). As an atheist, D'Amville believes neither in God nor the devil, but here he pretends to believe in the supernatural reality of the specter of Charlemont in order to cover his own misdeeds. Langbeau Snuffe, who postures as a Puritan chaplain but is actually a candle-maker (and client of prostitutes), becomes frightened by the sight of the supposedly dead Charlemont, claiming that the "ghost" must actually be a demon. While it is likely that

Snuffe is merely pretending to believe that Charlemont is a demon, Snuffe nonetheless struggles to make sense of the re-appearance of Charlemont:

> No, 'tis profane. Spirits are invisible. 'Tis the fiend i' the likeness of Charlemont. I will have no conversation with Satan. (3.2.22–24)

Charlemont himself pretends to be a spirit, but the ensuing fight between him and Sebastian reveals Charlemont to be a man of flesh and blood.

Later, Snuffe disguises himself as the ghost of Montferrers while attempting an assignation with Soquette. Charlemont then assumes the same disguise and is thus able to prevent D'Amville from raping Charlemont's fiancée (now D'Amville's daughter-in-law) Castabella. When D'Amville complains to Snuffe about a ghost lurking in the graveyard, Snuffe responds with classic skepticism, despite his earlier stated fear of demons: "Tush, tush, their walking spirits are mere imaginary fables. There's no such thing in *rerum natura*" (4.3.275–276).

But all of this parodic, skeptical discourse about ghosts, spirits, and demons does not seem to have the final word in Tourneur's play. The ghost of Montferrers appears in a dream to pronounce judgment on D'Amville. While D'Amville is skeptical about the dream, things turn out as predicted by the ghost, with D'Amville suffering the most astounding form of divine retribution imaginable when he brains himself with the very axe with which he intended to decapitate Charlemont. The many comic recastings of the ghost lore of *Hamlet* in *The Atheist's Tragedy* culminate in a moralistic lesson that vengeance belongs to God, not humans.

The Atheist's Tragedy is an unusual play in a number of respects, even in its sustained parody of *Hamlet*. As a Protestant play which atypically affirms the goodness of a ghost, as a revenge play which refutes revenge, and as a purported tragedy which emerges as a "divine" comedy, Tourneur's play makes some important contributions to *Hamlet*'s handling of revenge. Whereas the ghost in *Hamlet* has been variously identified as the departed spirit of Hamlet's father, a demon, or the projection of Hamlet's imagination, the ghost in Tourneur's play is cast as the mouthpiece for orthodox piety. In doing so, Tourneur's play accentuates the critique of revenge already implicit in *Hamlet* by having the ghost renounce violence, as it were. If *Hamlet* showcases the course of religiously countenanced violence by taking the ghost's rhetoric to its disastrous conclusion, Tourneur's play, despite its moralistic formulae, tellingly comments on the inherent incompatibility between violence and religion. The critique of violence that Shakespeare only implies, Tourneur makes brutally clear.

CHANGING KEYS: FROM REVENGE TO FORGIVENESS

But one does not need to believe in demons or even ghosts to observe that *Hamlet* deconstructs the violence unleashed in the play. Perhaps it does not even require consummate spiritual discernment to know that violence is a counter-productive way of dealing with one's putative enemies. Apparently, that simple ethical truth was lost on virtually entire generations of early modern Christians who sometimes literally killed each other over their divergent perspectives on such lovely ideas as salvation. Whereas the central figure of Christianity turned the other cheek to the very point of torture and death, his followers in the sixteenth and seventeenth centuries devised cruel and unusual punishments for those who understood him differently. That is the dark historical reaction to the Reformation, a darkness that enshrouded many Catholics and Protestants alike. The early modern period failed to grasp spiritual discernment any better than Hamlet did. That is precisely the point of Shakespeare's use of Petrine imagery. Shakespeare uses his fluency with the biblical text to refute the contemporary practice of countenancing violence with religious rhetoric.

However, the relationship between religion and violence in the early modern period (as in ours) is perhaps more complex than the popular imagination allows. William Cavanaugh opposes what he regards as an unhelpful distinction between religious violence and secular violence, a distinction which he sees as legitimizing violence by the state against the religious other (13). Cavanaugh even challenges the idea that religion was the main issue motivating early modern violence. According to his historiography, the rise of the nation state in early modern Europe was a *cause* of the wars, not their solution (11–12). In other words, religion may not be the primary factor in the so-called religious wars of the sixteenth- and seventeenth centuries. Cavanaugh acknowledges that the church was complicit in much of the violence, but he insists that the church did so because it capitulated to nationalist agendas (11–12). Cavanaugh challenges the notion that the modern nation state "saved Europe from the violence of religion" (12). Even if (as Cavanaugh suggests) secular nationalism is as inherently violent as religion, there is no escaping the fact that religious identity was a focal point for violence in the early modern period. The ghost's use of religious language to justify revenge and regicide conveys just how inextricable religion and politics were in the period. Hamlet's susceptibility to such religious rhetoric helps to identify him as a man of his times.

There is a change of key in the play when Hamlet turns from deliberating on revenge to fatalistically acquiescing to his own mortality: "There is special providence in the fall of a sparrow" (5.2.197–198 cf. Matthew 10:29). But the change comes too late, for the leaven of revenge has by now worked itself into the main characters' destinies. Claudius schemes that Laertes, "with a little shuffling" may "choose / A sword unbated" to kill Hamlet (4.7.135–136). All this from the same usurper who realized during prayer that no "shuffling" could deceive the Almighty (3.3.61). The violence that Hamlet ambivalently pursues throughout the play tragically has the final word: "The potent poison quite o'ercrows my spirit" (5.2.337). Whereas a cock crow had silenced the ghost in the first scene of the play, elucidating the spirit's dark origin, the "crow" at the end of the play is not that of a bird invoking the light, but of a violent victor of a cockfight surveying the bloody carnage. *Hamlet* is an elegy for the period's misguided religious violence.

However faintly, the play also changes keys from revenge to forgiveness. Much like the Johannine text is framed by Jesus's calling and reinstatement of Peter—"Follow me" (John 1:39–43 cf. John 21:19–22), *Hamlet* begins with a summons to follow the ghost—"I'll follow thee" (1.4.86)—and ends with Hamlet forgiving the dying Laertes for killing him: "Heaven make thee free of it. I follow thee" (5.2.316). The same framing statement that Hamlet makes to the ghost at the beginning of the play and to Laertes at the end of the play ("I follow thee"), has the effect of converting the ghost's Senecan (demonic?) mandate of vengeance into the Christian praxis of forgiveness. Hamlet and Laertes ultimately forgive each other, transposing the play from a revenge drama to a sublime work of spiritual transcendence.

4

Vicarious Atonement and the Failure of Ethics in *Measure for Measure*

GRAHAM HOLDERNESS OBSERVES THAT "*Measure for Measure* (1603) is Shakespeare's most explicitly religious play" (113) and N. W. Bawcutt states the obvious: "*Measure for Measure* is inescapably about sexuality" (31). But what exactly do religion and sexuality have in common in this play? I would submit that both are reliant on the principle of substitution— be it the infamous bed trick or the vicarious atonement of Christ. In fact, substitution theory is pervasive in *Measure for Measure*. Bawcutt observes that "Shakespeare seized on the concept of substitution, and made it ramify throughout the play. In its literal form, one person takes the place of another. In its more metaphorical form the characters are urged to imagine themselves in someone else's place, in order to achieve a more sympathetic understanding of his behaviour" (23). While (as Bawcutt observes) empathy for neighbor is sometimes the fruit of the widespread substitution in the play, in other cases the enforcement of substitution creates serious ethical problems. The bed trick in which Mariana pretends to be Isabella is a case in point, for both women are dishonored in this scheme. Another instance of unethical substitution is the Duke's suggestion that Barnardine be executed so that his decapitated head could be used as a proxy for Claudio's (in order to satisfy the demands of Angelo). *Contra* Bawcutt, the play parodies ideas of substitution as often as it upholds them. In particular, the play interrogates the substitutionary logic of the atonement of Christ, as articulated by Isabella. Ultimately, *Measure for Measure* suggests that it is a grave category error to force the principle of substitution found in Calvin's theory of Christ's forensic, vicarious atonement onto the jurisdictions of sexuality and law. Shakespeare highlights the impasse between soteriology and ethics as a cautionary picture of what happens when religion overreaches its bounds by impinging on secular authority.[1]

While the bed-trick is a convention of stage comedy, Shakespeare links it to questions of theology—vicarious atonement—in ways that are far from typical. Isabella's citation of the vicarious atonement of Christ effectively grounds the play's fixation with substitution in theology:

> Why, all the souls that were were forfeit once,
> And He that might the vantage best have took
> Found out the remedy. (2.2.74–76)[2]

---

1. Debora Shuger observes that in *Measure for Measure* penitential justice is the purview of the temporal ruler (the Duke), not the church (103). Shuger also argues that the play is not ultimately concerned with romantic love, but with a Christian vision of social justice (98). She suggests that there are two competing Christian visions of social justice, one based on law and another based on penance. Shuger affirms the play's celebration of social justice in terms of penance rather than law (137). I adopt Shuger's distinction between temporal and ecclesiastical domains of social justice, but I instead argue that the attempt to impose a Christian ethic through the temporal ruler is fraught with perils, as the Duke's unsatisfying handling of justice demonstrates. *Contra* Shuger, I do not think the play endorses a political vision based on penance. If anything, the play suggests that penitence is better handled by the church than by the temporal government.

Sarah Beckwith argues that Luther's idea of the two swords or the two kingdoms, spiritual and secular, lies behind the handling of sin in *Measure for Measure* (*Grammar* 65–68). Beckwith argues that Luther's idea that there should be a split between the sacred and secular realms effectively took power away from the church and gave it to the nation state. Moreover, Beckwith suggests that the play's problematic violation of human consent derives from the license Luther gave to the secular ruler to govern with force (66). Beckwith further notes that the reformed English church replaced the private arena of auricular confession to a priest with public acts of shaming by ecclesiastical courts, a pattern she sees as being followed in the play (68–69). While I am greatly indebted to Beckwith for giving me the Lutheran framework of the two swords as a hermeneutical approach to the play's political vision, I do not think Luther's idea is responsible for coercion or public shaming in the play. Rather, I see the secular power as overreaching its authority by imposing religious standards on its citizens. In my reading, the problem is with the Duke playing God, not with a distinction between religious and secular authority. Luther's idea of the two swords could be seen positively as offering a way forward by limiting the hegemonic powers of both church and state by holding them in balance. If the church were the domain of soteriology and the state were the domain of public law and order, the Duke would be prevented from enacting his flagrant spiritual abuse and coercive intrusions into private affairs. Luther's idea would prevent the Duke from exercising his godlike powers so unadvisedly.

2. I am using the Oxford Shakespeare edition of *Measure for Measure*, edited by N. W.

The idea that Christ died as a substitute for ethically fallen humanity forms the bedrock of Christian atonement theory. And yet, this theology that Isabella cherishes so devoutly becomes comically (cynically?) parodied in the unethical practices of the substitutionary bed trick and the proxy decapitation (albeit of a corpse, not a living person). Shakespeare seems to be pointing out the incongruity of substitution being foundational to soteriology and yet harmful to social order. This tension is part of the play's self-conscious exposing of the gap between soteriology and ethics. *Measure for Measure* is a problem play, not merely because of its generic hybridity, part tragedy, part comedy, but also because of its misappropriated soteriology.[3]

CALVIN'S FORENSIC, VICARIOUS ATONEMENT THEORY MEETS THE QUINTESSENTIAL "PROBLEM PLAY"

Measure for Measure grounds its examination of justice in the foundational soteriological concept of atonement. Isabella's pointed reference to the vicarious atonement (2.2.74–76) attempts to situate the play's penitential approach to justice in the soteriology of Anslem and Calvin. The presence of atonement logic thus underscores the play's vexed discourses about sexual ethics, justice, and forgiveness.

Christian theologians have advanced numerous theories of atonement to try to grapple with the unthinkable act of their human-God being crucified by Roman centurions. Origin's theory that God paid a ransom to the devil for sinful humanity perhaps finds its parallel in Angelo's request that Isabella sacrifice her body to him for the release of her brother Claudio. Isabella dismisses this scenario, and along with it, Origin's theory on which it may be based, as a specious instance of "foul redemption" (2.4.114). When the Duke "returns" to Vienna, he asks Isabella to present her grievance to Angelo for justice. Isabella's response

---

Bawcutt. For George Whetstone's *Promos and Cassandra*, Parts I and II (1578), I use the Chadwyck-Healey edition found on the *English Verse Drama Full-Text Database*.

3. The term "problem play" was first used by Frederick S. Boas in 1896 as a way of identifying Shakespearean plays which were particularly amenable to being read in terms of *fin de siècle* social realism (Widdicombe 147). While I realize that this term has been challenged because of its definitional instability (Widdicombe 147), I nonetheless find the term useful in highlighting Shakespearean plays that deal with ethical or social problems in a manner that critics continue to regard as controversial. In effect, Debora Shuger invokes the term in this way when she suggests that *Measure for Measure* "is, for us, a problem comedy: the play wrestles with a law that seems basically fruitloops" (9).

alludes to Origen's theory of God paying a ransom to the devil for humanity's salvation: "You bid me seek redemption of the devil" (5.1.30).

More germane to the play is Anselm's satisfaction theory of the atonement, namely that Christ died to assuage God's wrath over the sins of humanity. In *Cur Deus Homo*, Anselm argues that satisfaction must be paid for sin, rather than God indulgently forgiving sin without requiring any restitution by the offending party. In dialogue form, Anselm conveys the idea that mercy alone does not constitute grounds for sinners to receive forgiveness, but that atonement must be paid for sin:

> *Anselm.* Let us return and consider whether it were proper for God to put away sins by compassion alone, without any payment of the honour taken from him.
> *Boso.* I do not see why it is not proper.
> *Anselm.* To remit sin in this manner is nothing else than not to punish; and since it is not right to cancel sin without compensation or punishment; if it be not punished, then is it passed by undischarged.
> *Boso.* What you say is reasonable.
> . . .*Anselm.* There is also another thing which follows if sin be passed by unpunished, viz., that with God there will be no difference between the guilty and the not guilty; and this is unbecoming to God. (203)

In some ways, the ending of *Measure for Measure*, which allows Angelo such a free pardon, even for his intended crimes of rape and murder, conveys a variety of salvation imagined by Anselm's interlocutor (but which Anselm attempts to refute), a salvation which is freely given even without the sinner evincing genuine penitence or acknowledgment of wrongdoing. Admittedly, Angelo is subjected to a humiliating public exposure of his intentions, but his forced marriage to Mariana hardly constitutes an appropriate legal or moral response to his unethical behavior. If the conclusion of the play is read along these lines, i.e., that no sacrifice is required for forgiveness, then the play remains a "problem play" indeed. In the very imbalanced ethical world of the play, Angelo's sins of premeditating and willing himself to enact rape and murder are punished less harshly than Claudio's "crime" of ante-nuptial fornication with his betrothed, or Lucio's witty insults towards the Duke.[4] In spite

---

4. Angelo insists that he is merely enforcing the law when he elects to subject Claudio to the death penalty for fornication. From his own perspective, then, Angelo is not guilty of murder, but of hypocrisy and cruelty. However, when Isabella seeks justice from the Duke, she calls Angelo "a murderer" because she believes he has succeeded in

of all the Duke's veiled scheming, there emerges no adequate sense of justice, for the relative moral caliber of the characters and of their actions seems to have very little weight in the distributions of punishments and pardons at the end of the play. The forgiveness that Mariana requests Isabella to grant to Angelo and which the Duke rewards so generously seems to assume that forgiveness is possible without atonement or *bona fide* repentance.

Anselm would not have approved of such groundless forgiveness, and neither would Dietrich Bonhoeffer, who more recently disparaged such theology as "cheap grace." Anselm insisted that forgiveness for sin must be costly, very costly indeed, requiring nothing less than the death of the God-man Jesus. Anselm reasoned that because "a sinner cannot justify a sinner" (232), therefore, "no being, except the God-man, can make the atonement by which man is saved" (244). Anselm argues that "human salvation follows upon his [Jesus's] death" (283). For Anselm, Jesus's atonement for sin is the event that qualifies God to serve out both justice and mercy. In light of Anselm's Trinitarian and Incarnational theology, the atonement of Christ makes possible forgiveness for sinful humanity. For Anselm, Christ's death on the cross recovers the sense of God's compassion that otherwise seems illusive to sinful humanity.

> Now we have found the compassion of God which appeared lost to you when we were considering God's holiness and man's sin; we have found it, I say, so great and so consistent with his holiness, as to be incomparably above anything that can be conceived. For what compassion can excel these words of the Father, addressed to the sinner doomed to eternal torments and having no way of escape: 'Take my only begotten Son and make him an offering for yourself;' or these words of the Son: 'Take me, and ransom your souls.' For these are the voices they utter, when inviting and leading us to faith in the Gospel. Or can anything be more just than for him to remit all debt since he has earned a reward greater than all debt, if given with the love which he deserves. (286)

For Anselm, only the death of Christ authorizes God to forgive sins in an ethically responsible manner.

---

executing Claudio for a lesser crime than Angelo himself intended to commit against Isabella (5.1.40). I have chosen to maintain Isabella's language in describing Angelo's behavior (or, rather, intended behavior), even though I realize it may be problematic because of its emotional subjectivity.

In the *Institutes of the Christian Religion*, Calvin picks up on a number of Anselm's key points about the atonement, giving them fresh currency in the early modern period. Calvin reiterates Anselm's central point that only Christ's death could procure salvation for humanity: "When we say, that grace was obtained for us by the merit of Christ, our meaning is, that we were cleansed by his blood, that his death was an expiation for sin" (341). Calvin refers to the efficaciousness of Christ's redeeming blood in terms that recall Anselm's satisfaction theory of the atonement: "by that price the justice of God was satisfied" (341). However, Calvin was not content simply to rearticulate Anselm's theory of the atonement without qualification. In Calvin's mind, any salvation that derives from a source outside the person of Jesus is entirely suspect. For Calvin, such illegitimate sources of grace include what he perceives to be extrabiblical Roman Catholic sacraments and liturgical practices. Even as Calvin celebrates the merits of Christ and his sacrifice in the most rapturous of terms, he cannot resist from ending his peroration on a polemical note directed at his Roman Catholic detractors.

> When we see that the whole sum of our salvation, and every single part of it, are comprehended in Christ, we must beware of deriving even the minutest portion of it from any other quarter. If we seek salvation, we are taught by the very name of Jesus that he possesses it; . . .if we seek redemption, we shall find it in his passion; acquittal in his condemnation; remission of the curse in his cross; satisfaction in his sacrifice; purification in his blood; reconciliation in his descent to hell; mortification of the flesh in his sepulcher; newness of life in his resurrection; immortality also in his resurrection; the inheritance of a celestial kingdom in his entrance into heaven. . . . In fine, since in him all kinds of blessings are treasured up, let us draw a full supply from him, and none from any other quarter. Those who, not satisfied with him alone, entertain various hopes from others, though they may continue to look to him chiefly, deviate from the right path by the simple fact, that some portion of their thought takes a different direction. No distrust of this description can arise when once the abundance of his blessings is properly known. (338)

If Calvin is committed to securing the exclusivity of salvation in Christ over and against his Catholic counterparts (who assign soteriological efficacy to the church as well as to Christ), he nonetheless envisions a very capacious salvation and spiritual life made possible by Jesus alone.

VICARIOUS ATONEMENT AND THE FAILURE OF ETHICS

Calvin imagines the believer as vicariously participating in the progress of Christ's life, death, and resurrection, thus obtaining the salvific merits earned by Christ on behalf of humanity. Substitution theory thus forms the bedrock of Calvin's understanding of salvation.

Calvin's Christocentric soteriology owes much to Luther, who argued in the sixty-second of his Ninety-Five Theses that "The true treasure of the church is the Holy Gospel of the glory and the grace of God" (*Selections* 496). Luther is also widely attributed with describing John 3:16, one of the Bible's most succinct formulations of soteriology, as "the gospel in miniature": "For God so loued the worlde, that he hathe giuen his onely begotten Sone, that whosoeuer beleueth in him, shulde not perish, but haue euerlasting life" (Geneva Bible). *The Book of Common Prayer* prescribes the priest to pronounce John 3:16 immediately after the sacrament of communion (260). *Measure for Measure* likewise contains the most succinct restatement of the gospel to be found anywhere in Shakespeare's corpus. Crucially, Isabella's retort to Angelo at 2.2.74–76 stands as "the John 3:16 of Shakespeare."[5] Angelo, speaking in decidedly Lutheran terms about the death-dealing nature of law, insists to Isabella that her brother Claudio "is a forfeit of the law" (2.2.72). Isabella's soteriological response to Angelo invokes the symmetry and succinctness of the Johannine text so cherished by Luther:

> Why, all the souls that were were forfeit once,
> And He that might the vantage best have took
> Found out the remedy. (2.2.74–76)

Isabella's statement also recalls Calvin's idea of the forensic, vicarious atonement of Christ which was so central to Protestant orthodoxy. Isabella's use of the term "forfeit" speaks to Calvin's legal understanding of Christ's atonement as a payment for humanity's moral debt. Isabella's idea that God did not require payment of the "forfeit" from humanity, but instead accepted the life of his Son a substitute, recalls Calvin's emphasis on the vicarious nature of the atonement.

---

5. I owe this point to John Anonby (personal communication).

MEASURE FOR MEASURE AND THE PROBLEM OF THE GOSPEL

Despite Isabella's devout religious dogma, *Measure for Measure* is a play more concerned with social order than with theology proper. Moreover, does Isabella's insistence upon the truth of the gospel really resolve the ethical problems in the play? The play's problematic conclusion would seem to suggest otherwise. Katharine Eisaman Maus argues, "As the title suggests, *Measure for Measure* is obsessed with problems of equivalence, asking us to reflect on which things are commensurable to, or equal in value to, or might be substituted for, which other things" (2176). The squaring off of the play's problems in a set of three or four marriages hardly provides the necessary resolution to the play's disturbing situational ethics. Angelo's threatening proposal that Isabella compromise her religious and sexual integrity to save her brother's life is completely out of order. And yet her infamous response to such coercion also seems imbalanced: "More than our brother is our chastity" (2.4.186). The Duke's idea that Isabella's forgiveness of Angelo's egregious sexual harassment atones for Claudio's fornication with his fiancée also seems incommensurate, especially considering that Claudio is penitent but that Angelo is not (at least until his guilt is exposed). The Duke thus tries to put Angelo's sins on par with Claudio's, which counter-intuitively minimizes the cruelty of Angelo's behavior. If anything, the sense of justice and proportion that the play so concertedly works towards ultimately fails to deliver on its promise. This play, after all, is not a play about justice, nor about any of the equity or proportion that normally facilitates justice.

Maus attributes some of the topsy-turvy formulations of "equivalence" to the play's religious sensibilities. For Maus, Isabella's spirituality implies a lack of proportion: "Isabella's counterintuitive otherworldliness is central to Christianity, a religion founded on the spectacularly lopsided substitution of the blameless Christ for sinful humanity in the system of God's justice" (2177). More precisely, it appears that the lack of ethical proportion in the play actually derives from Isabella's restatement of Calvin's doctrine of the forensic, substitutionary atonement of Christ. As gratuitous as it may appear, Isabella's *carte blanche* forgiveness of Angelo may be a practical outworking of her previous endorsement of the gospel. Forgiven by Christ, Isabella comes to believe that she is responsible to forgive Angelo in kind.[6]

---

6. The fact that Angelo's sins are so much more egregious than either Isabella's or

The lesson that Isabella learns under the tutelage of the Duke as Friar is that she must practice the same kind of extravagant forgiveness to Angelo that she enjoined Angelo to grant to Claudio. Isabella's movement from accusing Angelo to forgiving him could be seen as an indication of the play's comic, redemptive structure (Cox 63). Yet I would qualify this interpretation by noting that the play troubles the notion of forgiveness as much as it affirms grace.[7] The ending of the play, therefore, may be only quasi-redemptive. From a skeptical perspective, Angelo's pardon amounts to a miscarriage of justice, in that the play refuses to make Angelo face the consequences of his unconscionable abuse of power. As the Duke himself acknowledges, "Well, Angelo, your evil quits you well" (5.1.499). Here the term "quits" is usually glossed as "repays" or "recompenses," indicating that Angelo is rewarded for being evil throughout the play by getting to marry a good woman who loves him despite his egregious faults. Either this is a case of truly amazing grace or it is an indication of the Duke's ethical incompetence.

In an ethical reading of the play, the Duke's forgiveness of Angelo seems to be problematic, in that he rewards Angelo for being evil. However, a soteriological reading of the play's ending would celebrate Angelo's forgiveness as the triumph of mercy over justice. This interpretive crux seems to hinge on the slippery meaning of the Duke's statement to Angelo, "your evil quits you well." Instead of glossing "quit" traditionally as "repay," we may interpret the verb in an alternate sense, "To leave or go away from (a place or person); to separate from or part with" (*OED*

Claudio's would indicate something of a reversal of Christ's parable of the unforgiving servant in Matthew 18:22–35. In Isabella and Angelo's case, a pious person is required to forgive a wicked hypocrite, whereas in Jesus's parable the servant forgiven an enormous debt is unwilling to forgive someone owing him a petty sum.

7. The Duke's experiment in keeping Isabella unaware that Claudio is still alive, while an unethical instance of emotional and spiritual abuse, becomes the mechanism for increasing the magnitude of Isabella's forgiveness of Angelo. The fact that such forgiveness is procured through unethical means complicates the notion of grace in the play. However, some critics persist in regarding the Duke's manipulations of Isabella in a positive light. Robert Bennett argues that Isabella undergoes a process of spiritual refinement under the tutelage of the Duke which requires that she be tested rigorously (128). Bennett interprets Isabella's forgiveness of Angelo as an important crux in the play which demonstrates that she has gained the spiritual maturity she previously lacked (147). Bennet's argument that Isabella's vicissitudes contribute to her spiritual purification has the undesirable effect of minimizing the Duke's and Angelo's mistreatment of her. Nevertheless, Bennet's argument seems to account for Isabella's belief that Christ's atonement makes possible her outrageous forgiveness of Angelo.

v.11.a). Using this definition, we might regard Angelo as experiencing a spiritual conversion by virtue of the fact that evil is leaving him.

Angelo has just had his sins publicly exposed, causing him to confess and repent of his wrongdoing. Initially, he craves the death penalty rather than forgiveness, but when he learns that Claudio is still alive, Angelo becomes open to the possibility of receiving mercy. The Duke then observes of Angelo, "Methinks I see a quickening in his eye" (5.1.498). The Duke's observation of new spiritual life in Angelo's countenance is paired with the recognition that "evil quits" Angelo "well." Perhaps the language here indicates a spiritual transformation in Angelo. Through the undeserved experience of mercy and grace, Angelo is given the power to expel evil from his heart and actions.

Such an interpretation of the play's ending as a celebration of amazing grace to the chief of sinners is an expression of classic Pauline soteriology: "But to him that worketh not, but beleueth in him that iustifieth the vngodlie, his faith is counted for righteousnes" (Romans 4:5). A hypocritical Puritan turned sexual harasser, Angelo is not beyond the purview of grace nor spiritual renewal. Whether one considers this good news or an affront to justice will likely shape one's affective response to both the Duke's leadership and the ending of the play. An ethical reading may object to Angelo being rewarded for his evil, while a soteriological reading will celebrate the renovation of a deviant like Angelo through divine grace.

The play evokes the scandal of how forgiveness operates in Christianity. In the play, as in Christian soteriology, the worst of people are shown mercy. Yet the uneasy ending of the play seems to ask if this gospel of grace is cause for celebration or if Christianity upsets the moral equilibrium of human culture so irresponsibly that its ethic of forgiveness should be dismissed. Is undeserved salvation workable or good? Or does unmerited mercy justifiably arouse a sense of moral outrage? While the Duke's penitential politics are certainly better than Angelo's Puritanical theocracy (as Debora Shuger argues), I would suggest that penitence itself is a flawed (or at least incomplete) basis for jurisprudence (137). Is not *Measure for Measure* a "problem play" in part because it forces penitence to serve as an overarching legal rubric? Soteriology may be fine enough on its own terms, but can it be used as a governing principle for all human affairs? The problematic ending of the play would suggest not.

The ending of the play denies Angelo any opportunity to corroborate his repentance as genuine, and so the audience is left wondering if the Duke's magnanimity was justified or gratuitous. From the perspective of Calvin's irresistible grace, the Duke's wholesale pardon of Angelo might not be justified by Angelo's behavior, but rather by divine election. Yet from another perspective, the Duke's exoneration of Angelo may be a judicially irresponsible decision that vexes the integrity of the play's turn to comedy. One "problem" in this problem play may be that not all viewers would be inclined to forgive a government official of blackmail, attempted rape, and attempted murder, nor to reward him with a loving wife. But in the straitjacket of comedy that this play is made to wear, Angelo's egregious immorality seems to dissolve inexplicably in a mist of mercy. Mercy is substituted for justice. Is this the gospel according to Shakespeare or an ethical fiasco?

THE FAILURE OF AN OVER-REALIZED SOTERIOLOGY IN *MEASURE FOR MEASURE*

Despite its soteriological emphases, *Measure for Measure* conveys a world of widespread ethical failure. The principle of "substitution" that Maus identifies as being so important to the play seems to work (at least for Isabella) in the realm of soteriology, but not in the realm of social ethics. In terms of Isabella's fervent articulation of Calvin's theory of the forensic, vicarious atonement of Christ, substitution works by having the sinless Christ die in the place of sinful humanity. The principle of substitution also works sacramentally, at least from a Protestant perspective, wherein communicants eat bread and drink wine rather than eating the actual body and drinking the actual blood of Christ (as in transubstantiation). Baptism, too, operates according to the principle of substitution. The priest sprinkles water on the infant so as to suggest her participation in the death and resurrection of Christ. Metaphorically and symbolically, the infant dies to sin through identification with Christ's crucifixion and is raised to newness of life through participation in Christ's resurrection. In baptism, substitution is also at work through the godparents, who make confessions of faith on behalf of the infant. Substitutionary atonement, in particular, becomes the theological principle which (from the perspective of Isabella) validates the invitation to repentance enjoined upon characters such as Angelo, Claudio, Julietta, and Barnardine. Isabella's theory of the atonement also serves as the theological basis for the gratuitous pardons at the end of *Measure for Measure*.

The play runs amuck ethically, however, when it attempts to force the soteriological principle of substitution upon the pragmatic domains of sexuality and law. The sexual substitution of Mariana for Isabella in the assignation arranged with Angelo is the ruse that the Duke uses to resolve much of the conflict in the play. The sexual substitution works to iron out some of the kinks in the plot, but only by introducing serious ethical violations into the play. Isabella the postulant (a candidate for the rigorous order of St. Clare) must pretend to use her sexuality to achieve political power, and she must actually require another woman to enact a sin similar to one that Isabella herself is unwilling to commit. This is muddy ethical terrain, indeed. While Mariana's prior contract with Angelo mitigates the worst of the legal difficulties of her duplicitous assignation with Angelo, early modern religion believed (at least in theory, if not in practice) that sexuality should be reserved for marriage.[8] Hence the Duke's eagerness for Angelo to marry Mariana in order to legitimate their sexual union. However, Isabella strongly protects her own sexual purity, but evinces little to no concern for the Duke's manipulation of Mariana's sexuality, nor for the social shame that the exposure of the bed trick might cause Mariana. The violations of Mariana's integrity and self-respect are further collateral damage from applying the principle of substitution to sexuality. A person who is sexually healthy wants to sleep with the partner he or she loves, not with a proxy. The play sends contradictory messages by trying to make Mariana a heroic character, while requiring her to disrespect herself and to deceive the unsafe man she foolishly loves into marrying her. In this context, the bed trick is an unwarranted application of substitution theory (so germane to soteriology) to sexual praxis.

The play also forces the soteriological principle of substitution upon the legal system, with disastrously unethical results. At one point, the Duke is suddenly willing to allow Angelo to execute the long-time prisoner Barnardine, simply so the Duke can use Barnardine's head in place of Claudio's. Ragozine's sudden death prevents the Duke from making this egregiously immoral legal decision of killing Barnardine for mere expediency. The Duke then rationalizes the opportunity to disguise Ragozine's head as Claudio's with religious rhetoric: "O, 'tis an accident that heaven

---

8. In early modern Catholic contexts such as Venice, fornication was often followed uneventfully by marriage. As long as the fornicating man was willing to marry the woman he slept with, his sex crime would be treated with lenity. In other words, the punishment for fornication was often forced marriage (Ruggiero 44).

provides" (4.3.74). Here and elsewhere, the Duke's religious claims reflect very poorly upon him and the penal substitution he imagines. The Duke's strategy of penal substitution relies on the unethical premise that a criminal's life is expendable. This iteration of substitution also theorizes that a person of lesser moral value can be sacrificed for an individual of greater moral value. The Duke's logic represents something of an inversion of how substitutionary atonement works in Christianity, where the flawless Jesus dies in the company of and for the sake of notorious criminals.

If substitution works in Christian atonement logic, it certainly does not work in the domains of human law. While Christian theology may locate salvation in Christ's sacrificial death, and while René Girard's anthropology may suggest that the death of the "scapegoat" can neutralize mimetic rivalry in the community, classical Western jurisprudence insists that only the criminal himself or herself can be punished for a crime he or she has committed. The play's attempt to apply the soteriological principle of substitution to the marriage bed and the death row prison cell creates enormous ethical problems. This theoretical conflation of theology with sexuality and law is one reason why the world of *Measure for Measure* is so religious, yet so unethical. The confusion in *Measure for Measure* is due not only to generic conflicts between comedy and tragedy, but also to category errors between soteriology and ethics.

THE TENSION BETWEEN CATHOLIC AND PROTESTANT PRE-CONDITIONS FOR FORGIVENESS

On the whole, *Measure for Measure* fails to align soteriology with ethics. The ubiquitous religion in the play fails to culminate in a coherent and constructive ethic. Does the fault lie in the drama's ethics or theology? Perhaps in both. In reformed English theology, the substitutionary atonement of Christ was the basis for salvation; nevertheless, the sinning subject could appropriate this salvation only through faith and repentance. *Measure for Measure* gives soteriological precedence to Isabella's impassioned articulation of the atonement, thus foregrounding the christological cause of salvation in the play. The individual bestowal of this salvation through faith and repentance, however, emerges less clearly in the play. Angelo's repentance is ambiguous at best, suggesting that the Duke's free pardon of Angelo might be unwarranted in some early modern soteriological schemas.

The problematic conclusion of the play thus begs the question: What are the reasonable conditions of forgiveness? The Duke forgives Angelo as soon as the Duke's identity is revealed. Angelo is recalcitrantly impenitent until he realizes that the Duke sees through him, indicating that Angelo has more respect for the power of the Duke than reverence for God or love of neighbor. The Duke's precipitous forgiveness of Angelo is likely to arouse moral objections in at least some audience members, particularly because the authenticity of Angelo's contrition is in question and his victimization of others has not been attended to.

The play's uneasy ending, in which tensions between forgiveness and ethics are left unresolved, speaks to what Paul Cefalu calls "a more systemic problem of integrating English Reformed soteriology. . . and ethical practice" (*Moral Identity* 2). Cefalu argues "that early modern theologians were often unable to incorporate a coherent theory of practical morality into their soteriological accounts of justification and sanctification" (2). The gist of this soteriological impasse is as follows: If God freely forgives my sins and justifies me by faith, then what motivation is there for me to perform the rigorous demands of ethics? However, antinomianism is only one of many concerns addressed by Cefalu's argument. More broadly, Cefalu observes that reformed soteriologies found it difficult to explain the relationship between sanctification and ethics (2). Cefalu argues that because "literary texts situate characters in ethically textured contexts" such works of the imagination sometimes reveal the limitations inherent in "the first-order distinction between justification and sanctification" (13). I would argue that *Measure for Measure* is one such text that interrogates the Reformation's collapsing of soteriology and ethics.

At the heart of the play's problematic ending lie competing Catholic and Protestant viewpoints on the pre-conditions for forgiveness. As with Isabella, Catholics and Protestants alike ground forgiveness in Christ's atonement. However, traditional Catholicism demands that sinners make satisfaction for their sins as a condition for their remission (or at least for the penitent's healing), whereas Luther allows for the total forgiveness of sin by faith alone. Aquinas designates the priest as being tasked with the responsibility to determine on Christ's behalf an appropriate satisfaction for the sin being confessed: "Hence, after the fault is taken away by contrition and the guilt of eternal punishment is relieved. . ., there sometimes persists an obligation to some punishment to maintain the justice of God which requires that fault be ordered by punishment" (280). In contrast,

Luther argues that the sinner may be completely forgiven simply by believing in Christ's atonement. Speaking of the imputed righteousness that is received by faith, Luther rhapsodizes:

> This is an infinite righteousness, and one that swallows up all sins in a moment, for it is impossible that sin should exist in Christ. On the contrary, he who trusts in Christ exists in Christ; he is one with Christ, having the same righteousness as he. It is therefore impossible that sin should remain in him. This righteousness is primary; it is the basis, the cause, the source of all our actual righteousness. (87–88)

The play seems to cast the Duke's free pardon of Angelo in the light of Luther's idea of complete and instantaneous justification *sola fide*. Divergent audience responses to Angelo's unmerited and unconditional forgiveness may, in both Shakespeare's time and ours, reflect competing soteriologies of forgiveness. Some may incline to Luther's radical ideas of grace, while others might hearken back to a Catholic theology that attempts to bridge soteriology and ethics through the means of reparation required by the sacrament of penance. Still others today might gravitate away from the forgiveness mandated by Christianity to a more pragmatic secular justice. Luther's view appeals to the tortured conscience yearning for immediate relief, while Aquinas's ideas have the psychological insight to integrate soteriology with ethical development. The problematic nature of the Duke's choice to forgive Angelo *without* requiring him to attend to his destructive actions suggests that the play recognizes the impasse between soteriology and ethics in standard reformed dogma.

MEASURE FOR MEASURE AND THE CONFLATION OF LUTHER'S "TWO GOVERNMENTS"

Another failed use of substitution in the play is the temporary replacement of the Duke by the deputy Angelo. If the Duke's laxity in enforcing law has resulted in widespread vice in Vienna, his scheme to have Angelo rectify the situation with Puritanical severity misses the mark. The Duke's exploitation of Angelo to enforce the laws with a harshness that the Duke had himself been unwilling to inflict reveals the Duke's hypocrisy. Of course, Angelo's policy of severity turns out to be more disastrous than the Duke's laxity, especially when Angelo himself becomes more corrupt than the population he attempts to reform. Both the Duke and Angelo compromise the integrity of their political office when they reverse their roles. Perhaps Shakespeare's political commentary here suggests a flattery of the newly installed King James. The failure of Angelo's moral severity resonates with James's personal dislike of Puritanism, and the failure of the Duke's divestment of power seems to be a backhanded compliment (whether sincere or opportunistic) to James's royal absolutism.

The Duke's disguise as a friar further conflates political and religious authority, with ethically unsettling results. Ever since Henry VIII had broken from Rome and proclaimed himself as head of the Church of England, political and religious authority had been united in a problematic way. While the contested jurisdiction of kings and the pope was often a sore spot in Catholic countries, the English Reformation effectively united the supreme religious and political offices in one person. It is ironic that the Protestant Reformation, which claimed scripture as its authority, would unite religious and political authority, when the Hebrew Bible had strictly enforced the separation of the offices of priest and king. In the Hebrew Bible, the prophetic office even spoke truth to royal power. Though the Duke adopts the identity of a Catholic cleric, his continued exercise of veiled ducal power suggests the Protestant English situation of absolute royal power rather than continental Catholic policy of monarchs in subjection (at least in theory) to papal authority.

Through the failed experiment of the Duke's performance of priestly duties, *Measure for Measure* highlights the danger inherent in the mixing of religious and political power in the English monarch.[9] In clerical disguise, the Duke procures confessions of penitence from Isabella and Claudio, but then ultimately uses his political power to expose Angelo's abuse of office. If the Duke had used his political power to stop Angelo's abuse of power as soon as it began, rather than pretending to provide interim religious solutions, much of the injustice in the play could have been prevented. The Duke seems almost to believe that he possesses the religious authority of a real priest when he says that he will bring Isabella spiritual consolation:

---

9. Sarah Beckwith observes, "The crown in parliament was the ultimate arbiter of ecclesiastical discipline and loyalty to the church and the state were indistinguishable as a result of the Erastian path taken in the English Reformation" ("Medieval" 196). Whereas Beckwith argues that Shakespeare's concern seems to lie in the encroachment of the state on the church, I suggest that the Duke's appropriation of a religious disguise has the opposite effect of emphasizing the danger inherent in religion impinging upon secular rule.

> But I will keep her ignorant of her good,
> To make her heavenly comforts of despair
> When it is least expected. (4.3.6–8)

In reality, the Duke is bullying Isabella with political power in the name of religion. By withholding from Isabella the information that her brother is alive, even lying to her that Claudio is dead, the Duke subjects Isabella to extreme psychological distress that is completely unnecessary. While the withheld information helps to establish his powerful exposure of Angelo's guilt at the end of the play, thus bringing the Duke greater glory, the pain that Isabella experiences and the further opportunities Angelo is given to persist in criminal behavior are gratuitous results of the Duke's Machiavellian abuse of power under the feigned auspices of religion. Shakespeare seems to be pointing out the potential dangers that arise when political and religious authorities are combined in one head. This political message would be less flattering to James, who saw himself as something like a spiritual shepherd for his English flock. Even Elizabeth had determined not "to make windows into men's souls," but the Duke displays a presumption of spiritual authority in hearing his subjects' confessions. His assumed religious authority becomes all the more dangerous when put to the service of his political power.

The failure of penitential justice in *Measure for Measure* thus becomes an object lesson about what happens when Luther's distinction between the "spiritual" and "secular" realms is not observed (Luther, *Selections* 370).[10] Luther argues that God's kingdom operates according to the sovereign love of the Holy Spirit, whereas human government requires the exercise of justice ("the secular sword") to maintain decency and order (370): "For this reason God has ordained the two governments; the spiritual, which by the Holy Spirit under Christ makes Christians and pious people, and the secular, which restrains the unchristian and wicked so that they must needs keep the peace outwardly, even against their will"

---

10. Debora Shuger briefly mentions Luther's distinction between the two realms in her study of *Measure for Measure*, but she does not dilate on its connection to the play (33). Sarah Beckwith engages in a sustained reading of the play in terms of Luther's two kingdoms (*Grammar* 65–68), but I take issue with her assumption that Lutheran thought is responsible for the play's violation of consent. Instead, I argue that the play's violation of Luther's distinction is what allows the Duke to act so unethically. Jonathan Goossen helpfully addresses the relationship between the spiritual and secular in the play, arguing that the Duke is a Puritan "attempting to deal with the personal spiritual issues of his subjects by means of the state's public law" (218). I build on Goossen's work by demonstrating how the play exposes the failure of soteriology when it is applied to specific legal and sexual contexts.

(370). While Luther's related idea that Christians do not need secular government to regulate their behavior is naïve and partisan, his distinction between spiritual and secular authority is a helpful heuristic for understanding the relationship between church and state in cultures where religious worldviews form a majority position. Early modern England did not observe Luther's distinction between sacred and secular authority, a fact which seems to trouble the political theology of Shakespeare's *Measure for Measure*.[11]

The Duke's failure to make Angelo face the legal consequences of his immoral actions suggests the Duke is unwisely conflating the spiritual realm of grace with the secular realm of justice. The very premise of the play, that the Duke's laxity in enforcing the laws in Vienna is the cause of widespread moral degeneracy, is a cautionary tale of the neglect of the secular realm. The Duke's political assessment of the moral climate in Vienna closely reiterates Luther's desire that secular justice be upheld, even in Christian societies: "Where. . . the spiritual government rules alone over land and people, there evil is given free rein and the door is opened for every kind of knavery; for the natural world cannot receive or comprehend spiritual things" (371–372). However, when the Duke exonerates Angelo at the end of the play—even rewarding him with a good wife—the Duke seems to have lost sight of the exigency for legal justice that he had championed at the beginning of the play. Whereas Luther insists that a Christian prince "must take heed that he deal justly with evil doers" (397), the Duke freely pardons Angelo. The Duke's enforcement of a soteriological solution of forgiveness in the case of Angelo, rather than an appropriate judicial sentencing, is ultimately a conflation of the offices of priest and secular magistrate. The application of the principles of soteriology to courtroom jurisprudence forces theology to do work more appropriately conducted by law. Shakespeare is demonstrating the failure of an over-realized soteriology when the Duke elides the distinction between Luther's "two governments."

---

11. Sarah Beckwith suggests that the Duke's disguise as a friar is "a thoroughgoing critique of the inseparability of church and state invested in the person of the monarch as supreme governor of the church" ("Medieval" 199). I argue that the soteriology in the play also critiques the relationship between church and state, but I draw a different conclusion than Beckwith. The play's over-realized soteriology paints a negative picture of religion meddling in secular affairs, not a picture of the church being overrun by secular power brokers.

MEASURE FOR MEASURE AND THE CULTURE WARS

The tension between the sacred and the secular derives from the play's diachronic context. The play was first staged roughly around the time of the Hampton Court Conference, during which King James faced off against the demands of Puritans for ecclesiastical reform, including church discipline. Earlier, the Puritan impulse to legislate morality had occasioned suggestions that the Mosaic legal code be reinstalled, which would make adultery a capital offense. In the tumultuous years of the Interregnum, this policy was briefly enshrined in English law. But for some moderates in late Elizabethan and early Jacobean England, apparently including Shakespeare himself (if Anne Hathaway's pregnancy at their wedding is any indication), Claudio's offense of fornication with his fiancée may have been regarded as a comparatively pedestrian offense.

By today's secular standards, the Viennese law prescribing the death penalty for premarital sex is ridiculously inhumane (Shuger 9). And while the idea that religion has jurisdiction over sexuality may seem absurd in the predominantly post-religious West, the basic premise of *Measure for Measure* cannot be adequately grasped without recovering an awareness of early modernism's widespread concern to inculcate sexual purity, understood in religious (and patriarchal) terms. Human nature, however, apparently has not changed very much since the heyday of the Globe Theater, and just as the Temperance Movement of the early twentieth-century resulted in a robust bootlegging industry, so did the Renaissance commercial theater revel in performing the very sexual misdemeanors that church and state were concertedly working to cleanse and/or punish. While the early modern theater was not a site of uncontained subversion, it was often transgressive, as in the bawdy humor of this Shakespearean drama, likely amplified by Middleton.

Isabella's sexual ethic of chastity, so alien to the ideology and praxis of postmodern secularism, is arguably what lies behind much of the critical disapproval of her behavior and attitude in the play.[12] The most notorious of Isabella's statements is her decision to prioritize her sexual ethic over her brother's life: "More than our brother is our chastity" (2.4.186). While this statement makes Isabella vulnerable to the moral disapproval

---

12. Peter Lake observes that critics see in Isabel "something like frigidity" (633). Lake himself writes pejoratively of Isabella's high valuation of her chastity: "overweening spiritual pride. . . lies behind her moral certainty of the transcendent social and spiritual value of her own sexual purity" (653).

of critics, I would suggest that Isabella's dilemma between acting according to her faith commitments or the welfare of her brother should not be dismissed so cavalierly. While I certainly do not consider Isabella to be an unqualified paragon of virtue, I nonetheless would argue that her predicament can be read more sympathetically or at least empathetically than much recent criticism would suggest.

Angelo's monstrous proposal is an outrageous request that Isabella substitute her body (sexuality) for the life of her brother. This sexual harassment involves the most unethical example of substitution in the entire play. Angelo tries to force Isabella to exchange her own self-respect for Claudio's pardon. The bargain is further complicated by the fact that Isabella's chastity is an expression of her religious commitment. In this proposed pact with the devil, Isabella is being asked to repudiate her conscience and faith, all for the lust of an unhinged government official. Sexual predation emerges as the governing principle which overturns the due process of law, violates a woman's right to her own sexual autonomy, and assaults a virtuous person's faith commitments. Isabella is being pressured to substitute her body for her faith, which transaction would result in extreme trauma. Critics sometimes seem to forget that Isabella is the victim here, not the perpetrator or accomplice.

Isabella's use of erotic language to describe martyrdom as she resists Angelo's advances has been cited as evidence that she was complicit in arousing Angelo's lust for her:

> . . .were I under the terms of death,
> The impression of keen whips I'd wear as rubies,
> And strip myself to death as to a bed
> That longing have been sick for, ere I'd yield
> My body up to shame. (2.4.100–104)

To be sure, such language does convey either an awakening or expression of latent sensuality in Isabella, despite her intention to join a monastic order. Rather than regarding Isabella as playing power politics with her sexuality or indicting her for hypocritically capitulating to sexual desire in a way that contradicts her religious vocation, I would suggest that Isabella should be seen more sympathetically as a victim of sexual harassment. After all, Angelo is using his power as deputy ruler not only to attempt to seduce Isabella, but to sexually blackmail her. The fact that she evinces a sensual response to Angelo, albeit in sublimated religious terms, does not mean that she is guilty of manipulating Angelo or irresponsibly

VICARIOUS ATONEMENT AND THE FAILURE OF ETHICS

contributing to his sexual arousal. Even if she were self-consciously trying to be sexy, such behavior would not excuse anyone sexually harassing her. Rather, she is a woman in a vulnerable position who is expressing negative behaviors that Angelo's abuse of power is scripting for her. As a victim of sexual harassment, Isabella experiences an egregious interpersonal violation which begins to shape her linguistic and subtextual responses to Angelo.

Isabella's harsh response to Claudio's request that she succumb to Angelo's monstrous proposal has also been regarded pejoratively by critics.

> O you beast!
> O faithless coward, O dishonest wretch!
> Is't not a kind of incest to take life
> From thine own sister's shame?
> . . .I'll pray a thousand prayers for thy death,
> No word to save thee. (3.1.139–143, 149–150)

It is easy to see why Isabella's cruel response to Claudio makes her an easy target for critical disapproval. However, I would suggest that her volatile response to Claudio can largely be attributed to the trauma she has sustained in her foregoing interaction with Angelo. She reacts so excessively here because her own brother, like Angelo, is enjoining her to violate her deeply held religious convictions about her sexual chastity. Her citation of incest, if not transgressive bawdy humor, is a tragic indication of the psychological damage she has sustained in being sexually harassed by Angelo. Moreover, as a postulant, she is experiencing from Angelo (and from a lesser degree, her own brother), a devastating violation of her cherished religious commitments with respect to sexuality. Angelo's violation of her is forcible, while Claudio's is opportunistic. She is thus a victim of both religious persecution and sexual abuse, her conscience and body being exploited by a high government official and by a close family member.

Criticism which neglects the religious contexts of the play will inevitably minimize the pain sustained by Isabella in having her cherished beliefs and her body bartered against each other by men who claim power over her. Although Isabella's responses to her dilemma are unpalatable, even unethical, the extreme duress she is under as a victim of an intense form of sexual harassment (which is tantamount to attempted rape) could perhaps mollify some of the harsh critical assessments made of her.

Angelo's monstrous proposal is obviously an even more unethical form of sexual substitution (and coercion) than the Duke's strategy of the bed trick, which itself degrades both Isabella and Mariana. If the Duke's abuse of assumed religious power speaks to the danger of religion encroaching on secular authority, Angelo's sexual predation is a counter-example of the danger of personal or political agendas impinging on religious beliefs and values. While *Measure for Measure* seems to be concerned that the monarchy and the church stay within their distinct jurisdictions, the play is also aware that secular and religious authorities alike can overstep their bounds.

Angelo's monstrous proposal is couched in soteriological language, which is all the more ironic for his attempt to violate Isabella's religious commitments. Angelo puts before her an offer to save her brother by forfeiting her soul (and her body):

> Which had you rather, that the most just law
> Now took your brother's life or, to redeem him,
> Give up your body to such sweet uncleanness
> As she that he hath stained? (2.4.52–55)

The scene becomes a kind of reverse Inquisition, where the victim is a devout believer and the tormentor is an apostate. Isabella maintains her integrity by resisting Angelo's advances that capitalize on religious language to sexually harass her. Using doublespeak, Angelo sharply focuses his attack on Isabella by emptying staple soteriological terms of their standard content and injecting them with sexually coercive force:

> Might there not be a charity in sin
> To save this brother's life? (2.4.63–64)

As we have seen, Isabella understands salvation and charity in terms of Christology, but Angelo manipulates such language into the rhetoric of sexual exploitation. For Angelo, salvation is nothing more than the gratifying of his most obscene desires. For Isabella, salvation of the soul translates into an attempt to literally save her brother's life. However, when Angelo pits the physical salvation of Claudio against Isabella's own religious integrity—which purity she deems to be a matter of her own salvation—Isabella will not budge to accommodate Angelo's blackmail:

> Better it were a brother died at once
> Than that a sister by redeeming him
> Should die for ever. (2.4.107–109)

For Isabella, spiritual loyalties trump even the most pressing demands of politics. Of course, Isabella's choice to preserve her chastity at the expense of her brother's life is not likely to find much sympathy in a postmodern context. Even some religiously inclined critics have regretted Isabella's predilection for chastity to charity (Cox 57). Nonetheless, Isabella's religious loyalty is not to be confused with rudimentary self-preservation or stubborn self-assertion. Admittedly, her response to Angelo belies a lack of self-knowledge and compassion for her brother, but the extremity of her position is really the result of her being pushed into a corner by Angelo, a male abusing political power.

Another instance of sexual and judicial substitution occurs in Angelo's determination to make an example of Claudio by executing him for fornication by suddenly implementing a severe law that hitherto had been unenforced. This policy represents an extreme and selective use of deterrence. Claudio is thus a scapegoat for the general Viennese "mass of perdition" (to use Augustine's phrase), as well as the victim of an unethical platform of political expediency. Claudio's status as a spiritual and political scapegoat indicates that his death sentence is a convenient cover-up of bad governance and widespread ethical malaise. As scapegoat, Claudio parodies Christ's redemptive death so cherished by Isabella. While Isabella focuses on the soteriological implications of Christ's substitutionary death, the biblical narratives indicate that political expediency also lay behind the substitutionary scapegoating of Christ, further linking Claudio's sentencing to Isabella's soteriology. (I do not aspire to allegorize Claudio as a 'Christ-figure' but to contrast how Shakespeare theorizes substitution in the respective domains of soteriology and social ethics.)

In John's gospel, the high priest Caiaphas argues, "Nor yet do you consider that it is expedient for vs, that one man dye for the people, and that that the whole nation perish not" (11:50). The immediate context suggests that Caiaphas's reasoning is based on political expediency, yet the biblical narrator interprets Caiaphas's statement as a prophecy with soteriological implications that Jesus would die for all God's children. Isabella's statement in 2.2.74–76 closely parallels the Johannine narrator's soteriological emphasis, whereas Angelo's determination to make an example of Claudio smacks more of political expediency. Even though substitution is integral to Isabella's Christian atonement theory, Shakespeare observes that attempts at judicial substitution become exercises in failure. Worse than Angelo's sentencing of Claudio to death for fornication is Angelo's sexual blackmail of Isabella. Worse yet is Angelo's subsequent persistence in the verdict of Claudio's execution. In the judicial realm, scapegoating results in escalating injustice. Again, *Measure for Measure* highlights the incompatibility of theories of salvation with social ethics.

MEASURE FOR MEASURE AND THE SOLUTION OF THE GOSPEL

The play, then, arguably fails to meet the demands of justice. Conversely, can the play really be said to offer a compelling vision of mercy? In her debate with Angelo, Isabella tries to shift the ideological foundation from justice to mercy, after the pattern of the gospel.

> Why, all the souls that were were forfeit once,
> And He that might the vantage best have took
> Found out the remedy. How would you be
> If He which is the top of judgement should
> But judge you as you are? O, think on that,
> And mercy then will breathe within your lips
> Like man new made. (2.2.76–80)

Isabella rhetorically moves from a statement of the atonement (lines 74–76) to an affirmation of God's justice to a plea for mercy, a virtue which she regards as evidence that a person has experienced the kind of ethical transformation enjoined upon believers in the Pauline epistles. Isabella's reference to "man new made" recalls the Pauline admonition to the Romans to "walke in newness of life" because "our olde man is crucified with him [Christ]" (6:4; 6:6). Isabella also echoes Paul's correspondence with the Corinthians, a city and church rife with sexual sin, much like Shakespeare's Vienna:[13] "Therefore if anie man be in Christ, let him be a new creature. Olde things are passed away: beholde, all things are become new" (2 Cor 5:17). Isabella sees ethical renewal as becoming possible only when the human subject deliberately identifies with God's mercy revealed in Christ. Her vision of substituting judgmentalism for mercy is distinctly Pauline, in that she describes an ethic of compassion as the natural and appropriate outgrowth of soteriology. Isabella's

---

13. Daniel Gates observes important parallels between Paul's Corinth and Shakespeare's Vienna, arguing that the "Duke resolves the city's disorder through compromises, in a manner consistent with the concessions Paul made in dealing with conflicting factions in Corinth and elsewhere" (512). Gates argues that although the play is "anti-puritan," it is nonetheless "Pauline," in that it envisions a "society that is inclusive but still only imperfectly reformed" (512).

theology intimates the Pauline methodology for ethical growth: personal identification with Jesus in his death and resurrection. The symbolism in the ritual of baptism thus becomes the template for a way of life for both Paul and Isabella.

Isabella's use of personification, "mercy then will breathe within your lips," also suggests the transforming agency of the Holy Spirit within the penitent. Possession by (surrender to?) the Holy Spirit is another Pauline soteriological commonplace. The immanent Holy Spirit substitutes for the transcendent (ascended) Christ, empowering disciples to achieve a measure of ethical renewal. The Hebrew Bible uses the term "ruach" or "wind, breath" for the Spirit of God and the Greek New Testament uses the term "pneuma" or "wind, breath" for the Holy Spirit. Hence, "pneumatology," or the doctrine of the Holy Spirit. Isabella's allusion to the insufflation of mercy into the human subject, thereby achieving "man new made," suggests the role of the Holy Spirit in repentance and regeneration. If Shakespeare foregrounds human agency as the basis for the failure or success of repentance (as in the case of Angelo), Isabella here cites the integral role of the Holy Spirit in effecting the transformation of human desire and character.

Isabella thus understands soteriology in distinctly Trinitarian terms. "He which is the top of judgement" refers to God the Father, the one who "Found out the remedy" is God the Son, and the one who "will breathe within your lips" is God the Holy Spirit. Isabella's rhetoric suggests that divine judgment gives way to divine mercy through Christ's sacrificial death, but that such mercy must be ardently appropriated by the human subject in committed identification with Jesus and in the willing reception of the Holy Spirit. In Isabella's soteriology, the penitent must welcome the gentle inbreathing of the Holy Spirit in order for Christ's mercy to result in ethical renewal.

Isabella's rhetorical substitution of justice with mercy also connects directly with the play's biblical title, an adaptation of a phrase from the Sermon on the Mount. This christological discourse reinterprets ethics as transcending mere adherence to law, instead requiring radical spiritual transformation. As rigorous as Jewish Law already was, Christ advocated a purity of heart that exceeded mere conformity to codes of conduct. Shakespeare's play begins with the premise that the laws of Vienna have been too laxly enforced, but its title invokes an ironic counter-perspective that would seem to undermine the notion of judgment itself: "Ivge not, that ye be not iudged. For with what iudgement ye iudge, ye shal be iudged, and with what measure ye mette, it shal be measured to you againe" (Matt. 7:1–2). For a play so concerned about curbing sexual vice, testing virtue, and exposing hypocrisy and criminal intent, the allusion to Christ's command not to judge seems out of place.

More than with most other Shakespearean plays, the trend among critics responding to *Measure for Measure* is to pointedly judge its characters, usually against standards that seem different from those which the play sets up. For instance, Isabella is variously read as a cruel, self-righteous prude or as a laudable picture of chastity graduating to charity. Angelo can be interpreted as a would-be rapist and murderer or as a victim of religiously imposed sexual repression. The Duke has been seen as a symbol of Providence or as a Machiavellian meddler. Although the Duke responds with impatience to Lucio's witty defamations of the Duke's character, a modern audience is likely to find Lucio's pluck delightful (presumably, so did early modern audiences). While King James likely would have approved of Lucio's chastening at the end of the play, modern audiences may be puzzled why Lucio's wit is punished more severely than Angelo's coercive sexual harassment. In short, this play seems to invite its audiences actively to judge the characters, in part because the Duke himself lacks the wisdom to address appropriately the ethical dilemmas in the play.

COMPETING DEFINITIONS OF SIN IN *MEASURE FOR MEASURE*

Christ's Sermon on the Mount (Matthew 5–7) would define sin invasively as both immoral action and a toxic state of mind. In Jesus's re-appropriation of Jewish Law, not only is murder a sin, but also unhealthy anger itself:

> Ye haue heard that it was said vnto thé of the olde time, Thou shalt not kil: for whosoeuer killeth, shal be culpable of iudgement. But I say vnto you, whosoeuer is angrie with his brother vnaduisedly, shal be culpable of iudgement. (Matt. 5:21–22)

Jesus similarly redefines sexual sin as encompassing both the act of adultery and sexual fantasies about adultery:

> Ye haue heard that it was said to them of olde time, Thou shalt not commit adulterie. But I say vnto you y^t whosoeuer loketh

on a woma[n] to lust after her, hathe committed adulterie w^t her already in his heart. (Matt. 5:27-28)

From any religious, ethical, or legal perspective, a murderer such as *Hamlet*'s Claudius would be guilty of sin/felony. However, under Jewish Law, and according to Isabella' ethical categories, Angelo's aberrant schemes would not constitute sin because they did not materialize in action. From the perspective of Christ's Sermon on the Mount, however, Angelo is guilty of sins of intent and thought. Nevertheless, Isabella forgives Angelo because he merely intended to sexually blackmail her, but did not actually perform the action of violating her:

> For Angelo,
> His act did not o'ertake his bad intent,
> And must be buried but as an intent
> That perished by the way. Thoughts are no subjects,
> Intents but merely thoughts. (5.1.451–455)

The play is a "problem play" in part because the audience is unlikely to find Isabella's exculpation of Angelo convincing. While Angelo did not actually rape Isabella and murder Claudio as he thought he had, Angelo's sexual harassment of Isabella is actual behavior that violates her personhood and the integrity of his political office. Contrary to Isabella's exoneration of him, Angelo is in fact guilty of immoral and illegal conduct. Equally problematic is Isabella's concession that Angelo acted legally in executing Claudio, and that Angelo thus should not face legal prosecution himself: "My brother had but justice, / In that he did the thing for which he died" (5.1.449–450). The inconsistency in Isabella imagining Claudio being punished for the same sin that Angelo receives a pardon for is excruciatingly obvious, and the sense of injustice here is not adequately resolved by the Duke's preservation of Claudio's life. Angelo does not deserve to be acquitted simply because the Duke intervenes to prevent Angelo from fulfilling the full measure of his criminal intent. In a more ethical world, Angelo's actual abuse of power (if not his unfulfilled criminal intentions of rape and murder) would face the due process of law.

The play's uneasy ethical formulas sit clumsily astride traditional legal notions of crime as harmful action and the Christian ethic of sin as both behavioral and *spiritual* unhealth. In *Measure for Measure*, legality and spirituality collide in such a way that the demands of neither are adequately realized. *The Book of Common Prayer*, of course, defines sin both legally and spiritually, enjoining communicants to repent of "our manifold sins and wickedness, which we from time to time most grievously have committed, by thought, word, and deed, against thy divine majesty" (259). Although Isabella dismisses Angelo's sin as mere "thoughts" or "intent," the liturgy of the Elizabethan church (following the Sermon on the Mount) would not exculpate Angelo (or admit him to the communion table) unless he first repented of his sins of intention ("thought"). Perhaps the play becomes inherently self-contradictory when it invites the audience to experience the destructiveness of Angelo's descent into evil, but then pardons and rewards him in the end. If nothing else, the play highlights the incongruity between soteriology and ethics.

ASCETIC RELIGION AND THE FAILURE OF ETHICS: ANGELO'S CAPITULATION TO TEMPTATION

If soteriology must confront its limits at the end of the play, the intervening action exposes the ethical failure of ascetic religion. There are two opposing varieties of ascetic religion in the play, the Roman Catholic Order of St. Clare (of which Isabella is a postulant) and Protestant Puritanism (represented by Angelo). The Duke comments, "Lord Angelo is precise," thus identifying Angelo as a Puritan in the language of Puritanism's detractors (1.3.50). While the play subjects Isabella to a necessary tempering process, her variety of religion, albeit flawed, emerges as superior to Angelo's hypocritical Puritanism. The play's critique of Angelo's religious zeal is highly pronounced, though perhaps not quite as caricatured as some of Ben Jonson's satirical Puritan figures (Tribulation Wholesome, Ananias, Zeal-of-the-Land Busy) or Shakespeare's own Malvolio. While the critique of Puritanism in *Measure for Measure* is fairly obvious, Peter Lake argues that "the play is not merely an anti-puritan, but also, potentially at least, an anti-Calvinist work" (669). Lake observes that Angelo is "elected" to be the deputy of the Duke, suggesting that the play seems to cast Angelo's spiritual pride as deriving from the Calvinist doctrines of unconditional election and irresistible grace (669–671). After making these and other bold anti-Calvinist claims, however, Lake confusingly backs down from his argument by concluding that "the evidence is too equivocal to allow a definitive answer" as to whether the play contains a "searching critique of Calvinist orthodoxy itself" (672). My argument that the play exposes the failure of ethics in reformed soteriology corroborates Lake's initial suggestion that the drama may be anti-Calvinist.

Yet much of the play's critique of Puritanism is more direct than my study of substitution theory would suggest. Shakespeare most obviously repudiates Puritanism, not through a critique of its soteriology, but through a critique of its hamartiology (doctrines of sin). The play implies that the failure of Puritanism lies not merely in its inability to connect salvation to ethics, but in its propensity to breed sin, especially hypocrisy and disordered desire. Although Angelo begins the play as one of Shakespeare's most religiously zealous characters, he quickly lapses into egregious moral failure when put to the test. Unwilling to seek the grace that would enable him to resist temptation, Angelo arrogantly displays the sin of presumption or hubris when he suggests he is impervious to the dangers of ethical failure: "'Tis one thing to be tempted, Escalus, / Another thing to fall" (2.1.17–18). Angelo's sense of moral superiority contradicts the Pauline admonition to the Corinthians, a church and city rife with sexual sin (like Shakespeare's Vienna): "Wherefore, let him y^t thinketh he standeth, take hede lest he fall" (1 Cor 10:12). Angelo imagines that his abstemious lifestyle gives him immunity to excessive or distorted sexual appetite, but his perceived insulation from common human failings sets him up for failure. *The Book of Common Prayer* prescribes a humble approach to temptation that recognizes personal vulnerability and fallibility: "Keep, we beseech thee, O Lord, the Church with thy perpetual mercy; and because the frailty of man, without thee, cannot but fall, keep us ever by thy help, and lead us to all things profitable to our salvation; through Jesus Christ our Lord. Amen" (198).

Angelo's desire to sleep with a woman whom he has been told is soon to be a nun, if not one already, indicates that his sexual desires have degenerated from health to distortion. All his Puritanical study and piety have not prepared him adequately to deal with natural human desire. In spite of (because of?) his ascetic spirituality, Angelo is prone to an obsession for harmful erotic behavior, which he will soon mask with hypocrisy. Even if Angelo's attraction to a postulant is in itself not amiss, his swift recourse to erotic coercion shows that he is not in control of his appetites. His unregulated lust is fast turning him into a monster. All this from a man who had the sterling reputation of the hotter sort of Protestant:

> . . .Lord Angelo is precise,
> Stands at a guard with envy, scarce confesses
> That his blood flows or that his appetite

> Is more to bread than stone. Hence shall we see
> If power change purpose, what our seemers be. (1.3.50–54)

The Duke plans to test this self-styled saint with power to see if Angelo is godly in reality or merely in show. The Duke's allusion to Matthew 4:3 is a subtle comment on the imminent Luciferian fall of Angelo, as putative "angel" of light: "If thou be the Sonne of God, commande that these stones be made bread." Whereas the fasting Jesus resists Satan's temptation to turn stones into bread, Angelo "scarce confesses / . . .that his appetite / Is more bread than stone." Angelo will not admit to himself or others that he has normal bodily appetites. Blinded by spiritual pride, Angelo fails to recognize his natural biological drives. By denying his basic human embodiment, Angelo becomes vulnerable to channelling his sexual energies in deviant ways, as in his reckless interaction with Isabella. Augustine ascribed Lucifer's fall to pride, whereas Milton in *Paradise Lost* would later attribute the making of the devil to envy of the Son. Angelo's spiritual pride transforms him with equal suddenness from a self-proclaimed "saint" to a devil incarnate, as it were.

Early in the play, when Escalus urges Angelo to relent in sentencing Claudio to death, Angelo insists that he would allow himself to be executed if ever he were to succumb to fornication. At the end of the play, Angelo judges himself as worthy of death—measure for measure—by his earlier pronouncement. Surprisingly, Angelo's ethical failure occurs in the context of the most poignant articulation of soteriology in the entire Shakespearean corpus. When Isabella visits Angelo to urge him to have mercy on Claudio by sparing his life, she marshals all her rhetorical skills, including a citation of the gospel by which God forgives sinners (2.2.74–80). Angelo is impervious to Isabella's rhetoric of the gospel. Their conversation continues as a deaf dialogue with Isabella begging for mercy for her brother and Angelo refusing to pardon him.

However, when Isabella asks Angelo to examine the desires of his own heart, he unexpectedly conflagrates with lust. Isabella's intention is to get Angelo to recognize that he too has inclinations to sin in the manner that Claudio did. However, when Angelo examines his desires, he suddenly realizes that he *wants* to sin. Instead of responding with remorse or contrition, realizing that he should thus show Claudio mercy (measure for measure), Angelo strategizes how he might satisfy his own desires in an illicit way. When Isabella finally gets the Puritan Angelo to admit his sinfulness, the result is not what either of them expects:

> ...Go to your bosom,
> Knock there, and ask your heart what it doth know
> That's like my brother's fault; if it confess
> A natural guiltiness, such as is his,
> Let it not sound a thought upon your tongue
> Against my brother's life. (2.2.138–143)

Whereas he had earlier ignored Isabella's plaintive articulation of the gospel, Angelo now speaks an aside which shows that for the first time he is paying attention to what Isabella is saying: "She speaks, and 'tis / Such sense that my sense breeds with it" (2.2.143–144). The thing that finally is able to stir Angelo's affect is not divine (or even human) mercy or justice, but his own lust. The next aside (spoken after he arranges for Isabella to return the next day) shows that Angelo is well on the way to sinning disastrously, inflamed by a sudden awakening to his own desire and to the prospect that he has the power to satisfy it however he wants.

The irony is that Angelo's strict adherence to religion has not made him immune to temptation or even to grievous ethical failure. Nor has his religion made him receptive to the gospel as articulated by Isabella. Paradoxically, his puritanical self-righteousness and spiritual pride have made him vulnerable to being tempted by virtue itself (Maus 2174). Like a religious fundamentalist—whose zeal may exacerbate (or overcompensate for) traits such as judgmentalism, greed, selfishness, and hypocrisy—Angelo's putative achievement of goodness has made him a worse, not a better person. Too late does he recognize his own proclivity to moral corruption:

> ...Most dangerous
> Is that temptation that doth goad us on
> To sin in loving virtue. (2.2.184–186)

Rather than being tempted by a common failing such as Claudio and Julietta's prenuptial fornication, Angelo's appetites have been perverted by spiritual pride in a more sinister direction. The goodness that he superciliously claims as his own degenerates into an obsession with violating a nun. Angelo's substitution of asceticism with unregulated lust is almost complete. In the case of Angelo, a puritanical obsession to eradicate total depravity in others seems to have unleashed it in himself. The play thus attacks Puritanism from both directions—soteriology and hamartiology.

The next time we see Angelo—two scenes later—he is still deliberating with himself in soliloquy, but he is now nearer to the crisis point of his criminal decision. More like a prayer than his first soliloquy, Angelo's second monologue also recalls the inner torment of Claudius's soliloquy in *Hamlet*.

> When I would pray and think, I think and pray
> To several subjects. Heaven hath my empty words,
> Whilst my invention, hearing not my tongue,
> Anchors on Isabel: Heaven in my mouth,
> As if I did but only chew his name,
> And in my heart the strong and swelling evil
> Of my conception. The state whereon I studied
> Is like a good thing, being often read,
> Grown seared and tedious; yea, my gravity,
> Wherein—let no man hear me—I take pride,
> Could I with boot change for an idle plume
> Which the air beats for vain. O place, O form,
> How often dost thou with thy case, thy habit,
> Wrench awe from fools and tie the wiser souls
> To thy false seeming! Blood, thou art blood.
> Let's write 'good angel' on the devil's horn,
> 'Tis not the devil's crest. (2.4.1–17)

Angelo's religion has not equipped him for the inevitable ethical testing that comes to all, particularly to those in positions of power. This soliloquy ostensibly begins as at attempt at prayer but quickly derails into a resolve to commit sin under the guise of hypocrisy.

Angelo's oblique Eucharistic reference helps to connect the ethical failure in this soliloquy to a more pervasive theological failure: "Heaven in my mouth, / As if I did but only chew his name."[14] This Folio reading, which may reflect the hand of a revising Middleton, holds back from the full-scale transubstantiation implied in John Jowett's speculative genetic edition of the play, which posits that the Shakespearean text originally read, "God in my mouth" (2.4.4). The Elizabethan prayer book also shuns transubstantiation when it enjoins communicants to eat the bread according to the theological formula of Calvin's virtualism:

---

14. Richard Wilson, building on John Jowett's genetic text of *Measure for Measure*, argues that the allusion to communion was more poignant in the original Shakespearean version of the play: "Of course, this Eucharist reference must originally have read 'God in my mouth'; so it is especially ironic that reference to the sacrament has been expurgated by Middleton's alteration of *God* to 'Heaven' throughout the Folio, in obedience to the 1606 Act of Abuses banning theaters from taking God's name in vain" (164–165).

> The body of our Lord Jesus Christ which was given for thee, preserve thy body and soul into everlasting life: and take and eat this, in remembrance that Christ died for thee, and feed on him in thy heart by faith, with thanksgiving. (264)

The reformed understanding of the Eucharist emerges in the prayer book's formula, "feed on him in thy heart by faith." (In contrast, Catholic transubstantiation envisions the communicant eating the body of Christ himself.) Although Angelo is willing to "chew his name," he does not allow his "heart" to feed on the body of Christ (as the prayer book enjoins), instead relishing sin deep within himself: "And in my heart the strong and swelling evil / Of my conception."

Through "composition of place" (to use the terminology of Ignatian spirituality recovered by Louis Martz) Angelo imagines himself as chewing the bread in communion, but not being able to swallow it. The sacrament of communion begins with the bread and continues with the cup of wine: "drink this in remembrance that Christ's blood was shed for thee" (264). Angelo, however, does not imagine himself as proceeding from the bread to the wine, as in the normal sequence of communion. In his corrupted state of mind, he associatively substitutes Christ's blood with his own burgeoning desire for Isabella: "Blood, thou art blood." At this point, Angelo jettisons a Eucharistic imagination for fleshly fantasies. Angelo's deliberation ends with a resolution to veil his demonic lust behind religious hypocrisy: "Let's write 'good angel' on the devil's horn, / 'Tis not the devil's crest." The anti-sacramental imagery here is a milder form of the inversion of the sacraments in Marlowe's *Doctor Faustus*, where Faustus's blood pact with the devil blasphemously parodies the Christian sacraments.

The ending of the play hardly offers a satisfying resolution to Angelo's moral unravelling. Religion and ethics remain at odds with each other. Angelo does not admit his duplicity until directly confronted by the Duke, whose rebuke evokes an articulation of penitence in Angelo that has been painfully absent thus far. Angelo responds to the Duke with abject humility and an admission of guilt, almost as if to God almighty:

> O my dread lord,
> I should be guiltier than my guiltiness
> To think I can be undiscernible,
> When I perceive your grace, like power divine,
> Hath looked upon my passes. Then, good prince,
> No longer session hold upon my shame,

> But let my trial be mine own confession.
> Immediate sentence, then, and sequent death
> Is all the grace I beg. (5.1.367–375)

When his guilt is exposed before the Duke, Angelo shows more fear than *Hamlet*'s Claudius does in the audience of God (*coram Dei*). The Duke's sudden—and apparently foolish—response to Angelo's admission of guilt is to require Angelo to marry Mariana. Angelo will not be punished after all, and the threatening storm clouds of tragedy are blown away by a (capricious?) gust of comedy.

However, another problem remains in this generically conflicted play. How can Mariana convincingly want to be married to a man who has just tried to violate a postulant? Why would she have agreed to marry Angelo, let alone sleep with him? The Duke's imposition of a religious solution of forgiveness and marriage for Angelo is at the cost of Mariana's self-respect, making *Measure for Measure* one of Shakespeare's most anti-feminist plays. If the audience were more convinced of Angelo's remorse, then perhaps his sudden salvation by marriage at the end of the play would be more palatable. John Cox, though unusually generous in his reading of Angelo's treatment of Isabella, eloquently assesses the final ambivalence of Angelo's supposed repentance, arguing that it is not clear "[w]hether Angelo learns anything about himself in the end" (54). If Claudius performs an abortive repentance in *Hamlet*, then Angelo makes an ambivalent, expedient, and eleventh-hour confession in the final moments of *Measure for Measure*.

A SOURCE FOR *MEASURE FOR MEASURE* AND THE PROBLEM OF ANGELO'S UNMERITED FORGIVENESS

My assessment of Angelo's pardon as problematic reiterates the force of Coleridge's conclusion: "For cruelty, with lust and damnable baseness, cannot be forgiven, because we cannot conceive of them as being morally repented of" (qtd. in Hawkins 90). However, my reading of the play's conclusion as an ethical failure which subverts the drama's soteriology is not likely to be universally appreciated.[15] Harriet Hawkins noted some

---

15. John Cox argues that it is "impossible to say" whether or not the ending of the play indicates Angelo's "transformation" (54). Jonathan Goossen's assessment of Angelo is in diametric opposition to my skeptical reading: "Angelo's repentance seems genuine" (235).

time ago that the critical jury was split on whether or not to accept the ending of *Measure for Measure* (91). For those dissenting critics who regard Angelo's repentance as genuine, Isabella's soteriology is arguably legitimated by the series of pardons at the end of the play. From such a perspective, the play's ethics and soteriology may be within reach of each other.

However, for those who regard the salvific conclusion of *Measure for Measure* as problematic, Shakespeare's source material provides some clues as to why the conflation of the sacred and secular realms results in chaos. The comic ending of *Measure for Measure*, in which soteriology overreaches its legally appropriate bounds, can be traced to Shakespeare's main source play, George Whetstone's *Promos and Cassandra* (1578). Shakespeare made some important revisions to Whetstone's drama in *Measure for Measure*, the most notable being Isabella's refusal to succumb to Angelo's monstrous proposal and the use of the bed trick in which Angelo sleeps with Mariana rather than Isabella (Bawcutt 23). However, Shakespeare closely parallels the conclusion of Whetstone's play in which King Corvinus of Hungary and Bohemia elects to forgive Promos (the Angelo figure) for his crime of rape and attempted murder, even giving him Cassandra (the Isabella figure) in marriage and restoring him to political office. Shakespeare adopts some of the plot from Whetstone's play when he has the Duke forgive Angelo and require him to marry Mariana. (If Shakespeare were following Whetstone more closely, Angelo would have married Isabella.) Some (but certainly not all) of the ethical failure in *Measure for Measure* may thus be an artistic failure from relying too heavily on weak dramatic source material.[16]

---

16. Other misogynist texts function as sources for *Measure for Measure*, including the Griselda story from Boccaccio's *Decameron*. The Marquess of Saluzzo marries the peasant Griselda and then tests her loyalty by pretending to kill their children and marry another woman. While the Duke's testing of Isabella in *Measure for Measure* is less cruel than Saluzzo's testing of Griselda, both men are renovated by seeing virtue enacted by the woman they love. From a feminist perspective, the ethical effect of these stories is repellant, in that men stand to profit spiritually by abusing women.

A major source for Whetstone's play, and thus directly or indirectly for *Measure for Measure*, is Giraldi Cinthio's *Hecatommithi* (also a major source for *Othello*). In one of Cinthio's stories, Epitia (the Isabella figure) actually sleeps with Juriste (the Angelo figure), who had blackmailed her by promising to free her brother. Nevertheless, Juriste kills her brother anyways. Epitia marries Juriste and then begs for him to be pardoned rather than executed. Her wish is granted. Again, from a feminist perspective, this source material is toxic, for women are rewarded for accepting abuse from men, while men are rewarded for abusing women. At least Shakespeare modified this repellent source material by having Isabella refuse to sleep with Angelo and by allowing Claudio

Shakespeare also took from Whetstone's play the important distinction between sins of thought or sins of action (a distinction deriving ultimately from Christ's Sermon on the Mount). The Gayler (Jailor) observes that Promos is guilty of both sins of intent and sins of commission in that he intended to kill Angrudio (the Claudio figure) and actually sexually assaulted Cassandra:

> . . .*Promos* long his rod can not escape:
> Who hath in thought, a wylfull murder wrought,
> Who hath in act performed a wicked rape. (Part I, Act 4, Scene 5)

While Whetstone's Promos actually commits the equivalent of rape against Cassandra, Shakespeare chose to leave Isabella's virginity intact by having Angelo intend to rape Isabella, but fail to enact it. Unlike Angelo, who shows almost no signs of remorse until the Duke exposes his guilt, Promos is reportedly conscience-stricken by his felony. As Phallanx (Promos's ruthless subordinate) observes of Promos,

> He fares as if a thousand Deuils were gnawing in his brest:
> There is sure some worme of griefe, that doth his conscience nip. . . . (I 5.1)

Nevertheless, Promos persists in his duplicity until confronted by the King. In one of the rare moments where Whetstone's play evinces ethical sophistication, King Corvinus describes Promos's use of political power to sexually harass and coerce Cassandra as a crime worse than rape by brute violence: "By worse then force, to spoyle her chastity" (II 3.2). On top of this evil of rape, Promos does not intend to spare Cassandra's brother Andrugio as promised, nor is he willing to marry Cassandra, as he had agreed to before violating her body. Angelo similarly refuses to spare Claudio's life after promising Isabella he would.

When Promos's sins come to light, the King's verdict is that Promos must marry Cassandra to restore her dignity and that he must be executed the following day, "In penaunce, that thou mad'st hir Brother dye" (II 3.2). The King authorizes his decision by quoting a variation on the Golden Rule of Matthew 7:12: "*Hoc facias alteri, quod tibi vis fieri*" (Do unto another that which you wish done unto you). The King's invocation of Christ's Golden Rule, however, is really a conflation with the *Lex Talionis*, in which retributive justice demands "an eye for an eye," or in

---

to live. However, some of the antifeminist logic of Shakespeare's sources troubles the sexual ethics of *Measure for Measure*.

this case, a life for a life. More accurately, the legal bind Promos faces is the result of his own violation of the Golden Rule, whereby he sentenced Andrugio to death for a crime that Promos himself had just committed. (Again, echoes of Angelo and Claudio.) Adherence to the Golden Rule would have prevented Promos's legal bind, for if he had given mercy, he would now be given mercy. But the Golden Rule cannot rescue Promos from his legal culpability, as the King's misinterpretation of Christ's ethic demonstrates.

At the end of the play, the King discovers that Andrugio is alive. This fact, coupled with Cassandra's grief that Promos is going to be executed, causes the King to pardon Promos for Cassandra's sake (II 5.5). Cassandra's implausible grief for Promos seeps into *Measure for Measure* in the form of Mariana's stubborn love for the unfaithful and unscrupulous Angelo. In an exchange between Promos and his wife Cassandra after he is pardoned for Cassandra's sake, we can also discern the source of some of *Measure for Measure*'s distasteful male chauvinism:

> Promos: *Cassandra*, howe shall I discharge thy due?
> Cassandra: I dyd, but what a wife, shoulde do for you. (II 5.5)

The idea that Cassandra merely performs her duty as a woman by pleading for the life of her rapist cum husband exposes the worst aspects of the period's patriarchal gender politics. This misogyny transfers into *Measure for Measure* as the degradation of Mariana sleeping with Angelo while she is pretending to be Isabella and then begging for his life to be spared so she can marry him.[17]

The highly (absurdly?) salvific conclusion of *Promos and Cassandra*, in which Promos, though guilty of actual rape (unlike Angelo's intended rape) is freely pardoned and even restored to political power, represents the apex of Whetstone's contribution to the over-realized soteriology in *Measure for Measure*. The King refers to Promos as the metaphorical lost sheep and returned Prodigal Son of Luke 15:

> If thou be wyse, thy fall maye make thee ryse.
> The lost sheep founde, for ioye, the feast was made. (II 5.5)

Whetstone takes Augustine's idea of *felix culpa* to an absurd extreme when he implies that Promos can benefit spiritually from having committed the

---

17. Thomas Heywood's *A Woman Killed with Kindness* and Shakespeare's own *Taming of the Shrew* furnish other well-known examples of misogynist drama.

equivalent of rape. Whetstone's play makes no sense of the female victim's perspective in all these male-dominated sexual politics.

Shakespeare unfortunately adopted some of this obfuscation of female victimization from Whetstone. Mariana's maxim in *Measure for Measure*—"They say best men are moulded out of faults"—imitates Whetstone's *apologia* for soteriology as the expense of women's dignity and safety (5.1.440 cf. *Promos* II 5.5). When King Corvinus reinstates Promos to political office, he urges Promos to "be good vnto the poore, / And Iustice ioyne, with mercie e[u]ermore" (II 5.5). Whetstone's untenable picture of the reconciliation between justice and mercy through the pardon of Promos and his forced marriage to Cassandra (the very woman Promos had raped) is adapted to *Measure for Measure* when Angelo is forgiven and married to Mariana. Both plays envision a salvific denouement after the pattern of the Prodigal Son (though the Lukan text is not explicit in *Measure*), but neither play requires the accurate self-knowledge and genuine repentance of the archetypal biblical parable. The result in *Measure for Measure* (even more pronounced in Whetstone) is a soteriology that short-circuits gender ethics.

MEASURE FOR MEASURE: AN UNHEEDED WARNING ABOUT POLITICAL THEOLOGY

Does the over-realized soteriology and its concomitant failure of ethics in *Measure for Measure* make it a play that is little more effective than its Whetstone source material? Emphatically, no. Whetstone's one-dimensional source play tends to flatten out any moral objections to Promos's pardon in particular, and to the general discontinuity between ethics and religion throughout the play. In contrast, Shakespeare's parodying of substitution theory from soteriology in the realm of social ethics suggests that he is self-consciously aware of the contradiction between religion and ethics in his own problem play. Shakespeare's three major alterations to the Whetstone source material indicate that Shakespeare was deliberately introducing new ideas about the relationship between religion and ethics. Bawcutt observes that Shakespeare changed the story by having Isabella refuse to succumb to the monstrous proposal, by making her a religious postulant, and by using the bed trick whereby Angelo sleeps with Mariana instead of Isabella (23–24). Bawcutt also observes that Shakespeare enlarged the role of substitution in the play (23). All of these changes Shakespeare made to his source material suggest that *Measure for Measure*'s increased use of substitution in the domain of sexuality connects to his larger critique of over-realized soteriology.

Some of the soteriological implications of these Shakespearean innovations are obvious: Isabella, a devoutly religious person, is saved from sexual violation by having Mariana take her place in bed with Angelo. One does not need to engage in largely discredited critical methods of religious allegory (for non-allegorical literature) to observe that the play makes some kind of link between Isabella's articulation of Christ's substitutionary atonement and the bed trick that Shakespeare deliberately introduced as a means to preserve Isabella by having Mariana take the fall. I certainly do not mean to suggest that *Measure for Measure* is a thinly veiled allegory of the gospel. Robert Bennet seems to fall into the trap of unwarranted religious allegory in his interpretation of Mariana's bed trick: "As Mariana's sexual union echoes the divine remedy of sacrificial death, it constitutes the paradox at the center of the play world's reformation history, the reunion of society with nature through the dynamic mediating power of the Heraclitean-Johannine Logos" (136). I would suggest that Bennet's articulation of the bed trick in such transcendently rapturous terms misses the mark. Bennet's overly earnest interpretation of the relationship between salvation and sexuality also does a disservice to the play's comedic spirit.[18] Nonetheless, Bennet is onto something when he suggests that the play opens up a conversation between soteriology and the bed trick. *Contra* Bennet, however, Shakespeare is parodying—not allegorizing—soteriology. As I have argued, Shakespeare is using parody to suggest that substitution works in Christian atonement but fails ethically when imposed on sexual praxis (and law).

The changes Shakespeare made to his sources indicate a concern that religious impositions on secular affairs—even in the name of salvation—may result in a miscarriage of justice. Just because Isabella is a

---

18. Some of the comedy involved in *Measure for Measure*'s handling of substitution arguably derives from Plautus. Plautus's *Two Menaechmuses* (*Menaechmi* in Latin) was a major source for *A Comedy of Errors*, and its playful substitution lies at the heart of *Measure for Measure*. In Plautus's play, the mistaken identity of the identical twins and the many resulting misadventures that result, including the twin sleeping with his brother's prostitute, find analogues in *Measure for Measure*, whether it be Marianna sleeping with Angelo in the place of Isabella or Ragozine's head being substituted for Barnardine's (and for Claudio's). Perhaps *Measure for Measure* could be described as an aesthetic fusion of Plautus and St. Paul. While my study focuses on the play's more serious theological dimensions, the bawdy humor of Mistress Overdone and Pompey contributes significantly to the play's enduring appeal.

postulant does not mean that Mariana should have to substitute (compromise) herself for the sake of Isabella. Just because Angelo perverts justice as the Duke's deputy and then later claims to be penitent when exposed does not mean that he should be delivered from the authority of the law. Just because someone is a criminal does not mean than his or her body is expendable, though the Duke may attempt to justify such brutality in the name of religion. Just because the Duke dresses up as a Friar does not mean he should be allowed to play God. These are only a few examples of religion conflicting with ethics in *Measure for Measure*, but the pervasive use of substitution theory here suggests that the tone of Shakespeare is deftly parodic as he speaks truth to power. In Whetstone, the over-realized soteriology becomes a smokescreen for an inadequate ethic, but in Shakespeare the overly salvific ending highlights the danger of the sacred realm impinging too aggressively on the secular realm. For Shakespeare, mercy must not obviate justice; grace must not degenerate into social chaos.

Shakespeare's Vienna is thus a thought experiment for what happens to a society when Luther's distinction between the sacred and secular realms is not honored. Such a warning was not irrelevant at the beginning of the reign of an English monarch (James I) who seemed to offer such promise in his initial policy of religious toleration but who later came to be associated more accurately with royal absolutism. The heavy-handed approach of his son Charles I to religion contributed significantly to inciting the Civil Wars, during which the early modern English debate over the respective boundaries of church and state reached its most violent expression. Apparently, Shakespeare's warning in *Measure for Measure* of the dangers of using religious solutions to solve political problems went largely unheeded by James and Charles Stuart, and by Puritans and Laudians alike.

5

"Thy Life's a Miracle"
Exorcism, Martyrdom, and Ecumenism in *King Lear*

IN *KING LEAR*, SHAKESPEARE negotiates soteriology by alluding generously to two contemporary works of religious polemic, Samuel Harsnett's *A Declaration of Egregious Popish Impostures* (1603) and Robert Southwell's *An Epistle of Comfort* (1587). Harsnett's vitriolic text is propaganda commissioned by the reformed English church to discredit the Jesuit missionaries' plans to re-establish the supremacy of the now persecuted Catholic church. Harsnett attempts to bring disrepute on the Jesuits by ridiculing one of their most controversial iterations of soteriology—the rite of exorcism. In borrowing liberally from Harsnett's satirical accounts of exorcism, Shakespeare does not endorse Harsnett's theology, but rather appropriates his imagery to meditate profoundly on human cruelty and the resulting trauma experienced by the victims. Shakespeare thus tacitly deflects the anti-Catholic agenda of Harsnett's tract, while harnessing its rhetorical power to explore the mysteries of suffering and healing.

Robert Southwell's *An Epistle of Comfort*, an impassioned piece of consolatory literature written to encourage recusants such as the imprisoned earl of Arundel, Philip Howard, in the face of religious persecution and potential martyrdom, is arguably also a Catholic polemic designed to discredit the heresy of Protestantism. Gary Kuchar suggests that the posthumous 1605 edition of *An Epistle of Comfort* was likely released to mitigate the fear of backlash against recusants following the Gunpowder

Plot ("Compassion" 140). The very fact that Shakespeare alludes to *An Epistle of Comfort* in *King Lear* (likely written in 1605) would at first glance suggest that Shakespeare employs his platform as a playwright to defend the cause of the beleaguered recusants. But upon closer analysis, Shakespeare's handling of the *Epistle* indicates that *King Lear* does not subscribe to the zealous fervor of Catholic martyrdom that Southwell advocates in his anti-Protestant rhetoric. Just as he neutralizes Harsnett's anti-Catholic agenda in *A Declaration of Egregious Popish Impostures*, so Shakespeare also softens the extremism of Southwell's Catholic discourse of martyrdom found in *An Epistle of Comfort*.

What emerges in *King Lear* from Shakespeare's spin on these two competing religious sources is a picture of *caritas* that is especially grounded in the reconciliation of familial relationships, rather than in faith or confessional affiliation. While the salutary (but more often senseless) suffering in the play suggests that it could be read nostalgically as a memorial for the salvific rituals and cruciform images of the old faith, *King Lear* can also be read skeptically, in that the play hesitates to venerate sacred Catholic performances of exorcism and martyrdom.[1] Yet in prioritizing love over faith, *King Lear* also parts company with the Protestant reformers' insistence on salvation *sola fide*. The play's approaches to salvation—whether defined theologically as the forgiveness of sin or metaphorically as the restoration of emotional and relational harmony—are generally oblique. Soteriology proper emerges mistily from the para-soteriological domains of exorcism and martyrdom. If salvation is attainable at all in the tragedy, it is proffered through endurance, kindness, forgiveness, and reconciliation. Such charity is reimagined cross-confessionally, perhaps even ecumenically.

EVIL AND EXORCISM IN *KING LEAR*

Much twentieth century criticism of *King Lear* is itself polarized along nihilist and religious lines, thus complicating any attempt to understand the play's mysterious dialectic between mental illness and demonology. Critics such as Harold Bloom, Jonathan Dollimore, and Stephen Greenblatt find the play devoid of transcendence and ominously silent in response to

---

1. While Protestant soteriology certainly incorporates christological suffering, the believer's suffering is greatly diminished from the soteriological heritage of medieval Catholicism found in such landmark texts as Dante's *Purgatorio*. See Jan Frans van Dijkuizen, *Pain and Compassion in Early Modern English Literature and Culture* (1–88).

the carnage splayed out on the stage. Those who have viewed the play as inherently religious, including W.H. Auden and David Beauregard, focus on its redemptive features, notably Cordelia's forgiveness of her father, Gloucester's salvation from suicide, and Lear's anagnorisis through suffering. Yet religious interpretations of the play need not only highlight its redemptive features, but can also account for the drama's ubiquitous cruelty, which Shakespeare metaphorizes as evil spirits. Seán Lawrence and Michael Edwards have effectively shown that a Christian interpretation of the play can be tragic, perhaps even pessimistic.[2] Certainly, a religious reading need not distort the play into something like the bowdlerized Nahum Tate adaptation, for suffering and tragedy are familiar terrain in theology and history, as any reader of Dostoevsky would know.

Many early moderns believed in the existence of an evil being who (through human complicity) "Brought death into the world, and all our woe" (Milton, *Paradise Lost* 1.3). Shakespeare's audiences and censors already had preconceived ideas about exorcism before seeing the ritual dramatically modified in *King Lear*, and for many of these spectators, the demonic was not reducible to metaphor. The rite of baptism in the early modern English church involved a renunciation of Satan, and this practice continues to the present day. Prior to the Reformation, baptism included a ritual of exorcism, and even after Trent, the Catholic church retained the rite of exorcism in baptism.[3] Thus, broadly speaking, exorcism could be conceived as coming under the rubric of soteriology. While the reformed English church was nervous about full-scale rituals of exorcism, the Jesuit missionaries to England practiced the ancient liturgical rite as a way of asserting the supremacy of the Roman Catholic church.[4] Despite the current critical assumption that demon possession

---

2. Seán Lawrence has astutely challenged "the general assumption, apparently held by many critics, that a Christian reading should be optimistic" (144). As Michael Edwards argues, "If we object to Cordelia's death not on exclusively aesthetic grounds but because it is *too much* both for the play and for our sense of life, we have missed, it seems to me, the meaning of the Fall" (27).

3. Luther removed several exorcisms from the Catholic baptism ceremony; he also took out the sacramental signs of salt, oil, chrism, and candles (Karant-Nunn 51, 70).

4. At this historical moment, general Catholic perspectives need to be decoupled from more particular approaches of the Jesuits, as the Archpriest controversy and the Appellant crisis indicate. Not all English Catholics were onside with the Jesuits. Elizabeth and Bancroft tried to divide the English Catholics through this situation, and Harsnett's scathing portrayal of the Jesuits conveys such official state policy. Shakespeare's refusal to demonize the Jesuits suggests that he was not taking the bait offered to the Appellants. Elizabeth's betrayal of the Appellants in 1602 may have reinforced

is a variety of madness, the play's ubiquitous diabolical imagery comes into sharpest focus when seen through the lens of the early modern recusants' belief in evil spirits and practice of exorcism.

Given the currency of the exorcism controversy, one might expect that demonic imagery would pervade Shakespeare's major tragedies, and *King Lear* does not fail to deliver. Joan Lord Hall notes that the word "devil" or "devils" appear twenty-two times in *Othello*, "whereas *Hamlet* and *Macbeth*, two other Shakespearean tragedies that are full of religious imagery, contain only eight and seven instances, respectively" (37). It is perhaps to be expected that these three plays, set in early modern or medieval Europe, would so extensively feature demonic imagery, yet *King Lear* engages even more extensively with demonology than the ostensibly religious tragedies.

While the terms "devil" and "devils" are each used only once in *King Lear*, the words "fiend" or "fiends" (usually in the form of "the foul fiend") are found twenty times. Moreover, "the Prince of Darkness," "witch," "black angel," "lake of darkness," "hell," "sulphury pit," and "spirit" (likely in the sense of demon) each appear in the play. More fascinating still are the outlandish names of the seven demons whom Poor Tom claims have possessed him: "Smolking" (11.126), "Frateretto" (13.6), "as of lust Obidicut, Hobbididence prince of dumbness, Mahu of stealing, Modo of murder, Flibbertigibbet of mocking and mowing, who since possesses chambermaids and waiting-women" (15.57–60).[5] Shakespeare lifts these names straight out of Harsnett, thus establishing Poor Tom as a demoniac and grounding the play in the contemporary exorcism controversy.

Shakespeare is obviously indebted to the Geneva Bible (the synoptic gospels and Acts of the Apostles contain numerous narratives of exorcism) and the medieval church traditions (including drama) for the recurring motif of demons in his major tragedies, but this fact is all the more pertinent to a discussion of *King Lear*, for Holinshed (one of Shakespeare's favorite sources) places Lear's reign in seventh century B.C.E. pagan Britain. For the distinctiveness of the demonology in *King Lear*, however, Shakespeare is largely indebted to Harsnett. Shakespeare's

---

Shakespeare's pro-Catholic sentiments in *King Lear*.

5. All citations of *The History of King Lear* are taken from *The Oxford Shakespeare King Lear*, edited by Stanley Wells and based on the 1608 Quarto version of the play. Citations from this version refer only to scene and line numbers because the *History* is not divided into acts. All references to Shakespeare's other works are taken from *The Norton Shakespeare*, edited by Stephen Greenblatt.

recasting of *A Declaration of Egregious Popish Impostures* brings the quasi-personal nature of evil, an historic concept usually ignored in modernist interpretations of *King Lear*, into the heart of the play's study of the problem of pain.

Many critics, beginning with Lewis Theobald in 1733, have commented on Shakespeare's borrowing of source material from Harsnett's 1603 *Declaration*, which was ready material for inclusion in *King Lear*, written in 1605–1606. Harsnett was chaplain to Richard Bancroft, bishop of London, (later archbishop of Canterbury), who commissioned him to write the polemical tract that would discredit the exorcisms conducted by Jesuit priests at Denham and elsewhere in 1585–1586.[6] Given the charged atmosphere in Elizabethan England during the brewing of the Babington plot to assassinate Elizabeth and install Mary Queen of Scots (only several years before the invasion of the Spanish Armada), the Church of England had ample cause for wanting to discount the exorcisms which were giving publicity to the Catholic cause.

EARLY MODERN THEOLOGIES OF EXORCISM

The imagery of exorcism in *King Lear* deserves focused attention because Shakespeare is responding to a key moment in intellectual history in which traditional views on demonology were being overturned by skeptical sectors within the church of England. The year before Shakespeare wrote the play, the English church had taken the unprecedented step of banning exorcism, a rite that had been an active feature of traditional Christianity since its inception. After Harsnett's attack on the Jesuit exorcisms, the English church adopted a rather stringent policy on exorcism, effectively forbidding a minister to cast out demons, decreeing in Canon 72 of 1604 that any exorcism must be approved by a bishop, which was "rarely if ever" done (Greenblatt, *Theory* 168). Canon 72 threatened that any minister who would continue to practice dispossession would be ejected from the clergy. This policy effectively eliminated the practice of exorcism by conformists in the Church of England throughout the seventeenth century, for it seems that such a license for exorcism was never granted (Thomas 485). The Canon even forbade a minister to practice

---

6 The recusant homes of Sir George Peckham in Denham, Buckinghamshire and of Lord Vaux in Hackney were the sites where a number of these exorcisms were performed (Thomas 488).

the spiritual disciplines of prayer and fasting as means to alleviate those afflicted with either demonic possession or oppression.[7]

The controversial nature of exorcism in Shakespeare's day was due not only to Catholic-Protestant rivalry, but also to the development of skepticism within Calvinism. The official restrictions on exorcism seem to have drawn strength from Calvinist theology. The reformer John Calvin was an outspoken proponent of cessationism, the doctrine that supernatural spiritual gifts had ceased after the period of the early church, and the early modern Church of England was heavily influenced by his *Institutes of the Christian Religion* and biblical commentaries. Calvin's cessationist views, as articulated in his commentary on 1 Corinthians, are reflected in Harsnett's passing comment:

> The gift of discerning of spirits spoken of by S. *Paul* being (as it is supposed) ceased in Gods Church, it becommeth a point of highest difficultie in the old and new exorcising craft, by what meanes a man shall come to be certaine whether the partie affected be possessed or no. (221)

The English church, with its growing trend towards cessationism, was ill-equipped ideologically to explain the phenomena of the Denham exorcisms. The Roman Catholic Church's claim to apostolic authority in exercising spiritual gifts such as discernment of spirits and exorcism would have empowered its adherents with an interpretive lens through which to view this doctrinal and political controversy.[8] The large crowds drawn to the exorcisms also attest to the element of popular appeal that the Jesuit priests were harnessing for the Catholic faith.

While most critics champion Harsnett and Bancroft's skeptical views on demon possession and exorcism (reports of miraculous relics understandably strain credulity), early modern Catholics would have seen these reformed English authorities as operating in opposition to historical Christianity. Medieval, patristic, and biblical Christianity had long established traditions of exorcism, all originating in the praxis of Jesus. However, Keith Thomas notes that by the end of the seventeenth century, many thinkers were skeptical even of biblical accounts of demon

---

7. The episcopacy of the early Jacobean church created a policy on exorcism which directly contradicted the teaching of Jesus, who advised his disciples that particularly recalcitrant demons can only be expelled by prayer and fasting (Mark 9:14–30).

8. Calvinism pejoratively refers to the belief in the ongoing practice of miraculous spiritual gifts as continuationism. The Catholic church, on the other hand, honored exorcism as a *bona fide* miracle.

possession, regarding the afflicted as epileptic or hysterical (490). While it is unsurprising that skeptics such as Reginald Scot and Thomas Hobbes espoused this view, even the godly Biblical scholar Joseph Mede believed that "these demoniacs were no other than such as we call madmen and lunatics" (qtd. in Thomas 490). Skepticism about demon possession and exorcism first emerged in England within the reformed church before becoming entrenched in later secular Enlightenment thought (490).

Shakespeare's naturalistic approach to exorcism in *King Lear* was therefore not original, but derived from the Calvinism within the English church. However, *King Lear* does not merely parrot official English church intolerance of exorcism, for the play retains a sense of wonder about the ritual, even after stripping exorcism of its metaphysical power.[9] Shakespeare's choice to write favorably about exorcism at a time when the ritual is losing prestige in the English church highlights the significance of the topic to his drama, precisely because of the play's counter-cultural perspectives. The afterglow of exorcism burns brightly in *King Lear*, even though the English church had effectively outlawed the ritual.

If demonology is a controversial subject today, it was even more so in Shakespeare's time. The academy now regards demonology critically as an arcane subject at best; at worst, as an outmoded superstition or even a tactic of terror adopted by the religious establishment. But for the recusants of Shakespeare's England, demons were believed to be active spiritual agents of Satan who could possess the wicked or torment the righteous. The only antidote for such spiritual oppression was the rite of

---

9. Shakespeare comments more overtly on the anti-supernatural impulse in English Calvinism in other plays. The Archbishop of Canterbury anachronistically conveys the idea of Calvinist cessationism in a comment to the Bishop of Ely about the sudden and unexpected "reformation" of Prince Hal:

> It must needs be so, for miracles are ceased,
> And therefore we must needs admit the means
> How things are perfected. (*Henry V* 1.1.67–69)

In *All's Well That Ends Well*, Lafeu reflects on recent currents of naturalistic thought:

> They say miracles are past, and we have our philosophical persons to make modern and familiar things supernatural and causeless. Hence is it that we make trifles of terrors, ensconcing ourselves into seeming knowledge when we should submit ourselves to an unknown fear. (2.3.1–5)

Lafeu, speaking as a French lord, could possibly be suggesting the skepticism of French authors such as Montaigne, but Lafeu's comment also speaks to the growing cessationism in the English church due to Calvinism. Lafue's suggestion that "philosophical persons" unwisely "make trifles of terrors" could suggest Shakespeare's suspicion of writers like Harsnett who are determined to void religion of mystery.

exorcism performed by a Jesuit priest who had been trained in exile in France and who had returned to England covertly, ministering under the threat of the death penalty.[10]

EXORCISM AND ECUMENISM IN *KING LEAR*

Emerging from the historical context of the exorcism controversy which reached a head around the time of *King Lear*, the polyvalent perspectives on exorcism in the play suggest a response that mediates between Calvinist skepticism about miracles and Catholic celebration of mystery. In defining demon possession in *King Lear* as inhumane cruelty and exorcism as the healing power of *caritas*, Shakespeare parts company with the play's contemporaneous polemical sources. Whereas Harsnett scapegoats the demoniac, Shakespeare—uniquely among his fellow dramatists and uniquely among his own plays—makes the demoniac a moral center in *King Lear*. Amy Wolf perceptively argues:

> Shakespeare uses the symbols, language, and details of Harsnett's *Declaration* to undermine the message of that pamphlet by contrasting possession with true madness, offering a sympathetic portrayal of demoniacs, and drawing a tragic portrait of human cruelty and evil that Harsnett's cynical politics do not admit. (252)

Shakespeare rejects the polemical aspects of Harsnett's tract, instead using its imagery of exorcism for his dramatic purposes.

---

10. While select Protestants, including John Foxe, author of the martyrology *Acts and Monuments*, also practiced exorcism, calling it instead dispossession, Shakespeare's use of source material in *King Lear* responds specifically to the Jesuit exorcisms. In some Puritan circles, the belief in and practice of dispossession were encouraged, but the English church episcopacy vehemently opposed such activity, especially when Puritan dispossessor John Darrell began to create too much of a sensation (Thomas 484). In *Twelfth Night*, Shakespeare parodies John Darrell in the mock exorcism of the puritan Malvolio, drawing upon Samuel Harsnett's *A Discovery of the Fraudulent Practises of One John Darrel Bachelor of Arts* (1599) (Brownlow, *Shakespeare* 60).

Brownlow sees Shakespeare as taking Harsnett's side in the case against John Darrell (*Shakespeare* 60). Brownlow suggests that when Feste in *Twelfth Night* dons a black clerical gown and pretends to dispossess Malvolio, that Feste is satirizing John Darrell: "I would I were the first that ever dissembled in such a gown" (4.2.5) (60). Brownlow also suggests that Ben Jonson's dramatization of fake possession in *Volpone* (5.12) and his allusion to the Darrell controversy in *The Devil Is an Ass* (5.8) reiterate Harsnett's satirical perspective on Darrell's dispossessions (60). The dramatic parodies of dispossession suggest that the popular imagination was captured by the scandal (60).

To my knowledge, *King Lear* is unique among early modern drama in its paradoxical treatment of exorcism from both a skeptical *and* therapeutic perspective.[11] In other words, the play takes a distinctive stance on exorcism by portraying it as a ritual that effects healing, even without the miraculous power that the church had traditionally ascribed to it. For the variety of exorcisms practiced in *King Lear*, no priest or liturgical script is needed, but only the compassion of the healer for the loved one in pain. Nonetheless, the ecclesiastical rite of exorcism is the contextual framework for the poetic faith exercised by Edgar in healing his father's despair through a mock suicide interpreted as a mock exorcism; the rite is also the precedent for Gloucester's receptivity to healing through such fictions.

At a time when it was common practice for Protestants and Catholics to accuse each other of being "of the Devil's party without knowing it" (to invert Blake's ironic commendation of Milton's poetry), *King Lear* stages a radical scenario in which a demoniac (the ultimate social pariah) turns out to be an agent of good. Poor Tom, a despised demoniac, becomes a center of moral gravity in the play. Tom claims, "The Prince of Darkness is a gentleman," and this attribution of goodness to the devil would identify him as a demoniac, for in the popular imagination it was believed that demoniacs obtained their supernatural power by making a pact with the devil (11.129).[12] (One thinks of Marlowe's *Doctor Faustus*.)

11. *Twelfth Night* contains a mock exorcism that is entirely satirical and skeptical, Marlowe's *Doctor Faustus* is both orthodox and transgressive in its demonology, Thomas Dekker's *If this be not a good play, the Devil is in it* uses demonology to satirize Guy Fawkes, and Ben Jonson's *The Devil Is an Ass* is a curious blend of satire and skepticism. The irony in Jonson's play is that Fitzdottrel seems to be unaware that his prayer to be visited by the devil actually has been answered. More surprising yet, the devil in question here (Pug) is no formidable foe, such as Mephistopheles was, but a fool of like mind as Fitzdottrel himself. Jonson's concern is more with social satire than demonology proper, perhaps indicating that Jonson himself may be skeptical about demons and demonic possession (as Shakespeare seems to be in *King Lear*). Unlike Jonson's *The Devil Is an Ass*, however, *King Lear* is entirely devoid of satire in its skepticism about exorcism. (The fool's witty satire does not seem to reproach Poor Tom's demonic bondage or therapeutic deliverance.)

12. Poor Tom's statement could also be interpreted as an indictment of the rich in a play that has been seen as promoting significant proto-Marxist sensibilities about the exigency of redistributing wealth. However, as Debora Shuger argues, the play's concern for the poor is a legacy of patristic and medieval Christianity rather than an indication of early modern radicalism ("Subversive Fathers" 49–53). Shuger contends that "Lear's prayer does not voice subversive heterodoxies—whether popular or humanist—but the social teachings of the medieval church. In a painful epiphany, the pagan king for a moment grasps the nature of Christian *caritas*" (53). However, Judy

And yet this poor, naked man who identifies himself as a demoniac, is himself an agent in Lear's healing. While Edgar counterfeits demon possession and madness, he perceives that Lear is suffering the onset of mental illness, and invokes a priestly blessing on Lear: "Bless thy five wits" (13.52).[13] The supposed demoniac turns out to be a healer in the making, a therapist for Lear's delusional fears.

Poor Tom expresses his desire to save Lear in terms that convey self-sacrifice. When the imaginary dogs (projections of Lear's daughters) pose a threat to Lear, "Tom will throw his head at them.—Avaunt, you curs!" (13.58–59). Through the exorcising power of love, the demoniac becomes the healer. In redefining the demoniac in such therapeutic terms, *King Lear* disabuses its audiences of common religious prejudices. The play's conciliatory handling of exorcism might have had ecumenical implications for the audience. By granting an unlikely gift of friendship to Lear and Gloucester in the person of a demoniac, the play encourages its audiences to consider affinities between the self and the other that may have been previously unrecognized. The Catholic demonized by the Protestant polemicist might in fact be a loving neighbor. The heretic repudiated by the Catholic controversialist may be a friend.

Even though the playwright's beliefs about demonology are irrecoverable, Shakespeare imbues Harsnett's polemical caricature of demon possession with a profound compassion that deepens Shakespeare's own exploration of human suffering and possibly suggests that the play invokes an ecumenical sense of salvation. The play's ecumenism, like its soteriology, is obliquely intimated in the conciliatory position the drama assumes in its handling of polarized Protestant and Catholic polemical source texts.

Kronoenfeld insists, "Whatever the limits of Reformation Protestant social thought, it supplies the moral frame of *King Lear*" (199). Kronenfeld suggests that the play's impulse towards charity is limited by the constraints of the period: "Thus 'distribution' and 'charity' as used in Reformation discourse specifically exclude egalitarian communal sharing; the explicit injunctions against the Anabaptists in all of the Reformation creeds, including the Forty-two and Thirty-nine Articles of the Anglican Church, deny the idea of common property while urging almsgiving" (184).

13. This benediction is possibly an echo of the character Five Wits in the morality play *Everyman*, thus giving *King Lear* another oblique connection to soteriology. While *Everyman* is a classic statement of late medieval Catholic soteriology, *King Lear* partially adopts Marlowe's subversion of the morality play in *Doctor Faustus*, in that Shakespeare's play foils hopes of an anticipated deliverance. Shakespeare's soteriology, unlike that of the morality play, is tragic.

READING *KING LEAR*'S DEMONOLOGY SKEPTICALLY OR HISTORICALLY?

My contention that Shakespeare takes exorcism seriously in *King Lear* is complicated by the fact that the demon possession of Poor Tom is merely the role-playing of Edgar as a Bedlam beggar. The demon possession in the play, then, is feigned rather than "real." Furthermore, Edgar's persona of Poor Tom is a Bedlam beggar, which would seem to indicate that Poor Tom is mentally ill rather than demon possessed. Moreover, many of the references to "fiends" in the play can be taken metaphorically, and those utterances that are intended literally are mostly spoken by Edgar as Poor Tom, i.e., by a man in danger pretending to be insane. Most significantly, the exorcisms in the play—both of Poor Tom and of Gloucester—are imaginary or dramatic, rather than literal or liturgical.

In other words, it would be possible to argue that all of the demonology in the play is reducible to metaphor. I concede that most, if not all, of the demonology in the play is metaphorical, not realistic or "empirical," but I nonetheless insist that Shakespeare's metaphors and dramatizations of exorcism are integral to the play and that they can only be adequately appreciated by seeing them as the first audiences would have seen them—in the light of contemporary discourses of demonology, both skeptical (Harsnett and the majority of the English bishops) and literal/liturgical (the Jesuits and select Puritans).

THE APPROPRIATION OF NICHOLAS MARWOOD'S EXORCISM IN *KING LEAR*

One of the most dramatic reports of exorcism in Harsnett's *Declaration* (hence its appropriation by Shakespeare in *King Lear*) is that of a recusant named Nicholas Marwood, a servant of the notorious Sir Anthony Babington.[14] According to Brownlow, "the possession of Marwood, Babington's servant, is the weakest part of Harsnett's case for fraud" (32). Brownlow also observes that Harsnett did not interview Marwood (123). Unlike the four demoniacs who provided confessions and renunciations of their exorcisms which were endorsed by the English church authorities and appended to the *Declaration*, Marwood never gave any indication

---

14. Babington was the Catholic nobleman executed for conspiring to assassinate Queen Elizabeth I in order to install her imprisoned cousin, Mary, Queen of Scots, on the English throne (the Babington Plot).

that he had a change of heart about his exorcism. Given the fact that Marwood's exorcism was the first in a series and apparently a catalyst for those that followed, Harsnett's failure to obtain any kind of confession or renunciation from him is noteworthy.

Nicholas Marwood was eventually imprisoned for refusing to take the oath of allegiance to Elizabeth, and the queen's Principal Secretary, Sir Francis Walsingham, kept files on his utterances during his exorcism. His exorcist was John Edmunds, who went under the pseudonym of William Weston, whose sincerity Brownlow maintains (32–33). Shakespeare's choice to focus on the possession of Marwood rather than of the less credible witnesses suggests that the playwright is determined to give exorcism a fair hearing in the play. The focus on Marwood is also a rhetorical strategy which favours the Catholic over the English church in the debate.

The account of Marwood's exorcism, which Harsnett borrows from the lost *Miracle Book* of the Catholics, furnishes Shakespeare with graphic images of demon possession:

> Edmunds *had scarcely begun his adjuration, and layd his hand on* Marwoods *head, but he presently falls into a furie, stretches out his body, beats with his feete and hands, snatches at the priests hand, makes all to ring with crying, swearing, and blaspheming.* (Harsnett 259)

Marwood's response to being exorcised is equally bizarre:

> *Heere srange tragicall exclamations filled all our eares. Devils why come yee not? And thou* Pippin *(which was the name of the tormenting devill) doost thou not revenge my quarrell? is there no ayde, no succour left in hel? Take mee miserable caytife and hurle mee into the infernall flames.* ... (259)

The verbiage evokes violence, confusion, and a high degree of self-hatred from which the demoniac is reluctant to be freed, all of which are reproduced in the malingering speech of Edgar as Poor Tom.

Poor Tom's litany of self-destructive tendencies allude to those voiced by Nicholas Marwood—Harsnett's leading demoniac—during his exorcism. Edgar as Poor Tom expresses a violent self-loathing, oxymoronically boasting of and lamenting his death wish:

> Who gives anything to Poor Tom, whom the foul fiend hath led through fire and through ford and whirly-pool, o'er bog and quagmire; that has laid knives under his pillow and halters in

his pew, set ratsbane by his potage, made him proud of heart to ride on a bay trotting-horse over four-inched bridges, to course his own shadow for a traitor. (11.45–51)

Poor Tom's suicidal ravings echo those of Marwood:

you launces, swords, and knives dash thorough me: fire, dogs, plague, mischief consume me, house fall upon me, earth swallow mee, lightning from heaven devoure mee: who can beare my burden? who can endure my heate? who can be thus torne in peeces, being rent with a thousand nayles? (Harsnett 259)

Not only does Shakespeare extensively borrow language from Harsnett's demoniac, but also posture and movement. The Gollum-like crouching, averted eyes, spastic motions, and other paranoid or dangerous gestures that Poor Tom typically makes in productions are embodiments of the speech acts of Marwood as he is being exorcized. Remarkably, there is no anti-Catholic polemic in Shakespeare's portrayal of Edgar's feigned demonization, but rather a sympathetic awareness of human frailty and guilt.

Bizarre as Marwood's exorcism was, its witnesses nevertheless lauded the Roman faith of the officiating Jesuit priest:

O the Catholique faith, O the faith Catholique, truly faith, holy, pure, powerfull faith: Thou art terrible to devils, formidable to hell, troupes submit to thee, legions of devils doe tremble at thy voice, they flie from thy unresistable command, they quake, and dare not abide thy sound. (Harsnett 261)

In the context of early modern England, a Jesuit exorcism was a victory for the miracle-working Roman Catholics and a defeat for the cessationist Protestants. Shakespeare's choice to stage favorably in *King Lear* at least two adaptations of the exorcism of Marwood suggests that the playwright was countering Harsnett's episcopally commissioned spin on the Denham exorcisms. The play seems to suggest that the Jesuits were not the enemy, but rather the intolerant Protestant clerics who sought to demonize them. Even though he does not subscribe to the Jesuits' miraculous formulae, Shakespeare nevertheless appears determined to legitimate their religious practices insofar as they are motivated by compassion and charity.

THE DEMONIZATION OF EXORCISM

Harsnett, however, deconstructs the Catholic assessment of Marwood's exorcism as a miracle by demonizing the Catholic church. As Greenblatt observes, "In the case of Catholic exorcists, Harsnett is prepared to locate the demonic in the very figures who profess to be the agents of God": the Jesuits themselves (*Negotiations* 104). Using theatrical metaphors, Harsnett identifies William Weston and the other exorcists as demons themselves because of their bizarre practices of burning sulfur under the demoniacs' noses and requiring them to drink an unpleasant potion of sack and herbs:

> Gentle spectators, we have held you som-what long ere our play begin; but now you see the devils are come upon the stage in their proper colours, Belzebub, alias *Weston*, and his twelve gracious assistants. For if the devils themselves should have devised a devillish potion to have intoxicated poore creatures and cause them to play the devils, they could not have invented a more potent potion then this. (238)

Another feature of the Jesuit exorcisms that Harsnett disparages is their empowerment by martyrdom. This component of the exorcisms is perhaps the most implausible for a modern readership. The girdle of the martyred Jesuit priest Edmund Campion, which supposedly came from Jerusalem and which Campion had worn at his execution at Tyburn, was used by Weston to diagnose Marwood as possessed because the martyr's relic was considered threatening to demons. Harsnett seizes the opportunity to satirize the miraculous power of Campion's relic: "*Campians* dreadful girdle had so heat the devil and intoxicated his braine as it made the devil to cry out, as you have heard: *O me stultum et infelicem, qui ista dicerem!* O foole and wretch that I am for saying thus much! Heere you see the devil was cleane gone, and confesseth himselfe to be out of his wits. And this was but an admotion, or touch, of the girdle" (269–270). This type of indulgent mockery of saints' relics was commonly enjoyed by Protestants of the Reformation period, and such bitter humor had deeply theological roots. The *Miracle Book* from which Harsnett is quoting depicts Marwood as being relieved of the demon by the application of pieces of Campion's body, precisely at the moment Marwood called out

Campion's name, "Edmunde, Edmunde" (296).[15] The absence of relics in the play's portrayals of exorcism corroborates Shakespeare's skepticism.

The most egregious injustice of the entire affair of the exorcisms was not sustained by the demoniacs, but rather by the Jesuit priests themselves. Brownlow perceptively observes that the Puritan dispossessor John Darrell was only imprisoned for two years, whereas three of the Jesuit exorcists were hanged, drawn, and quartered, and the remainder who were apprehended were incarcerated for 17 years before being sent into exile (59; 61). William Weston and a couple of other Jesuit exorcists were suffering in jail while Harsnett was collecting his data for the *Declaration* (80). Shakespeare's portrayal of exorcism as therapeutic could also be regarded as a bold political gesture which contradicted official English church prohibition of the rite. Perhaps some Catholics among the play's original audiences would even have interpreted the play's staging of exorcisms as a *de facto* vindication of the Jesuit exorcists who were so brutalized by the Elizabethan regime.

BIBLICAL SOURCES FOR THE EXORCISMS IN *KING LEAR*

In contrast to Harsnett's satirical exposé of demoniacs, Shakespeare portrays the guilt-laden Poor Tom with profound compassion, both as a persona created by the virtuous Edgar and as a destitute figure himself.

---

15. Harsnett's distinctly Protestant response to this report is to feel threatened that a miracle would be attributed to a Catholic saint rather than to Christ himself: "The sound had beene harsh, and the period not worth a point, if it had runne thus, *O Christe, Christe, O Salvator, Salvator,* O Christ, ô Saviour; but ô *Edmund,* ô *Edmund* falls with a goodlyer grace" (296). Earlier Harsnett had expressed a similar rationale for discrediting the exorcisms—a fear that Jesuit priests would be performing greater miracles than Christ (254). Again, the Calvinist doctrine of cessationism desires to limit the exercise of miraculous power to Christ and his apostles, rather than to see it wielded by the contemporary church. Correspondingly, Protestant soteriology is stripped of any overtly miraculous effects. For Protestants, full-scale exorcism was no longer part and parcel of soteriology, but for early modern English Catholics, even a saint martyred for Christ had the power to expel a demon, so great is the measure of the delegation of divine power. Harsnett's concern that a martyr's relic would have more power in expelling a demon than the name of Jesus (295) also draws attention to key theological controversy about prayer. Whereas Protestants prayed in the name of Jesus alone, Catholics were happy to invoke the panoply of saints. And yet Harsnett's posture of offense at hearing a report of a miracle performed by invoking a martyr may be less theologically than politically motivated. Even though the Puritan John Darrell used extemporary prayer (not martyrs' relics) to dispossess demons, he was the target of Harsnett's most bitter antipathy. Harsnett and Bancroft were clearly uncomfortable with the very idea of exorcism/dispossession, whether practiced according to Catholic or Protestant formulae.

Shakespeare's handling of a demoniac with compassion is almost unique to the period, whether in drama, poetry, or polemical prose. The resulting pathos the audience experiences for Poor Tom and Edgar himself contributes significantly to the play's recovery of a biblical *compassio* as the appropriate response to suffering, including demonic possession. In the ecclesiastical Latin of the Vulgate, the term often used for "compassion" is not the noun *compassio*, but a verb—*misereri*—and perhaps more forcefully than its English equivalent ("to have pity on"), bears a religious gravity that locates reprieve for suffering in divine intent.[16] The compassion that Shakespeare evokes for the demoniac seems to be a recovery of earlier Christian praxis and a rejection of the polemically inflected demonology of the early modern period.[17]

In its portrayal of demon possession and exorcism, *King Lear* not only exploits the powerful metaphorical/linguistic texture of its contemporaneous sources, but also draws upon accounts of exorcism from the synoptic gospels. Stanley Wells affirms that "both the Book of Job and the parable of the Prodigal Son have been regarded as deep sources of the play" (29). To these archetypal backdrops to the play, I would add the narratives of the Gadarene demoniac (Mark 5:1-20; Matthew 8:28-34; Luke 8:26-39). Harsnett's account of the exorcism of Marwood and Shakespeare's dramatization of the demon possession of Poor Tom both parallel and counterpoint the biblical stories of the Gadarene demoniac. The Markan text portrays the demoniac as habitually self-harming: "And alwayes bothe night & day he cryed in the mountaines, and in the graues, and stroke him self with stones" (5:5). Marwood and Edgar merely threaten to harm themselves with knives, whereas the Gadarene demoniac actually practices self-harm. Like the biblical text, the play associates the demonic with violence to self and others. In addition to harming the human subject, the "Legion" of demons kills a nearby herd of pigs: "Then the vncleane spirits went out & entred into the swine, and the herd ran headling from the high ba[n]ke into the sea" (5:13). Like the biblical text,

---

16. The deponent verb *misereri* ("have pity on") is used to convey the compassion of Jesus in a number of synoptic texts, including Mt. 9:36: "Videns autem turbas misertus est eis quia erant vexati et iacentes sicut oves non habentes pastorem." The Geneva Bible uses a noun for compassion in place of the Vulgate's verb: "he had compassion vpon them." The Authorized Version instead uses the more poetic formulation, "he was moved with compassion," relying on the usage of the noun (as in the Geneva Bible).

17. Biblical and patristic Christianity are replete with narratives of exorcisms that emphasize compassion and that refrain from the scapegoating that is so characteristic of early modern demonology.

Harsnett and Shakespeare associate the demonic with animals. Whereas the pigs in the biblical texts are the innocent victims of unclean spirits, the demon possessed Poor Tom (taking his cue from Harsnett) metaphorizes his own sin as animals.

The Lukan account narrates that the demoniac "ware no clothes, nether abode in house, but in the graues" (8:27). Similarly, Edgar removes his clothes, smears himself with dirt, and lives in isolation in a hovel on the heath. Like the Gadarene, Poor Tom is solitary, yet tormented by indwelling demons. The Gadarene demoniac displays superhuman strength in breaking the chains that were intended to subdue him: "nether colde anie man tame him" (Mark 5:4).[18] Poor Tom, however, is frail and vulnerable; a foil to the intimidating Gadarene. Healing comes to the Gadarene in the compassion of Jesus, and Edgar likewise finds consolation in the presence of others—Lear, the Fool, Kent, and Gloucester. The exorcism of Edgar, which occurs when he jettisons his persona of Poor Tom and decides to save his father from despair, involves him donning clothes and resuming noble speech, thus echoing the exorcised Gadarene, "bothe clothed, & in his right minde" (Mark 5:15). While abandoning the supernatural dimensions of his biblical sources, Shakespeare appropriates from these texts the demoniac's rehumanization through the cure of *compassio*.

CRUELTY FIGURED AS THE DEMONIC

While Edgar's role as Poor Tom and Gloucester's struggle with despair are important studies of human *victimization by* evil and subsequent liberation from its power, Shakespeare also probes the problem of human *perpetration of* evil, which he similarly invests with demonic imagery.[19] *King*

---

18. This text suggests the argument in James's *Daemonologie* that one of the tell-tale signs of demon possession is superhuman strength.

19. Shakespeare associates villains with demons not only in *King Lear*, but also in other major tragedies. After being destroyed by Iago, Othello looks for cloven hooves as a sign of Iago's devilry: "I look down towards his feet, but that's a fable. / If that thou beest a devil I cannot kill thee" (*Othello* 5.2.292–293). Of course, Iago is mortal, and his evil machinations finally catch up with him when he is apprehended by the Venetian state. Lady Macbeth invokes demonic spirits before persuading her husband to kill the innocent King Duncan. She eventually becomes psychologically unhinged by her guilt, and perhaps her story would also make for an interesting study of demon possession. Hamlet, albeit a tragic hero rather than a villain, struggles to discern if the ghost he sees is a demon or the spirit of his murdered father. From a Catholic perspective, the specter of Hamlet's father could be his ghost from Purgatory, but from a Protestant perspective the sighting would more likely be interpreted as a deceiving demon. In *Hamlet*, as in

Lear thus figures cruelty against the backdrop of demonology. Whereas Harsnett had polemically imagined the demonic in the Catholic other, *King Lear* identifies evil as the infliction of suffering on others for the sake of self-gratification. As the play unfolds, acts of cruelty proliferate, giving evil an enormous scope. Gonoril and Regan abuse their father, Edmund betrays his own brother, Cornwall barbarically blinds Gloucester, Gonoril poisons her own sister before committing suicide, Edmund has the innocent Cordelia hanged, and Lear dies of a broken heart, as will Kent (shortly after the play is over).

The deep structure of the play figures the spread of evil as the onset of demonic possession; the active resistance of such evil is imagined as exorcism. The kingdom begins to disintegrate as soon as Lear foolishly rejects Cordelia's understated love. Into the moral vacuum created by the rejection of Cordelia enters a cruelty that the play metaphorizes as demonic oppression. Lear imagines the cruel ingratitude of Gonoril as portending the onset of demon possession, helplessly declaiming, "Darkness and devils!" and "Ingratitude, thou marble-hearted fiend" (4.243; 4.251).

Whereas Harsnett satirically demonizes the Jesuit rituals of exorcism, *King Lear* reimagines the scene of Gloucester's torture as the fallout of truth speaking to power.[20] Cornwall decides to mutilate Gloucester on a mere whim arising "from sense of injured merit" (*Paradise Lost* I.98). Like Milton's Satan, who strategizes the destruction of humanity because his own ambitions have been foiled, Cornwall mutilates Gloucester because Cornwall's own sense of self-justification is inflated beyond the tempering reach of ethics. Shortly afterwards, Edmund, the *gentil* villain, will also begin to show his true colors when he offers himself to Gonoril: "Yours in the ranks of death" (16.25). Distressed by the moral degeneracy all around him, Albany desires something like divine intervention to restrain the villains:

King Lear, Shakespeare complicates the relationship between madness and demonology as he explores the depths of evil and suffering.

20. Richard Strier argues that this scene reveals the play as radically resistant to oppressive political and religious authorities (*Resistant Structures* 199). Strier notes that when the servant commands his master, the Duke of Cornwall, to refrain from blinding Gloucester, that the servant legitimates his resistance to his master as loyalty (199). Strier describes this scene as expressing "the paradox of service through resistance" (193–194). Strier assesses *King Lear* as a particularly radical play: "If, after *Lear*, Shakespeare never again so clearly espoused active resistance, the distinction between the good servant who disobeys immoral commands and the wicked who will do anything becomes a fundamental axiom" (199).

> If that the heavens do not their visible spirits
> Send quickly down to tame these vile offences,
> It will come,
> Humanity must perforce prey on itself,
> Like monsters of the deep. (16.45–49)

Deliverance seems to be imminent with the return of Cordelia, accompanied by the French troops, perhaps referencing the Jesuit exorcists arriving from France who were themselves feared to be spearheading a foreign Catholic invasion.[21] Like the spiritual army of Jesuits, Cordelia claims her French army is motivated by love rather than political ambition:

> No blown ambition doth our arms incite,
> But love, dear love, and our aged father's right. (18.28–29)

The play thus identifies love as the only power capable of dislodging the demonic stronghold of cruelty. Love is powerfully at work in the play, reconciling Gloucester to Edgar, and Lear to Cordelia, but even so, *caritas* only prevails at a staggering cost, for both fathers die momentarily after being forgiven by the child they have wronged. Even love herself, Cordelia (whose name derives from *cor*, the Latin word for heart), must die in the capricious tragic logic of the play. When Lear and Cordelia are apprehended as prisoners, Lear enjoins Cordelia to celebrate her virtue even as she is being persecuted:

> Upon such sacrifices, my Cordelia,
> The gods themselves throw incense. (24.20–21)

In light of the loving Cordelia's imminent death, the suggestion of sacrifice recalls the doctrine of the vicarious atonement of Christ or perhaps Southwell's canonical death as a martyr. In the pagan context of the play, however, the unresponsive gods do not seem to hearken to the gratuitous deaths of Cordelia, Gloucester, and Lear. When Cordelia is hanged in a murder framed as a suicide, Lear changes his tune about the beauty of Cordelia's sacrifice, instead arraigning the gods for her death.

---

21. Arthur Marotti observes that Elizabeth's royal proclamation "Declaring Jesuits and Non-Returning Seminarians Traitors" conveys the widespread fear that Jesuits were the vanguard of a Catholic military invasion (11). Marotti clarifies the exaggerated nature of such fears: "Although in the 1580s and 1590s only a couple dozen Jesuits came to England, one would think from the government's actions and from the rash of anti-Jesuit polemical activity that a secret army of thousands had landed on England's shores to prepare the way for foreign invasion" (11).

Angry at the divine, Lear desires "That heaven's vault should crack" (24.255). Perhaps the play cannot decide if the self-sacrifice of love is more powerful than the demon of violence. In any case, the perennial critical debate about whether the tragedy conveys a nihilist or redemptive worldview finds expression in the way the play's pervasive demonic specters encounter the challenge of exorcism. While the agents of evil in *King Lear* are no longer the literal demons of early modern Christian theology, nor the ideological scapegoats of religious polemic, these naturalistic villains retain enough of the cruelty of their metaphysical forebears to weight the play with a profound—even apocalyptic—sense of suffering.[22]

DEMONOLOGY AND MENTAL ILLNESS

In naturalizing the evil in *King Lear*, Shakespeare parts company with the morality play (and with Marlowe's transgressive subversion of the genre in *Doctor Faustus*). This fact raises the pertinent question as to whether demonic possession in the play is reducible to mental illness. Admittedly, the distinction between mental illness and demon possession in the play is tricky, and often critics conflate the two conditions by assuming that demonization is an archaic idiom for mental illness. Conversely, many early modern writers, including Shakespearean characters in *Twelfth Night* and *The Comedy of Errors*, comically ridicule mental illness as the work of Satan. While most scholarship today has no category for metaphysical evil, early modern scholarship was obsessed with demons, but had little understanding of mental illness.

Some early modern thinkers, however, considered mental illness and demon possession to be different afflictions. In *De praestigiis daemonum*, continental demonologist Johann Weyer distinguishes mental illness from demon possession, even though he suggests that these conditions often occur concurrently (346–347). In the sixteenth century, suicide was often linked to demonic possession, but rarely so by the end of the seventeenth century (Watt 2–8). Jeffrey R. Watt argues that the proscription of self-harm and its association with demons derive from historic Christianity (2). During the Enlightenment, attitudes towards suicide began to take their cue from rationalism rather than theology (4):

---

22. Gary Kuchar observes that Edmund (with fiendish delight) and Gloucester (with ethical horror) adopt apocalyptic imagery from the gospel of Mark to articulate the unleashing of evil in the world of the play ("Compassion" 138).

"Suicide as we know it—decriminalized, secularized, and medicalized—had taken hold among Europeans by the late 1700s" (8).

The current scholarly speculation on Edgar's mental health is quite extensive, and Andreasen suggests that "Edgar feigns classic schizophrenia as Poor Tom" (qtd. in Truskinovsky 344). Physician Alexander Truskinovsky claims certainty in his diagnosis of Edgar: "Without a doubt, his case is one of malingering as an adaptive behavior to escape persecution. Although clinically inconsistent at times, it safeguards his survival" (351). Truskinovsky's qualification that Edgar's behavior is "clinically inconsistent" is interesting, for it suggests that Poor Tom's condition does not clearly reflect any straight diagnostic category. Perhaps this medical ambiguity leaves room for the controversial possibility that Edgar is not only impersonating a psychiatric illness such as schizophrenia, but also is mimicking a state of demonic possession (as understood by English recusants).

Many psychiatrists have also tried to diagnose Lear, proposing various maladies, including "senile dementia, mania, delirium, brief reactive psychosis, involutional melancholia, and others" (Truskinovsky 343). Truskinovsky suggests that Lear suffers from bipolar I disorder, including episodes of psychotic mania (351). Lear himself fears the onset of the Mother, or "Histerica passio" ("suffering of the womb") (7.225; Wells 165 n224–5), a rather strange self-diagnosis (especially for a man) which comes from Harsnett's *Declaration*. Perhaps Shakespeare is the best analyst of his own character when, through Edgar, he comments on Lear's mental condition: "O, matter and impertinency mixed— / Reason in madness!" (20.163–64). Shakespeare represents a monumental advance in medical understanding from some who preceded him, such as Thomas More, who had a former Bedlamite (that is, one who had been a patient in London's Bethlem Hospital for the mentally ill) publicly tied and whipped for relapsing (Neely 170).[23]

---

23. If *King Lear* humanizes demon possession and exorcism through the rhetoric of *caritas*, play also conveys Lear's mental illness with *compassio*. In losing his wits, Lear learns to identify with the basest of men and thereby discover the true meaning of kingship. When Lear is turned away by his daughters to brave the ferocity of the storm, he empathizes for the first time with the poor who must endure the vicissitudes of life without the insulating comforts of wealth:

> Take physic, pomp,
> Expose thyself to feel what wretches feel,
> That thou mayst shake the superflux to them
> And show the heavens more just. (11.30–33)

It is worth noting that Lear considers Poor Tom mad, but not (as the Bedlamite had described himself) demon possessed. Edgar, in adopting the persona of Tom, also sees himself as playing the role of a patient from St. Mary of Bethlehem hospital who has been released to beg. Discerning Shakespeare's own perspective on his polyvalent writing is always a slippery undertaking, but Lear and Edgar's views here seem to be close to Shakespeare's own. Perhaps for Shakespeare, as Stephen Greenblatt insists, there is only madness, but no such thing as demon possession (*Theory* 175). But Shakespeare's use of demonic imagery is so pervasive that it becomes difficult to evade the contextual reality behind the metaphor. If Edgar is feigning madness, but is not really mad, his behavior still affords insights into mental illness. Similarly, if Edgar is also feigning demon possession (as I am arguing), then perhaps his posturing points to a spiritual disorder that had its basis in the recusants' worldview. In the mind of Elizabethan recusants, demon possession was believed to be a spiritual problem that required a spiritual cure. Many early moderns were not always careful to distinguish the perceived work of Satan from mental illness, but Shakespeare's understanding of madness as a medical condition is rather astounding. Nonetheless, Shakespeare also relies heavily on demonic imagery to convey his concerns about the magnitude and cruelty of evil. If, indeed, the recusants felt they could make a distinction between mental illness and demon possession, the former would be the province of human frailty and the latter would be the domain of "motiveless malignity," to borrow from Coleridge's description of Iago (150).

Debora Shuger notes that "'Superflux' is a Shakespearean coinage, a translation of a technical term from medieval canon law referring to that percentage of a person's income or goods that is *owed* to the poor" ("Subversive Fathers" 53). Lear's speech is a preface to the entrance of Poor Tom, thus giving Lear the opportunity to practice his newfound impulse towards social justice. Edgar says to Lear, "Do Poor Tom some charity, whom the foul fiend vexes" (11.53). Rather than judging Poor Tom for his sins, self-proclaimed demon possession, and madness, Lear identifies with him, joining the demoniac in his nakedness: "Unaccommodated man is no more but such a poor, bare, forked animal as thou art. Off, off, you lendings!" (11.96–98). During the onset of his own madness, Lear nonetheless "discerns" that Poor Tom is mad and in need of compassion. By becoming poor in spirit, Lear shows "the heavens more just." Divesting himself of power, he discovers the true meaning of justice through his solidarity with Poor Tom, a character who is destitute materially, intellectually, and spiritually.

EXORCISM AND THE ACADEMY

Most academics today are skeptical about demon possession, assuming it to be a superstitious diagnosis of a well established medical condition such as epilepsy or schizophrenia. Moshe Sluhovsky observes that "the rationalizing tendency of modern scholarship. . . assumes that possession as such did not really exist, that it was always something else" (3). H.C. Erik Midelfort challenges the common misconception that that the medieval and early modern periods regarded all mental illness as demonic, when in fact they often maintained a distinction between organic mental illness and demonic affliction (19). Midelfort observes a rise in demonic obsessions in the later sixteenth century, insisting that these cases should not be assumed to be synonymous with schizophrenia and other modern diagnoses (19): "Before we can seek to translate such disorders into our terms, we need to see what they meant in their own historical context" (19).

Sluhovsky makes an argument similar to Midelfort's, articulating the danger of defining demonic and divine possession in modern psychiatric terminology (2). Sluhovsky insists that early modern distinctions between "organic" sickness such as mental illness and spiritual disorders such as possession should not be cavalierly dismissed by current scholarship (2–3). Sluhovsky praises the "coherence" of the early modern "system of organizing knowledge" with regards to possession (3). Taking my cue from the historiography of Midelfort and Sluhovsky, I am attempting to recover the significance of early modern theologies of exorcism in Shakespearean drama. While this essay focuses specifically on the demonology, mental illness, and martyrdom in *King Lear*, all of these topics existed in a dynamic cultural context, not just in the play and its source texts.

In the early modern period Satan was believed to be responsible for an alarming array of misfortunes, including demon possession. Theology, as the queen of the sciences, had developed compendious theories to explain the world, but medical science was still operating by Galenic humoral theory, making many Renaissance medical diagnoses obsolete by today's scientific standards.[24] Unsurprisingly, the pre-modern diagnosis of demon possession has been superseded by the naturalistic science of psychiatry. Nonetheless, there are still a number of academics who remain committed to the study of religious experiences for which psychiatry may not yet have produced adequate explanations. A philosopher,

---

24. From the perspective of modern science, Robert Burton's *Anatomy of Melancholy* is an alien medical landscape.

Phillip Wiebe insists that religious experiences should not be dismissed out of hand merely because they defy current scientific explanation. If an academic such as Wiebe is willing to consider demon possession on its own terms even in the twenty-first century, it could be argued that theories of exorcism have an even greater exigency for the study of early modern contexts.

In *God and Other Spirits: Intimations of Transcendence in Christian Experience*, Wiebe scrutinizes a number of recent claims of demonic possession and exorcism, subjecting such reports to the rigors of evidentialist academic analysis. Wiebe concludes that "claims that God and other spirits are real are rationally defensible" (152). Wiebe argues that it would be irresponsible to dismiss all reports of encounters with evils spirits simply because such reports cannot be easily harmonized with materialist scientific assumptions. Wiebe suggests that both religious experiences and scientific theories can be subjected to similar standards and methods of scrutiny (112–113):

> This process of developing conjectures to explain events having religious significance and then assessing their rationality is seemingly no different than that which occurs in science and in other settings where critical judgment is exercised. Explanations that postulate the existence of spirits can be reconstructed to form a rational system of thought, although this claim is very different than asserting that views about spirits as we usually find them—inside or outside the church—are rational. Defenders of naturalism often portray the belief in spirits as irrational, so in asserting that theories that refer to spirits could be rational, I am contesting an influential position. (112–113)

Wiebe observes that in science the method of "abduction" (hypothesis) is used to postulate phenomena that are normally unobservable. Wiebe argues that the method of abduction can be used with similar effectiveness in the investigation of reported religious experiences such as demonic possession or exorcism (113).

Subjecting both biblical and present day reports of exorcism to the method of abduction, Wiebe observes how patters of evidence correspond between the exorcism of the Gadarene demoniac by Jesus as narrated in the synoptic gospels and present day testimonies of exorcism that subjects reported to Wiebe. While some of Wiebe's conclusions may be suspect to the broader academic community, his insistence that religious experience, even of the bizarre variety of demonic possession and exorcism, should come under the purview of rigorous scholarly investigation, is audacious and well taken.²⁵ If select scholars today can regard exorcism as a legitimate field of inquiry, then perhaps Shakespeare's interest in demonology deserves greater consideration than the modern academy has afforded it.²⁶ Certainly, demonology was an active subset

---

25. A survey of Wiebe's rigorous academic work on evil spirits could be supplemented by the eye-witness narratives of journalist Matt Baglio, who shadowed an American Catholic priest who went to Rome for training in exorcism. Baglio's observations are recorded in a winsome, if untechnical style in *The Rite: The Making of a Modern Exorcist* (Doubleday, 2009).

26. Transpersonal psychotherapy is a field which takes demon possession seriously on its own terms. On the fringes of mainstream psychology, transpersonal psychotherapy understands itself "as the melding of the wisdom of the world's spiritual traditions with the learning of modern psychology" (Cortright 8). In *Psychotherapy and Spirit: Theory and Practice in Transpersonal Psychotherapy* (State University of New York Press, 1997), Brant Cortright categorizes demon possession as a form of "spiritual emergency," which occurs when "spiritual experience erupts so forcefully that the usual integrative capacities of the person are overwhelmed and psychological functioning is disturbed. New energies, beings, planes of experience bombard the person, resulting in confusion, fear, and attempts to control what is going on. At this point, spiritual emergence becomes spiritual emergency" (159). Although transpersonal theory remains a minority view in psychology, spiritual emergency as a category is now nevertheless in the DSM, indicating that the diagnosis itself is widely recognized. Cortright seems to validate belief in evil spirits and to legitimate therapeutic techniques of expelling them from the human subject:

> Most spiritual traditions warn about the dangers of possession and have rituals designed to remove invading entities. In the Bible, part of the proof of Christ's divinity was his commanding ability to cast out the demons from people who were possessed. While phenomenological descriptions of possession have also been reported since the birth of modern psychology, they have always been interpreted as signs of mental illness, for example, in intrapsychic terms such as an invasion of the ego by the id's impulses and energies. Transpersonal psychotherapy raises the possibility of holding both the spiritual and psychological points of view. That is, sometimes we may be witnessing purely psychotic phenomena, other times we may be witnessing pure possession states, and at other times we may be witnessing a mixture where the person is indeed psychotic *and* possessed. The implications of such a possibility are so vast that it is beyond the scope of this discussion to explore them. Admitting spiritual realities into our scientific and psychological worldview opens up immense new possibilities, which transpersonal psychotherapy is only beginning to explore. (166–167)

Cortright's numinous approach to psychology recalls Hamlet's comment to Horatio after seeing the ghost of his own father: "There are more things in heaven and earth, Horatio, / Than are dreamt of in your philosophy" (1.5.168–169).

of theology and church discipline in Shakespeare's period, so the playwright's fascination with it warrants attention.

THE DRAMA AND POETRY OF EXORCISM IN *KING LEAR*

Shakespeare's pictures of exorcism are some of the most touching and hopeful features of the play and have been significantly underrepresented in the ongoing debate about whether *King Lear* is ultimately redemptive or nihilistic (or somewhere in between). Poor Tom undergoes an exorcism of sorts when he abandons his self-harming speech and rituals, and instead practices the virtue of charity in saving the blind Gloucester from suicide. As Poor Tom the demoniac reaches out in love to Gloucester, he is transformed into a person of dignity, even exchanging his garbled prose for the measured tones of blank verse! Gloucester notices Tom's sudden rehabilitation:

> Methinks thy voice is altered, and thou speak'st
> With better phrase and matter than thou didst. (20.7–8)

Poor Tom does not concede that he has relinquished his afflicted identity:

> You're much deceived. In nothing am I changed
> But in my garments. (20.9–10)

Just before leading Gloucester through a mock suicide, however, Poor Tom completely disappears, along with all his demons, never to return again. After leading Gloucester safely through the ritual (but not the reality) of self-slaughter, Edgar adopts a new identity as a sane individual who describes the old Poor Tom not as a person but as a demon from folklore:

> As I stood here below, methoughts his eyes
> Were two full moons. A had a thousand noses,
> Horns whelked and wavèd like the enridgèd sea.
> It was some fiend. (20.69–72)

Here, Edgar's new persona fails to differentiate between the demon and the demoniac, between the agent of evil and the human being tormented by it. Gloucester, however, is unwilling to demonize Poor Tom; instead, he humanizes him, beautifully demonstrating the play's compassionate impulse:

> That thing you speak of,
> I took it for a man. Often would it say
> 'The fiend, the fiend!' He led me to that place. (20.77–79)

We could say that Edgar's strategic changing of roles means that Poor Tom is redemptively transformed into a new person. Or we could say that Tom o'Bedlam has been exorcised and is now clothed and in his right mind (like the healed Gadarene demoniac). The old Bedlamite is gone, and the new creation has come, one who practices charity instead of self-harm. But Poor Tom's life is not the only one that has been saved by an exorcism; so has Edgar's. When Edgar first adopted the role of Poor Tom, he had renounced himself: "Edgar I nothing am" (7.186). But just after jettisoning the role of the demoniac, he calls Gloucester "father" (20.72), regaining his true identity as the rightful son and heir, loving and beloved. Of course, he will not reveal himself to Gloucester yet, and when he does, the sheer weight of the reconciliation is too much for Gloucester's weakened heart to bear. But here we see that the key to Tom's exorcism and Edgar's salvation is forgiveness. When Edgar forgives Gloucester, proving it by saving his life, Edgar is released forever from the identity of Poor Tom and his legion of demons. Poor Tom the demoniac thus becomes Edgar the exorcist, bringing the course of redemption full circle. Humanity can be deeply wounded by evil, but it can also enjoy tremendous healing through love.

Edgar's saving his estranged father from suicide is one of the most stirring scenes in all of literature, and Shakespeare imbues it with the imagery of demonic affliction and divine deliverance. In his new role as exorcist, Edgar describes the demon of despair and then assures Gloucester of his release from its torment:

> Think that the clearest gods, who made their honours
> Of men's impossibilities, have preserved thee. (20.73–74)

The conditional language here suggests that Edgar is inviting Gloucester to exercise a kind of "poetic faith" (à la Richard McCoy)—rather than an actual belief in God—in an effort to grasp a renewed hold on the hope that life is worth living.[27]

From a literal perspective, it is not the gods, but Edgar, who saves Gloucester from his suicidal despair. And yet the trick of the mock suicide actually works, effecting the literal salvation of Gloucester from

---

27. McCoy relates, "I now see faith in Shakespeare as more theatrical and poetic than spiritual. The credibility of his characters and stories derives from no higher power than literature. Faith in Shakespeare is a profoundly paradoxical experience because his scripts in performance allow us to believe in dramatic illusions that move and engage us even as we see through them" (ix). Gloucester's mock suicide and mock exorcism are poignant examples of such "dramatic illusions."

death by suicide. Edgar's recommendation of faith in "the clearest gods" may be misplaced, or it may even be a skeptical formula which manipulates Gloucester into believing that life has value, but it seems to work, even if it does not accord with fact. Undergirding Edgar's well-meaning deception of his father is perhaps a faith that overcomes the impossible, even if it is as small as a mustard seed, or even if it looks more like doubt than faith. Embedded in Edgar's reference to the pagan pantheon is Jesus's statement, "With men this is vnpossible, but with God all things are possible" (Matthew 19:26). Edgar deceives the blind Gloucester into believing that he has jumped off the cliffs of Dover but has been supernaturally preserved: "Thy life's a miracle" (20.55). In reality, Gloucester had attempted suicide by falling forward on level ground, thanks to the life-preserving stratagem of Edgar. Gloucester, in gratitude for being yet alive because of the "miracle" of Edgar's intervention, determines to go on bearing the burdens of his life.

Shakespeare here presents exorcism in a positive light, indeed. Leo Salingar connects this scene to the current exorcism controversy: "Edgar's trick to exorcise his father's despair seems to follow the same line of thought set going by Harsnett, even though no verbal echoes from Harsnett have been traced in the Dover Cliff scene" (138). But this statement is somewhat misleading, for Edgar's exorcism of his father's suicidal ideation is entirely effectual, even if it does involve a ruse, whereas Harsnett accuses the Jesuits of diabolical cunning. If Edgar is reminiscent of the Jesuit exorcists, Shakespeare is clearly determined to place him in the most favorable light. David Beauregard argues, "There is the positive attitude toward exorcism and 'miracles' as kind of benevolent fraud practiced for the spiritual good of the individual, just as Edgar tricks his father out of his despair" (206). Beauregard also traces a recusant perspective in Edgar's persecution and escape, recalling the Jesuit priests who were forced into hiding under Elizabeth (205).

The play's exploration of exorcism through the lens of *caritas* is more Johannine and Catholic than Pauline and Protestant.[28] From a recusant perspective, the exorcism of Marwood (recorded in Harsnett's *Declaration*) inspired a favorable response from the attendant crowd towards Catholicism, and Shakespeare's exorcism of Gloucester seems to be faintly Catholic, even if the playwright is unwilling to invest it with truly miraculous powers. There are other interesting connections between the

---

28. Here I am applying to *King Lear* the language and conceptual framework of Paul Cefalu's *The Johannine Renaissance in Early Modern English Literature and Theology*.

case of Marwood and the fiction of Gloucester's exorcism. Marwood claimed to have been delivered from a barrage of self-harming thoughts, words, and actions when Weston exorcised him. Shakespeare may have had Marwood's case in mind when he portrayed Gloucester's deliverance from a self-destructive impulse, described (at least metaphorically) as demonic in origin. In this sense, Edgar operates much like a Jesuit priest, administering salvation through mysterious rituals.

However, there are other aspects of the play's handling of exorcism that convey a Protestant slant. Whereas the Jesuits saw themselves as agents of God who could release the oppressed through their spiritual vocation, Shakespeare endows the alienated Edgar with the same therapeutic powers to lift the burden of despair that had previously been attributed to priests. Recalling Luther's idea of the priesthood of all believers, Shakespeare's assignment of a priestly role to Edgar suggests that humans have the capacity to administer grace to each other, even as they have the tendency to hurt one another. The play also makes a concession to Calvinist skepticism about exorcism by portraying the healing of Poor Tom and Gloucester through therapy rather than miracle.

The skepticism in the play extends well beyond the bounds of Calvinist cessationism, threatening to engulf Christianity or even theism. Yet if the action in the play operates without recourse to any supernatural intervention, human life itself emerges as something that is sacred. After Gloucester has survived his suicide attempt, Edgar says: "Thy life's a miracle" (20.55). In the early modern context, miracles such as exorcism were regarded as rare feats achieved by herculean faith, thus giving them currency in the contest between competing domains of Christianity. In the violent world of *King Lear*, miracles are reimagined as exceptional acts of love, intimations of a salvation that is ultimately elusive. For Shakespeare, acts of kindness, such as Edgar's healing of his father's despair, are in fact worthy of being designated "miracles," even if they can be explained naturalistically. In its balancing of Catholic and Protestant approaches to exorcism, the play thus portrays the ritual cross-confessionally, if skeptically. Whereas its polemical sources handled exorcism like an Occam's razor of heterodoxy, *King Lear* imagines exorcism ecumenically as the healing of alienated parties through forgiveness.

That same ecumenical impulse may be discerned in the play's handling of martyrdom. A number of the Jesuit priests who practiced exorcism were executed for treason, effectively making them martyrs from a Catholic perspective. The martyr who looms largest in *King Lear* is

Robert Southwell, whose memory emerges in a controversial allusion to *An Epistle of Comfort*.

MARTYRDOM IN *KING LEAR*

Henry Garnet recorded that his fellow Jesuit, Robert Southwell, was given the unusually humane treatment of being hanged to death before being disembowelled (Marotti 25). Customary Elizabethan practice was for convicted traitors to be cut down from the scaffold while still alive, so they would be sentient while being disembowelled. Garnet, and all Catholics in his wake, have styled Southwell's execution as the death of a martyr. Certainly no one could deny the courage that Southwell exhibited in withstanding relentless interrogation and torture while incarcerated; his unflinching death was the culmination of his life quest to be a martyr. Because his death seemed to draw respect from Catholics and Protestants alike, Southwell becomes an important icon in the confessionally contested landscape of late-Elizabethan and early Jacobean England. Shakespeare's decision to reference Southwell's martyrdom ten years later in 1605 in *King Lear* shows that Southwell's death was still producing aftershocks. This chapter seeks to ascertain the meaning of Shakespeare's potentially volatile allusion to Southwell's death in *King Lear*.

If the approach to exorcism in *King Lear* reveals a softening of entrenched confessional differences, the play's handling of martyrdom makes a similarly ecumenical gesture. In appropriating source material from *An Epistle of Comfort*, Shakespeare neutralizes the polemical thrust of Southwell's anti-Protestant prose by acknowledging the heroism of suffering bravely in the face of injustice, while contemning the divisive politics responsible for such persecution. By echoing Southwell at a key moment in the play—the prison scene—Shakespeare makes a tacit connection between the unjust suffering of Lear and Cordelia and the excessive cruelty endured by Southwell.[29] But as I will argue, Lear's

---

29. The question as to whether *Lear* is a play that values compassion and forgiveness in response to unjust suffering or to pretty much any suffering may be more difficult to answer. It seems that Shakespeare creates some empathy for Edmund's demise, but his longstanding victimization as a "bastard" and an eleventh hour repentance (of sorts) nudge the audience to reassess his status as villain. The death of Cornwall, however, falling hard on the heels of his barbaric mutilation of Gloucester, arguably excites precious little audience compassion. The disguise of the virtuous Edgar as a Bedlam beggar implicitly communicates the idea that the suffering of the poor, sick, and marginalized is undeserved, despite the prejudiced unconcern of those insulated by wealth and

prison-bound repudiation of "the packs and sects of great ones" (24.18) belies an impatience with the religious politics that provide the scaffolding for such persecution. *King Lear* thus reaches across confessional divides by rejecting the Protestant extremism of Harsnett and reining in the Catholic martyrological zeal of Southwell. Ideologically speaking, *King Lear* situates itself in a precarious middle space between the radically polarized politics of its two foremost contemporary religious sources.

Commenting on Southwell's prose, John Klause asserts, "Martyrdom for a Catholic was salvific: blood from martyrs' wounds purified even more powerfully than the waters of baptism" (100). It is thus not surprising that martyrdom should feature so prominently throughout Robert Southwell's literary corpus (and in his biography).[30] In *An Epistle of Comfort*, Southwell's first printed work of prose, the Jesuit who will himself be imminently martyred makes a soteriological connection between the wounds of Christ and the scars of the martyrs: "O how comfortable to all Saynctes, but especiallye to Martyrs, who shall not onlye reioyce in them [the wounds of Christ], as assurances of theyre saluation, certyfycates of Christes loue towards them, and pledges of perpetuitye in blisse: but also in that they themselues are scarred in like manner, and haue a more particular resemblance of that glorye" (450). Southwell attributes soteriological assurance to martyrdom, whereas Puritans sought assurance through experimental predestinarianism.

Susannah Brietz Monta explains the significance of Southwell's *Epistle* to Catholic-Protestant martyrological controversy:

> The tract mounts four principal arguments about suffering: suffering provides assurance of Christian identity; suffering is an imitation of Christ; martyrdom provides passage to security in heaven; and martyrdom offers a supreme sort of merit. These arguments seem designed both to comfort Southwell's readers and to respond to competing forms of consolation and comfort offered in Foxe's *Actes and Monuments*. (120)

---

comfort (such as Lear before his own ethical transformation through suffering).

30. Arthur Marotti observes that Southwell's martyred body furnished English Catholics with relics, and that his writings were similarly esteemed posthumously. Referring to Southwell, Marotti observes that "Despite confessional differences and despite the atmosphere of polemical viciousness in print culture, the literary remains of a Catholic author could be preserved *and venerated*" (31). Marotti explains how Reformation developments influenced the posthumous reception of a martyr's writings. When the "Catholic visual imagery and oral communication" gave way "to Protestant fetishizing of the word and the book," the literary corpus of a martyr began to assume an importance comparable to the martyr's own mutilated body (27).

In the sixteenth century, martyrdom gave credence to competing sectors of Christianity.

Because *An Epistle of Comfort* was primarily aimed at recusants, encouraging them to be constant to their Catholic faith in the face of persecution, the text's advocacy of martyrdom is more zealous and extreme than in *An Humble Supplication to her Maiestie*, which is written with a tenuous blend of flattery for and indictment of the Protestant Queen Elizabeth, whose government is responsible for egregious acts of intimidation and violence against the Catholic minority.[31] Yet even in *An Humble Supplication*, Southwell persists in imagining martyrdom as the highest path towards salvation: "We come to shedd our owne, not to seeke the effusion of others bloud. The weapons of our warrfare are spirituall, not offensive. We carry our desires soe high lifted aboue soe savage purposes, that we rather hope to make our owne Martyrdomes our steppes to a glorious eternity, then others deaths our purchase of eternall dishonour" (32).[32] *An Humble Supplication* is thus a formal, public plea for the toleration of Catholics and the practice of their faith.

Southwell's landmark narrative lyric, *Saint Peters Complaynt*, also provides another important variation on Southwell's theme of martyrdom.[33] The poem meditates on the guilt and shame Saint Peter experiences after denying Christ three times, where Peter is analogous to the recusants who are experiencing the temptation to apostatize from the Catholic to the English church. In this sense, the poem is an escape clause for a beleaguered Catholic who, like Southwell himself, may be steeling himself towards martyrdom, but is unsure if he can withstand the temptations and tortures which would urge him to renege on his faith. However,

---

31. Susannah Brietz Monta observes, "Southwell makes some of the period's boldest claims for martyrdom's power, insisting that the willingness to suffer for one's faith is the only sure foundation upon which to construct a stable, integrated self" (118). Monta emphasizes the theological and literary import of Southwell's writings, noting that they invited clergy and laity alike to offer themselves as martyrs. Southwell introduced both tears-literature and continental ideas of martyrdom to England (120).

32. Monta suggests, "This insistence that martyrdom ushers in a glorious eternity explains Southwell's elevation of martyrdom over baptism in certain respects" (125). Monta suggests that Southwell conceives of martyrdom in sacramental terms: "suffering assimilates martyr-soldiers to their captain so fully that they become typological fulfillments alongside him, enacting, in flesh and blood, sacramental figurations" (121–122). Southwell's sacramental understanding of martyrdom corroborates my inclusion of martyrdom in a study of the play's soteriology.

33. Gary Kuchar, following Louis Martz and Allison Shell, argues that *Saint Peters Complaynt* is the mainspring of the poetry of tears in English Renaissance devotional literature (*The Poetry of Religious Sorrow in Early Modern England*).

as Southwell would console the English recusant with the example of Peter, there is hope of forgiveness for the Catholic who lapses under duress.

Marie Magdelens Fvneral Teares also flirts with the theme of martyrdom, for Southwell portrays Mary as surpassing the male disciples in devotion to her Lord in that she was willing to die with Christ when they fled from him (13). The baroque prose text also favorably contrasts Mary's courage with Peter's cowardly denial of Christ (127). In both *Marie Magdelens Fvneral Teares* and *Saint Peters Complaynt*, Southwell is careful to note that Peter denied Christ while attempting to placate a maid, a rather overt allusion to the threatening anti-recusant policies of the virgin Queen Elizabeth.

REVERBERATIONS OF SOUTHWELL'S *EPISTLE OF COMFORT* IN *KING LEAR*

Shakespeare's poignant allusion to *An Epistle of Comfort*, Southwell's tract advocating recusant martyrdom, is strategically placed in the scene in which Cordelia and Lear are apprehended as prisoners, shortly before Cordelia is killed and Lear dies of a broken heart. For the original audiences of *King Lear*, among whom there would be some, like Shakespeare, who had secretly read Southwell's *Epistle*, the allusion to the martyred Southwell must have been electric. Lear's quotation of Southwell while Lear is apprehended as a prisoner who will die momentarily must have struck informed members of the original audience as something like an appearance of the ghost of the Jesuit who had been martyred at Tyburn some ten years earlier in 1595.

F.W. Brownlow first noted Shakespeare's important allusion to *An Epistle of Comfort* in *King Lear*, arguing that it was "a sign of the personal element in Shakespeare's engagement with Harsnett as well as its seriousness that he should allow the dead poet-priest to speak through the mouth of his player king at this moment of the tragedy" (*Shakespeare* 131). Brownlow helpfully contextualizes the allusion in terms of its religio-political significance: "That the play should have been performed at court, on St. Stephen's of all nights, in the year after the Gunpowder Plot, is a sign of Shakespeare's cool and cunning authority in the face of his times" (131). (Stephen was the first Christian martyr, in whose death Saul of Tarsus [eventually the Apostle Paul] was complicit.) By painting an allusive overlay of Jesuit torture and martyrdom onto the approaching execution of Cordelia (also a miscarriage of justice) and the resulting death of Lear from grief and exhaustion (Kent later refers to Lear being stretched upon the rack), Shakespeare must have struck a few chords, to say the least.

This allusion to Southwell, quoted and analyzed below, shows Shakespeare getting his hands much dirtier in political controversy than is typical of him. By mapping Southwell's martyrdom onto the dethroned and abused Lear, the play comes precariously close to vocalizing a critique of the Elizabethan regime for its mistreatment of Catholics such as Southwell. Even so, Shakespeare showed some restraint in responding to such injustice by waiting to reference Southwell in such a potentially dangerous manner until James was well ensconced in his reign.

There were strong popular hopes that the reign of James would be characterized by a Solomonic peace rather than the fractious religious tensions of the late Elizabethan reign. The Gunpowder Plot threatened to disrupt such a rapprochement, but *King Lear* gestures towards a revitalization of pacific hopes. James's temperate response to the Gunpowder Plot (at least with respect to the broader Catholic community) might have given Shakespeare the window he needed to voice his own concerns about the dangerous potential for the reactive mistreatment of Catholics. Hence the uncharacteristically daring allusion to Southwell's *Epistle of Comfort*. The echo of Southwell by Lear, whose own sufferings strongly elicit audience sympathy, arguably belies Shakespeare's sense of outrage at the state sanctioned torture and murder of his Jesuit relative. Indeed, the location of this extended allusion might give the impression that Shakespeare daringly champions the cause of his cousin (as defined in the period), the martyred Jesuit poet, polemicist, and priest.

However, a closer reading of Shakespeare's appropriation of Southwell's voice in *King Lear* reveals a more nuanced response to Southwell's Catholic missionary agenda. While the allusion to *An Epistle of Comfort* inevitably would have created or encouraged empathy for Southwell's memory in many audience members, it is unlikely that Shakespeare's allusion to Southwell was widely perceived as an obvious endorsement of Southwell's Jesuit ministry and martyrdom, for if it had, Shakespeare might have landed in jail like Ben Jonson and Thomas Middleton for tackling politically loaded religious controversies. And while Shakespeare certainly honors the suffering of his Jesuit relative—the play keenly honors all types of unjust suffering—the adaptation of the allusion in the play mutes, possibly even critiques, the confessional politics of Southwell's martyrdom. The play thus impugns Elizabeth's cruel anti-recusant policies without necessarily endorsing the Catholic culture of martyrdom that emerged in response to her persecutions.

A comparison of Southwell's source material with Shakespeare's appropriation of it reveals a striking contrast in the two texts' responses to suffering. Southwell's metaphor of a bird singing in a cage depicts the external bondage but spiritual freedom of the persecuted recusant. Like a bird, which sings more melodiously in a cage than at liberty, the recusant can hope to advance in spiritual devotion while being incarcerated for his or her beliefs:

> Honorable it is in Gods quarell, to be abridged of bodilye libertye, for mainteyning the true libertye and freedome of our soule. The birdes beinge vsed and naturallye delighted with the full scope of the ayre, though they be neuer so well fedd in the Cage yet are they all wayes pooringe at euery cranie to see whether they may escape. . . . Lett vs not in this be lyke the senseless byrdes, but rather imitate them in an other propertye, which is, that in the cage they not onlye singe their naturall note, both sweetlyer and oftener, then abroade, but learne also diuerse other, farre more pleasant, and delightsome: So we both keepe, and oftener practise our wonted deuotions, and besydes learne new exercises of vertue, both for our owne comfort, and example of others. (223–225)

Shakespeare poignantly echoes Southwell's recusant rhetoric in Lear's response to being unjustly incarcerated with Cordelia. Like Southwell's recusant, Lear determines that he and Cordelia "will sing like birds i'th' cage," in spite of their misfortunes:

> . . .Come, let's away to prison.
> We two alone will sing like birds i'th' cage.
> When thou dost ask me blessing, I'll kneel down
> And ask of thee forgiveness; so we'll live,
> And pray, and sing, and tell old tales, and laugh
> At gilded butterflies, and hear poor rogues
> Talk of court news, and we'll talk with them too—
> Who loses and who wins, who's in, who's out,
> And take upon's the mystery of things
> As if we were God's spies; and we'll wear out
> In a walled prison packs and sects of great ones
> That ebb and flow by th' moon. (24.8–19)

Shakespeare's citation of Southwell's metaphor of the caged bird would initially seem to evoke a Catholic sense of martyrdom. Yet Shakespeare reconfigures Southwell's text in ways that suggest the playwright is critical of the Jesuit's zealous confessional rhetoric. Significantly, Shakespeare replaces Southwell's partisan martyrological discourse with a soteriological emphasis on personal forgiveness and blessing in the context of close familial relationships needing reconciliation. Shakespeare's emphasis in the prison scene is on the healing of Lear and Cordelia's relationship, rather than on divisive religious politics. If salvation is attainable at all in the play, it is through charity rather than confessional affiliation or theological dogma.

Much like the exorcisms in *King Lear* that are therapeutic without being denominationally inflected, the "martyrdoms" of Cordelia and Lear are conspicuously devoid of theological controversy. Frankie Rubinstein further notes that "Lear's packs and sects are the Catholic and Protestant sects, whose controversies split families and the nation on religion and politics as well" (249). Rubinstein also rightly observes that Catholics would consider Protestants to be members of as sect, and that Protestants had a similar estimation of Catholics (245). Lear's desire to evade the contentious "packs and sects" of competing religious communities arguably puts an irenic spin on Southwell's resistant metaphor of the singing caged bird. Shakespeare's soteriological emphasis here (as in the romances) is on forgiveness, whereas Southwell's soteriological emphasis is on martyrdom in *An Epistle* and the majority of his other works.

In *An Epistle of Comfort*, Southwell himself endorses the inflammatory language surrounding religious identity in the sixteenth-century. "Scismatickes" are Catholics who conform outwardly to Protestantism and "Nicodemites" are Protestants who conform outwardly to Catholicism (386; 398). Southwell is at times as extreme and hateful in his description of Protestants as Harsnett is of Catholics. Arians, Lutherans, and Calvinists are "no longer members of Christ, but the sinagoge of antichrist" (169). Southwell likens church papists raising their children in the English church to those pre-exilic biblical Jews and ancient near east gentiles who sacrificed their children to demons (400). To Harsnett, the Jesuits are demonic; to Southwell, the Protestant heretics are demonic.

Southwell imagines his determination to suffer for his Catholic faith as a weapon against Protestant heresy: "But we are now in a battayle, not onlye agaynst men of our tymes, who are both *Epicures* in conditions, *Iewes* in malice, and *Heretickes* in proud and obstinate spirittes: But agaynst the whole rable and generation of all heretiks, that since Christes tyme haue ben, & in a manner with Satan the father of lying, and his whole armye" (183). Southwell accordingly sees martyrdom as the most effective strategy against the Elizabethan settlement. Perhaps it would be unfair to blame Southwell for demonizing Protestants, for they were the ones imprisoning, torturing, and executing his fellow Jesuit missionaries, and Southwell himself would pay the ultimate price for his Catholic commitments by being hanged, drawn, and quartered on charges of treason, i.e., for being a practicing Catholic priest in late Elizabethan England.

While Southwell glorifies Catholic martyrdom in soteriological terms as a baptism of blood (*Epistle* 319), he refuses to acknowledge the similar courage and conviction of the Protestant Marian martyrs.[34] Instead, Southwell condemns the martyrs celebrated in Foxe's *Acts and Monuments* as belonging to the same heretical and ephemeral tradition as Arius (431). In repudiating the Protestant martyrs, Southwell cites and glosses on 1 Corinthians 13:3: "For in trueth as S. *Paule* sayeth, though I deliuer my bodye to be burned, and haue no charitye and vnion with God, and his true Church: it auayleth me nothinge" (433–434). Southwell interpolates into the Pauline text, "vnion with God, and his true Church," thus reinterpreting the Pauline rhetoric of charity as a defense of Catholic martyrdom and a rebutting of Protestant martyrdom.

Lear's desire to "wear out / In a walled prison packs and sects of great ones," far from affirming Southwell's partisan politics and polemics of martyrdom, suggests a weariness with the very religious disputation and intolerance advocated from opposite ends of the spectrum by Harsnett and Southwell. At this moment in the play, Lear recalls the deposed Richard II, who emerges as an ironic, self-appointed Christ figure in his solipsistic melancholy. But just as Richard II only partially mirrors the suffering Christ, so too does Lear only partially reflect the Jesuit martyr he references. Like Southwell, Lear is victim of injustice and cruelty. But while Southwell in *An Epistle of Comfort* glorifies martyrdom for confessional affiliation, Lear would rather suffer in a fashion that transcends the partisanship of religious "sects," focusing instead on his own need for

---

34. Of course, Protestantism also had a well developed veneration for martyrdom, as seen in the most compendious martyrology ever written in English, Foxe's *Actes and Monuments*. Foxe's antipathy for Catholicism is even more pronounced than Southwell's antipathy for Protestantism. Brad Gegory's *Salvation at Stake: Christian Martyrdom in Early Modern Europe* conveys the confessional dimensions of martyrdom, be it Catholic, Reformed, or Anabaptist.

forgiveness and reconciliation. Like Flannery O'Connor, Lear knows that *The Life You Save May Be Your Own.*

The penultimate quotation in *An Epistle of Comfort* is from St. Bernard on the necessity of perseverance and patience, which Southwell defines as a willingness to suffer for the Catholic faith (501). When Lear utters his agonized cry, "I will be the pattern of all patience" (9.37), he conceivably echoes not only Job and Christ, but also Southwell. While clearly not reading the play in Calvinist terms, Gary Kuchar has astutely noted the significance of perseverance in *Lear*, suggesting that Shakespeare is responding to the debates about such Calvinist theology in the Hampton Court conference ("Compassion" 139). Indeed, the play parts company with both Calvinist and Catholic doctrines of perseverance. While Calvinism was determined to signify perseverance as a mark of unconditional election, and Southwell to interpret perseverance as the making of a Catholic saint, Shakespeare imagines Lear's sufferings in terms of neither theological idiom, but rather as an expression of the universal heroism of enduring the vicissitudes of life and making peace with broken relationships, as in the prison scene with Cordelia.

The universal effect of Shakespeare's dramaturgy is achieved as the tragedy encourages the audience to perceive similarities across confessional divides. The agonies of Lear and, by allusive extension, the torments of Southwell, are not to be celebrated as confessionally specific examples of heroic fortitude. In *King Lear*, the *division* of the kingdom is what precipitates the violence in the first place. The biggest split in the late Elizabethan kingdom was between the Catholic minority and the Protestant majority, not to mention the tension within the English church between the Puritan majority and the episcopal containment of it. Lear's repudiation of sectarianism even as he is being wrongfully treated counterpoises the period's preoccupation with hatred and violence along confessional lines.

Shakespeare's handling of his partisan source materials, either Catholic or conforming, provides an alternate response to the period's vitriolic approach to religious controversy. For Harsnett, the Jesuits are diabolical practitioners of a fraudulent craft of exorcism, but for two of the characters in *King Lear*, exorcism becomes a metaphor for the healing power of forgiveness and a cathartic release from despair and self-hatred. For Southwell, the greatest weapon a Catholic can wield at Protestant heresy is to offer his life as both a political and spiritual statement. In *King Lear*, the salutary response to unjust suffering is relocated from martyrdom to forgiveness. When Kent articulates his desire to die in solidarity with Lear, the focus of his impending martyrdom is not confessional loyalty or theological precision, but tenacious relational fidelity. Hence my use of the inadequate descriptor "universal" to capture the cross-confessional dimensions of the play's impulses towards compassion and endurance.

The theological skepticism in *King Lear* is not confined to exorcism and martyrdom, but also broaches the more central soteriological terrain of sin and forgiveness. Southwell, too, advances his own hamartiology or doctrine of sin. The title of chapter five of *An Epistle* is as follows: "The fifte comfort in tribulation is that our punishmentes are but easy in comparison of our desertes" (120). Directly refuting Southwell's religious rhetoric, Lear makes the self-vindicating claim, "I am a man more sinned against than sinning" (9.60). Lear's utterance is a consummate reiteration of monotheism's most persistent paradox—the problem of evil. Lear's statement also seems to interrogate the justice of the Lord's Prayer, "And forgive us our debts, as we forgive our debtors" (Mt. 6:12).

Indeed, Lear's suffering at the hands of Gonoril and Regan is in excess of his desserts, but then again, so is Cordelia's mistreatment by Lear grossly undeserved. But by the end of the play, Lear is willing to seek forgiveness from Cordelia, though he will not live long enough to struggle through the process of forgiving Gonoril and Regan, even if he wanted to. Shakespeare reserves forgiveness of that magnitude for *The Tempest*. The religious skepticism in Lear's perspective on his suffering contrasts sharply with the zealous hunger for self-authenticating martyrdom that hangs over Southwell's poetry and prose almost like a death wish.

SOUTHWELL'S POETRY AND *KING LEAR*

In *King Lear*, Shakespeare possibly echoes one of Southwell's poems which circulated only in manuscript in the period because of its dangerous topicality—"I dye without desert." Davidson and Sweeney believe this poem to be ventriloquizing the persona of the earl of Arundel (159), the same man who inspired Southwell's *Epistle of Comfort* (Brownlow, *Robert Southwell* 26). The speaker in this poem is styled as a victim of religious persecution and potential martyrdom. In metaphorically depicting the plight of the English recusant, Southwell's poet persona uses language and ideas which Shakespeare seems to recast in Edgar's speech and situation:

> Left orphane like in helpelesse state I rue
> With onely sighes and teares I pleade my case
> My dying plaints I daylie do renewe
> And fill with heavy noyse a desert place
> Some tender hart will weepe to here me mone
> Men pitty may but helpe me god alone. (13–18)

In recounting his reconciliation with his father, Edgar says to Albany,

> —O, our lives' sweetness,
> That with the pain of death would hourly die
> Rather than die at once! (24.181–183)

Edgar's statement is obviously a recasting of the Pauline confession, "I die daily" (1 Cor 15:31), as is Southwell's poetic complaint, "My dying plaints I daylie do renewe," but Shakespeare's text arguably has more affinities with Southwell's than St. Paul's. Edgar is "orphane like" in being disowned by his father and must "fill with heavy noyse a desert place" when he assumes the pitiful persona of Poor Tom on the stormy heath, uttering insane verbiage. But if Shakespeare is drawing some of his imagery from Southwell's poem, he reappropriates the lyric for much different purposes than Southwell. The peroration of Southwell's poem is a celebration of recusant martyrdom: "God doth sometimes first cropp the sweetest flowre / And leaves the weede till tyme do it devoure" (35–36). For Southwell, the supreme form of salvation is the reward promised to the faithful martyr.

Shakespeare instead imagines salvation in this context as human compassion meeting human need, particularly in close, familial relationships. Salvation for Edgar is reconciliation with his father, much like Lear's salvation is reconciliation with his only faithful daughter. Both reconciliations are achieved through the grace of forgiveness. Again, we see this play resisting the confessional agendas of its polemical sources, even as it borrows their powerful metaphors. In Southwell's poem "I dye without desert," martyrdom is figured as a glorious entrance to salvation, but in this parallel passage in *King Lear*, Edgar recounts his compassion for Gloucester which "saved him from despair" (24.188). Edgar effects Gloucester's salvation by intervening in his suicide attempt through a pseudo-exorcism, thus redefining soteriology in terms of psychological and spiritual health rather than confessional allegiance.

Gary Kuchar has noted that Southwell's poem, "Decease release," is echoed in the prison scene with Lear and Cordelia (personal communication). The poem imagines Mary Queen of Scots as a monarch turned saint, a glorious Catholic martyr. Peter Davidson and Anne Sweeney note that this poem, too, was only available in manuscript form in the early modern period because of its political volatility (158–159). To possess this poem could cause one to be guilty of treason (158–159). But the imprisoned Lear's situation is only partly analogous to Mary's, and therefore Shakespeare's echoing of Southwell's poem should not be interpreted as a holistic endorsement of the poem's martyrological perspectives. By the end of the play, Lear may be spiritually saved through repentance and forgiveness, but he is no saint in the Catholic sense of the word. Cordelia, coming from France as queen consort to provide relief to the English resistance movement, then suffering a treacherous death by an unauthoritative execution, would be a closer parallel to Southwell's martyred queen.

Indeed, Cordelia's presence is one of the strongest Catholic resonances in the play. An unnamed character tells Lear, "Thou hast one daughter / Who redeems nature from the general curse" (20.194–195). This statement alludes to Jesus, the Son of God (he is feminized as Lear's "one daughter"), the redeemer of the world (Cordelia also "redeems nature"), the second Adam ("the general curse" of the first Adam is reversed by Christ). Cordelia's redemptive presence in the play is a much needed corrective to Lear's misogyny. In spite of Shakespeare's determination to distance himself from the martyrological zeal of Southwell, Cordelia as quasi-saint and martyred queen possibly has Catholic resonances, especially when considered in relation to Mary, Queen of Scots. Loosely speaking, Lear and Cordelia undergo what Southwell would call a baptism of blood, thus associating them with martyrdom.

Gary Kuchar and Richard Wilson have drawn attention to the martyrological connections between *Saint Peters Complaynt* and Shakespeare's *Venus and Adonis* (Kuchar "Alchemy"; Wilson 297–316). While Southwell's poem obviously promotes martyrdom, Wilson suggests that "at its core, *Venus and Adonis* is a critique of martyrdom" (301). If, as Wilson contends, these two narrative poems are in conversation with each other, then it is possible Shakespeare continued the discussion with *Saint Peters Complaynt* in *King Lear*. I have argued that *Saint Peters Complaynt* is Southwell's thought experiment for the grief-stricken and conscience-smitten recusant who has conformed under pressure to the church of England. I have also argued that *King Lear* responds to Southwell's martyrdom by reimagining it without its confessional politics, as I have tried to prove in Shakespeare's handling of his allusion to *An Epistle of Comfort*.

Whether or not Shakespeare intended it, there is a triangulation of the bird in a cage metaphor in *An Epistle of Comfort*, *Saint Peters Complaynt*, and *King Lear*. In one of *Saint Peters Complaynt*'s most striking sixain stanzas, Peter as persona relates how he has become demonized by denying his Lord. (The demonic imagery here in *Saint Peters Complaynt* also reverberates in both Harsett's *Declaration* and *King Lear*.) While striking to a religiously minded reader today, the idea that Peter, the first pope, could have seen himself as a former demoniac, was arguably normative in the sixteenth century when serious Christians often reflected on whether their spirituality was genuine or inspired by the devil.

In *Saint Peters Complaynt*, we also observe a sixteenth century work of religion choosing to demonize its hero rather than its polemical opponents. In the cases of Harsnett's *Declaration* and Southwell's *Epistle of Comfort*, not to mention nearly every work of religious disputation in the period, it is typically one's enemies on the other side of the confessional divide who are demonic. Interestingly, the self-examination and self-recrimination of the apostolic persona are as robust as in the spirituality found in any work of Puritan or other form of Protestant devotion (such as John Bunyan's Restoration autobiography, *Grace Abounding to the Chief of Sinners*). Southwell's Peter, instead of demonizing his enemies, demonizes himself in a posture of penitence.

In an apostrophe to the disciple John, whose acquaintance with the high priest helped to secure Peter's entrance into the palace where Peter denied that he knew Christ, Peter castigates himself in the most severe terms:

> Why didst thou lead me to this hell of evils:
> To shew my selfe a feind among the divels? (233–234)

Southwell represents Peter as a demonized denier of Christ by reworking the image of a bird in a cage:

> The dispossessed devels that out I threw,
> In *Jesus* name, now impiously forsworne,
> Triumph to see me caged in their mew,
> Trampling my ruines with contempt and scorne,
> My perjuries were musick to their daunce:
> And now they heap disdaines on my mischaunce. (607–612)

Peter is captive in a "mew," or cage for hawks, but his only songs are discordant "perjuries" of his Lord.

In contrast, the persecuted recusants of *An Epistle of Comfort* "in the cage . . . not onlye singe their naturall note, both sweetlyer and oftener, then abroad, but learne also diuerse other, farre more pleasant, and delightsome" (224). Also unlike Peter, Lear determines to sing while being unjustly imprisoned with Cordelia:

> . . .Come, let's away to prison.
> We two alone will sing like birds i'th' cage. (24.8–9)

Instead, Peter laments that his denial of Christ was the music to which demons danced. Analogously, Southwell thus demonizes confessional disloyalty and apostasy. The pathos of Lear and Cordelia in prison, though ultimately tragic, is comparatively free of the self-hatred of Southwell's lapsed Peter.

Saint Peters Complaynt conveys the extreme psychological pressures acting upon English Catholics determined to be loyal to their faith in the face of escalating persecution. While it may be difficult to prove that Shakespeare is deliberately echoing the caged bird metaphor from *Saint Peters Complaynt* in the prison scene in *King Lear*, these imagistically related but thematically contrasting passages again reveal that Shakespeare's play is more concerned to evoke compassionate and redemptive responses to suffering than to promote confessionally weighted strategies of self-recrimination or self-vindication.

The dreaded rack is another metaphorical link between Southwell's long narrative poem and Shakespeare's tragedy. For Southwell's Peter, the bitter pain of his denial of Christ is paradoxically curative:

> Sorrow, the smart of evill, Sinnes eldest child:
> Best, when unkind in killing who it bred,
> A racke, for guilty thoughtes, a bit, for wild.
> The scourge, that whips, the salve that cures offence. . . .
> (734–737)

While the sin of Peter's denial evokes profound pain, that pain has the penitential effect of restoring Peter's faith. Peter's pain is analogous to the lapsed recusant's guilty conscience, which presents a far worse prospect for Southwell than anything he would inevitably suffer under Elizabethan interrogation and torture.

The image of the rack reappears at a critical juncture in the last scene of *King Lear*, when Kent urges Edgar to accept Lear's death as a cessation of the king's agonies:

> Vex not his ghost. O, let him pass. He hates him
> That would upon the rack of this tough world
> Stretch him out longer. (24.308–310)

Some in Shakespeare's audiences would recall that Southwell himself had been subject to a lengthy solitary confinement where he was brutally tortured on a recurring basis before finally being hanged, drawn and quartered.[35] The Elizabethan state claimed Southwell's life as a traitor; the Catholic church has since canonized him as a saint.[36]

While the rack has strong religious and political associations in the early modern period, Kent employs the image metaphorically to represent Lear's pain of living with a host of vicissitudes—broken family

---

35. Marotti provides a riveting and detailed account of Southwell's execution which shows the impulse of the recusant community to venerate the relics of their martyrs (25). The fact that Shakespeare does not ridicule relics in *King Lear*, even though Harsnett satirized the use of Edmund Campion's relics in the Denham exorcisms, possibly suggests that Shakespeare was too respectful of the gravity of Southwell's martyrdom (which also produced relics) to allow the play to degenerate into such disrespectful confessional mudslinging. Marotti claims that Southwell's death had a number of striking features, including the compassion of the crowd. Shakespeare seems to have capitalized on such compassion by echoing Southwell's martyrdom in *King Lear*. Marotti recounts that the hangman, contrary to standard procedure, allowed Southwell to die before disembowelling him. Marotti then quotes from Garnet's account of Southwell's martyrdom:

> [Instead he] pulled on his legs—an act of courtesy and humanity that is unusual. One of the executioners several times made to cut the rope, but was stopped by the Lord [Mountjoy] and by the whole crowd, which cried out three times: 'Let him be, let him be.' The executioner took him down with great reverence and carried him in his own arms, assisted by his companions, to the place where he was to be quartered, whereas in all other cases it is the custom to drag [the bodies] brutally along the ground. When he was being disemboweled, his heart leaped into the hands of the executioner. All those who stood around spoke of him with respect, and there was none to cry 'Traitor' according to custom. (25)

The humane elements that intervene in Southwell's otherwise brutal execution make it an effective martyrdom for Shakespeare to reference in *King Lear*. Because his death seemed to draw respect from Catholics and Protestants alike, Southwell thus becomes an important icon in Shakespeare's campaign against cruelty in *King Lear*.

36. Monta suggests that the Elizabethan authorities felt so threatened by the rhetorical power of Southwell's writings that they rarely gave him access to writing materials during his imprisonment (118).

relationships, disloyal children and servants, civil war, the loss of power and prestige, mental illness, faulty character, bad judgment, senility, grief over the plight of the sick and poor, and exposure to the elements. Again, these are "universal" experiences of human suffering rather than persecutions engineered along confessional fault lines. Perhaps one of the implications that emerges from the play is the awareness that the early moderns had enough problems without fighting over religious and other ideological differences. Southwell, however, saw things differently. He believed that capitulation to the political and religious consensus would wrongfully extirpate his voice and his church's voice from his culture. He was willing to pay with his blood for the hope of seeing his faith granted minority status, or better yet, for the dream of his faith becoming reestablished as the consensus it once was.

CONCLUSION: SOTERIOLOGY IN *KING LEAR*

Much like Southwell's brutal death can be regarded either as either a dreadful expression of human cruelty or a glorious triumph of spiritual courage, *King Lear* has been identified as both a wasteland of barbarism and an arena of heroic endurance. Perhaps some readers will regard my attempt to trace soteriological discourse in *King Lear* as missing the mark. The play has been so persistently regarded as an eloquent, yet ultimately hopeless, response to human suffering, that nihilism might be more germane to the tragedy than soteriology.

Yet the two modes of para-soteriological discourse that I have identified in the play—exorcism and martyrdom—are perhaps as deeply implicated in suffering as in healing. One of the basic assumptions of early modern soteriology is that suffering can produce salutary as well as destructive results. The theological underpinnings of exorcism suggest that the subject can be deeply distorted and afflicted by evil originating from self, others, and even immaterial, quasi-personal beings before she experiences therapeutic relief and spiritual cleansing. *King Lear* may not traffic in the supernatural dimensions of exorcism, but the specter of evil in the play assumes staggering dimensions, whether or not "the foul fiend" is personified (as in early modern theology) or merely metaphorized (as in the emerging skepticism of Harsnett and perhaps even Shakespeare).

Martyrdom, too, precariously straddles the knife edge of suffering and glory. While early modern Catholics attributed salvation (including exorcism) to martyrdom, there was always the risk that the supreme sacrifice of faith could degenerate into confessional politics. The theology of martyrdom is *imitatio Christi* taken to the extreme—a saint's death can produce life through the power of self-giving love. And yet even the putatively salvific dimensions of the deaths of martyrs like Edmund Campion and Robert Southwell are causally linked to the most barbaric and inhumane tortures of the period—all of which were inflicted in the name of God and the Queen.

In *King Lear*, salvation may never fully emerge Phoenix-like from the ashes of suffering, but there are precious glimpses of kindness and compassion even in the bleak tragic landscape. In the play, the weakness and vulnerability of humanity are put on display, but this kenosis has the unexpected effect of ennobling some of the characters, who are, in effect, renovated by their sufferings. Lear, Gloucester, the Fool, Kent, and Edgar, far from being diminished by their subjection to unjust suffering, are instead augmented by it, growing in self-knowledge, contrition, humility, compassion, generosity, and perseverance. To this extent, the play intimates the soteriological idea that suffering can enhance or express *caritas*.

While critics have long-noted that Lear's grief-stricken entrance with the murdered Cordelia in his arms is like a gender reversed Pietà, it is important to observe that Shakespeare's soteriological perspective here is distinctly Johannine, perhaps indicating something of the turn from what John Coolidge called *The Pauline Renaissance* to what Paul Cefalu calls *The Johannine Renaissance*. *King Lear's* privileging of charity to faith corroborates Cefalu's thesis that the preoccupation with faith in the literature of the sixteenth century evolved into an emphasis on charity in the poetry of the seventeenth century.

When Lear had entered the stage mad, "*crowned with weeds and flowers*" (s.d. 20.79) instead of thorns, Edgar exclaims, "O thou side-piercing sight!" (20.85). This biblical allusion to the piercing of Christ with a spear is found only in John's gospel (Cefalu "Johannine" 1047) and has important implications for soteriology. As Paul Cefalu observes, "Augustine's emphasis on the result of the wounding rather than the piercing itself allows for his typological and intertextual glossing of the passage: from the opening flows the sacraments, vehicles of the blood (justification) and water (baptismal sanctification)" (1052). Shakespeare's biblical allusion, taken in the context of the play's relentless preoccupation with pain, faintly echoes a soteriology based on Christ's sufferings and the sacraments.

This is not to suggest that Shakespeare is endorsing every aspect of traditional soteriology, for the play's bleak ending would seem to deny the very salvific hope it intimates. Lear hopes that the murdered Cordelia is alive, for that would "redeem all sorrows / That ever I have felt" (24.262–263). But Lear's hope that the feather stirring in front of Cordelia's mouth is evidence that she is alive turns out to be an insane delusion, much like the audience's hope that the play's unbearable suffering will be alleviated or vindicated. Even as *King Lear* would seem to evoke a nostalgia for the mysterious rituals of exorcism and the cruciform images of martyrdom, Shakespeare underscores his soteriological discourse with nagging doubts about the credibility of the resurrection. *King Lear* ultimately places a heavy burden of proof on Christian soteriology. Does God have the power or even the desire to save this world from itself?

From a skeptical perspective, the play may be calling into question the meaning of both suffering and salvation. Lear rants and raves during the storm that the gods are now discovering all the secret sins and crimes (which Lear apparently attributes to others, not to himself) having previously gone undetected:

> Close pent-up guilts, rive your concealèd centres
> And cry these dreadful summoners grace.
> I am a man more sinned against than sinning. (9.58–60)

At this point, it is unclear whether the senile king is resisting self-knowledge or legitimately objecting to his mistreatment at the hands of his elder daughters and disloyal subjects. By the end of the play, Lear is willing to admit his folly to Cordelia and to seek forgiveness from her in a kind of private ritual of penance. But it could be argued that even in this moment of anagnorisis, Lear's reconciliation with Cordelia is compromised by his delusional, childlike regression. The ambiguous efficacy of Lear's conversion, the unrelenting affliction of the virtuous characters, and the rich biblical and theological language in the play all suggest that Shakespeare is putting salvation to the litmus test of suffering.

On the one hand, if the soteriology of *King Lear* is somewhat skeptical, on the other hand, it may be somewhat ecumenical. The play is ecumenical in the sense that it evades religious polemic, while simultaneously drawing upon contentious Catholic and Protestant perspectives of exorcism and martyrdom, and somehow harmonizing them (or, at least, attempting to do so). The play is skeptical in that its exorcisms do not require "direct" divine intervention. And just how skeptical is the play? The lack of apparent divine intervention means that Catholics likely would have rejected the soteriology of the play. Stripping exorcism of its metaphysical power is a profoundly radical move for Catholics and even for many Protestants, the recent English outlawing of exorcism notwithstanding. Yet to reduce the play's soteriological tendencies to "secularism" diminishes in an untenable way the repeated and insistent references to exorcism and martyrdom. The demons from which Edgar and Gloucester are delivered may be metaphorical rather than literal, but these characters nonetheless experience a profoundly salvific and humanizing experience of *gratia* and *caritas*, which are central concerns of early modern religious dogma, if not practice.

The overall thrust of the religious allusions in *King Lear* is cross-confessional rather than partisan. In absorbing powerful images from such confessionally antithetical authors such as Harsnett and Southwell, while carefully expunging their volatile polemics, the soteriology of *King Lear* arguably becomes as ecumenical as it is skeptical. If *King Lear* can mute the acerbic Protestant bias of Harsnett's pamphlet and divest Southwell's consolatory prose of its confessional extremism, perhaps the play recognizes the exigency for soteriology to break denominational barriers, rather than entrenching them in the manner of its sources.

Conclusion

I BEGAN THIS VOLUME by citing Anthony Dawson's assessment that the Claudius prayer scene in *Hamlet* is ambiguous in terms of its confessional affiliation (239). I retorted that such ambiguity calls for further inquiry into historical theology. This study has been precisely such an exploration of the relationship between historical theology and Shakespearean drama. A question that naturally arises at the end of a book about Shakespeare's handling of the bitterly controversial topic of soteriology is this: "What is Shakespeare's perspective on soteriology?" In other words, where might a critic position Shakespeare along the great Reformation divide?

A REFORMATION CONTINUUM OR REFORMATION DIVIDE?

Before answering this question, some clarification about my overarching terminology of "the Reformation divide" is in order. The question of where Shakespeare might be positioned "along" the Reformation divide suggests a continuum of theological positions, maybe a plurality or constellation. But the word "divide" suggests a dichotomy. So which is it: a Reformation continuum or a Reformation divide? At times this study acknowledges a spectrum of soteriological positions, even in a single play, as in my chapter on agency in *Hamlet*. At other times, this study negotiates entrenched hostility between antithetical Catholic and Protestant soteriologies, as in the debate between justification by faith or works in *The Merchant of Venice*. It seems as though Shakespeare transcends the language I use to describe Reformation soteriological controversy.

Many of the polemical religious writings of the early modern period are characterized by polarizing rhetoric, substantiating my terminology of a Reformation "divide." One thinks of Samuel Harsnett's *Declaration of Egregious Popish Impostures* and Robert Southwell's *Epistle of Comfort*, confessionally antithetical source texts for *King Lear*. Even the theological writings of the magisterial Reformers such as Luther and Calvin and the responses of Bellarmine and Moore are dripping with Catholic-Protestant hostility. Again, a theological "divide." The Renaissance commercial theater frequently registered the Catholic-Protestant hostility of the Reformation "divide." Nonetheless, this study conveys Shakespeare's rich engagement with a variety of soteriological views, reminding us of the spectrum of theological positions represented in his diverse audiences. Perhaps a Reformation "continuum" after all?

Nevertheless, I have chosen to retain the language of a "Reformation divide" because it captures the religio-political polarization of the period. However, I recognize that alternate terminology, such as a theological continuum or constellation more accurately reflects the sheer variety of soteriological positions represented by different strains of Protestantism and Catholicism. I believe Shakespeare's plays effectively capture such soteriological variety in a way that many of the polemicists, theologians, and even some other playwrights could not, stuck as they were in the religious gridlock of the period. Recent historiography, such as that of Alec Ryrie, Alexandra Walsham, and Peter Marshall, has helped to convey the rich diversity of religion in the period, and Shakespeare studies are working to recover this theological polysemy.

It is disappointing when the Reformation "divide" registers in the tone of particular literary critics in a way that perpetuates some of the polarization of the past. The religious polarization in the early modern period is also a cautionary tale against the current political polarization in North America, as Holly Nelson so astutely argues. The Reformation divide often fostered hatred between Catholics and Protestants, even though both claimed to be Christians. History likewise shows present day North Americans that we might be in danger of forgetting the humanity we have in common with our ideological "enemies," be they political or social conservatives or liberals.

So where might we position Shakespeare along the Reformation divide? Before answering this question, another word of caution is in order. Brian Cummings rightly observes that Shakespeare and religion studies have all too often been misguidedly biographical (14). I do not intend to fall into the trap of identifying Shakespeare the man with any particular confessional position, whether it be related to soteriology in particular or to religion more generally. Another word of caution comes from Erin Kelly, who tells her graduate students of drama and religion, "We don't have to fight the Reformation all over again." Any attempt to co-opt Shakespeare to a particular confessional position is likely to be a disingenuous political gesture, especially considering that the actual biographical evidence for Shakespeare's beliefs is so scant. While soteriology is not likely to produce the kind of violence today that it did in the sixteenth and seventeenth centuries, many religiously minded readers of Shakespeare in the twenty-first century are likely to have strong feelings about the topic, be they Catholic or Protestant. Identifying Shakespeare with either branch of Christianity arguably involves making a politically charged statement. Plays such as *Othello* and *The Merchant of Venice* are also likely to trigger emotions for present day Muslims and Jews. Agnostics and atheists may have personal responses to the positing of a believing or irreligious Shakespeare. To conscript Shakespeare to a particular religious position is therefore inadvisable on intellectual grounds and perhaps even affective ones, unless of course, more substantial evidence is brought forward.

IDENTIFYING SOTERIOLOGICAL POSITIONS IN SHAKESPEAREAN DRAMA

Nonetheless, at the end of this study, I do submit that it is possible to perceive particular theological leanings or colorings in particular plays. While certainly not exhaustive, my analysis of Shakespeare's handling of soteriology in four plays has shown him to be engaged with such theology as an informed thinker and not merely as an impartial observer. While the theological perspectives I have elicited from Shakespeare's plays are not confessionally uniform nor obviously rhetorical, their subtlety and sophistication suggest elements of keen interest and intervention.

So how do the plays at hand convey soteriological leanings? First, I want to emphatically state that I do not think a Catholic, Protestant, or even ecumenical Shakespeare can be consistently deduced from his drama. Nevertheless, particular Catholic, Protestant, or ecumenical ideas and sentiments may all be construed at particular moments in particular plays. For a case study, let's start with the Claudius prayer scene in *Hamlet*, probably the most important soteriological action in Shakespearean drama.

I argue that the prayer scene in the first quarto of *Hamlet* is highly predestinarian, and thus Calvinist, in its theological orientation. With respect to the more authoritative second quarto of *Hamlet*, I present evidence for influences of both Lancelot Andrewes's "avant-garde conformity" and Jesuit Molinism (via an allusion to Robert Southwell).[1] Andrewes—a high ranking clergy in the church of England—and Southwell—a Jesuit priest and martyr—both advocate for free will in salvation, in contradistinction to Calvinism, which emphasizes the sovereignty of God through the doctrine of double predestination.

Laying questions of authorship aside, here we see that the first quarto contains theological perspectives which are challenged in the second quarto. To speak a little reductively, the Protestant first quarto is overturned in the second quarto by emerging theology derived from within the Protestant church of England *and* from the Roman Catholic church. If it is even possible to speak of the second quarto as resisting Calvinism, the fact that the play's theology of agency draws strength from both the English and the Roman churches makes it virtually impossible to definitively identify the play with a particular theological camp. That is not to say that Shakespeare was uninvested in theology, for the careful nuancing of Claudius's prayer conveys Shakespeare's ability to negotiate the tricky and volatile landscape of early modern soteriology in a way that impacts the audience, which also would have been aware of competing theological perspectives in the drama.

If Dawson is convinced that the confessional orientation of the Claudius prayer scene "is never clear" (239), perhaps some of the lack of clarity is owing to our relative illiteracy about Reformation theological controversy. Nevertheless, my attempt to ground the dramatic scene in its theological contexts fails to produce any simple explanation for *Hamlet*'s confessional orientation. Rather, the play, in its first and second quartos taken together, evinces flashes of Calvinism, proto-Arminianism, and Catholicism. Theologically speaking, this is not light reading. An engagement with historical theology thus reveals more of the ideological deftness and versatility of Shakespeare's dramatic art without reducing his plays to any kind of political, religious, or moral patronization.

The essay on *The Merchant of Venice* is in some ways the most controversial of my chapters, if considered in the light of Reformation debate. In arguing that *The Merchant of Venice* represents Shakespeare's ethical

---

1. "Avant-garde conformity" is Peter Lake's coinage for the theological orientation of Lancelot Andrewes and others in his circle.

critique of the cardinal doctrine of the Reformation, justification by faith alone (*sola fide*), I come perilously close to positioning Shakespeare on a particular side of the Reformation divide. However, when the argument is seen in the context of a close reading of one play and in the context of other essays in this study, it appropriately shrinks down to an assessment of one moment where a play's theological coloring is particularly vivid rather than suggesting an overarching identification of Shakespeare with a particular religious denomination.[2]

A personal engagement with Reformation controversy over Luther's doctrine of justification by faith alone produced some of the passion that was the catalyst for this study. Although I will not disclose whether my personal predilections are for or against Luther's quintessential Reformation dogma, I will reveal that with respect to this debate I began on one side of the Reformation divide, moved over to the other side, and then moved back to my original position, more convinced than ever of its compelling beauty and freedom. Such was the level of my personal engagement with these historically rich ideas during the drafting of this study. Regardless of my personal beliefs, however, I have attempted to let the theology in the plays speak for itself, rather than imposing my own preferences on the reader. I hope there is much here to interest critics who lean to either side of the Reformation divide, as well as those who celebrate the rise of secularism in Western culture out of a predominantly religious past.

The chapter on the discernment of spirits in *Hamlet* and the chapter on exorcism in *King Lear* are likely to be regarded as the most arcane portions of my engagement with early modern soteriology, and for good reason. In the interests of historical accuracy, I have not shied away from these topics, even though they are often fraught with academic suspicion. The controversies about demonic possession and exorcism that flared up in the early modern English church find expression in several of Shakespeare's plays, thus justifying the inclusion of such intellectually problematic topics in this study. The work of philosopher Phillip Wiebe

---

2. While I argue that *The Merchant of Venice* treats Luther's doctrine of justification by faith in rather pejorative terms, I regard *Measure for Measure* as upholding Luther's political distinction between the sacred and secular realms. Rather than suggesting that Shakespeare's theology can be reduced to either pro- or anti-Lutheran sentiments, I regard the plays as having very particular responses to specific aspects of Luther's theology, responses that are variously favorable or dissenting. For a reading of *Measure for Measure* as upholding a Catholic political vision, see Sarah Beckwith's *Shakespeare and the Grammar of Forgiveness*.

on religious experience brings these bizarre historical obsessions into the current scholarly conversation. In researching exorcism in Shakespeare, Stephen Greenblatt also draws connections between historical theology and present day anthropological studies.[3] While my research on the demonic in *Hamlet* and *King Lear* makes no explicit conclusions about how such historical phenomena might be understood by the current academy, I hope that my work will prompt further inquiry into possible intersections between religious experience of the past and present.

SOTERIOLOGY IN *THE WINTER'S TALE*

Ideally, this study would have included a soteriological analysis of one of the romances, but space did not permit. So here I will briefly sketch out how my argument could be advanced by a subsequent chapter on *The Winter's Tale*, perhaps the most soteriologically resonant of the romances. The spirituality of Shakespeare's romances derives its flavor from a unique blend of classical paganism, Renaissance magic, and Reformation theology. One of Shakespeare's preoccupations in the romances is with psychological maturation, which he illuminates in part with the discourses of soteriology, especially sanctification.

The Winter's Tale subjects the rash and impulsive Leontes to a spiritual maturation that Shakespeare articulates by reconciling and harmonizing Catholic and Protestant soteriologies. The ubiquitous references to faith and grace in the play are obvious throw-away lines to his predominantly Protestant audience. Shakespeare also playfully toys with the Pelagian idea of humanity's innate goodness in Polixenes's disavowal of original sin:

> ...we knew not
> The doctrine of ill-doing, nor dreamed
> That any did. Had we pursued that life,
> ...we should have answered heaven
> Boldly, 'not guilty', the imposition cleared
> Hereditary ours. (1.2.68–74)

(The legal language of exoneration also recalls Luther and Calvin's forensic renderings of justification by faith.)

---

3. See Greenblatt's "Shakespeare and the Exorcists" and *Shakespearean Negotiations* for an analogy between demonic possession in an anthropological study in Ethiopia and exorcism in Shakespearean drama.

But Leontes's phantasmagoric attack of jealousy soon exposes his need for renewal and maturation, despite his supposedly innocent origins. It also soon becomes clear that the Paulina of Shakespeare's romance is not the Protestant Paul of Luther and Calvin, for she subjects Leontes to a sixteen-year penance for his paranoid accusation of Hermione's infidelity, which resulted in the death of Mamillius, the exposure of the baby Perdita to a possible death, and the deaths of Antigonus and his mariners. Cleomenes suggests that it is only through sustained remorse for the supposed death of Hermione (for which Leontes believes himself responsible), that Leontes can find sufficient salvation to atone for his sin:

> . . .No fault could you make
> Which you have not redeemed; indeed, paid down
> More penitence than done trespass. At the last,
> Do as the heavens have done, forget your evil;
> With them forgive yourself. (5.1.2–6)

In Roman Catholic terms, Leontes has made the requisite satisfaction to validate his sacramental penance.

When Hermione is revealed to be alive, Leontes's hard won sanctification is finally complete (in terms of what the play requires of him). The first gentleman, expressing his determination to see the sculpture of Hermione, announces, "Every wink of an eye, some new grace will be born" (5.2.108–109). This statement, immediately preceding Hermione's "parousia," is a timely recasting of St. Paul's teaching on the resurrection of the body in 1 Corinthians 15:52: "In a moment, in the twinkling of an eye at the last trumpet: for the trumpet shal blowe, and the dead shal be raised vp incorruptible, and we shalbe changed" (Garber 850). Fascinatingly, Paulina also calls for music before performing the pseudo-resurrection of Hermione, as if to further establish the play's connection with the trumpet of Pauline eschatology. The "change" that we find in the play is not a literal resurrection, but a feigned one, as Richard McCoy rightly points out (142). And yet the ethical transformation of Leontes that Hermione's "resurrection" mirrors is all too real, even if both metamorphoses have been achieved without a miracle.

The generic transposition of this romance from tragedy through pastoral to comedy finds its resolution in the final scene of justifying faith. It is not until the last scene of the play that Shakespeare attributes salvific power to faith, when Paulina asks Leontes to secure his reunion with Hermione by exercising his faith: "It is required / You do awake your faith" (5.3.94–95). Shakespeare thus frontloads the play with Leontes's sanctification through penance, only resolving the drama with Leontes's justification by faith at the conclusion. Shakespeare thereby reverses the typical Protestant *ordo salutis*, in which salvation is caused by election, secured by justification, demonstrated by sanctification, and consummated by glorification. For Leontes, faith is the final principle which gives benediction to the strenuous remorse of his penance, whereas the reformers believed that the initial activation of justification by faith obviated the need for penance.

Ironically enough, Leontes's experience of faith as a postscript to a protracted period of introspective self-loathing is the spiritual method that Luther's life illustrates, if not his theology. In Shakespeare's art, both faith and grace are put into the service of an elaborate scheme of penance. The playwright thus harmonizes competing Catholic and Protestant soteriologies to convey his vision of personal transformation, which the early moderns' theorized as sanctification, but which critics today are more likely to describe as ethical and/or cognitive development.

THE RELIGIOUS IDENTITIES OF OTHER MAJOR EARLY MODERN ENGLISH PLAYWRIGHTS

Maurice Hunt argues that Shakespeare was able to syncretize Catholic and Protestant ideas in his plays to a much greater extent than his peers (ix). This study of soteriology certainly would lend credence to Hunt's observation, even if biographical clues as to Shakespeare's personal religious identity prove elusive at almost every turn. And since my study brings up Shakespeare's biography (as not relevant to my argument but worth mentioning), it might be à propos to consider by way of comparison the religious identities of several other major Renaissance playwrights—Marlowe, Jonson, and Middleton.

Christopher Marlowe is arguably the most transgressive of the major English Renaissance playwrights, his plays depicting a theologian's capitulation to the devil (*Doctor Faustus*), the burning of the Koran (*Tamburlaine, Part 2*), and the murder of a king by sexual assault (*Edward the Second*). Indeed, Marlowe's plays "are filled with the energy of the sacred and its desecration" (Romany and Lindsey xi). His Cambridge education was intended to prepare him for ministry in the Church of England, but Marlowe instead ventured into some shadowy activity that may have included spying as a double agent on Catholics and counterfeiting money. While early biographical assessments of Marlowe are problematic, in that they tend to be written by his detractors, Marlowe's reputation emerges as an "atheist."

The charge of atheism in the early modern period did not necessarily mean disbelief in the existence of God, yet the atheism that the vindictive informant Richard Baines attributes to Marlowe in the infamous Baines Note includes a litany of heterodox beliefs, many of which flaunt traditional assumptions about the deity and holiness of Jesus Christ (qtd. in Romany and Lindsey xxxiv–xxxv). While The Baines Note should be taken with a large grain of salt, Marlowe's plays do seem to subvert the religious status quo in a determined manner. Marlowe's early death in a bar-room brawl (that may or may not have involved intrigue) prevented him from achieving the fulness of his dramatic potential, but his bequest to Shakespearean drama is invaluable, even if the tone Shakespeare was to adopt would be more guarded, perhaps more conservative than Marlowe's. For example, the reckless violence in *The Jew of Malta* is enacted by people of various faiths (including Christians, Jews, and Muslims), whereas the entrenched stereotypes of *The Merchant of Venice* perpetuate longstanding policies of Jewish persecution by Christians.

Ben Jonson seems to have taken a more deliberate stance on his religious identity than Shakespeare. Jonson took religion seriously enough to convert to Roman Catholicism for a duration of twelve years, according to the testimony of William Drummond. Jonson converted to the old faith while in prison for murdering fellow actor Gabriel Spencer. The priest who was responsible for Jonson's conversion is likely Thomas Wright, author of *The Passions of the Minde in Generall*, for which Jonson wrote a commendatory poem (Crowley 56–59). In light of the fact that recusants were persecuted and that it was illegal even to seek spiritual direction from a Catholic priest, Jonson's conversion in prison while under the watchful eye of the late Elizabethan regime is a notably courageous act that speaks of the force of his personal religious convictions (53–56). In the event, Jonson escaped hanging for his crime by pleading benefit of clergy, a loophole made possible by his knowledge of Latin (likely in reading and translating *Miserere*, Psalm 51). Jonson's religious identity is further complicated by his explicit return to the English Protestant church in the wake of the Gunpowder Plot.

Jonson is perhaps best known today for his satirical portrayals of Puritanism, including characters Tribulation Wholesome and Ananias in *The*

Alchemist and Zeal-of-the-Land Busy in *Bartholomew Fair*. Playwrights such as Ben Jonson and Thomas Dekker[4] helped to associate the theater with antipathy to Puritanism. (Dekker was also forcefully anti-Catholic.) Archbishop Laud championed the theater because it satirized Puritans (Knapp, "Jonson" 58). Indeed, Jonson enjoyed the favor of some sectors of the church, as indicated in a posthumous collection of verse in praise of him entitled *Jonsonus Virbius* (1638), in which nearly one-third of the contributors were clergy or were soon to become such (58). Although *Twelfth Night* satirizes the Puritan Malvolio, Shakespeare does not go for the ideological cheap shot against Puritans in the concerted manner of Jonson and Dekker. Nor would Shakespeare ever overtly identify himself with Catholicism, as Jonson did with such courage, notwithstanding Gary Taylor's overstated claim that Shakespeare "was almost certainly a church papist" and that he "might have become a recusant" (298).

Middleton's exact religious identity is perhaps more difficult to pin down than Jonson's, but Middleton self-identified broadly as a Protestant, as the patriotic and anti-Catholic *A Game at Chess* makes amply clear, despite its government censorship. Gary Taylor considers Middleton to be "a moderate Puritan" (289), while Lori Anne Ferrell argues that Middleton is a Calvinist who came to be identified as a Puritan when the religio-political situation polarized in England during the looming threat of the Spanish match (682). Ferrell correctly identifies a number of Calvinist strains in Middleton's work of religious prose, *The Two Gates of Salvation Set Wide Open* (1609), such as an occasional reference to election and reprobation.

However, Ferrell caricatures Middleton's prose work by accentuating his treatment of double predestination into a major theme (681), when in fact, such controversial Calvinist ideology is only a minor feature of the text. Instead, Middleton's work highlights a myriad of examples of Old Testament prophecies achieving their fulfillment in the saving work and person of Jesus Christ. Middleton prefaces his harmony of scripture with a resounding statement of the centrality of Christ: "By him are *the gates of salvation set wide open*, in him alone all debts are paid, through his means the *prophets* and *evangelists* hold hands and embrace" (684–685). Many of his marginalia also connect soteriology to Christology: "This shows that in Christ only we should seek remedy in all our miseries" (691), "There is no other name under heaven to be saved by" (713), "The

---

4. Dekker's *If this be not a good play, the Devil is in it* (1611), ends by mocking a Puritan who is burning in hell.

true deliverance from sin and Satan" (714), and "Salvation, which was purchased by Jesus Christ" (717). In other words, Middleton's prose work is strongly christological and soteriological, and only secondarily, Calvinist (in any controversial sense). Most of Middleton's arguments, taken as they are from a Christocentric reading of scripture, would sit comfortably in any mainstream early modern Protestant tradition.

While there are elements of Calvinist predestinarian thought in Middleton's prose work of soteriology, the stronger emphasis lies in his use of "rhetorical theology," to borrow the coinage of Maria Devlin (174). Devlin observes that systematic Reformed theology typically advanced a doctrine of soteriological determinism. However, she argues that much practical reformed theology of the period, what she terms "rhetorical theology," "re-opens a place for temporality, indeterminacy, and human agency" (175). Devlin claims that such rhetorical theology fostered hope, whereas deterministic systematic theology inculcated despair (175). Middleton concludes his prose tract with a poem that is a quintessential example of rhetorical theology, enjoining his readers to willingly and freely partake of the gift of salvation:

> *What heaven calls his, call yours: be glad, and feast;*
> *There is no price set on a heavenly guest:*
> *Milk, water, wine—life, grace, th'Eternal love—*
> *All three are free, and so I hope you'll prove.* (719)

There is arguably an incongruity between the high rhetoric of Middleton's religious tract and the bawdy and violent humor of his plays, which often luxuriate in sexual deviance, violence, and social disorder. It is hard for me to imagine the author of *A Mad World, My Masters*, *The Revenger's Tragedy*, and *A Chaste Maid in Cheapside* being a Puritan in any recognizable sense of the term. These plays, and many others by Middleton, are replete with the very species of course humor that the Puritan anti-theatricalists found so objectionable.

Nevertheless, Taylor argues of Middleton, "The vocabulary and psychology of his major tragedies is strongly Calvinist" (289). I grant that Middleton's plays assume a low view of human nature, one embroiled in total depravity, so to that extent they may reflect Calvinist ideology. However, the very prurience with which Middleton's plays respond to such depravity runs counter to the severe moralism characteristic of Puritanism and also of Calvinism more generally. Even if some of the Puritan anti-theatricalists may show signs of repression when they argue so vociferously against the immorality of the theater, Calvinism on the whole did not give license to the distorted varieties of sexuality conveyed in Middleton's drama. In short, I question Taylor and Ferrell's identification of Middleton as a Puritan, even if my evidence to the contrary may be inchoate.

Unlike Middleton, Shakespeare did not leave us a religious prose tract to help substantiate his religious identity. And while Shakespeare has great affective range in registering social concerns, from the high tragic vision of *Hamlet* and *King Lear* to the bawdy underworld of *Measure for Measure*, I would suggest that he ultimately conveys a more redemptive picture of human nature and society than Middleton does. There is often more to love and admire in Shakespeare's characters than in Middleton's, or even Marlowe's or Jonson's, for that matter. Even though Shakespeare's religious identity may be less accessible (or recoverable) than the identities of his playwrighting peers, the plays of Shakespeare nonetheless negotiate the Reformation divide with a deftness that attests to his theological sophistication.

CODA: SALVATION... FROM AUGUSTINE TO LUTHER TO SHAKESPEARE

Perhaps a fitting case study of soteriology with which to close this study would be the conversion of St. Augustine, who continues to exert such a strong theological influence on both sides of the Reformation divide. Augustine's emphasis on grace contributed massively to Luther and Calvin's doctrine of salvation *sola gratia*, while Augustine's celebration of the Church and her sacraments helped Roman Catholicism navigate Trent. Sitting under a fig tree, weeping for his sins, Augustine hears the words spoken by a child, "*Tolle lege*" ("Pick up and read"). Reading the first passage to which his Bible opens, Augustine discovers the words of Saint Paul (another radical sinner turned radical saint): "'Not in riots and drunken parties, not in eroticism and indecencies, not in strife and rivalry, but put on the Lord Jesus Christ and make no provision for the flesh in its lusts' (Rom. 13:13–14)" (*Confessions* 153). Augustine's lengthy spiritual quest was over in an instant: "I neither wished nor needed to read further. At once, with the last words of this sentence, it was as if a light of relief from all anxiety flooded into my heart. All the shadows of doubt were dispelled" (153). Augustine's conversion evinces the faith of a child and a love of the Bible, both of which passions would be recovered by an Augustinian monk in the sixteenth century. In turn, the theological innovations of Luther and their concomitant controversies would captivate the mind of the greatest playwright who has ever lived.

Bibliography

PRIMARY SOURCES

Andrewes, Lancelot. *Apospasmatia sacra*. London, 1657, STC 2104. *Early English Books Online*.
———. *Ninety-Six Sermons*. Vol. 5. Edited by John Henry Parker. Oxford: Oxford University Press, 1843.
Anselm. *Basic Writings: Proslogium; Monologium; Gaunilon's on Behalf of the Fool; Cur Deus Homo*. Edited by S. N. Deane. La Salle, Il: Open Court, 1962.
Aquinas, Thomas. *Summa Contra Gentiles. Book Four: Salvation*. Translated by Charles J. O'Neil. Garden City, NY: Doubleday, 1960.
———. *Summa Theologiae: Latin Text and English Translation, Introductions, Notes, Appendices, and Glossaries*. Cambridge: Blackfriars, 1964.
Athanasius. *Life of Antony*. Edited and translated by Carolinne White. Early Christian Lives. London: Penguin, 1998.
Augustine. *The City of God*. Translated by Marcus Dods, New York: Modern Library, 1950.
———. *Confessions*. Translated by Henry Chadwick. Oxford: Oxford University Press, 1992.
———. *On Christian Teaching*. Translated by R. P. H. Green. Oxford: Oxford University Press, 2008.
———. *The Trinity (De Trinitate)*. Translated by Stephen McKenna, Washington, D. C.: The Catholic University of America Press, 1963.
———. *Trilogy on Faith and Happiness (The Happy Life, Faith in the Unseen, The Advantage of Believing)*. Translated by Roland Teske et al. Hyde Park, NY: New City, 2010.
Beard, Thomas. *Theatre of Gods Judgements*. London, 1581, RSTC 1659.
Bellarmine, Robert. *Of the Seaven Wordes Spoken by Christ upon the Crosse*. Edited by D. M. Rogers, *English Recusant Literature 1558-1640*, London: The Scolar, 1974.
Biblia Sacra Iuxta Vulgatam Versionem. 5th ed. Stuttgart: Deutsche Bibelgesellschaft, 2007.
Boccaccio, Giovanni. *The Decameron*. Translated by Richard Aldington, New York: Dell, 1966.
The Book of Common Prayer 1559: The Elizabethan Prayer Book. Edited by John Booty. The Folger Shakespeare Library. Charlottesville: University Press of Virginia, 1976.
The Book of Common Prayer: The Texts of 1549, 1559, and 1662. Edited by Brian Cummings. Oxford: Oxford University Press, 2011.

The Books of Homilies. 1547; 1571. *The Anglican Library.* http://anglicanlibrary.org/homilies/.

Bunny, Edmund. *A booke of Christian exercise appertaining to resolution, that is, shewing how that we should resolve our selves to become Christians indeed: by R.P. Perused, and accompanied now with a treatise tending to pacification: by Edm. Bunny.* London, 1584, STC 19355. Early English Books Online.

Bunyan, John. *The Pilgrim's Progress.* Oxford: Oxford University Press, 1984.

Calvin, John. *Calvin's Commentaries.* 22 vols. Translated by Calvin Translation Society, 1843–1855. Repr. Grand Rapids: Baker, 1979.

———. *Commentary on a Harmony of the Evangelists, Matthew, Mark, and Luke.* Translated by William Pringle. Grand Rapids, MI: Christian Classics Ethereal Library.

———. *Commentaries on the Epistles of Paul the Apostle to the Corinthians.* Translated by William Pringle. Grand Rapids, MI: Christian Classics Ethereal Library.

———. *Institutes of the Christian Religion.* 1559. Translated by Henry Beveridge, Hendrickson, 2008.

Coleridge, Samuel Taylor. "[Comments on *Othello*]." In *Othello*, edited by Alvin Kernan, 149–51. London: Penguin, 1998.

Dekker, Thomas. *The Dramatic Works of Thomas Dekker, Volume 3: The Roaring Girl. If This Be Not a Good Play, the Devil Is in It. Troia-Nova Triumphans. Match Me in London. The Virgin Martyr. The Witch of Edmonton. The Wonder of a Kingdom.* Cambridge: Cambridge University Press, 1958.

———. *The Whore of Babylon by Thomas Dekker: A Critical Edition.* Edited by Marianne G. Riely. New York: Garland, 1980.

Dekker, Thomas, et al. *Old Plays: Patient Grissel, Thomas Dekker, Henry Chettle and William Haughton. Timon. Sir Thomas More. Ralph Roister Doister, by Nicholas Udall. the Tragedie of Gorboduc, by Thomas Norton and Thomas Sackville.* Nendeln: Kraus, 1966.

Donne, John. *Devotions upon Emergent Occasions.* Edited by Anthony Raspa. Oxford: Oxford University Press, 1987.

———. *Pseudo-martyr.* Edited by Anthony Raspa. Montreal, Canada: McGill-Queen's University Press, 1993.

———. *Sermons.* Edited by George R. Potter and Evelyn M. S. Simpson. Berkeley: University of California Press, 1953.

Erasmus, Desiderius, and Martin Luther. *Luther and Erasmus: Free Will and Salvation.* Edited by E. G. Rupp and Philip S. Watson. Philadelphia: Westminster, 1969.

Erasmus, Desiderius. *De Libero Arbitrio.* Translated and edited by E. Gordon Rupp. *Luther and Erasmus: Free Will and Salvation,* Philadelphia: Westminster, 1969.

———. *Enchiridion Militis Christiani: An English Version.* Edited by Anne M. O'Donnell. Oxford: Oxford University Press, 1981.

———. *The Praise of Folly and Other Writings.* Translated and edited by Robert M. Adams. New York: W.W. Norton, 1989.

Forbes, John. *[H]ow a Christian man may discerne the testimonie of Gods spirit, from the testimonie of his owne spirit, in witnessing his adoption.* Middelburg, 1616, STC 11131, Early English Books Online.

Foxe, John. *The Unabridged Acts and Monuments Online* or *TAMO.* Sheffield: HRI Online Publications, 2011. http//www.johnfoxe.org.

Geneva Bible: A Facsimile of the 1560 Edition. Peabody, MA: Hendrickson, 2007.

Gerson, Jean. *Early Works*. Translated by Brian Patrick McGuire. New York: Paulist Press, 1998.

Gosson, Stephen. *The School of Abuse: Containing a Pleasant Invective against Poets, Pipers, Players, Jesters &c*. Edited by John P. Collier. New York: AMS, 1970.

Gosson, Stephen, Salvian, and Anthony Munday. *A Second and Third Blast of Retrait from Plaies and Theaters*. New York: Garland, 1973.

Harsnett, Samuel. *A Declaration of Egregious Popish Impostures*. In *Shakespeare, Harsnett, and the Devils of Denham*, edited by F.W. Brownlow, 183–413. Newark: University of Delaware Press, 1993.

———. *Three sermons preached by the reverend, and learned, Dr. Richard Stuart, Dean of St. Pauls, afterwards Dean of Westminster, and clerk of the closset to the late King Charles. To which is aded [sic], A fourth sermon, preached by the right reverend Father in God, Samuel Harsnett, Lord Arch-bishop of Yorke*. London, 1656. STC 184684. Early English Books Online.

Heywood, Thomas. *The First and Second Parts of King Edward IV*. Edited by Richard Rowland, Manchester, UK: Manchester University Press, 2005.

———. *If You Know Not Me, You Know Nobody*. Edited by Madeleine Doran, London: Printed for the Malone Society by J. Johnson at the Oxford University Press, 1935.

The Holy Bible. King James Version (Authorized Version). Grand Rapids: Zondervan, 1989.

Hooker, Richard. *A Learned Discourse of Justification, Works, and how the Foundation of Faith is Overthrown*. 1612. *Christian Classics Ethereal Library*, Calvin College. www.ccel.org/ccel/hooker/just.i.html.

———. *Of the Laws of Ecclesiastical Polity*. Edited by Arthur Stephen McGrade. Cambridge: Cambridge University Press, 2004.

———. *Of the Laws of Ecclesiastical Polity*. Edited by W. S. Hill et al. Binghamton, NY: Medieval & Renaissance Texts & Studies, 1993.

Ignatius of Loyola. *The Spiritual Exercises of St. Ignatius: Based on Studies in the Language of the Autograph*. Translated by Loius J. Puhl. Chicago: Loyola University Press, 1951.

James I. *Daemonologie*. New York: Da Capo, 1969.

Jewel, John. *An Apology of the Church of England*. Edited by J. E. Booty. Ithaca: Cornell University Press, 1963.

Johnson, Samuel. *Dr. Johnson on Shakespeare*. Edited by W. K. Wimsatt. New York: Penguin, 1960.

Jonson, Ben. *The Devil Is an Ass and Other Plays*. Edited by Margaret J. Kidnie. Oxford: Oxford University Press, 2009.

Jonson, Ben, et al. *Eastward Ho!*, Edited by Michael Neill. London: Bloomsbury, 2015.

Kyd, Thomas. *The Spanish Tragedy*. Edited by Clara Calvo and Jesus Tronch. London: Bloomsbury, 2013.

Lodge, Thomas, Robert Greene. *A Looking Glasse for London and England: A Critical Edition*. Edited by George A. Clugston. New York: Garland, 1980.

Luther, Martin. *De Servo Arbitrio*. In *Luther and Erasmus: Free Will and Salvation*, translated and edited by Philip S. Watson. Philadelphia: Westminster, 1969.

———. *Lectures on Romans*. Edited and translated by Wilhelm Pauck. London: S. C. M., 1961.

———. *Luther's Works*. 55 vols. Edited by Jaroslav Pelikan and Helmut Lehmann. Philadephia: Muehlenberg and Fortress, and Saint Louis: Concordia, 1955–1986.

———. *Martin Luther: Selections from His Writings*. Edited by John Dillenberger, Garden City, NY: Doubleday, 1961.

———. *Treatise on Good Works*. Auckland: The Floating Press, 2009. ProQuest Ebook Central, https://ebookcentral-proquest-com.ezproxy.library.uvic.ca/lib/uvic/detail.action?docID=502282.

Marlowe, Christopher. *The Complete Plays*. Edited by Frank Romany and Robert Lindsey. London: Penguin, 2003.

Marprelate, Martin. *The Martin Marprelate Tracts*. Edited by Joseph L. Black. Cambridge: Cambridge University Press, 2008.

Mayer, John. *A Commentarie Vpon the New Testament. Representing the Diuers Expositions Therof, Out of the Workes of the most Learned, both Ancient Fathers and Moderne Writers, and Hereby Sifting Out the True Sense of Euery Passage, for the Benefit of all that Desire to Read with Vnderstanding: Containing the Seuen Smaller Epistles, Called Catholike, and the Booke of the Reuelation / by Iohn Mayer*. London, 1631. STC 17731.7. *Early English Books Online*.

Middleton, Thomas. *Thomas Middleton: Five Plays*. Edited by Bryan Loughrey and Neil Taylor, London: Penguin, 2006.

———. *Thomas Middleton: The Collected Works*. Edited by Gary Taylor and John Lavagnino. Oxford: Oxford University Press, 2010.

Milton, John. *Paradise Lost*. Edited by Stephen Orgel and Jonathan Goldberg. Oxford: Oxford University Press, 2004.

Modena, Leon. *The Autobiography of a Seventeenth-Century Venetian Rabbi: Leon Modena's Life of Judah*. Translated and edited by Mark R. Cohen. New Haven, CT: Yale University Press, 1988.

More, Thomas. *The Confutation of Tyndale's Answer*. In *The Complete Works of St. Thomas More*, edited by Louis A. Schuster et al., vol. 8, parts 1–3. New Haven, CT: Yale University Press, 1973.

———. *Responsio ad Lutherum*. In *The Complete Works of St. Thomas More*, edited by John M. Headley and translated by Sister Scholastica Mandeville, vol. 5, parts 1–2. New Haven, CT: Yale University Press, 1969.

———. *Utopia*. Translated by Paul Turner. London: Penguin, 2003.

Munday, Anthony, et al. *Sir Thomas More: A Play by Anthony Munday and Others, Revised by Henry Chettle, Thomas Dekker, Thomas Heywood, and William Shakespeare*. Edited by Vittorio Gabrieli and Giorgio Melchiori. Manchester: Manchester University Press, 1990.

A New Ballad Intituled, Daniels Siftyng in these our Dayes Aptly Applyed to the True Preachers of the Gospell. what God Hath Wylled Vs, to that Good Eare Geue: For Daniels are Abroad: Siftyng with their Seeue. London, 1572. STC 6235. *Early English Books Online*.

Nowell, Alexander. *A Catechism Written in Latin By Alexander Nowell... Translated into English by Thomas Norton* [1570]. Edited by G. E. Corrie. Cambridge: Parker Society, 1853.

Parsons, Robert. *The first booke of the Christian exercise appertayning to resolution*. Rouen: Printed at Fr. Parson's, 1582. STC (2nd ed.) 1953. *Early English Books Online*. https://search-proquest-com.ezproxy.library.uvic.ca/eebo/docview/2240875750/99857114/A8D4349DD82D4332PQ/1?accountid=14846.

Peele, George. *The Dramatic Works: The Araygnement of Paris. David and Bethsabe. The Old Wives Tale*. Edited by Charles T. Prouty. New Haven, CT: Yale University Press, 1970.

Perkins, William. *A golden chaine: or The description of theologie containing the order of the causes of saluation and damnation, according to Gods word*. Cambridge: John Legate, 1600.

———. *The Work of William Perkins*. Edited by Ian Breward. Appleford: The Sutton Courtenay Press, 1970.

Plautus. *The Two Menaechmuses*. In *Plautus*, edited and translated by Wolfgand de Melo, 2:428–548. Cambridge, MA: Harvard University Press, 2011.

Prynne, William. *Histrio-Mastix : The players scovrge, or, Actors Tragaedie, divided into two parts : wherein it is largely evidenced, by divers Arguments . . . that popular stage-playes . . . are sinfull, heathenish, lewde, ungodly spectacles, and most pernicious corruptions . . . and that the profession of play-poets, of stage players, together with the penning, acting, and frequenting of stage-playes, are unlawfull, infamous and misbeseeming Christians / by William Prynne, an Vtter-Barrester of Lincolnes Inne*. London: Printed by E.A. and W.I. for M. Sparke, 1633.

Satan sifting, or, The oyl of joy for the spirit of heaviness. London, 1692. STC 12013. *Early English Books Online*.

Shakespeare, William, adapted by Thomas Middleton. Measure for Measure: *A Genetic Text*. In *Middleton (Taylor and Lavagnino)*, edited by John Jowett, 1542–1585.

Shakespeare, William, adapted by Thomas Middleton. *Measure for Measure: A Genetic Text*, edited by John Jowett. In *Thomas Middleton: The Collected Works*, edited by Gary Taylor and John Lavagnino, 1542–1585. Oxford: Oxford University Press, 2010.

Shakespeare, William. *Hamlet*. Edited by Ann Thompson and Neil Taylor. Arden Shakespeare 3. London: Bloomsbury, 2006.

———. *Hamlet: The Texts of 1603 and 1623*. Edited by Ann Thompson and Neil Taylor. Arden Shakespeare 3. London: Bloomsbury, 2006.

———. *Hamlet. The Norton Shakespeare*. 1st ed. Edited by Stephen Greenblatt et al. New York: W. W. Norton and Company, 1997.

———. *Henry IV Part One*. Edited by David Bevington. Oxford: Oxford University Press, 2008.

———. *The History of King Lear*. Edited by Stanley Wells. Oxford: Oxford University Press, 2000.

———. *Macbeth*. Edited by Nicholas Brooke. Oxford: Oxford University Press, 2008.

———. *Measure for Measure*. Edited by N. W. Bawcutt. Oxford: Oxford University Press, 2008.

———. Measure for Measure: *Texts and Contexts*. Edited by Ivo Kamps and Karen Raber. Boston: Bedford/St. Martin's, 2004.

———. *The Merchant of Venice: A Longman Cultural Edition*. Edited by Lawrence Danson. New York: Pearson, 2005.

———. *The Merchant of Venice*. Edited by Jay Halio. Oxford: Oxford University Press, 2008.

———. *The Merchant of Venice*. Edited by John Drakakis. Arden 3, London: Bloomsbury, 2010.

———. *The Norton Shakespeare*. 3rd ed. Edited by Stephen Greenblatt et al., New York: W. W. Norton, 2016.

———. *Othello*. Edited by Michael Neill. Oxford: Oxford University Press, 2008.
———. *Shakespeare's Sonnets*. Edited by Katherine Duncan-Jones. London: Bloomsbury, 1997.
———. *Titus Andronicus*. Edited by Eugene Waith. Oxford: Oxford University Press, 2008.
———. *The Winter's Tale*. Edited by Stephen Orgel. Oxford: Oxford University Press, 2008.
Southwell, Robert. *Collected Poems*. Edited by Peter Davidson and Anne Sweeney. Manchester: Fyfield, 2007.
———. *An Humble Supplication to Her Maiestie*. Edited by R. C. Bald. Cambridge: Cambridge University Press, 1953.
———. *Robert Southwell's* Epistle of Comfort: *An Edition*. Edited by Desmond Patrick Burke-Gaffney. New YorkL Fordham University Press, 1964.
———. *Robert Southwell's* Marie Magdelens Fvneral Teares: *An Edition*. Edited by Richard John Gappa. St. Louis: St. Louis University Press, 1968.
Spenser, Edmund. *The Faerie Queene*. London: Penguin, 1987.
Teresa of Ávila. *The Life of Saint Teresa of Ávila by Herself*. Translated by J. M. Cohen, London: Penguin, 1957.
Tourneur, Cyril. *The Atheist's Tragedy*. In *The Revels Plays*, edited by Irving Ribner, 1–118. Cambridge, MA: Harvard University Press, 1964.
Tyndale, William. *Answer to Sir Thomas More's 'Dialogue.'* 1530. Edited by Henry Walter. Cambridge: Cambridge University Press, 1850.
———. *The Obedience of a Christian Man*. Edited by David Daniell. London: Penguin, 2000.
Weyer, Johann. *Witches, Devils, and Doctors in the Renaissance: De praestigiis daemonum*. Edited by George Mora and translated by John Shea. Binghamton, NY: State University of New York, 1991.
Whetstone, George. *Promos and Cassandra*, Parts I and II (1578). Cambridge: Chadwyck-Healey, 1994. *English Verse Drama Full-Text Database*. ProQuest. https://literature-proquest-com.ezproxy.library.uvic.ca/searchFulltext.do?id=Zo00129484&childSectionId=Z000129484&divLevel=0&queryId=3057679160407&trailId=1635B71E1E9&area=drama&forward=textsFT&queryType=findWork.

SECONDARY SOURCES

Adelman, Janet. *Blood Relations: Christian and Jew in* The Merchant of Venice. Chicago: University of Chicago Press, 2008.
Åklundh, Jens. "Voices of Jewish Converts to Christianity in Late Sixteenth-and Seventeenth-Century England." *Seventeenth Century* 29 (2014) 45–71. *MLA Database*, http://search.proquest.com.ezproxy.library.uvic.ca/docview/1803149812?accountid=14846.
Allen, Don Cameron. "Vaughan's 'Cock-Crowing' and the Tradition." *ELH* 21 (1954) 94–106. www.jstor.org/stable/2872018.
Anderson, David K. *Martyrs and Players in Early Modern England: Tragedy, Religion and Violence on Stage*. Burlington, VT: Ashgate, 2014.
Anderson, Judith H., and Jennifer C. Vaught. *Shakespeare and Donne: Generic Hybrids and the Cultural Imaginary*. New York: Fordham University Press, 2013.

BIBLIOGRAPHY

Auden, W.H. *Lectures on Shakespeare*. Edited by Arthur Kirsch. Princeton: Princeton University Press, 2000.

Baglio, Matt. *The Rite: The Making of a Modern Exorcist*. New York: Doubleday, 2009.

Bailey, Michael. *Fearful Spirits, Reasoned Follies: The Boundaries of Superstition in Late Medieval Europe*. Ithaca: Cornell University Press, 2013.

Barber, C L. *Shakespeare's Festive Comedy: A Study of Dramatic Form and Its Relation to Social Custom*. Princeton, NJ: Princeton University Press, 1959.

Bawcutt, N. W. "Introduction." In *Measure for Measure* by William Shakespeare, 1–82. Oxford: Oxford University Press, 2008.

Beauregard, David. *Catholic Theology in Shakespeare's Plays*. Newark: University of Delaware Press, 2008.

——. "Human Malevolence and Providence in *King Lear*." *Renascence: Essays on Values in Literature* 60 (2008) 199–223.

——. *Shakespeare and Catholicism*. Leiden: Brill, 2001.

Beckwith, Sarah. "Medieval Penance, Reformation Repentance and *Measure for Measure*." In *Reading the Medieval in Early Modern England*, edited by Gordon McMullen and David Matthews, 193–204. Cambridge: Cambridge University Press, 2007.

——. *Shakespeare and the Grammar of Forgiveness*. Ithaca: Cornell University Press, 2011.

Belsey, Catharine. "Gender and Family." In *The Cambridge Companion to Shakespearean Tragedy*, edited by Claire McEachern, 123–41. Cambridge: Cambridge University Press, 2002.

Bennett, Robert. *Romance and Reformation: The Erasmian Spirit of Shakespeare's Measure for Measure*. Newark: University of Delaware Press, 2000.

Benson, Sean. *Shakespearean Resurrection: The Art of Almost Raising the Dead*. Pittsburgh: Duquesne University Press, 2009.

Berman, Ronald. "Shakespeare and the Law." *Shakespeare Quarterly* 18 (1967) 141–50.

Berry, Edward. "Laughing at 'Others.'" In *The Cambridge Companion to Shakespearean Comedy*, edited by Alexander Leggatt, 123–38. Cambridge University Press, 2002.

——. *Shakespeare's Comic Rites*. Cambridge: Cambridge University Press, 1984.

Bevington, David. "The Debate about Shakespeare and Religion." In *Shakespeare and Early Modern Religion*, edited by David Loewenstein and Michael Witmore, 23–39. Cambridge: Cambridge University Press, 2015.

Bloom, Harold, ed. *Modern Critical Interpretations: William Shakespeare's* Measure for Measure. New York: Chelsea House, 1987.

Bloom, Harold. "Introduction." In *Modern Critical Interpretations: William Shakespeare's Measure for Measure*, edited by Harold Bloom, 1–6. New York: Chelsea House, 1987.

Bloom, Harold, ed. *Modern Critical Interpretations: William Shakespeare's* The Merchant of Venice. New York: Chelsea House, 1986.

Bloom, Harold. *Shakespeare: The Invention of the Human*. New York: Riverhead, 1998.

Boitani, Piero. *The Gospel According to Shakespeare*. Translated by Vittorio Montemaggi and Rachel Jacoff. Notre Dame, IN: Notre Dame University Press, 2013.

Bonfil, Robert. *Jewish Life in Renaissance Italy*. Translated by Anthony Oldcorn, Berkeley: University of California Press, 1994.

Bonhoeffer, Dietrich. *The Cost of Discipleship*. New York: Macmillan, 1963.

Booty, John. "Editorial Matter." In *The Book of Common Prayer 1559: The Elizabethan Prayer Book*, 327–84. Charlottesville: University Press of Virginia, 1976.
Bourus, Terri. *Young Shakespeare's Young Hamlet: Print, Piracy, and Performance*. London: Palgrave Macmillan, 2014.
Bowers, Fredson. *Hamlet as Minister and Scourge and Other Studies in Shakespeare and Milton*. Charlottesville: University of Virginia Press, 1989.
Boyle, Marjorie O'Rourke. "Angels Black and White: Loyola's Spiritual Discernment in Historical Perspective." *Theological Studies* 44 (1983) 241–57.
Bradbrook, M. C. "Authority, Truth, and Justice in Measure for Measure." In *Modern Critical Interpretations: William Shakespeare's Measure for Measure*, edited by Harold Bloom, 7–22. New York: Chelsea House, 1987.
Bradley, A. C. *Shakespearean Tragedy*. London: Penguin, 1991.
Brayton, Dan. "'Angling in the Lake of Darkness': Possession, Dispossession, and the Politics of Discovery in *King Lear*." *ELH: English Literary History* 70 (2003) 399–426.
Brownlow, F. W. *Robert Southwell*. New York: Twayne, 1996.
———. *Shakespeare, Harsnett, and the Devils of Denham*. Newark: University of Delaware Press, 1993.
———. Review of *Shakespeare, the Earl, and the Jesuit*. John Klause. *Shakespeare Quarterly* 61 (2010) 132–34.
Buccola, Regina, and Lisa Hopkins, eds. *Marian Moments in Early Modern British Drama*. Aldershot: Ashgate, 2007.
Bucholz, Robert, and Newton Key. *Early Modern England 1485–1714*. 2nd ed. Oxford: Wiley-Blackwell, 2009.
Bullough, Geoffrey, ed. *Narrative and Dramatic Sources of Shakespeare. Vol. 2: The Comedies, 1597–1603*. London: Routledge and Kegan Paul, 1958.
Bynum, Caroline Walker. *Wonderful Blood: Theology and Practice in Late Medieval Northern Germany and Beyond*. Philadelphia: University of Pennsylvania Press, 2007.
Caciola, Nancy. *Discerning Spirits: Divine and Demonic Possession in the Middle Ages*. Ithaca: Cornell University Press, 2003.
Cavanaugh, William T. *The Myth of Religious Violence: Secular Ideology and the Roots of Modern Conflict*. New York: Oxford University Press, 2009.
Cefalu, Paul. "The Ethics of Pardoning in Measure for Measure." In *Early Modern Drama and the Bible: Contexts and Readings, 1570–1625*, edited by Adrian Streete, 105–17. New York: Palgrave Macmillan, 2012.
———. "Johannine Poetics in George Herbert's Devotional Lyrics." *ELH: English Literary History* 82 (2015) 1041–71.
———. *The Johannine Renaissance in Early Modern English Literature and Theology*. Oxford: Oxford University Press, 2017.
———. *Moral Identity in Early Modern English Literature*. Cambridge: Cambridge University Press, 2004.
———. *Revisionist Shakespeare: Transitional Ideologies in Texts and Contexts*. New York: Palgrave Macmillan, 2004.
Cefalu, Paul, and Bryan Reynolds, eds. *The Return of Theory in Early Modern English Studies: Tarrying with the Subjunctive*. New York: Palgrave Macmillan, 2011.
Coleman, David. *Drama and the Sacraments in Sixteenth-Century England: Indelible Characters*. Basingstroke: Palgrave Macmillan, 2007.

Collinson, Patrick. *The Elizabethan Puritan Movement*. Berkeley: University of California Press, 1967.
———. *From Cranmer to Sancroft: Essays on English Religion in the Sixteenth and Seventeenth Centuries*. London: Hambledon Continuum, 2006.
———. *Godly People: Essays on English Protestantism and Puritanism*. London: Hambledon, 1983.
———. *The Reformation*. London: Weidenfeld & Nicolson, 2003.
Coolidge, John S. *The Pauline Renaissance in England: Puritanism and the Bible*. Oxford: Clarendon, 1970.
Copeland, Clare, and Jan Machielsen, eds. *Angels of Light?: Sanctity and the Discernment of Spirits in the Early Modern Period*. Leiden: Brill, 2013.
Cortright, Brant. *Psychotherapy and Spirit: Theory and Practice in Transpersonal Psychotherapy*. Albany: State University of New York Press, 1997.
Cox, John. *The Devil and the Sacred in English Drama, 1350–1642*. Cambridge: Cambridge University Press, 2000.
———. *Seeming Knowledge: Shakespeare and Skeptical Faith*. Waco, TX: Baylor University Press, 2007.
Coyle, Martin, ed. *New Casebooks:* The Merchant of Venice: *William Shakespeare*. London: Macmillan, 1998.
Cressy, David, and Lori Anne Ferrell, eds. *Religion and Society in Early Modern England: A Sourcebook*. 2nd ed. New York: Routledge, 2005.
Crowley, James P. "'He Took His Religion by Trust': The Matter of Ben Jonson's Conversion." *Renaissance and Reformation/Renaissance et Réforme* 22 (1998) 53–70.
Cummings, Brian. *The Literary Culture of the Reformation: Grammar and Grace*. Oxford: Oxford University Press, 2002.
———. *Mortal Thoughts: Religion, Secularity and Identity in Shakespeare and Early Modern Culture*. Oxford: Oxford University Press, 2013.
Cummings, Brian, and James Simpson, eds. *Cultural Reformations: Medieval and Renaissance in Literary History*. Oxford: Oxford University Press, 2010.
Cunningham, John, and Stephen Slimp. "The Less into the Greater: Emblem, Analogue, and Deification in The Merchant of Venice." In *The Merchant of Venice: New Critical Essays*, edited by John Mahon and Ellen Macleod Mahon, 225–82. New York: Routledge, 2002.
Curran, John, Jr. Hamlet, *Protestantism, and the Mourning of Contingency: Not to Be*. Aldershot: Ashgate, 2006.
Curran, Kevin, ed. *Shakespeare and Judgment*. Edinburgh: Edinburgh University Press, 2017.
Davidson, Clifford. *History, Religion, and Violence: Cultural Contexts for Medieval and Renaissance English Drama*. Aldershot, Hampshire: Ashgate, 2002.
Davidson, Peter, and Anne Sweeney, eds. *St. Robert Southwell: Collected Poems*. Manchester: Fyfield, 2007.
Dawson, Anthony. "Claudius at Prayer." In *Religion and Drama in Early Modern England: The Performance of Religion on the Renaissance Stage*, edited by Jane Hwang Degenhardt and Elizabeth Williamson, 235–48. Farnham: Ashgate, 2011.
Degenhardt, Jane Hwang, and Elizabeth Williamson, eds. *Religion and Drama in Early Modern England: The Performance of Religion on the Renaissance Stage*. Surrey, England: Ashgate, 2011.

Degenhardt, Jane Hwang. *Islamic Conversion and Christian Resistance on the Early Modern Stage.* Edinburgh: Edinburgh University Press, 2010.
de Grazia, Margreta. Hamlet *without Hamlet.* Cambridge: Cambridge University Press, 2007.
Devlin, Maria. Devlin, Maria. "'If it were made for man, 'twas made for me': Generic Damnation and Rhetorical Salvation in Reformation Preaching and Plays." In *Sin and Salvation in Reformation England*, edited by Jonathan Willis, 173–89. Surrey, England: Ashgate, 2015.
Diehl, Huston. *Staging Reform, Reforming the Stage: Protestantism and Popular Theater in Early Modern England.* Ithaca: Cornell University Press, 1997.
Dollimore, Jonathan. "*King Lear* (ca. 1605-1606) and Essentialist Humanism." In *Shakespeare: An Anthology of Criticism and Theory 1945-2000*, edited by Russ McDonald, 535–46. Oxford: Blackwell, 2004.
———. *Radical Tragedy: Religion, Ideology and Power in the Drama of Shakespeare and His Contemporaries.* Durham: Duke University Press, 1993.
Duffy, Eamon. "Bare Ruined Choirs: Remembering Catholicism in Shakespeare's England." In *Theatre and Religion: Lancastrian Shakespeare*, edited by Richard Dutton et al., 40–57. Manchester: University of Manchester Press, 2003.
———. *The Stripping of the Altars: Traditional Religion in England, C.1400-C.1580.* 2nd ed. New Haven, CT: Yale University Press, 2005.
Edelman, Charles, ed. *Shakespeare in Production:* The Merchant of Venice. Cambridge: Cambridge University Press, 2002.
Edwards, Michael. "*King Lear* and Christendom." *Christianity and Literature* 50 (2000) 15–29.
Fee, Gordon. *God's Empowering Presence: The Holy Spirit in the Letters of Paul.* Peabody, MA: Hendrickson, 1994.
Felsenstein, Frank. *Anti-Semitic Stereotypes: A Paradigm of Otherness in English Popular Culture, 1660–1830.* Baltimore: The Johns Hopkins University Press, 1995.
Fernie, Ewan, ed. *Spiritual Shakespeares.* London and New York: Routledge, 2005.
Ferrell, Lori Anne. "Introduction." In *Thomas Middleton: The Collected Works*, edited by Gary Taylor and John Lavagnino, 679–82. Oxford: Oxford University Press, 2010.
Flaherty, Jennifer. "Heaven and Earth: Confession as Performance in *Hamlet* and *Measure for Measure*." *Theatre Symposium* 21 (2013) 78–89, 143.
Foakes, R. A. *Shakespeare and Violence.* Cambridge: Cambridge University Press, 2003.
Freinkel, Lisa. *Reading Shakespeare's Will: The Theology of Figure from Augustine to the Sonnets.* New York: Columbia University Press, 2002.
Frye, Roland Mushat. *Shakespeare and Christian Doctrine.* Princeton: Princeton University Press, 1963.
Fulton, Thomas, and Kristen Poole, eds. *The Bible on the Shakespearean Stage: Cultures of Interpretation in Reformation England*, Cambridge: Cambridge University Press, 2018.
Gallagher, Lowell, ed. *Redrawing the Map of Early Modern English Catholicism.* Toronto: University of Toronto Press, 2012.
Garber, Marjorie. *Shakespeare After All.* New York: Anchor, 2004.
Gates, Daniel. "The Law made Flesh: St. Paul's Corinth and Shakespeare's Vienna." *Christianity and Literature* 62 (2013) 511–30.

Gazal, André. "'Appareled in Christ': Union with Christ in the Soteriology of John Jewel." In *Sin and Salvation in Reformation England*, edited by Jonathan Willis, 39–52. Surrey, England: Ashgate, 2015.

Girard, René. *A Theatre of Envy*. Oxford: Oxford University Press, 1991.

———. "To Entrap the Wisest." In *Modern Critical Interpretations: William Shakespeare's The Merchant of Venice*, edited by Harold Bloom, 91–106. New York: Chelsea House Publishers, 1986.

Goddard, Harold. "Portia's Failure." In *Modern Critical Interpretations: William Shakespeare's The Merchant of Venice*, edited by Harold Bloom, 27–36. New York: Chelsea House Publishers, 1986.

———. "Power in Measure for Measure." In *Modern Critical Interpretations: William Shakespeare's Measure for Measure*, edited by Harold Bloom, 23–44. New York: Chelsea House, 1987.

Goossen, Jonathan. "'Tis Set Down so in Heaven, but Not in Earth': Reconsidering Political Theology in Shakespeare's *Measure for Measure*." *Christianity and Literature* 61 (2012) 217–39.

Gottschalk, Paul. "*Hamlet* and the Scanning of Revenge." *Shakespeare Quarterly* 24 (1973) 155–70.

Graham, Kenneth J. E., and Philip D. Collington. *Shakespeare and Religious Change*. Basingstoke, England: Palgrave Macmillan, 2009.

Graham, Kenneth J. E. "The Reformation of Manners and the Grace of the Reformation: *Measure for Measure*'s Disciplinary Mingle-Mangle." *Religion and Literature* 49 (2017) 162–71.

Greenblatt, Stephen. *Hamlet in Purgatory*. Princeton, NJ: Princeton University Press, 2001.

———. "Shakespeare and the Exorcists." In *Shakespeare and the Question of Theory*, edited by Patricia Parker and Geoffrey Hartman, 163–87. New York: Methuen, 1985.

———. *Shakespearean Negotiations: The Circulation of Social Energy in Renaissance England*. Berkeley: University of California Press, 1988.

———. *Shakespeare's Freedom*. Chicago: University of Chicago Press, 2010.

———. *Will in the World: How Shakespeare Became Shakespeare*. New York: W.W. Norton, 2004.

Gregory, Brad S. *Salvation at Stake: Christian Martyrdom in Early Modern Europe*. Cambridge, MA: Harvard University Press, 1999.

———. *The Unintended Reformation*. Cambridge: Harvard University Press, 2012.

Griffiths-Osborne, Claire. "'The terms for common justice': Performing and Reforming Confession in *Measure for Measure*." *Shakespeare* 5 (2009) 36–51.

Gross, John. *Shylock: Four Hundred Years in the Life of a Legend*. London: Chatto and Windus, 1992.

Gross, Kenneth. *Shylock is Shakespeare*. University of Chicago Press, 2006.

Groves, Beatrice. *Texts and Traditions: Religion in Shakespeare, 1592–1604*. Oxford: Clarendon, 2007.

Hadfield, Andrew. "Shakespeare: Biography and Belief." In *The Cambridge Companion to Shakespeare and Religion*, edited by Hannibal Hamlin, 18–33. Cambridge: Cambridge University Press, 2019.

Haigh, Christopher. *English Reformations: Religion, Politics, and Society Under the Tudors*. Oxford: Clarendon, 1993.

Halio, Jay. Introduction. *The Merchant of Venice*, by William Shakespeare, 1–98. Oxford: Oxford University Press, 2008.

Hall, Joan Lord. *Othello: A Guide to the Play*. Westport, CT: Greenwood, 1999.

Hamilton, Donna, and Richard Strier, eds. *Religion, Literature, and Politics in Post Reformation England, 1540–1688*. Cambridge: Cambridge University Press, 1996.

Hamilton, Sharon. *Shakespeare's Daughters*. Jefferson, North Carolina: McFarland, 2003.

Hamlin, Hannibal. *The Bible in Shakespeare*. Oxford: Oxford University Press, 2013.

Hamlin, Hannibal, ed. *The Cambridge Companion to Shakespeare and Religion*. Cambridge: Cambridge University Press, 2019.

Harris, Jonathan Gil. *Untimely Matter in the Time of Shakespeare*. Philadelphia: University of Pennsylvania Press, 2009.

Hassel, R. Chris, Jr. *Shakespeare's Religious Language*. Bloomsbury, 2015.

Hawkins, Harriett. "'The Devil's Party': Virtues and Vices in *Measure for Measure*." In *Modern Critical Interpretations: William Shakespeare's Measure for Measure*, edited by Harold Bloom, 81–94. New York: Chelsea House, 1987.

Hirsch, Brett D. "Jewish Questions in Robert Wilson's *The Three Ladies of London*." *Early Theatre: A Journal Associated with the Records of Early English Drama* 19 (2016) 37–56.

Hirschfeld, Heather. *The End of Satisfaction: Drama and Repentance in the Age of Shakespeare*. Ithaca: Cornell University Press, 2014.

Holderness, Graham. *The Faith of William Shakespeare*. Oxford: Lion Hudson, 2016.

Houliston, Victor. "Filling in the Blanks: Catholic Hopes for the English Succession." *SEDERI : Journal of the Spanish Society for English Renaissance Studies* 25 (2015) 77–104, 228–29.

Hsia, R. Po-Chia. *The Myth of Ritual Murder: Jews and Magic in Reformation Germany*. New Haven, CT: Yale University Press, 1988.

———. *Trent 1475: Stories of a Ritual Murder*. Chelsea, MI: Book Crafters, 1992.

Hunt, Maurice. *Shakespeare's Religious Allusiveness: Its Play and Tolerance*. Aldershot: Ashgate, 2004.

Jackson, Ken, and Arthur Marotti, eds. *Shakespeare and Religion: Early Modern and Postmodern Perspectives*. Notre Dame: University of Notre Dame Press, 2011.

Jackson, Ken and Arthur Marotti. "The Turn to Religion in Early Modern English Studies." *Criticism: A Quarterly for Literature and the Arts* 46 (2004) 167–90.

Jackson, Kenneth S. *Shakespeare and Abraham*. Notre Dame, IN: Notre Dame University Press, 2015.

Jackson, MacDonald P. "Introduction." In *Thomas Middleton: The Collected Works*, edited by Gary Taylor and John Lavagnino, 543–47. Oxford: Oxford University Press, 2010.

Jeffrey, David Lyle, ed. *A Dictionary of Biblical Tradition in English Literature*. Grand Rapids: Eerdmans, 1992.

Jensen, Phebe. *Religion and Revelry in Shakespeare's Festive World*. Cambridge: Cambridge University Press, 2008.

Jones, Ernest. *Hamlet and Oedipus*. New York: Norton, 1976.

Jowett, John. "Introduction." In *Thomas Middleton: The Collected Works*, edited by Gary Taylor and John Lavagnino, 1542–46. Oxford: Oxford University Press, 2010.

Karant-Nunn, Susan C. *The Reformation of Ritual: An Interpretation of Early Modern Germany*. London: Routledge, 1997.

Kastan, David Scott. *A Will to Believe: Shakespeare and Religion*. Oxford: Oxford University Press, 2014.
Katz, David S. *Philo-Semitism and the Readmission of the Jews to England 1603-1655*. Oxford: Clarendon, 1982.
Kaufman, Peter Iver. *Religion Around Shakespeare*. University Park, Pennsylvania: Pennsylvania State University Press, 2013.
Kearney, Richard. *Anatheism: Returning to God After God*. New York: Columbia University Press, 2011.
Keefe, Maryellen. "Isolation to Communion: A Reading of *The Merchant of Venice*." Mahon and Mahon, pp. 213-224.
Kelly, Erin E. "*Conflict of Conscience* and Sixteenth-Century Religious Drama." *English Literary Renaissance* 44 (2014) 388-419.
Kendall, R. T. *Calvin and English Calvinism to 1649*. New York: Oxford University Press, 1979.
Kermode, Frank, ed. *Four Centuries of Shakespearian Criticism*. New York: Avon, 1965.
Kinney, Arthur, ed. Hamlet: *New Critical Essays*. New York: Routledge, 2002.
———. *The Oxford Handbook of Shakespeare*. Oxford: Oxford University Press, 2012.
Kinney, Arthur, ed. *Renaissance Drama: An Anthology of Plays and Entertainments*. 2nd ed. Oxford: Blackwell, 2005.
Klause, John. "Catholic and Protestant, Jesuit and Jew: Historical Religion in *The Merchant of Venice*." In *Shakespeare and the Culture of Christianity in Early Modern England*, edited by Dennis Taylor and David N. Beauregard, 180-221. New York: Fordham University Press, 2003.
———. *Shakespeare, the Earl, and the Jesuit*. Madison: Fairleigh Dickinson University Press, 2008.
Knapp, James. "Penitential Ethics in *Measure for Measure*." In *Shakespeare and Religion: Early Modern and Postmodern Perspectives*, edited by Ken Jackson and Arthur Marotti, 256-86. Notre Dame: University of Notre Dame Press, 2011.
Knapp, Jeffrey. "Jonson, Shakespeare, and the Religion of Players." *Shakespeare Survey: An Annual Survey of Shakespeare Studies and Production* 54 (2001) 57-70.
———. *Shakespeare's Tribe: Church, Nation, and Theater in Renaissance England*. Chicago: University of Chicago Press, 2002.
Knight, G. Wilson. *The Wheel of Fire: Interpretations of Shakespearian Tragedy*. 4th ed. London: Methuen, 1972.
Kronenfeld, Judy. King Lear *and the Naked Truth: Rethinking the Language of Religion and Resistance*. Durham: Duke University Press, 1998.
Kuchar, Gary. "Alchemy, Repentance, and Recusant Allegory in Robert Southwell's *Saint Peters Complaint*." In *Redrawing the Map of Early Modern English Catholicism*, edited by Lowell Gallagher, 159-84. Toronto: University of Toronto Press, 2012.
———. "Compassion, Affliction, and Patience." In *The Cambridge Companion to Shakespeare and Religion*, edited by Hannibal Hamlin, 134-50. Cambridge: Cambridge University Press, 2019.
———. "Decorum and the Politics of Ceremony in Shakespeare's *Titus Andronicus*." In *Shakespeare and Religion: Early Modern and Postmodern Perspectives*, edited by Ken Jackson and Arthur Marotti, 46-78. Notre Dame, IN: University of Notre Dame Press, 2011.
———. *Divine Subjection: The Rhetoric of Sacramental Devotion in Early Modern England*. Pittsburgh: Duquesne University Press, 2005.

———. *George Herbert and the Mystery of the Word: Poetry and Scripture in Seventeenth Century England*. Cham, Switzerland: Palgrave Macmillan, 2017.

———. "Introduction: Distraction and the Ethics of Poetic Form in *The Temple*." *Christianity and Literature* 66 (2016) 4–23.

———. "'Loves Best Habit': Eros, Agape, and the Psychotheology of *Shakespeare's Sonnets*." In *The Return of Theory in Early Modern English Studies: Tarrying with the Subjunctive*, edited by Paul Cefalu and Bryan Reynolds, 211–36. New York: Palgrave Macmillan, 2011.

———. *The Poetry of Religious Sorrow in Early Modern England*. Cambridge: Cambridge University Press, 2008.

Laing, John. "Middle Knowledge." *Internet Encyclopedia of Philosophy*. 2019. https://www.iep.utm.edu/middlekn/.

Lake, Peter. *Anglicans and Puritans?: Presbyterianism and English Conformist Thought from Whitgift to Hooker*. London: Unwin Hyman, 1988.

———. "Lancelot Andrewes, John Buckeridge, and Avant-Garde Conformity at the Court of James I." In *The Mental Word of the Jacobean Court*, edited by Linda Levy Peck. 113–33. Cambridge: Cambridge University Press, 1991.

———. *Moderate Puritans and the Elizabethan Church*. Cambridge: Cambridge University Press, 1982.

Lake, Peter, and Michael C. Questier. *Conformity and Orthodoxy in the English Church, C. 1560–1660*. Woodbridge, Suffolk: Boydell, 2000.

Lake, Peter, with Michael Questier. *The Antichrist's Lewd Hat: Protestants, Papists and Players in Post-Reformation England*. New Haven, CT: Yale University Press, 2002.

Lander, Jesse K. *Inventing Polemic: Religion, Print, and Literary Culture in Early Modern England*. Cambridge: Cambridge University Press, 2006.

———. "Maimed Rites and Whirling Words in *Hamlet*." In *The Bible on the Shakespearean Stage: Cultures of Interpretation in Reformation England*, edited by Thomas Fulton and Kristen Poole, 188–203. Cambridge: Cambridge University Press, 2018.

Lawrence, Sean. *Forgiving the Gift: The Philosophy of Generosity in Shakespeare and Marlowe*. Pittsburgh: Duquesne University Press, 2012.

———. "'Gods That We Adore': The Divine in *King Lear*." *Renascence: Essays on Values in Literature* 56 (2004) 143–59.

Leggatt, Alexander, ed. *The Cambridge Companion to Shakespearean Comedy*. Cambridge University Press, 2002.

Leo, Russ. *Tragedy as Philosophy in the Reformation World*. Oxford: Oxford University Press, 2019.

Lesser, Zachary. *Hamlet After Q1: An Uncanny History of the Shakespearean Text*. University of Pennsylvania Press, 2015.

Levith, Murray. "Shakespeare's Merchant and Marlowe's Other Play." In *The Merchant of Venice: New Critical Essays*, edited by John Mahon and Ellen Macleod Mahon, 95–106. New York: Routledge, 2002.

Lewalski, Barbara. "Biblical Allusion and Allegory in *The Merchant of Venice*." *Shakespeare Quarterly* 13 (1962) 327–43.

Loewenstein, David, and Michael Witmore, eds. *Shakespeare and Early Modern Religion*. Cambridge: Cambridge University Press, 2015.

Low, Anthony. "*Hamlet* and the Ghost of Purgatory: Intimations of Killing the Father." *English Literary Renaissance* 29 (1999) 443–67.

Lualdi, Katherine Jackson, and Anne T. Thayer, eds. *Penitence in the Age of Reformations*. Aldershot: Ashgate, 2000.

Lupton, Julia. *Citizen-Saints: Shakespeare and Political Theology*. University of Chicago Press, 2005.

———. *Thinking with Shakespeare: Essays on Politics and Life*. University of Chicago Press, 2011.

The Lutheran World Federation and the Catholic Church. *Joint Declaration on the Doctrine of Justification*. 1999. http://www.vatican.va/roman_curia/pontifical_councils/chrstuni/documents/rc_pc_chrstuni_doc_31101999_cath-luth-joint-declaration_en.html.

Mahon, John, and Ellen Macleod Mahon, eds. *The Merchant of Venice: New Critical Essays*. New York: Routledge, 2002.

Maltby, Judith D. *Prayer Book and People in Elizabethan and Early Stuart England*. Cambridge: Cambridge University Press, 1998.

Marno, David. *Death Be Not Proud: The Art of Holy Attention*. Chicago: University of Chicago Press, 2016.

Marotti, Arthur F. *Religious Ideology and Cultural Fantasy: Catholic and Anti-Catholic Discourses in Early Modern England*. Notre Dame: University of Notre Dame Press, 2005.

Marshall, Peter, and Alexandra Walsham, eds. *Angels in the Early Modern World*. Cambridge: Cambridge University Press, 2006.

Marshall, Peter. "Choosing Sides and Talking Religion in Shakespeare's England." In *Shakespeare and Early Modern Religion*, edited by David Loewenstein and Michael Witmore, 40–56. Cambridge: Cambridge University Press, 2015.

———. *Reformation England 1480–1642*. 2nd ed., London: Bloomsbury Academic, 2012.

Martz, Louis. *The Poetry of Meditation*. New Haven, CT: Yale University Press, 1962.

Matheson, Peter. *The Imaginative World of the Reformation*. Minneapolis: Fortress, 2001.

Maus, Katharine Eisaman. "Introduction." In The Norton Shakespeare, 3rd ed., edited by Stephen Greenblatt et al., 2171–78. New York: W. W. Norton, 2016.

Mayer, Jean-Christophe. *Shakespeare's Hybrid Faith: History, Religion, and the Stage*. Basingstoke: Palgrave Macmillan, 2007.

McCarthy, Dennis. "Harvey's 1593 'To Be and Not To Be': The Authorship and Date of the First Quarto of *Hamlet*." *Critical Survey* 31 (2019) 87–100. EBSCOhost, search.ebscohost.com/login.aspx?direct=true&db=mzh&AN=201916660596&login.asp&site=ehost-live&scope=site.

McClusky, Colleen. "Medieval Theories of Free Will." *Internet Encyclopedia of Philosophy*, 2018. https://www.iep.utm.edu/freewi-m/#SH4a.

McCoy, Richard. *Faith in Shakespeare*. Oxford: Oxford University Press, 2013.

McCullough, Peter. "'Avant Garde Conformity' in the 1590s." *The Oxford History of Anglicanism, Volume 1: Reformation and Identity c.1520–1662*. Oxford University Press, February 16, 2017. Oxford Scholarship Online. https://www-oxfordscholarship-com.ezproxy.library.uvic.ca/view/10.1093/acprof:oso/9780199639731.001.0001/acprof-9780199639731-chapter-20.

McEachern, Claire, and Debora K. Shuger, eds. *Religion and Culture in Renaissance England*. Cambridge: Cambridge University Press, 1997.

McEachern, Claire. *Believing in Shakespeare: Studies in Longing*. Cambridge: Cambridge University Press, 2018.

McGrath, Alister. *Christian Theology: An Introduction*. 6th ed. Oxford: Blackwell, 2017.
———. *Iustitia Dei: A History of the Christian Doctrine of Justification*. 2nd ed. Cambridge: Cambridge University Press, 1998.
———. *Luther's Theology of the Cross: Martin Luther's Theological Breakthrough*. Oxford: Basil Blackwell, 1985.
———. *Reformation Thought*. 3rd ed. Oxford: Blackwell, 1999.
Menzer, Paul. "'Tis Heere, Tis Heere, Tis Gone': Q1 *Hamlet* and Degenerate Texts." *Analytical and Enumerative Bibliography* 12 (2001) 30–49.
Radford, Michael, dir. *The Merchant of Venice*. Beverly Hills: Metro-Goldwyn-Mayer Studios, 2004.
Midelfort, H. C. Erik. *A History of Madness in Sixteenth-Century Germany*. Stanford: Stanford University Press, 1999.
Milner, Stephen J., ed. *At the Margins: Minority Groups in Premodern Italy*. Minneapolis: University of Minnesota Press, 2005.
Monta, Susannah Brietz. *Martyrdom and Literature in Early Modern England*. Cambridge: Cambridge University Press, 2005.
Morris, Ivor. *Shakespeare's God: The Role of Religion in the Tragedies*. London: Allen and Unwin, 1972.
Muir, Kenneth. "Madness in *King Lear*." *Aspects of* King Lear, edited by Kenneth Muir and Stanley Wells, 23–33. Cambridge: Cambridge University Press, 1982.
Mullaney, Steven. *The Reformation of Emotions in the Age of Shakespeare*. Chicago: University of Chicago Press, 2015.
Murphy, John L. *Darkness and Devils: Exorcism and* King Lear. Athens, OH: Ohio University Press, 1984.
Nahshon, Edna, and Michael Shapiro, eds. *Wrestling with Shylock: Jewish Responses to* The Merchant of Venice. Cambridge University Press, 2017.
Neely, Carol Thomas. *Distracted Subjects: Madness and Gender in Shakespeare and Early Modern Culture*. Ithaca: Cornell University Press, 2004.
Nelson, Holly Faith. "What Seventeenth- and Early Eighteenth-Century Literature Has to Teach Us About Living in a Polarized Age." Christianity and Literature Study Group (allied with ACCUTE). Congress of the Humanities and Social Sciences, University of British Columbia, June 3, 2019. Conference Keynote Address.
Novy, Marianne. *Shakespeare and Outsiders*. Oxford: Oxford University Press, 2013.
O'Connell, Michael. "'The Juice of Egypt's Grape': Plutarch, Syncretism, and *Antony and Cleopatra*." In *Religion and Drama in Early Modern England: The Performance of Religion on the Renaissance Stage*, edited by Jane Hwang Degenhardt and Elizabeth Williamson, 195–208. Surrey, England: Ashgate, 2011.
Palfrey, Simon. *Poor Tom: Living* King Lear. Chicago: University of Chicago Press, 2014.
Parker, John. *The Aesthetics of Antichrist: From Christian Drama to Christopher Marlowe*. Ithaca: Cornell University Press, 2007.
Paster, Gail Kern, et al., eds. *Reading the Early Modern Passions: Essays in the Cultural History of Emotion*. Philadelphia: University of Pennsylvania Press, 2004.
Patterson, Mary H. *Domesticating the Reformation: Protestant Best Sellers, Private Devotion, and the Revolution of English Piety*. Madison: Fairleigh Dickinson University Press, 2007.
Pearce, Joseph. *The Quest for Shakespeare: The Bard of Avon and the Church of Rome*. San Francisco: Ignatius, 2008.

Peck, Linda Levy, ed. *The Mental World of the Jacobean Court*. Cambridge: Cambridge University Press, 1991.

Pilarz, Scott R. *Robert Southwell and the Mission of Literature, 1561–1595: Writing Reconciliation*. Farnham, Surrey: Ashgate, 2004.

Pohle, Joseph. "Molinism." In *The Catholic Encyclopedia* 10. New York: Robert Appleton Company, 2019. http://www.newadvent.org/cathen/10437a.htm.

Pollard, Tanya, ed. *Shakespeare's Theatre*: A Sourcebook. Malden: Blackwell, 2004.

Poole, Kristen. *Radical Religion from Shakespeare to Milton: Figures of Nonconformity in Early Modern England*. Cambridge, UK: Cambridge University Press, 2000.

Preedy, Chloe K. *Marlowe's Literary Scepticism: Politic Religion and Post-Reformation Polemic*. London: Arden Shakespeare, 2012.

Price, Joseph, ed. Hamlet: *Critical Essays*. New York: Garland, 1986.

Prosser, Eleanor. *Hamlet and Revenge*. 2nd ed., Stanford University Press, 1971.

"Quit, V., Sense II.11.a." *Oxford English Dictionary*. Oxford: Oxford University Press, 2023.

Ranson, Angela. "Separating the Universal Bishop from the Universal Church in the Jewel-Harding Controversy." In *Sin and Salvation in Reformation England*, edited by Jonathan Willis, 53–68. Surrey, England: Ashgate, 2015.

Ratcliffe, Stephen. *Reading the Unseen: (Offstage) Hamlet*. Denver: Counterpath, 2010.

Romany, Frank, and Robert Lindsey. "Introduction." In *Christopher Marlowe: The Complete Plays*, xi–xxxiii. London: Penguin, 2003.

Rossiter, A. P. "Measure for Measure." In *Modern Critical Interpretations: William Shakespeare's Measure for Measure*, edited by Harold Bloom, 45–60. New York: Chelsea House, 1987.

Rubin, Miri. *Gentile Tales: The Narrative Assault on Late Medieval Jews*. New Haven, CT: Yale University Press, 1999.

Rubinstein, Frankie. "Speculating on Mysteries: Religion and Politics in *King Lear*." *Renaissance Studies: Journal of the Society for Renaissance Studies* 16 (2002) 234–62.

Ruggiero, Guido. *The Boundaries of Eros: Sex Crime and Sexuality in Renaissance Venice*. Oxford: Oxford University Press, 1985.

Ryrie, Alec. *Being Protestant in Early Modern England*. Oxford: Oxford University Press, 2013.

———. *Protestants: The Faith that Made the Modern World*. New York: Viking, 2017.

Salingar, Leo. *Dramatic Form in Shakespeare and the Jacobeans*. Cambridge: Cambridge University Press, 1986.

Schleiner, Louise. "Providential Improvisation in *Measure for Measure*." Bloom, pp. 95–110.

Scholl, Edith. "The Mother of Virtues: <discretio>." *Cistercian Studies Quarterly* 36 (2001) 389–401.

Schreyer, Kurt A. *Shakespeare's Medieval Craft: Remnants of the Mysteries on the London Stage*. Ithaca: Cornell University Press, 2014.

Schuster, Louis A. Introduction. "Thomas More's Polemical Career, 1523–1533." In *The Confutation of Tyndale's Answer*, by Thomas More, 1135–268. New Haven, CT: Yale University Press, 1973.

Seiden, Melvin. Measure for Measure: *Casuistry and Artistry*. Washington, DC: The Catholic University of America Press, 1990.

Shaheen, Naseeb. *Biblical References in Shakespeare's Plays*. Newark: University of Delaware Press, 2011.
———. *Biblical References in Shakespeare's Tragedies*. Newark: University of Delaware Press, 1987.
Shapiro, James. *Shakespeare and the Jews*. New York: Columbia University Press, 1996.
———. *A Year in the Life of William Shakespeare—1599*. New York: HarperCollins, 2005.
Shell, Alison. *Shakespeare and Religion*. London: Bloomsbury, 2010.
Short, Hugh. "Shylock is Content: A Study in Salvation." In *The Merchant of Venice: New Critical Essays*, edited by John Mahon and Ellen Macleod, 199–212. Mahon, New York: Routledge, 2002.
Shuger, Debora. *Political Theologies in Shakespeare's England: The Sacred and the State in Measure for Measure*. New York: Palgrave, 2001.
———. "Subversive Fathers and Suffering Subjects: Shakespeare and Christianity." In *Religion, Literature, and Politics in Post-Reformation England, 1540–1688*, edited by Donna Hamilton and Richard Strier, 46–69. Cambridge: Cambridge University Press, 1996.
Sierra, Horacio, ed. *New Readings of* The Merchant of Venice. Newcastle upon Tyne: Cambridge Scholars, 2013.
"Sift, V., Sense 2.a." *Oxford English Dictionary*. Oxford: Oxford University Press, 2023.
Simpson, James. *Burning to Read: English Fundamentalism and Its Reformation Opponents*. Cambridge: Harvard University Press, 2007.
———. *The Oxford English Literary History: Reform and Cultural Revolution*. Oxford: Oxford University Press, 2004.
Sluhovsky, Moshe. *Believe Not Every Spirit: Possession, Mysticism, and Discernment in Early Modern Catholicism*. Chicago: University of Chicago Press, 2007.
Sterrett, Joseph. *The Unheard Prayer: Religious Toleration in Shakespeare's Drama*. Leiden: Brill, 2012.
Stevens, Paul. "*Hamlet, Henry VIII*, and the Question of Religion: A Post-Secular Perspective." In *Shakespeare and Early Modern Religion*, edited by David Loewenstein and Michael Witmore, 231–57. Cambridge: Cambridge University Press, 2015.
Stevenson, Kenneth W. "'Human Nature Honoured': Absolution in Lancelot Andrewes." In *Like a Two-Edged Sword: The Word of God in Liturgy and History: Essays in Honour of Canon Donald Gray*, edited by Martin R. Dudley, 113–38. Norwich: The Canterbury, 1995.
Stow, Kenneth R. "Stigma, Acceptance, and the End to Liminality: Jews and Christians in Early Modern Italy." In *At the Margins: Minority Groups in Premodern Italy*, edited by Stephen J. Milner, 71–92. Minneapolis: University of Minnesota Press, 2005.
Streete, Adrian. "Lucretius, Calvin, and Natural Law in *Measure for Measure*." In *Shakespeare and Early Modern Religion*, edited by David Loewenstein and Michael Witmore, 131–54. Cambridge: Cambridge University Press, 2015.
———. *Protestantism and Drama in Early Modern England*. Cambridge: Cambridge University Press, 2008.
Streete, Adrian, ed. *Early Modern Drama and the Bible: Contexts and Readings, 1570–1625*. New York: Palgrave Macmillan, 2012.
Strier, Richard. *Resistant Structures: Particularity, Radicalism, and Renaissance Texts*. Berkeley: University of California Press, 1995.

———. *The Unrepentant Renaissance: From Petrarch to Shakespeare to Milton.* Chicago: University of Chicago Press, 2011.
Swift, Daniel. *Shakespeare's Common Prayers: The Book of Common Prayer and the Elizabethan Age.* Oxford: Oxford University Press, 2013.
Targoff, Ramie. *Common Prayer: The Language of Public Devotion in Early Modern England.* Chicago: University of Chicago Press, 2001.
———. "The Performance of Prayer: Sincerity and Theatricality in Early Modern England." *Representations* 60 (1997) 49–69.
Taylor, Dennis, and David N. Beauregard, eds. *Shakespeare and the Culture of Christianity in Early Modern England.* New York: Fordham University Press, 2003.
———. *Shakespeare and the Reformation.* Leiden: Brill, 2003.
Taylor, Gary. "Forms of Opposition: Shakespeare and Middleton." *English Literary Renaissance* 24 (1994) 283–314.
Thomas, Keith. *Religion and the Decline of Magic.* New York: Charles Scribner's Sons, 1971.
Thomas, Vivien, and William Tydeman, eds. *Christopher Marlowe: The Plays and their Sources.* London: Routledge, 1994.
Tillich, Paul. *The Courage To Be.* New Haven, CT: Yale University Press, 1952.
Truskinovsky, Alexander M. "Literary Psychiatric Observation and Diagnosis Through the Ages: *King Lear* Revisited." *Southern Medical Journal* 95 (2002) 343–52.
Turner, Victor W. *The Ritual Process: Structure and Anti-Structure.* Chicago: Aldine, 1969.
Tutino, Stefania. *Shadows of Doubt: Language and Truth in Post-Reformation Catholic Culture.* New York: Oxford University Press, 2014.
Tyacke, Nicholas. *Anti-Calvinists: The Rise of English Arminianism, c. 1590–1640.* Oxford: Clarendon, 1987.
van Dijkuizen, Jan Frans. *Pain and Compassion in Early Modern English Literature and Culture.* Cambridge: D.S. Brewer, 2012.
Van Gennep, Arnold. *The Rites of Passage.* Chicago: University of Chicago Press, 1960.
Walsham, Alexandra. "Afterword." In *Sin and Salvation in Reformation England*, edited by Jonathan Willis, 259–75. Surrey, England: Ashgate, 2015.
———. *Catholic Reformation in Protestant Britain.* Rev. ed. Aldershot, Hamps: Ashgate, 2014.
———. *Church Papists: Catholicism, Conformity, and Confessional Polemic in Early Modern England.* Woodbridge, Suffolk, UK: Boydell, 1993.
Watt, Jeffrey R., ed. *From Sin to Insanity: Suicide in Early Modern Europe.* Ithaca, New York: Cornell University Press, 2004.
Watts, Cedric. *Penguin Critical Studies: William Shakespeare:* Measure for Measure. London: Penguin, 1986.
Weil, Herbert, Jr. "Form and Contexts in *Measure for Measure.*" In *Modern Critical Interpretations: William Shakespeare's Measure for Measure*, edited by Harold Bloom, 61–80. New York: Chelsea House, 1987.
Wells, Stanley. "Introduction." In *King Lear*, 1–93. Oxford: Oxford University Press, 2000.
———. *Shakespeare and Co.* New York: Vintage, 2006.
———. *Shakespeare, Sex, and Love.* Oxford: Oxford University Press, 2010.
Werrell, Ralph. "Sin and Salvation in William Tyndale's Theology." In *Sin and Salvation in Reformation England*, edited by Jonathan Willis, 23–38. Surrey, England: Ashgate, 2015.

Widdicombe, Toby. *Simply Shakespeare*. New York: Longman, 2002.

Wiebe, Phillip. *God and Other Spirits: Intimations of Transcendence in Christian Experience*. Oxford: Oxford University Press, 2004.

Williams, Rowan. "Afterword: Finding the Remedy." In *The Cambridge Companion to Shakespeare and Religion*, edited by Hannibal Hamlin, 285–92. Cambridge: Cambridge University Press, 2019.

Willis, Jonathan. "Introduction." In *Sin and Salvation in Reformation England*, edited by Jonathan Willis, 1–19. Surrey, England: Ashgate, 2015.

———. "'Moral Arithmetic' or Creative Accounting? (Re-)defining Sin through the Ten Commandments." In *Sin and Salvation in Reformation England*, edited by Jonathan Willis, 69–84. Surrey, England: Ashgate, 2015.

———, ed. *Sin and Salvation in Reformation England*. Surrey, England: Ashgate, 2015.

Wilson, John Dover. *What Happens in* Hamlet. Cambridge: Cambridge University Press, 1964.

Wilson, Richard. "A Bloody Question: The Politics of *Venus and Adonis*." *Religion and the Arts* 5 (2001) 297–316.

———. "As Mice by Lions. Political Theology and *Measure for Measure*." *Shakespeare* 11 (2015) 157–77.

———. "When the Cock Crew: The Imminence of *Hamlet*." *Shakespeare* 3 (2007) 1–17.

"Winnow, V., Sense 1.b." *Oxford English Dictionary*. Oxford: Oxford University Press, 2023.

Wolf, Amy. "Shakespeare and Harsnett: 'Pregnant to Good Pity'?" *SEL Studies in English Literature, 1500–1900* 38 (1998) 251–64.

Woods, Gillian. *Shakespeare's Unreformed Fictions*. Oxford: Oxford University Press, 2013.

Wright, N. T. *Justification: God's Plan and Paul's Vision*. Downers Grove, IL: InterVarsity Press Academic, 2009.

Young, Francis. *A History of Anglican Exorcism: Deliverance and Demonology in Church Ritual*. London: I.B. Tauris, 2018.

———. *English Catholics and the Supernatural, 1553–1829*. Farnham: Ashgate, 2013.

Zysk, Jay. "In the Name of the Father: Revenge and Unsacramental Death in *Hamlet*." *Christianity and Literature* 66 (2017) 422–43.

Subject Index

abduction, 228
Abraham, 68
Abrahamic faiths, 33
absolution, 87
absolutism, royal, 180, 204
Adelman, Janet, 60
affliction, 146
agency, 23, 83, 101, 117
allegory, 24
Allen, D. C., 135
anatheism, 120
Andrewes, Lancelot, 80
Anonby, David, xii
Anonby, John, 171 fn5
Anselm, *Cur Deus Homo*, 168–69
anti-Calvinism, 192
anti-Catholicism, 35, 41, 59–60
anti-Judaism, 34, 54–59
antinomianism, 73
anti-Semitism, 34, 68
anti-theatricalists, 263–64
atonement, 165–71
Antony, Saint, 126
Aquinas, Thomas, 108, 178
Arden, 32
Aristotle, ix, 23
Arius, 240–1
Arminianism, 36, 73, 81, 90, 256
Arminius, Jacobus, 81
asceticism, 192
Athanasius, 126
atheism, 5, 261

atonement, 81
Augustine, 28, 39, 44, 51, 72, 108, 150–51, 187, 194, 201, 264
avant-garde conformity, 80, 108, 256

Babington, Anthony, 215
Babington Plot, 209
Baines Note, 261
Baines, Richard, 261
Bale, John, 26
Bancroft, Richard, 209
baptism, 96, 175, 189, 207
Bawcutt, N. W., 165
bawdy humor, 183, 263
Beauregard, David, 232
Beckwith, Sarah, 19, 166 fn1
bed trick, 165, 176
benefit of clergy, 261
Bennet, Robert, 203
Bernard of Clairvaux, 131, 242
Berry, Edward, 35
bias, 12, 20, 24
Bible, 219–21, 264
biblical irony, 156
Blake, William, 213
blasphemy, ix
blood libel, 54–55
Bonhoeffer, Dietrich, 169
Book of Common Prayer, The, 2, 95, 191–3, 196–7
Book of Homilies, The, 47 fn8
bowdlerizing, 14, 207

SUBJECT INDEX

Bradley, A. C., 10
Brownlow, F.W., 215–16, 237
Bucer, Martin, 23
Bunny, Edmund, 125
Bunyan, John, 246
Burbage, Richard, 54

Cain, 84
Calvin, John, 15, 27–28, 51, 70, 71, 103, 129–130, 133, 146, 170, 210
Calvinism, 87, 97, 99–101, 233, 256, 263
Campion, Edmund, 218
canon, scriptural, 71
caritas, 39, 41, 76, 206, 212, 223, 232, 250
Catholicism, 177–79, 192, 217, 256
Cavanaugh, William, 163
cessationism, 210, 233
Cecil, Robert, 88
Cefalu, Paul, 21, 178, 250
chapter summaries of this book, 30–31
Charles I, 204
chastity, 183
Christianity, 67, 172, 177, 233, 261
Christology, 262
church discipline, 183
church papists, 240, 262
circumcision, 65
Civil Wars, English, 204
Coleridge, Samuel Taylor, 15, 125, 198, 226
comedy, 32, 162, 167, 198
commercial theater, 4, 183
communion, 95, 175, 197
compassion, 169, 188, 214, 220
confessional divides, 242, 246
conformist, 17
conscience, 47, 114
consolation, 129
contrition, 99
conversion, 26, 37, 55–61, 79, 261, 264
conversos, 58
Council of Trent, The, 39, 72, 86
Cox, John, 20, 198
Cranmer, Thomas, 2, 57
Cromwell, Oliver, 55
cruelty, 221
crypto-Catholicism, 80

culture wars, 183–88
Cummings, Brian, 2, 254

damnation, 152
Darrell, John, 130, 219
Davidson, Peter, 139
Dawson, Anthony, 1, 10, 13–14, 253
deep structure, 222
Dekker, Thomas, 4, 10, 262
demon, 121–2, 126, 153, 211
demoniac, 131, 213, 216
demonic possession, 131, 215
demonization, 218, 240, 246
demonology, 206, 208, 224
desolation, 129
despair, 100, 263
determinism, 104, 263
devil, 150, 153
Devlin, Maria, 23, 263
discretio spirituum, 120–21, 124–32
dispossessor, 130
Dominicans, 111
Donne, Henry, 77
Donne, John, 59, 77, 144
Dostoevsky, Fyodor, 106, 207
double justification, 74
dramatic irony, 137
Drummond, William, 261

ecumenism, 73, 212, 214, 251
Edward I, 59
Edwards, Michael, 207
Edmunds, John, 216
election, 1
Elizabeth I, 4, 35, 140, 144, 181, 236
Erasmus, Desiderius, 1, 15
eros, 76
Esau, 85
eschatology, 259
ethics, 29, 37, 175–77, 188–89, 192, 202
Eucharist, 95, 136, 196–97
evil, 106, 114, 206
exorcism, 205, 206–14, 257
experimental theology, 130

faith, xi, 15, 41, 68, 70, 250, 259–60
fasting, 126
fatalism, 102–3

SUBJECT INDEX

felix culpa, 201
feminism, 36
Ferrell, Lori Anne, 262
Forbes, John, 130
Foreman, Gary, 22 fn11
forgiveness, 95, 116, 117, 163–64, 177–79, 233, 243
forensic salvation, x, 28, 45, 50, 171, 258
Foxe, John, 130, 144, 241
free will, 112, 114, 256
Freud, Sigmund, 105
Frye, Roland Mushat, 13–14
fundamentalism, 195

Gadarene demoniac, 220, 231
Galenic humoral theory, 227
Garnet, Henry, 234
generic hybridity, 167
Gerson, Jean, 127
ghost, 123, 153, 159, 161
Girard, René, 177
God the Father, 97, 189
godly, 17
Goethe, Johann Wolfgang von, 125
golden rule, 200–201
gospel, 3, 72, 171–75, 188–90
grace, 11, 29, 32, 82, 117, 118, 169, 174, 182
Greenblatt, Stephen, 14, 226, 258
Gross, Kenneth, 63–64
Gunpowder Plot, 205–6, 237–38, 261

habit, x–xi
Hall, Joan Lord, 208
hamartiology, 193, 195
Hamlin, Hannibal, 9, 13
Hampton Court Conference, 183, 242
Harsnett, Samuel, 28, 88, *A Declaration of Egregious Popish Impostures*, 205
Hathaway, Anne, 183
Hebrews, epistle, 86
hell, 152, 155, 158
Henry VIII, 180
Herbert, George, 26
heterodoxy, 261
Heywood, Thomas, 10

Hirschfeld, Heather, 19
Hobbes, Thomas, 211
Holderness, Graham, 165
Holinshed, Raphael, 208
Holocaust, 34
Holy Spirit, 64, 97, 126, 129, 132, 181, 189
Hooker, Richard, *Laws of Ecclesiastical Polity*, 3, *A Learned Discourse of Justification*, 73
Howard, Philip, earl of Arundel, 205, 243
humanism, 149
Hunt, Maurice, 260
hypocrisy, 195

idolatry, 39
Ignatian meditation, 92, 197
Ignatius of Loyola, 128
imitatio Christi, 250
impenitence, 108, 114, 117
imputed righteousness, 45, 72
intolerance, 11, 32
intrafaith tensions, 34
irenicism, 74
Isaac, 68
Islam, 9, 24, 33, 40, 41, 64, 67, 255, 261

James, epistle, 71
James I, 55, 59, 78, 180, 183, 190, 204, 238
Jesuits, 59, 77, 111, 128, 205, 217, 219
Jesus Christ, 3, 26, 28, 29, 45, 47, 51, 63, 66, 92, 93, 141, 163, 164, 166–67, 170–71, 172, 175, 177, 179, 188–89, 210, 232, 242, 245, 262
Job, 220, 242
Johnson, Samuel, 125, 152
Jones, Ernest, 105
Jonson, Ben, 5, 17, 192, 238, 261–62
Jowett, John, 196
Joyce, James, 10
Judaism, 9, 24, 33, 41, 255, 261
judgmentalism, 188, 195
justification, 33–79
justice, 50, 175, 182

Kastan, David Scott, 6, 120
Kearney, Richard, 120
Kelly, Erin, 4, 255
Kierkegaard, Søren, 41
Klause, John, 34–35, 138, 235
Kuchar, Gary, ix, 16, 27, 31, 138, 144, 205–6, 242, 244–5
Kyd, Thomas, 98, *The Spanish Tragedy*, 154–57

Lake, Peter, 80, 192
Lander, Jesse, 18
Laud, William, 81, 87, 262
Laudians, 204
law, 38, 40, 48, 49, 64, 176
Lawrence, Seán, 207
Lewalski, Barbara, 56
lex talionis, 142, 200
Lord's Prayer, 243
love, 90, 103
Lupton, Julia, 5, 66
Luther, Martin, 1, 15, 37, 45, 47, 55, 61, 62, 70, 87, 137, 171, 178, 179, 181, 204, 233, 257, 260, 264–65
Lutherans, x, 16

Marcion, 71
Marian martyrs, 241
Marlowe, Christopher, 5, 25, 51, 260–1, *Doctor Faustus*, 53, 103, 147–9, 197, *The Jew of Malta*, 33
Marno, David, 107
Marshall, Peter, 22–23
Martyrdom, 53, 77, 143, 145, 206, 218, 234–37
Martz, Louis, 197
Marwood, Nicholas, 215
Mary Stuart, 144, 209, 245
Mary Tudor, 3
Maus, Katharine Eisaman, 172
Mayer, John, 147
McCoy, Richard, 15, 231, 259
McCullough, Peter, 88
McEachern, Claire, 21
McGrath, Alister, 44
Mede, Joseph, 211
Melanchthon, Philip, 43–44
memorial reconstruction, 98

Menghi, Girolamo, 131–2
mental illness, 102, 206, 215, 224
mercy, 38, 92, 175, 188–89
merit, 40, 45, 118
metatheatricality, 155
methodology of this book, 25
middle knowledge, 112
Middleton, Thomas, 5, 83, 196, 238, 262–64, *The Revenger's Tragedy*, 113–17, *The Two Gates of Salvation Set Wide Open*, 262–64
Midelfort, H. C. Erik, 227
Milton, John, 194, 213, 222
miracles, 233, 259
misogyny, 201, 245
Molina, Luis de, 111
Molinism, 81, 111
monstrous proposal, 184, 202
Monta, Susannah Brietz, 235
More, Thomas, 15, 21, 37, 52–53, 225

narcissism, 18, 116
nationalism, 163
Nazism, 64
Nelson, Holly, 254
Nicodemites, 240
nihilism, 230, 249
Norden, John, 107
Novy, Marianne, 57

Oath of Allegiance, 59, 78
Oath of Supremacy, 35, 76
O'Connor, Flannery, 242
Olivier, Laurence, 56
ordo salutis, 71, 260
Origen, 168
orthodoxy, 78
overreach of religion, 24, 202
Ovid, 158

parousia, 259
Parsons, Robert, 125
passive righteousness, 72
pastoral genre, 259
Patristic era, 2
Paul, 43–44, 50–51, 62–63, 97, 259, 264
Pelagius, 258

penance, 16, 19, 179, 259–60
penitential psalm, 100
Perkins, William, 45, 90
persecution, 78
perseverance, 242
Peter, 122, 133, 150, 164
Pietism, 71
Pius V, Pope, 140
polarization, 36, 42, 87, 235, 253–54
polemics, 88, 212
political theology, 182, 202
prayer, 117, 126
predestination, 83, 84, 89, 101, 256
prevenient grace, 111
problem of evil, 243
problem play, 168, 174, 191
prodigal son, 201–2, 220
prophecy, 141
proselyte, 77
Protestantism, 177–79, 205, 217
psychology, 120
psychopath, 159
Purgatory, 121, 149, 157
Puritanism, 36, 43, 74, 130, 147, 174, 180, 183, 192, 204, 235, 261–63

racism, 36, 60–62, 68
reconciliation, 76, 117
recusants, 18, 35, 43, 59, 143, 205, 226, 239
Reformation, xii, 1, 2
Reformation continuum, 253
Reformation divide, 253, 257, 264
relic, 218
religious allegory, 203
religious difference, 40, 77
religious experience, 228–89, 258
religious identity, 260
religious minorities, 79, 249
religious violence, 123, 163–64
repentance, 1, 96, 116
reprobate, 83, 110
ressentiment, 79
resurrection, xi, 45, 259
revenge, 154–57,
revenge genre, 157, 162, 164
rhetorical theology, 23, 95 fn10, 263
romances, 258

Romans, epistle, 71
Ryrie, Alec, 2

sacraments, 39, 175, 250
salvation, 1, 18, 177, 203, 264
sanctification, 71, 146, 178, 259–60
Santayana, George, 5
Satan, 159, 207
satisfaction, 99
scapegoating, 188, 224
Scot, Reginald, 211
secularization, 10, 11, 76, 79, 183, 203, 252, 257
self-condemnation, 47
self-deception, 94
self-justification, 47
Seneca, 153, 156
Sermon on the Mount, 189–92, 200
sermons, 81
sexuality, 176, 183
Shakespeare, John, 5
Shakespeare, Susanna, 5
Shakespeare, William, *Antony and Cleopatra*, xi, Bible, 9–10, 119–20, biography, 5–6, xi, *The Comedy of Errors*, 31, *Hamlet*, 1, 80–118, 119–64, 255–56, 257–58, *1 Henry IV*, 7, *King Lear*, 3, 205–52, 257–58, *Macbeth*, 31, *Measure for Measure*, 165–204, *The Merchant of Venice*, 33–79, 256–57, *Othello*, 31, religion, 7–16, *Richard II*, 11, 31, 241, sonnets, ix, *Sonnet 73*, 40, *Sonnet 138*, x, soteriological positions, 255–8, soteriology, 16–32, *The Tempest*, 32, *Timon of Athens*, 25, *Titus Andronicus*, 158–59, *Twelfth Night*, 5, 9, 31, 43, *Venus and Adonis*, 145, 245, *The Winter's Tale*, xi, 15–16, 31, 258–60
Shell, Alison, 10, 150
Short, Hugh, 56
Shuger, Debora, 166 fn1
sin, 18, 50, 62, 86, 89, 93, 101, 114, 179, 190–92, 243

SUBJECT INDEX

skepticism, 162, 209–10, 215, 227, 243, 251
Sluhovsky, Moshe, 227
sola fide, 15, 34, 36, 53, 86, 179, 206, 257
sola gratia, 53, 107, 264
sola scriptura, 2
solus Christus, 47 fn8, 53
soteriological deep structures, 27–29
soteriology, 18–19, 27, 175–77, 188–90
Southwell, Robert, 3, 78, 143–5, "Decease release," 244–5, *An Epistle of Comfort*, 144, 205, 234–35, 237–43, *An Humble Supplication to Her Maiestie*, 236, "I dye without desert," 243–44, *Mans Civill Warre*, 1, 108, *Marie Magdelens Fvneral Teares*, 237, *Saint Peters Complaynt*, 133–34, 138–43, 236–37, 246
Spanish Armada, 209
Spanish Inquisition, 59
Spencer, Gabriel, 261
spiritual pride, 195
St. Mary of Bethlehem hospital, 226
Stephen, martyrdom of, 237
substitution, 165, 170–71
subversion, 183
suffering, 251
suicide, 231
Sweeney, Anne, 139
syncretism, 121, 161
synoptic gospels, 220

Tansillo, Luigi, 139
Tate, Nahum, 207
Taylor, Gary, 262
temptation, 111, 192
Teresa of Ávila, 128
theism, 233
Theobald, Lewis, 209
Thomas, Keith, 210–11
Thomism, xi, 81
Topcliffe, Richard, 143
torture, 247–8
total depravity, 263
Tourneur, Cyril, *The Atheist's Tragedy*, 159–63
tragedy, 162, 167, 198
transubstantiation, 28, 43, 175, 197
treason, 245
Trinity, 189
Truskinovsky, Alexander, 225
turn to religion, 16, 27, 120
Tyndale, William, 51–52
typology, 69

victimization, 221
violence, 122, 161, 224
virtualism, 196
voluntarism, theological, 28
Vulgate, 156, 220

Walsingham, Francis, 216
Wells, Stanley, 28
Weston, William, 216
Weyer, Johann, 224
Whetstone, George, *Promos and Cassandra*, 198–202
Wiebe, Phillip, 228–29, 257–58
Williams, Rowan, 13
Willis, Jonathan, 18
Wilson, Richard, 145, 245
Wolf, Amy, 212
Woodes, Nathaniel, *Conflict of Conscience*, 4
Woods, Gillian, 14–15
works, 38, 68
Wright, N. T., 44
Wright, Thomas, 261

zeal, 161, 195

www.ingramcontent.com/pod-product-compliance
Lightning Source LLC
Chambersburg PA
CBHW061432300426
44114CB00014B/1643